Killing the Messiah

KILLING THE MESSIAH

The Trial and Crucifixion
of Jesus of Nazareth

NATHANAEL J. ANDRADE

OXFORD
UNIVERSITY PRESS

OXFORD
UNIVERSITY PRESS

Oxford University Press is a department of the University of Oxford.
It furthers the University's objective of excellence in research, scholarship,
and education by publishing worldwide. Oxford is a registered trade mark of
Oxford University Press in the UK and in certain other countries.

Published in the United States of America by Oxford University Press
198 Madison Avenue, New York, NY 10016, United States of America.

© Oxford University Press 2025

All rights reserved. No part of this publication may be reproduced, stored in a retrieval system, transmitted, used for text and data mining, or used for training artificial intelligence, in any form or by any means, without the prior permission in writing of Oxford University Press, or as expressly permitted by law, by license or under terms agreed with the appropriate reprographics rights organization. Inquiries concerning reproduction outside the scope of the above should be sent to the Rights Department, Oxford University Press, at the address above.

You must not circulate this work in any other form
and you must impose this same condition on any acquirer

Library of Congress Cataloging-in-Publication Data
Names: Andrade, Nathanael J., author.
Title: Killing the Messiah : the trial and crucifixion of Jesus of Nazareth / Nathanael J. Andrade.
Description: New York : Oxford University Press, 2025. |
Includes bibliographical references and index.
Identifiers: LCCN 2024030491 | ISBN 9780197752487 (hardback) |
ISBN 9780197752500 (epub)
Subjects: LCSH: Jesus Christ—Trial. | Jesus Christ—Crucifixion.
Classification: LCC BT440 .A46 2025 | DDC 232.96/2—dc23/eng/20240917
LC record available at https://lccn.loc.gov/2024030491

DOI: 10.1093/oso/9780197752487.001.0001

Printed by Marquis, Canada

To Oliver and Stella, truest loves
John and Marceline Nadeau, truest disciples

Contents

Acknowledgments	ix
Chronology of Jesus' Judaea	xi
Introduction: Pilate's Path to Crucifixion	1

PART I: *Politics and People*

1. Places, Peoples, Empire	13
2. The Governing Order	36
3. Dissenters	52

PART II: *Jesus of Nazareth and the Gospels*

4. The New Testament Gospels and Jesus	71
5. Jesus, Herod Antipas, and Galilee	86

PART III: *Arresting Jesus*

6. Jesus, the Temple, and the Chief Priests	97
7. Jesus' Arrest	118

viii   *Contents*

PART IV: *Jesus' Trial and Death*

8. Jesus and "the Sanhedrin"   131

9. Pilate and Sedition   144

10. Pilate's Path, Jesus' Trial   165

PART V: *Aftermaths and Apostles*

11. Jesus' Followers on Trial (until 250)   185

Epilogue: Crossing Paths with Pilate   204

Appendix 1: Policing, Arresting Parties, and the New Testament Gospels   207

Appendix 2: Josephus on Jesus   211

Appendix 3: Greek and Hebrew/Aramaic Names   215

Appendix 4: Note on Texts, Translations, and Abbreviations   217

Notes   219

Bibliography   251

Index   275

Acknowledgments

I HAVE ALWAYS found acknowledgments challenging to write. I always worry that my words will not do justice to my gratitude. I fear that I will overlook people whose mention here is already just a paltry recompense. I have decided to be brief. But readers should know that I did not toil alone. I relied on the intellect, wisdom, kindness, generosity, and friendship of others at every moment that I researched and wrote. I also relied on the work of many scholars I have met and many I have not. Without them, this book would not exist. Without them, I would not have kept trying.

Stefan Vranka and Oxford University Press guided the project through its most critical stages. I am grateful for their support, encouragement, and advice amid all the challenges that it faced. The external readers deserve special recognition for their balanced, insightful critiques. The Alexander Von Humboldt Foundation supported a critical summer and fall semester of the project from June 2021 to February 2022, as did The American Friends of the Alexander Von Humboldt Foundation with a William Calder III fellowship. Under their auspices, I was able to make great progress at the Cluster for Excellence in Politics and Religion at WWU-Münster. I thank Michael Blomer, Achim Lichtenberger, and above all Engelbert Winter, my host, for their generous hospitality and encouragement while I was there. I am eternally grateful. The Department of History and the MAP Project at Université de Toulouse–Jean Jaures, especially Corinne Bonnet, were also generous hosts at this time. The Department of History, the Institute for Advanced Studies in the Humanities, and Harpur College at Binghamton University conferred invaluable research support. Alexander Angelov and the Medieval and Renaissance Studies Seminar at William and Mary College enabled me to share material and refine ideas. To Oliver Andrade, Stella Andrade, Jinny Prais, Paul Andrade, Marcia Chase, Derick Alexandre, Jessica Place, Ellie Geake, Abby Geake, Joseph Ricker, Kent Schull, Tina Homberg: deepest, deepest thanks. I hope you know why.

Binghamton University and the Department of History made my research possible through a Dean's Research Leave (spring 2020) and a sabbatical (spring 2023). The Institute for Advanced Studies in the Humanities there enabled me to make great headway in fall 2022. Colleagues, scholars, and students have enriched my thinking immensely. These include Anne Bailey, Michael Bird, Elisa Camiscioli, Elizabeth Casteen, John Chaffee, Alex Chase-Levenson, Heather DeHaan, Arnab Dey, Sean Dunwoody, Kathleen Fedorchak, Philip Harland, Ted Kaizer, Jonathan Karp, Maia Kotrosits, John Kuhn, Danielle Larose, Meg Leja, Keith Limbach, Colleen Marshall, Eva Miller, Hailee Milligan, Rob Parkinson, Gail Place, Michael Place, Tyler Rancourt, Rubina Raja, C. J. Rice, Bradley Skopyk, Diane Sommerville, Julia Walker, Wendy Wall, Katriella Weingarten, Heather Welland, and Heidi Wendt. My gratitude.

Chronology of Jesus' Judaea

4 BCE: Death of Herod I
4 BCE–6 CE: Jesus of Nazareth is born
6 CE: Roman prefects begin to govern Judaea
     Annas becomes High Priest at Jerusalem
     Antipas becomes Client Dynast of Galilee and Peraea
     Philip becomes Client Dynast of Territories east of Galilee
14 CE: Emperor Augustus dies, Tiberius succeeds him
15 CE: Annas deposed as High Priest
18 CE: Caiaphas becomes High Priest
26 CE: Pontius Pilate becomes Prefect of Judaea
c. 30 CE: Antipas executes John the Baptizer
     Jesus of Nazareth begins preaching
c. 33 CE: Pilate executes Jesus of Nazareth
34 CE: Philip the Tetrarch dies
36 CE: Pilate is recalled
     Caiaphas is deposed
     Aretas defeats Antipas near Gamala
37 CE: Emperor Tiberius dies, Caligula succeeds him
c. 37–40 CE: Paul escapes Damascus and convenes with Jesus' followers
     at Jerusalem
39 CE: Antipas is deposed, Agrippa succeeds him
41 CE: Agrippa I becomes King of Greater Judaea
44 CE: Agrippa I dies

Introduction

PILATE'S PATH TO CRUCIFIXION

*Pilate asked [Jesus], "Are you the King of the Jews?" He said
to him in response, "You are saying it."*

—MARK 15:2

LONG AGO, ON a spring morning in Jerusalem, a Roman governor passed
judgment on a mysterious preacher. The preacher was disfigured by scourges
and nailed to a cross shortly after. He died in agony. The effects of this verdict
have reverberated throughout the world. They have shaped two millennia of
history. Today billions of people embrace the executed convict as their savior.
His judge is remembered as his impious murderer. The Nicene Creed, treasured by so many Christians, names only one man for crucifying Jesus of
Nazareth. This is Pontius Pilate.

When Pontius Pilate put Jesus to death, he did not know it was a pivotal
moment in human history. It was just one of many cases he judged. Jesus of
Nazareth was a unique defendant. He posed a host of problems. But Pilate
judged and executed many people while governing Judaea, and with few last-
ing consequences. He even ordered large-scale massacres until dismissed for
his violent excesses. His encounter with Jesus was typical of Passover week,
well known for its social volatility. All the New Testament Gospels claim the
chief priests of Jerusalem had petitioned his court to put Jesus on trial. He
heard the case, and he rendered a verdict. This verdict would make Jesus' trial
the most famous one ever.

Yet the trial remains shrouded in mystery even today. The New Testament
Gospels do not clearly communicate what charges Pilate judged. They also
portray Pilate as embracing Jesus' innocence before having him killed anyway.
We are left with more questions than answers. Why did Pontius Pilate con-
demn a man he believed innocent? Or did Jesus commit a crime? What was
Pilate's role in Jesus' execution? What was his path to crucifixion?

These are important questions to address. Despite Pilate's role as Jesus' judge, centuries of anti-Semitism have blamed Jews for Jesus' death. It has motivated any number of atrocities that Christians have inflicted. It factors into the genocidal evils of the Holocaust. It is also in keeping with how the New Testament Gospels portray Jesus' trial. These probably reworked earlier traditions in which Jesus had antagonized Roman authority. In this sense they craft a misleading portrait of Pilate as crucifying Jesus from personal weakness or indifference. They claim he did not think Jesus was a criminal. They blame the chief priests or, as phrased by the Gospel of John, "the Jews" for engineering Jesus' death by pressuring Pilate. In this way they frame members of Jesus' movement, both past and contemporary, as innocent of any criminal sedition against Roman governance. But the Gospels do not bear sole responsibility. Late ancient Christians argued that an "innocent" Pilate had never tried and convicted Jesus of a crime at all. Instead, he just had Jesus executed, reluctantly. Their arguments have reverberated through the centuries. Once becoming Christian, Romans embraced a paradox. They celebrated a man executed as a criminal by a Roman judge as the protector of their legal system. Many Europeans and their colonial descendants have done the same. They have also blamed Jews for Jesus' death or embraced the hatred such blame has inspired. Each spring the timing of Easter haunts the holiday of Passover.[1]

This book traces Pilate's path to crucifying Jesus. It determines why and how Pilate deemed Jesus guilty of criminal behavior and the roles people played in ensuring it. It probes how their motivations and social obligations affected how they assessed Jesus' criminality, and it situates Jesus' trial in the legal practices of the Roman Middle East, especially Judaea. In the decades before Jesus' lifetime, and throughout the centuries that followed, Roman courts determined the outcomes of millions of trials throughout the region. Jesus' trial happened in the same legal framework as all of these. Perhaps by understanding the Roman Middle East and its courts, we can learn about Jesus' death.

Jesus' Crucifixion: The Conundrum

The trial and execution of Jesus have long attracted attention. Just about every detail from the ancient sources has been subject to critique. Jesus' fame is not the only reason why. The New Testament Gospels on which we rely abound in ambiguities. It does not help that they were written decades later than what they describe. It does not help that they contradict one another and pursue their own literary goals. The legal justifications for Jesus' execution are unclear.

Introduction

Many scholars have confronted the topic in the past several centuries. Their conclusions present us with many scenarios founded upon many different understandings of the Gospel accounts as historical, literary, and theological sources. This fact gives us a keen sense of the problem. Our sources pose so many challenges that consensus is near impossible.[2]

In this book, we will not sift through all the different theories in minute detail. We also will not explore the apocryphal Gospels or the works purportedly written by Pontius Pilate that circulated in late antiquity. Our focus will be the New Testament Gospels, the works of the Jewish historian Josephus, and legal source material from the Roman Empire. Through them, we will communicate what the most probable legal justification for Jesus' crucifixion by Pilate was. Scholars vary tremendously in their views. They dismiss many different aspects of the Gospel narratives as fabricated while making sense of Jesus' trial. In truth, the historical validity of few (if any) Gospel episodes escape challenge. Not even the Gospel of Mark is beyond suspicion. Most deem it the earliest and most historical gospel. But what it says about Jesus' preaching, trial, and death at Jerusalem attracts withering scrutiny. Experts suspect that it even contrives entire episodes to fulfill evangelical purposes.[3]

The spectrum of views is vast. These range from Pilate's executing Jesus for convenience to his not having executed Jesus at all. They also reflect a host of different yet overlapping features, even if we give them basic schemes. One common theory, aligned with the Gospels' testimony, maintains that Pilate thought of Jesus as innocent of any crime. But he had him executed to accommodate the chief priests, the attending crowd, or a local court's sentence against Jesus for blasphemy, perhaps while convicting him of sedition for cover. Deferring to Jewish legal custom or immense political pressure, he exploited his discretionary powers to execute Jesus without believing him guilty of any criminal behavior. If he hesitated, it was because he was hostile to Jews and did not want to kill an innocent man. This viewpoint and variations on it are common. Some even posit that Pilate did not actually put Jesus on trial but executed him without convicting him of any crime.[4]

Almost universally dismissed is the opposite premise, one espoused by rabbinic texts written centuries after Jesus' death. It is that Jesus was convicted of blasphemy and stoned by a court of Jewish priests and scribes called the Sanhedrin. The New Testament Gospels surely did not fabricate his execution by Pilate. If anything, they frame members of Jesus' movement as innocuous to Roman authority and blame the hostility of the chief priests, not Pilate, for his death. If the chief priests and allied scribes really had stoned Jesus, the

Gospels would not portray Pilate as sentencing him to a crucifixion that Roman judges normally inflicted on insurrectionists. The rabbinic material in fact parodies the New Testament Gospels. It identifies Jesus as a blasphemer worthy of death and celebrates Jewish judges for securing it. But it does not support that the chief priests or allied scribes had the legal authority to execute Jesus centuries earlier.[5]

More promising is the widespread argument that Pilate saw Jesus as a politically dangerous or subversive figure. But why? Many scholars surmise Pilate had Jesus executed because he associated the preacher with social instability. But they differ in what they deem Jesus' message and activity to be. Did he believe divine intervention would destroy the known world and judge the people in it? Or did he envision it would restore an autonomous Israel to righteous Jews? Did Jesus claim to be a kingly Messiah, a term connoting "anointed one" in Hebrew and Aramaic? Did he become known as Christ, the Greek translation of "Messiah," because of it? Did he pose as a heaven-sent agent, or just a prophet or wise man? Not surprisingly, scholars also differ about Pilate's motivations. Why did Pilate deem Jesus a seditionist figure? Because of his message or "regal" pretensions? Because of his activity at the Temple precinct during Passover? Because he was organizing some sort of armed insurgency?

Scholars address the questions just posed with amazing variety. To make their perspectives intelligible, we again organize their views into basic schemes here. But these often cross-pollinate and diverge with differing combinations. Some conclude that Pilate executed Jesus for sedition because he preached against the chief priests, on whom Pilate relied for governance. When Jesus brought his message to Jerusalem and the Temple and the merchants and moneychangers there, he threatened Roman authority and prompted Pilate to execute him. In such theories, Jesus was not necessarily an apocalyptic visionary foreseeing a world-ending moment wrought by God. In some versions, he was a Galilean peasant prophet who sought to restore Israel's self-governance and commitment to the Torah through popular protest against the chief priests and the Romans. In others, he was a wise sage, or even a rural Cynic like the famed Diogenes, who criticized the Temple leadership for unjust acts. His message and conduct at the Temple motivated Pilate to execute him for sedition during his final pilgrimage to Jerusalem. Yet quite a few scholars describe Jesus as a Messianic preacher who denounced the Roman occupation of Judaea and, relatedly, the Temple's management while posing as "King of the Jews." Pilate in response had him arrested and executed, or at least supported charges brought by the chief priests of Jerusalem. The Gospels,

Introduction

bent on shifting the blame to the Jewish elite, made Pilate seem committed to his innocence.[6]

In many reckonings, Jesus' alleged posturing as a Messiah, a king, was enough for Pilate to classify him as guilty of seditious activity, especially since he did so at the Temple precinct during the volatile period of Passover week. For some, Pilate's decision aligned with the legal proceedings of the chief priests, who believed false prophecies warranted death. But for others, the Gospels retain "distorted memories" that misleadingly shift responsibility for Jesus' death from Pilate to the chief priests or even "the Jews" to portray them as the killers of prophets or Messiahs. Within decades of his crucifixion, tensions between believers in Jesus Christ and other Jews shaped how the Gospels or their sources exaggerated or even contrived certain episodes from Jesus' final Passover. These include his "royal" entry into Jerusalem, his confrontation of moneychangers and merchants at the Temple, his arrest, Pilate's belief in his innocence, the pardon of a seditionist named Barabbas, and Pilate's accommodation of the chief priests and crowd at Jesus' trial. Jesus' regal claims were enough for Pilate to execute him, and if he hesitated, it was because he usually resisted complying with the chief priests or their compatriots. But Pilate believed Jesus was criminally responsible for claiming to be "King of the Jews."[7]

In some accounts, Pilate convicted Jesus of "treason" (*maiestas*) for staking a claim as "King of the Jews" but without believing he had done something seriously criminal or seditious. Pilate was caving to pressure from the chief priests or the crowd witnessing the trial, despite his misgivings. What proved decisive in Jesus' conviction by Pilate were his Messianic aspirations, his confessing to them at trial, and his otherwise uncooperative conduct, not his activity in Jerusalem or at the Temple. Even so, Pilate conceived of Jesus as an eccentric making a bizarre and unenforceable claim of kingship, not a dangerous political subversive. He perhaps construed it as the toothless assertion of the mentally disturbed and had him (and only him) executed as such. But ultimately, if Pilate convicted Jesus of treason or sedition for his regal claims, it was because he was pressured by the chief priests or the crowd present at Jesus' trial.[8]

Some scholars maintain Jesus did not merely die for his preaching. He was organizing insurgency against the Romans and maybe making an earthly claim to Messianic kingship (with divine support). An armed seditionist, he was arrested, tried, and executed by Pilate, along with some followers. The Gospel accounts in turn disguised this to shift blame to the Jewish elite and to obscure Jesus' seditious stature. But despite this, they could not disguise that Pilate condemned Jesus to death by crucifixion, typically imposed upon insurgent seditionists. This had become too well established and widely known.[9]

Some theories shift Pilate's motives from Jesus' conduct to the crowds in Jerusalem that celebrated him as a Messiah during his final Passover. Jesus may not have promoted himself as Messiah, but he still posed a threat to crowd stability because of his Messianic reputation, and Pilate had to act. As such, Jesus' trial before a court convened by the chief priests probably never happened. His famous confrontation of moneychangers and merchants at the Temple and his prediction of its destruction may not have either. These were Gospel inventions. Instead, the chief priests and Roman soldiers collaborated to have Jesus arrested, and Pilate acted on his powers as Roman prefect to use violence to keep the peace. He had Jesus convicted and crucified for sedition. But Pilate did not execute Jesus publicly because he had committed a recognizably criminal act or posed a real danger to regional stability. He did it as a precaution, to prevent any violence at Jerusalem that Jesus' incendiary reputation could arouse during Passover week. This would also explain why only Jesus and none of his followers was crucified.[10]

Another strand of thought emphasizes Jesus' impact on crowds as well. But it suggests Jesus was inciting crowd violence at the Temple precinct during his final Passover. After all, the Gospels report that the chief priests were concerned with it during their Passover encounters with Jesus. They also state that Pilate had Jesus tried alongside an insurrectionist named Barabbas and had him executed with two seditionists or brigands. Even if these had no relationship with Jesus' activity, it points to Pilate's recognition of Jesus as one among several figures engaged in incendiary, criminal activity during Passover week. He crucified Jesus for it.[11]

Why has there been such variation in modern understandings of Jesus' execution? We can note several factors. One boils down to how scholars variously reconstruct Jesus of Nazareth and his message from the Gospel accounts. These have different literary and theological goals, often fulfilled by borrowing material from one another (as opposed to providing independent corroboration). A point of debate is whether the Gospel of Mark, often understood as written right after the Romans destroyed Jerusalem's Temple in 70, is accurate or anachronistic in portraying Jesus as hostile to the Temple's management and predicting its destruction (Parts II–III). After all, what Jesus preached, how he was understood by others, and whether he was inciting sedition all have a bearing on how Pilate or the chief priests dealt with him.

Introduction

Another factor is that the Gospel narratives of Jesus' trial and execution do not make sense. They depict a Pilate who believes Jesus innocent of any crime but decides to placate the chief priests and attending crowds by eliminating him. To this end, he kills Jesus (and him alone) through a conspicuously gruesome execution allotted to seditionists and violent criminals. The problem is not just Pilate's decision to execute but how he does it. After all, he could have decided to have Jesus quietly eliminated or detained him until after Passover week before executing him. He did not need to have Jesus viciously scourged, grotesquely crucified, and humiliated in public under the mocking title of "King of the Jews" within a day of his arrest. But all the Gospels agree he did just that.[12]

A third factor is the confessional stakes and their bearing on how Jesus is understood. Scholars of Jesus and the New Testament share many methods, worldviews, and terms of debate. Their confessional beliefs, whether religious, secularist, or atheistic, do not necessarily negate rigorous scholarship. But such beliefs (including mine) can create confirmation biases despite best efforts. They seemingly affect the range of views on how historical the Gospels are. These include arguments favoring the historical validity of the Gospels and "mythicist" ones maintaining that Jesus never existed outside the minds of his believers, who first conceived of him as a celestial being.[13]

A final serious problem is the vicious, violent history of anti-Semitism the Gospel accounts have fed. The Gospels arguably shift responsibility for Jesus' death from Roman authorities to the chief priests and pilgrims at Jerusalem. They assert that the chief priests engaged in selfish, unethical plotting to secure Jesus' death and manipulated the crowd at his trial to demand his crucifixion. They ignore any moral concerns that motivated the chief priests and treat them as simple foils to Jesus' spiritual mission. They state that Pilate knew Jesus was innocent and reluctantly conceded to have him killed. This dynamic in the Gospels has long fueled hateful rhetoric that blames Jews for Jesus' death. Even after the Holocaust, accounts of Jesus' trial based on the Gospel accounts have portrayed Jesus as antithetical or transcendent of all other contemporary Jews and their practices. A valid counterpoint challenges their treatments of the chief priests and Jesus' Jewish compatriots. Some assert that the chief priests and Judas Iscariot played little or no role in Jesus' arrest or death. A few surmise that they even tried to protect him from the Romans bent on his demise. Altogether the atrocious purposes for which people have historically exploited the Gospels give us pause. We must be mindful of them when we assess the role in Jesus' death they assign to the chief priests or Jews at Jerusalem. Even when the Gospels appear to agree, we should worry they depend on common traditions or one another and replicate the same harmful distortions.[14]

Despite centuries of attention, the following questions persist: What was the nature of Jesus' activity in Jerusalem during his final Passover? Was he a Messianic preacher, an apocalyptic messenger, a peasant philosopher, a prophet, or an armed insurrectionist? Did he think God would create an autonomous Israel or end the entire earthly order? What happened when Jesus entered Jerusalem? Was it really the elaborate public affair that the Gospels report? What happened when Jesus preached at the Temple during his final Passover week? Did Jesus and his core followers really act aggressively against moneychangers and merchants and predict the Temple's destruction? Who arrested Jesus? Was it a band organized by the chief priests or Roman soldiers? What charge did a *synhedrion*, or council, at Jerusalem (misleadingly called "the Sanhedrin") bring against him? Was Jesus even tried by it? On what charge did Pilate convict Jesus? Did Pilate give Jesus a formal trial or simply execute him? Is it true that Pilate did not execute any of Jesus' followers? Why not?

Such questions will probably never have definitive answers. All we can do is create historically plausible narratives based on critical readings of the source material and weigh them against their alternatives. This book operates in this spirit. It confronts the questions just posed to identify the most plausible legal path for Pilate's crucifixion of Jesus. Its interpretation of Jesus' arrest and trial owes deep debts to the scholarship with which it engages. Its narrative would be impossible without it. But its orientation is different in some meaningful ways. As can be expected, my approach involves pondering the Gospel narratives, assessing their relationships to one another, and evaluating their historical value for Jesus' trial. But it also contemplates how Roman imperialism and its regional authorities provided the legal framework for Jesus' encounter with Pilate. It outlines how the mechanisms of different courts and judges in the Roman Middle East can enable historical inquiry into Jesus' trial and execution. None of the accounts attributed to Pilate are authentic or can be proven so. We have no testimony from the high priests Annas and Caiaphas. But they all plausibly believed they were fulfilling a vital social obligation by securing Jesus' trial and execution.[15]

This book is foremost intended for the general reader. It will not trace the vast array of scholarly arguments with intractable detail or dense footnotes. But its narrative will stake certain positions in a broader field of scholarly engagement. It takes seriously that Jesus and his followers, largely Galilean laborers by origin, acted on their moral convictions to oppose the ruling order

Introduction

of Roman Judaea, including the chief priests of Jerusalem's Temple. It also takes seriously that the chief priests, being wealthy municipal elites at Jerusalem, acted on their moral convictions in arresting and prosecuting him for sedition. It recognizes that Pilate, a Roman magistrate, deemed Jesus responsible for a capital crime.

Jesus was executed by a man who embodied Roman governance and its repressive violence. His trial was given form by the legal cultures of its provinces and client kingdoms. By identifying their machinery and mechanisms, we can cast light on Pilate's path to crucifying Jesus. We now start with the peoples, places, and key players of the Middle East during Jesus' lifetime.

PART I

Politics and People

I

Places, Peoples, Empire

*Then in his reign's 18th year...Herod threw himself into
an unprecedented work: to build the Temple of God on his
own initiative.*

—JOSEPHUS, *Ant.* 15.380

*On the fourth day of the festival, some Roman soldier
exposed himself and showed his genitals to the Temple's
crowd. Those who saw it were angry and frustrated. They
did not claim that they were being outraged but that God
was being treated impiously.*

—JOSEPHUS, *Ant.* 20.108, on a Passover Week during the 50s

WHEN PILATE KILLED Jesus, Rome had governed greater Judaea for a century. "Judaea" was more or less what people called "Israel" in Greek and Latin,
but the territories encompassed by both terms could vary. For much of Jesus'
life, it was under the sway of the Roman emperor Tiberius. Beneath him,
Jerusalem and lesser Judaea were governed by prefects from Italy. These held
the rank of equestrian, basically a wealthy Roman citizen who was not a senator. Jesus' home region of Galilee and other territories were allotted to
Herodian dynasts. These were Jewish by ancestry and piety but Roman by citizenship. Both the prefects and Herodian dynasts embodied Roman authority.
They were made or broken by the emperor's approval. The long arm of Roman
imperialism defined where Pilate and Jesus would cross fatal paths. But why
was Jesus subject to Roman authority? Why were Galileans like him Jewish?
What was a Roman prefect doing in Jerusalem during his final Passover?

Judaea in the Roman Empire

In 64–63 BCE, the Roman general Pompey arrived in the Levant. There he
encountered the last reigning members of the Seleucid dynasty. This dynasty

had come to govern the Middle East after Alexander the Great's conquest but had lapsed into dysfunction. Deposing it, Pompey created the province of Syria. While doing so, he marched south to Damascus and then southwest into greater Judaea, now governed by Jews as their ancestral territory (*Eretz Israel* in Hebrew). There two brothers named John Hyrcanus (II) and Aristobulus (II) were locked in civil war. These were the scions of the Hasmonaean dynasty, the ruling priestly family. Over the prior century, it had freed lesser Judaea from Seleucid rule and annexed the surrounding regions of Idumaea, Samaria, and Galilee. But in 63, the Hasmonaeans were mired in fratricidal bloodletting. Pompey picked sides. He besieged Aristobulus in the Temple precinct of Jerusalem and slaughtered his followers. Once victorious, he sacrilegiously entered the Temple's inner spaces, though he left its treasury alone. Promoting Hyrcanus as high priest, he had Aristobulus brought to Rome and paraded in triumph.

This was how the Roman Republic annexed greater Judaea as a "client kingdom." It would be in the Roman Empire over 600 years, as either "client" or provincial territory. From the start, it was a satellite of the province of Syria. This was governed by a Roman senator of consular rank. It was also surrounded by territories managed by ancestral dynasts who answered to him. In greater Judaea, Hyrcanus was the face of ancestral Jewish rule. But his henchman, an Idumaean named Antipater, came to dominate politics. Many turbulent decades later, Antipater's son Herod became Rome's client king over greater Judaea and some surrounding territories. The king ruled them with an iron fist, a proclivity for violence, and ambitious building. Much of what we know about Herod comes from two accounts written by the Jewish historian Josephus in the late first century: the *Jewish War* and the *Jewish Antiquities*. Josephus pursues his own goals by portraying the rule of Herod (but not of Romans, despite some terrible governors) as hostile to Jewish traditions. The sources he used and their narrative goals remain controversial. Even so, some aspects of Herod's reign are clear. Herod created much of the impressive Temple precinct at Jerusalem that Jesus frequented in his final days. Murdering most priests of Hasmonaean lineage, he appointed men from other families, often with origins in the Jewish Diaspora, not greater Judaea. When Herod died in 4 BCE or so, his kingdom was parceled to some of his sons. Archelaus received lesser Judaea, which consisted of Jerusalem and surrounding territory. Antipas (or Antipater) got Galilee, and Philip controlled adjacent parts of southern Syria. He executed John the Baptizer and was governing Galilee when Jesus lived there.[1]

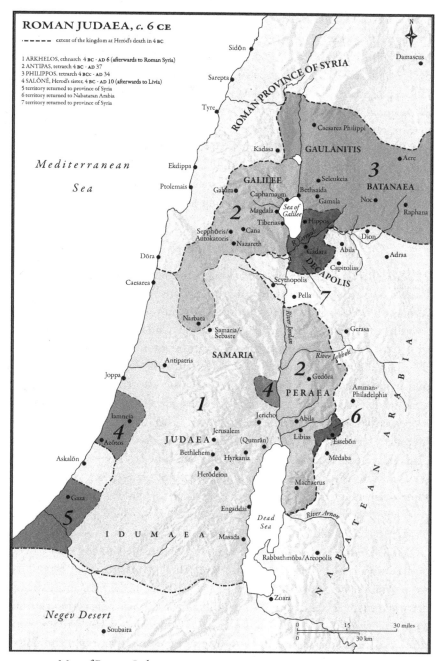

MAP 1.1 Map of Roman Judaea.
After *The Herodian Kingdoms* © Ian Mladjov: https://drive.google.com/file/d/1KQBQppx AXfpHSdZSsI13i5X0hco-1Or8/view

No son of Herod earned the title king from the Roman emperor Augustus. Even so, Antipas and Philip enjoyed long reigns. Archelaus mismanaged lesser Judaea, and Augustus had him deposed and executed in 6 CE (or so). He also decided to transfer lesser Judaea to the province of Syria, to be managed by Italian prefects of Roman equestrian rank. Pontius Pilate, Jesus' judge, is easily the most infamous.

Such was the political situation in greater Judaea when the paths of Jesus and Pilate crossed (Map 1.1). But who were the people of greater Judaea and the regions around it? Why were Galileans like Jesus also Jews who made pilgrimages to Jerusalem? We turn to the peoples and places that the Romans were governing in the Middle East during Jesus' lifetime.[2]

Syrians, Arabians, and Greeks

The lands around Roman Judaea belonged to their ancestral populations. In Roman Syria, these were Aramaeans, or "Syrians" in Greek. For Greeks and Romans, "Syrian" had many meanings. Broadly defined, they used both "Syrian" and "Assyrian" for people in the Levant and Mesopotamia descended from Aramaic-speaking ancestors. They thought these populations called themselves Aramaeans in Aramaic. More narrowly, "Syrian" described peoples living west of the Euphrates River or just east of it. Yet after Pompey annexed the Levant, Roman authorities classified everyone living north of Judaea as Syrian, whoever their ancestors were. This definition stuck. By Jesus' lifetime, everyone living north and east of Galilee was Syrian, including the Canaanite peoples of coastal Lebanon. This is how Jesus reportedly encountered a "Syro-Phoenician" woman at the city of Tyre (Mark 7:26). While Phoenician (Canaanite) by descent (Matt 15:22), she was a Roman Syrian provincial. When lesser Judaea was joined to the province of Syria in 6 CE, people conceived of it as part of Syria too (Matt 4:24).[3]

More ambiguous were the people who had settled in the client kingdoms surrounding the province of Syria. Their ancestors often originated from Arabia and spoke Arabian languages. As such, Greeks and Romans classified them as "Arabians." Being polytheists, they wove together the cultural traditions of Greeks, Aramaeans, and Canaanites with Arabian traditions. At Emesa (modern Homs) were the Emesene dynasts. In the Bekaa Valley and adjacent highlands of Lebanon were the Ituraeans. Centered at the marvelous city of Petra, but controlling much of Transjordan and northern Arabia, were the Nabataeans. The Nabataeans have left a host of inscriptions in their Aramaic dialect, but they spoke a northern Arabian

Places, Peoples, Empire

language resembling Arabic. When Arabians forged a national consciousness as Arabs in late antiquity, they derived the classical script of Arabic from the Nabataean one. In the seventh century, Arabs would conquer Judaea, by then divided by the Romans into several provinces called Palestine. Their descendants, and those of the people they governed, now bear the name "Palestinian."[4]

The Syrian province was centered on the stretch of the Levant north of Samaria and Galilee. But a cluster of Greek polities to the east of Galilee and Judaea were in it too. The ancient sources sometimes describe these as part of the "Decapolis" (Matt 4:25; Mark 7:31) or "Coele-Syria." Even so, these were ambiguous concepts, and different authors place different cities or regions in them. Some just speak of "Greek cities" east of Galilee. The Gospels claim Jesus sometimes entered their territory. He reportedly cured a demoniac at Gerasa or Gadara.[5]

Who were the Greeks populating the cities surrounding greater Judaea? After Alexander the Great's conquests, Greco-Macedonian kings established settlements of Greeks throughout the Levant, including at existing urban areas. Even so, members of some ancestral Middle Eastern populations adopted Greek cultural life and fashioned relationships with other Greek communities. Phoenicians notably did this. The controversial Seleucid king Antiochus IV is infamous for patronizing Greek practices among priests of Jerusalem, along with subsequent repressive and sacrilegious measures. When Pompey arrived in Syria in 64–63, he restored the preeminence of the Greek communities in Hasmonaean territories. Yet he also populated them with people of Syrian, Phoenician, or Arabian ancestries. This practice became increasingly standard throughout the Roman period. This is why the "Syro-Phoenician" Jesus encountered is also identified as a Greek by the Gospel of Mark (7:26).[6]

Judaea and Jews (or Judaeans)

During Jesus' lifetime, Judaea had many definitions. In its narrowest sense, it referred to Jerusalem and adjacent territory. This definition corresponded to the Iron Age kingdom of Judah and, under Persian rule, the district of Yehud. This was the ancestral land of the Jews. It explains why the Gospel of Luke claims Jesus' natal household traveled from Galilee to Bethlehem "of Judaea" for the census of 6 CE. Other Gospels distinguish Jerusalem and Judaea from Galilee, Peraea (the region "across" the Jordan River), Idumaea, and the cities of Syria or Nabataea.[7]

Even so, the Hasmonaean kingdom shifted and expanded what Judaea meant. During the later second and early first century BCE, the Hasmonaeans conquered Galilee, Idumaea, Samaria, Peraea, and coastal Palestine (the Greek term for "Philistia"). The Hasmonaeans settled Judaeans in many of these territories, and in Galilee and Idumaea many people became Jews who venerated the Temple at Jerusalem. The Hasmonaeans also destroyed the Samaritan temple at Mount Gerizim. As people became Jews or lived under Hasmonaean governance, their territories became part of what Jews called "the Jewish/Judaean land" (*ge Ioudaia*) in Greek or *Eretz Israel* in Hebrew. Jews conceived of this territory and their cities as belonging to Jews. This explains why Jesus, a Galilean, was also a *Ioudaios* in Greek. He venerated the Temple of Jerusalem and the Torah like other Jews, but he originated from Galilee, now a part of greater Judaea.[8]

When Pompey intervened in Judaea in 63, he recognized only part of the Hasmonaean claim. Entrusting most of Samaria to the Samaritans, he identified Greek communities as preeminent in coastal Palestine's cities. Jews there had some privileges and protections. But they did not determine the visible features of their civic landscapes, which Greeks speckled with temples and statues of gods and emperors. Instead, Pompey defined lesser Judaea, Galilee, and Peraea as belonging to Jews. There Jews had civil authority and could maintain civic spaces void of polytheist temples and statues. Remarkably, statements attributed to Jesus reflect this definition of Judaea or *Eretz Israel*. "Do not go out onto the road of the peoples [*ethne*] or enter a city of the Samaritans. Travel instead to the lost sheep of the house of Israel" (Matt 10:5–6). Here "the lost sheep" of Israel are the populations of lesser Judaea, Peraea, and Galilee. Samaria and the Greek peoples surrounding the land of the Jews are apparently off limits.

In 6 CE or so, the Romans created the district of Judaea in the province of Syria. The district integrated lesser Judaea and various parts of the land of the Jews. But it also included the Greek polities along the coast and Samaria. The district represents yet another meaning the term "Judaea" could take during Jesus' lifetime. Here we repeat what "Judaea" could variously mean under Roman rule:

Lesser Judaea:
The region surrounding Jerusalem, formerly the kingdom of Judah and the Persian district of Yehud.

Greater Judaea (Jewish definition):

The territory once ruled by the Hasmonaean kings and where Jews represented the governing order while they ruled. It corresponded with the broadest definition of the land of Israel and included lesser Judaea, Samaria, Galilee, immediate Transjordan, Idumaea, and coastal Palestine. Jews expected its public landscapes to be void of polytheist temples and statues.

Greater Judaea (Roman definition):

This included lesser Judaea, immediate Transjordan, Idumaea, and Galilee. Smaller in scale than the Jewish definition, it was where Romans treated Jews as the governing population that maintained public landscapes void of polytheist temples and statues.

The district of Judaea:

a Roman provincial unit, it included greater Judaea (Roman definition), Samaria, and coastal cities of Palestine.

By Jesus' lifetime, the *Ioudaioi* were all the inhabitants of greater Judaea (including Galilee), minus Samaria. For them, the Jewish Temple of Jerusalem was their ancestral cultic center. Their name had obvious ethnic and regional connotations. Because of this, scholars sometimes argue *Ioudaios* is best translated as "Judaean," not "Jew." Even so, by Jesus' lifetime *Ioudaios* could also describe any people who worshiped the ancestral God of Judaea, embraced the Torah as law, and venerated the Temple at Jerusalem. Their ancestors did not have to originate from lesser Judaea or even be *Ioudaioi* themselves. This is why Jesus' Galileans were *Ioudaioi* by his lifetime. Whether *Ioudaioi* were foremost an ethnicity or a civil community of worshipers that an individual could join was never resolved in antiquity. *Ioudaioi* themselves had different criteria for their definitions and differed in their perspectives. Since the term carried both connotations, we will refer to *Ioudaioi* as Jews.[9]

The inhabitants of Samaria were distinct from most nearby Jews. Yet it remains debated whether we should classify them as Jews too. They claimed descent from Israelites deported by the Assyrians in 722 BCE. But Jews asserted they were descended from Persians settled there by the Assyrians (2 Kings 17:5–6, 24). The Samaritans also maintained many of the same languages, perspectives, and cultural practices as Jews, or at least variations on them. But unlike Jews, who had their temple at Jerusalem, the Samaritans maintained theirs at Mount Gerizim. Excavations show it existed as early as the Persian period, even if Josephus associates it with Alexander's conquests.

The Hasmonaeans had destroyed it c. III BCE, but worship persisted there during Jesus' lifetime. Roman authorities clearly thought of Samaritans as distinct. They excluded Samaria from the ancestral territory of Jews (while including it in the district of Judaea). This sense of profound difference born of disturbing similarity explains why some Jews considered Samaritans outsiders. In the Gospels, Samaritans are not *Ioudaioi* (John 4 generally), even if they are Israelites. They also foreshadow how non-Jews could embrace Jesus by the time the Gospels were being written. One of Jesus' parables narrated how one of them, known today as "the Good Samaritan," aided a man beaten by robbers after two pious Jews concerned with corpse impurity left him in the dirt. Another celebrates how Jesus healed lepers at the border of Samaria and Galilee, with only a Samaritan thanking him (Luke 10:25–37, 17:11–19). Pontius Pilate would end his career by massacring Samaritans marching to Mount Gerizim, the site of their destroyed temple.[10]

As noted, Herod I came to power through Roman support. His territories corresponded to greater Judaea and adjacent regions. They also included regions that Romans had variously entrusted to Greek or to Jewish communities. Herod largely maintained such distinctions, which had a huge impact on urban terrain. At Jerusalem, he promoted the Jewish Temple. There sculptures were largely absent. Jews usually paid the Temple tax and other dues with Tyrian shekels that bore images of the Phoenician god Melqart. They sometimes used coins engraved with likenesses of Roman emperors that had been minted and circulated elsewhere. Imperial and royal likenesses were mostly absent from cities, towns, and villages in lesser Judaea, Galilee, and Transjordan. In cities where Greeks were preeminent, Herod promoted the Roman imperial cult and Greek polytheism. Sculptures and coins with imperial likenesses abounded. When Herod executed massive building programs throughout greater Judaea, they largely perpetuated such patterns. They also created the infrastructure that subsequent Roman governors would exploit and made the Temple precinct an even more contested space for Jews than ever before. Pilate and Jesus would confront each other in the urban world Herod built.[11]

Herod and His Cities

Herod's building program was ambitious. His foundations defined the Judaean topography Jesus and Pontius Pilate came to inhabit and were part of the Jerusalem where they had their fatal encounter. Recent excavations illuminate Herod's urban and monumental foundations and how volatile they were in Jesus' lifetime.[12]

Some of Herod's notable foundations were not cities; they were fortified palaces. At Jericho, Herod expanded on the work of his Hasmonaean predecessors by building three new palaces and a complex for horse races and other spectacles. Near Bethlehem, he built his tomb. His "Herodeion" involved a fortified palace at the top of a large mount with artificial slopes and another palace at its base. At the rocky outcropping of Masada, known for where Jewish insurgents confronted the Romans in 74, Herod built a palace site overlooking the surrounding countryside. In distinct stages, he constructed a complex on its western side and a truly remarkable one on its northern end. The northern complex was built on several terraces in conformity to shifts of elevation in the bedrock. Nearby was an impressive bathhouse (Figure 1.1). Altogether, Herod's palaces and monuments at Jericho, Herodeion, and Masada were made by current techniques, technologies, and materials from Roman Italy and the Greek-speaking eastern Mediterranean. So was his work in cities like Jerusalem, Caesarea, and Samaria.

Samaria was Herod's earliest major urban re-foundation. He dubbed it Sebaste to honor the emperor Augustus and built a temple to both Rome and Augustus there. He also established a theater, a temple (probably to Persephone-Kore), an aqueduct, and perhaps a stadium. It enabled Herod to maintain a cluster of veterans, many being polytheists, in the territory of Israelite Samaritans, who desired to revive their Temple at Mount Gerizim. Subsequently, the city would become one place where the Romans recruited soldiers for their cohorts.

The gem of Herod's new cities was Caesarea Maritima, or Caesarea-by-the-Sea, which he built principally from 22 to 10 BCE. Once again, we know much about it through excavations and the testimony of Josephus. At a city called Strato's Tower, Herod built a massive artificial harbor complex that had two massive concrete breakwaters and a lighthouse. Overlooking the harbor, he constructed a large temple dedicated to Rome and Augustus. He also built a large palace, a hippodrome (a circus for horse racing), and a theater. Outfitting this renewed city with an aqueduct, he renamed it after the emperor Augustus Caesar (Figure 1.2).

Caesarea was a very important city thereafter. When Judaea was integrated into provincial space in 6 CE, its palace became the headquarters of Roman prefects like Pontius Pilate. It was also where Rome's military strength was concentrated. No legions were stationed there, but prefects commanded six infantry cohorts and one cavalry unit, overwhelmingly recruited from Samaria-Sebaste and Caesarea. Most of these were normally stationed at Caesarea. The city was volatile. Its very existence fostered the worship of

FIGURE 1.1 Aerial view of Herod's palace at Masada. © Andrew Shiva/Wikimedia Commons CC BY-SA 4.0.

FIGURE 1.2 Aerial view of Herod's palace and Roman prefect's *praetorium* at Caesarea Maritima. © Abraham Graicer/Wikimedia Commons CC BY-SA 4.0.

Roman emperors, and its population consisted largely of non-Jews. It was replete with temples, cult statues of gods, and images of the imperial family. The local Greek and Syrian population asserted themselves as the city's governing population, with imperial support. But Caesarea had been built by a Jewish king in a region the Hasmonaeans had defined as belonging to Jews. The substantial local Jewish population could claim they rightfully governed it.[13]

Caesarea Maritima is never mentioned in the Gospels. Its existence is merely implied when a centurion seeks out Jesus at Capernaum. It figures more prominently in the Acts of the Apostles. It claims a centurion named Cornelius became a believer in Jesus and a supporter of Simon Peter. Paul was reportedly detained there for two years by the prefect Felix after the chief priests and allied scribes accused him of seditious behavior. He was then tried before the governor Festus and the Herodian king Agrippa II. Otherwise, Caesarea was a port through which Jesus' followers moved between Judaea and Mediterranean locations (Matt 8:5–13; Luke 7:1–10; Acts 9:30, 10, 18:22, 23–27).

Above all, Caesarea has fielded a vital trace of Pontius Pilate, Jesus' judge. While prefect (c. 26–36), Pilate restored a lighthouse named after the emperor Tiberius and celebrated it with a dedicatory inscription that bore his name. A fragment of the inscription survives, though its building does not. When Pilate was not maintaining order and administering justice, he was often involved in building and restoration. His work has left traces in the Jerusalem Herod created too.

As impressive as Caesarea was, Herod's most notable achievements involved Jerusalem. Despite venerating Rome's imperial household, Herod was a devout Jew who lavished huge expenses on Jerusalem's Temple. In this respect, he was intervening in a sacred terrain that had existed for centuries. But before Herod's reign, Jerusalem had also been the primary residence of the Hasmonaean priests, who had maintained the Jewish Temple and an autonomous Israel for a century prior. An upstart, Herod funded work that still shapes the topography of Old Jerusalem today. On its western hill, and along its existing circuit wall, Herod established an elaborate palace. On its north end, he built several defensive towers. After Herod's death and the deposition of his son Archelaus, the palace became the headquarters (*praetorium*) of Roman governors, who would judge cases outside it. It was here Jesus would be sentenced to death by Pilate.

Even so, Herod's most impressive building at Jerusalem was the Temple. The initial Temple attributed to King Solomon by the Hebrew Bible had been

Places, Peoples, Empire

destroyed by Babylonians in 586 BCE. Jews who inhabited Jerusalem under Persian and Seleucid rule maintained a less impressive one. After Antiochus IV's sacrilegious activity, Hasmonaeans had safeguarded it from imperial aggressors until Pompey's arrival in 63 BCE. It was this Temple that Herod overhauled on a grand scale, and even if Roman soldiers destroyed it in 70 CE, its location remains a sacred space for Jews even today. Around 23 BCE, he initiated work on a new building and the massive walled courtyard that would encompass it. The Temple building and its surrounding fortification walls were completed first, within a decade. Within its walls, there were two courtyards where ritually pure worshipers could make offerings, one for Israelite women (and men) and another just for Israelite men. Non-Jews who entered these were to be put to death. In the 50s, the preacher Paul reportedly stood accused of violating the prohibition by bringing non-Jews there (Figures 1.3 and 1.4).[14]

Work on the Temple's massive walled courtyard took much longer. It remained unfinished for decades after Jesus' lifetime. To create it, Herod had to make the Temple Mount into a massive, level terrace that had not existed before (Figures 6.1, 6.2, 10.2; Map 6.1). The courtyard was outfitted with colonnaded porticoes flanking each side and, beyond them, a vast wall. The famous Wailing Wall is a part that survives (Figure 1.5). Non-Jews could visit this massive courtyard even if they could not enter the Temple itself. At the northwest corner of the Temple precinct was a fortress previously built by the Hasmonaeans and amplified by Herod. He had named it Antonia, after Mark Antony. From it, Herod's soldiers monitored the Temple precinct and kept order.

Herod's work made Jerusalem an unprecedented center for Jewish pilgrimage. Ideally those living in greater Judaea would come several times a year for major festivals. Jews from the Diaspora also traveled to Jerusalem at an accelerated scale. According to the Gospels of Luke and John (Chapter 6), such pilgrimages brought Jesus to Jerusalem on many occasions in his life. In Acts of the Apostles (2:5–13), Jews traveled to Jerusalem from all over the known world, bringing their languages with them. Ultimately, it was on such a pilgrimage that Jesus made his fatal trip to the city. In his final days, he and his followers reportedly preached an incendiary message in the Temple's outer courtyard.

When Jesus made his final pilgrimage, the Temple and its senior priests had ample economic means. As an institution, it owned farmland that produced animals, grains, and vegetables for offerings. It also claimed fines for sacred infractions and offerings (called a *qorban*). But to maintain its sacrifices

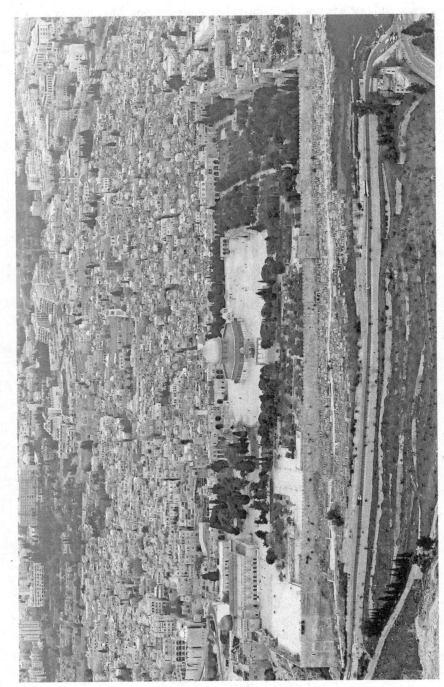

FIGURE 1.3 Aerial view of contemporary Jerusalem. © Andrew Shiva/Wikimedia Commons CC BY-SA 4.0.

FIGURE 1.4 Model of Jerusalem in the Second Temple period. Photo by N. Andrade. © Holyland Tourism 1992, Ltd. Courtesy of The Israel Museum, Jerusalem, at the Israel National Museum. Place names inserted by N. Andrade.

FIGURE 1.5 Western Wall of Herod's courtyard terrace. Photo by N. Andrade.

and grandeur, Herod's priests expected devout Jews to pay priestly tithes and a Temple tax. Both had precedents in the Torah, but with serious changes originating under the Hasmonaeans. What had justified tithes was that priests did not own land. They acquired agricultural produce from others for their maintenance. But priests had now become the most powerful landowners in Judaea. They collected tithes anyway. The Torah also obliged Jews to make one donation of a half-shekel to the Temple during their lifetime. The chief priests requested that Jews pay it each year. These innovations enabled the amplified Temple to accommodate vast numbers of pilgrims and sacrifices during festivals. Under the priests' supervision, the Temple's outer courtyard even became a vital center of commerce and exchange. Merchants, vendors, tax and tithe collectors, and moneychangers regulated by the chief priests, or even being their clients or dependents, were active there. This was normal at ancient temples. But at Jerusalem, it could attract criticism if priests profited from poor Jews or attached commercial ventures to how they collected sacred revenues. Some were apparently collecting surcharges for money exchanges that enabled pilgrims to pay the Temple tax or selling offerings (like doves) at premium costs in the Temple's external courtyard. These enterprises enabled pilgrims to engage in pious acts. But some dissenting Jews thought these taxes,

Places, Peoples, Empire

tithes, and commercial enterprises were unjust, violated communal obligations to the poor, or enabled priests to profit from what belonged to God. Jesus' famous confrontation with moneychangers and merchants at the Temple precinct (Chapter 6), if historical, was plausibly motivated by such concerns.[15]

Herod's urban foundations and promotion of the Temple precinct of Jerusalem were remarkable. But they were also firmly embedded in longstanding social rivalries his activity exacerbated. In his major cities like Caesarea and Samaria-Sebaste (though not Jerusalem), he had even built temples for the Roman emperor. By the time Jesus reached manhood, some Jews did not deem the Romans, Herodians, or chief priests of the Jewish Temple, being enmeshed in uneasy alliance, to be legitimate. Dissidents were issuing challenges from the villages of Galilee and the shore of the Dead Sea to the crowds of the Temple precinct.

Social Tensions at the Time of Jesus' Birth

When Jesus was born, his native region of Galilee as well as greater Judaea was rife with social tensions. By many criteria, the violent charismatic Herod had managed a long, successful reign. He had earned the trust of the emperor Augustus and the consular governors of Syria. But his regime and complicity with Roman authority also fed conflicts. These defined the world Jesus came to inhabit. They shaped the Judaea Pontius Pilate had to govern.

Ancient empires encompassing vast territories had to overcome serious obstacles to their cohesion. They governed diverse populations, with their own unique social practices and traditions. Imperial authorities expected them to cooperate. These often had to forge (more) amiable relationships with their traditional enemies. Before Pompey's arrival, the Jews of Judaea, the Samaritans, the Nabataeans, and the Greek polities speckling coastal Palestine, southern Phoenicia, and Transjordan had tense relationships, which sometimes became violent. These tensions persisted, and Roman authorities aimed to manage them peacefully. As we have seen, their solution was to map areas where Jewish communities were governing populations (Judaea, Galilee, Peraea, and Idumaea) and those where they were not (Samaria and the Greek cities of coastal Palestine, Phoenicia, and southern Syria). This distinction endured under Herod, whose realm included regions where Jews, Greeks, or Samaritans were preeminent civic populations. It had to be recognized by subsequent Roman prefects and Herodian dynasts too.[16]

Another obstacle was the limitations of ancient technology. These put serious constraints on how Roman authorities governed populations. Human movement and communication were very slow, and coordination was hard. The Roman imperial bureaucracy of Pilate's lifetime was small. Military garrisons, which attracted provincial recruits, enabled it to administer provinces and client kingdoms. Otherwise, Roman authorities promoted and cooperated with regional and municipal elites that managed the ancestral traditions of their peoples. In greater Judaea, they had so identified the Herodian dynasts and the chief priests of Jerusalem. In fact, the emperor Augustus (reigned 27 BCE–14 CE) envisioned the Herodians and other client kings as members of the empire's governing elite. These exercised authority just like the Italian elites dispatched to govern provinces. Augustus could even pit them in competition, to his benefit.

Governing elites like the Herodians and chief priests faced serious challenges. They were a vital link between Roman authorities and subject populations. In exchange for political and economic privileges, they helped persuade their compatriots to comply with the established order. But this was tricky. Elites had to coordinate with Roman authorities well enough to be useful to them. But if they were too compliant or advantaged, their compatriots could accuse them of self-promoting corruption and betrayal. For this reason they had to serve the needs of their ancestral populations, even if it meant criticizing or sometimes resisting Roman authorities. If they did not manage such intersecting interests well, Roman authorities could replace them. Augustus deposed Herod's son Archelaus in 6 CE or so when Jewish and Samaritan elites accused him of acts of violence and extortion. Even so, starting in 66 some of the Temple's priests spearheaded an insurgency against Roman authority. Others opposed it. The outcome was the destruction of the Temple and the dispersal of the chief priests by the Roman government.[17]

When Herod died in 4 BCE or so, the Romans did serious reshuffling. The emperor Augustus divided the kingdom among Herod's surviving sons without giving any of them the title of king. Herod had already killed some of his many children by his many wives, especially Mariamne. Antipas acquired Galilee. Herod's territories in adjacent southern Syria and Lebanon, populated mostly by non-Jews, were given to Philip. Archelaus received lesser Judaea, Samaria, and the Greek polities of coastal Palestine.

Archelaus was not up to the task. His reign was plagued by hostility from Jewish and non-Jewish subjects, who accused him of misgovernance. Deposing him in 6 CE or so, Augustus made Judaea a district of the province of Syria. Quirinius, Syria's consular governor, conducted a census. The district of Judaea was now governed by an equestrian prefect who maintained his headquarters at Caesarea Maritima. In Jerusalem, lesser Judaea, and the

Places, Peoples, Empire

hinterland of Samaria, Jewish and Samaritan populations were the majority. They expected their Roman overseers to respect the integrity of civic terrains in which human and animal likenesses were mostly absent. But in the Greek polities of southern Syria and coastal Palestine, especially Caesarea, polytheist temples and statues dotted the landscape.

Herod's iron fist and talent for survival had kept social conflicts under restraint. But his reign did not end enduring tensions and may have made them worse. After his realm was parceled out to his descendants or Italian outsiders, ensuring order became harder. Many factors fed conflict. One was that Roman governors were foreign intruders who at times treated Jews violently or sacrilegiously. In 63 BCE, Pompey besieged the Temple precinct, slaughtered the people in it, and entered the interior of the Temple itself. As governor of Syria (57–55 BCE), Aulus Gabinius suppressed an insurgency in Judaea. In 53 BCE, Crassus pillaged the Temple. During the Roman civil war period, Marcus Cassius extracted heavy taxes and enslaved certain Judaean cities that did not pay. Roman legions put Herod in power by besieging Jerusalem in 37 BCE, and Herod inflicted much violence on opponents while authorized by the Romans (or without their preventing him). Such violence resumed after Herod's death. During Jesus' lifetime, in 4 BCE or so, a procurator named Sabinus brutally suppressed an insurrection at Jerusalem. Shortly after Jesus' death, military action against the Nabataeans encouraged Vitellius, the governor of Syria, to march through Judaea with legions and their standards. The chief priests had to petition him not to do so.[18]

Acts of outrage by individual soldiers were hard to prevent, even if they were sometimes punished. We hear how, after Jesus' crucifixion, a soldier at the Antonia fortress exposed his genitals and posterior to worshipers during Passover week and incited a lethal riot. Another soldier publicly burned a Torah scroll, was tried by the governor, and was executed in front of an attending crowd. The First Jewish Revolt erupted in 66 when the governor Florus tried to steal from the Temple's treasury and responded to demonstrations with repressive slaughter and mass executions, including the scourging and crucifixion of Jews who were Roman citizens and even equestrians. Altogether, the Jews of Judaea lived under Rome's constant potential for sacrilege and violence. Negotiations often resolved conflicts. But sometimes at critical moments they did not.

Another factor had to do with problems of legitimacy faced by Herod and his priestly elite. Herod's political talents and flair for repressive violence had disguised these weaknesses during his reign. But under his successors, such fissures became more visible. Since Herod was an upstart placed in power by the Romans, his ancestors had not been recognized rulers of Judaea. Through his father Antipater, Herod gained access to the Hasmonaean court and controlled John Hyrcanus II, whom he eventually killed. He even married a member of the Hasmonaean line, Mariamne, so that some of his children could claim legitimacy. But none of the sons who succeeded him had been born to her. Executing most men with links to the Hasmonaean dynasty, including his own sons, Herod had also populated the priesthood at Jerusalem with people of diasporic origins. These same men, as well as veterans in Herod's large army, had benefited from allotments of land and control over agricultural labor. All these factors shaped the perceptions of those who believed the Herodian dynasts, the priests of Jerusalem, and the landed elite of Judaea were not true ancestral authorities. They were illegitimate, all backed by Roman rule. These factors affected the criticisms that Jesus reportedly made against all of them, for these were connected.[19]

Another factor was the promotion of the Temple precinct as a pilgrimage center for all Jews. The work and wealth that Herod and his priests poured into it made it a place of sharp Roman surveillance. Now densely populated during festivals, it became a locus of crowd disturbance and volatile social action. After Herod's death, the dynast Archelaus massacred a crowd at the Temple that had been motivated to violence by its ringleaders, and the procurator Sabinus brutally suppressed an insurrection staged by Jews at the Temple precinct during Pentecost, when the area was crowded. The Acts of the Apostles (21:31–32) refers to the troops at the Antonia as keeping watch for a public disturbance and arresting the preacher Paul to defuse one. Moreover, the promotion of the Jewish Temple at Jerusalem fed tensions between Jews and Samaritans, whose temple at Mount Gerizim had remained in ruins since the Hasmonaeans destroyed it. By Jesus' lifetime, Roman magistrates and Jewish worshipers recognized the potential for violence at Jerusalem, especially when travelers flooded the city for festivals, including many Galileans who crossed Samaria to get there. When Jesus preached in the Temple precinct in his final days, he did so in a very turbulent space.[20]

Another factor was the strife between Greek and Jewish communities. A legacy of Seleucid Greek imperialism and Hasmonaean expansion, disputes between Greek and Jewish communities often surfaced in local contexts. But sometimes the violence and strife assumed regional proportions. The Greek communities of coastal Palestine and Transjordan long had troubled relationships with Jews in their cities and the nearby regions of Judaea and Galilee. Their cities had once been governed by the Hasmonaean kings, who promoted the Jewish populations in them and declared them part of the land of the Jews. But these same cities had been restored to local Greek civic management by the Romans in 63 BCE. As mentioned previously, Roman authorities (including the Herodians) drew a distinction between territories in which Jews represented the predominant governing order (lesser Judaea, Peraea, Galilee, and Idumaea) and those in which they did not. This generated serious tensions between local Greek and Jewish populations, who often inhabited the same urban landscapes and claimed governance over them. The Greeks in many cities of coastal Palestine even created civic calendars that began with the arrival of Pompey and the termination of Hasmonaean governance. After Herod's death, such tensions persisted. In Iabneh (Iamneia), Greeks and Jews fought over whether an altar could be established for the emperor Caligula (reigned 37–41). Not much later, the Greeks of Doris provoked local Jews by placing a statue of the emperor Claudius in a synagogue, and Greeks and Jews living near Amman attacked one another.[21]

In certain ways, Herod's rule had made such hostility worse. For example, in 59 the Greeks and Jews of Caesarea Maritima erupted into violence over who governed the city. The Jews' position was that Herod was its founder. The Greeks maintained that a city named Strato's Tower had preceded Herod's foundation. Herod had anyhow established temples and statues in recognition of Greek preeminence. When the First Jewish Revolt broke out in 66, Greeks and Jews attacked one another as Roman authority in the region became severely compromised. We hear of massacres of Jews, sometimes Greeks, at Amman, Gerasa, Hippos, Gadara, and Scythopolis–Beth Shean, Askalon, Ptolemais, and Tyre. As the Romans suppressed Jewish insurgency, they posed as protectors of the Greek polities and paraded Jewish captives to this effect.

Yet another factor in the prevailing tensions was economic. The stable (if violent) rule of Herod, and Judaea's integration into the broader Roman economy, had created prosperity and increased agrarian production. But it also fed social displacement. Whether the agrarian economy of greater Judaea under the Romans differed drastically from what preceded it is debatable. Many surmise that the laboring classes of cities and rural areas suffered greater want than ever before at the hands of governing elites (including the Temple's priests) or other landowners, who also profited from the revenues of tax collection. The critiques of the wealthy aired by the New Testament Gospels would undoubtedly reflect this. Others maintain that Roman and Herodian rule did not dramatically alter patterns of landowning and tenancy. It did not lead to increased taxes. In fact, Judaea's integration into the main current of the Roman economy created opportunities and probably greater wealth overall. The Herodians' urban foundations and promotion of Jerusalem as a pilgrimage center generated markets and labor demand. The wealthy were investing in commercial agriculture, their Mediterranean-wide contacts, their own patterns of consumption, and their patronage of social subordinates. Some middling sorts benefited from new economic opportunities and were not much worse (or better) off than before. The relationship between the wealthy and the broader population had simply shifted to meet the demands of the new imperial context and its economic life.[22]

Despite debate, many recognize that Roman rule, in one way or another, did create conditions in which the Herodians and their priestly elites benefited from access to landed property and profits from tax collection. They also enjoyed the fruits of profitable enterprises at the Temple precinct, whose treasury and commercial spaces they regulated. Their activity typified landed elites throughout the Roman Empire and its regional ordering of wealth. But competitors for social capital could exploit this in their preaching. Even if their situation did not differ drastically from that of their forebears, the laboring and unlanded of Judaea still suffered serious hardships common throughout antiquity. They could resent people who overwhelmingly accumulated land and money under Roman governance. The benefits of increased wealth were not distributed evenly. A small elite segment controlled most of it, and some middling sorts lived above mere subsistence or enjoyed serious mobility. Everyone else lived in unceasing vulnerability, fending off deprivation on a near-daily basis. Many farmers did not fully control the land they tended or the produce from it. Landless wage earners weathered a vulnerable, subsistence-level existence. Tax and tithe collection favored the governing order or its immediate clients. From Josephus and the New Testament Gospels we can infer that many agrarian laborers worked for daily wages or paid rent to the powerful as tenants. A fair amount owed debts or arrears to local landowners, who could then opt to seize their possessions or exploit their labor to their greater benefit. When Jesus reportedly exhorted people to relinquish their wealth and not deprive the poor of it (Chapters 3 and 5), this was the situation he was addressing.

If the economic situation of Judaea and the Galilee was consistent with what preceded it, many agrarian and urban laborers *experienced* it as oppressive. The continued concentration of land and wealth in the hands of governing landowners like the Herodians and chief priests inflicted real hardship and suffering on the poor, who often controlled little or no land of their own. Those who opposed them could always exploit this in their rhetoric. It worked to their advantage that the elite's ancestors had not governed Judaea.

Places, Peoples, Empire

Its members had come into such power and status under Roman rule. In general, their economic activity typified governing elites throughout the Roman Empire and indeed the ancient world. But so did its effects on the working poor. As villagers struggled to control agrarian wealth, earn wages, or participate in Temple sacrifices, charismatic figures like Jesus sometimes pointed fingers at the governing order. Competing with the Herodians or chief priests for social capital and authority, they could and did seize upon their acquisition of status and wealth as evidence of disrepute and injustice, whether fairly or not. Inspired by traditional ideals of communal support and obligation, they also advocated that people stop accumulating wealth and instead distribute it to poorer Jews.[23]

During Jesus' lifetime, the economic tensions and fracturing of ruling legitimacy in Judaea enabled aspiring leaders to present their moral vision and authority as alternatives to the governing order and its injustices (Chapters 2 and 3). Some of these were brigands, insurrectionists, or armed insurgents. Figures like Judas the Galilean and his sons rebelled against Roman authority. Others were dissenting preachers who challenged the conduct and privileges of the Herodians and the Temple's priests. At Qumran and other locations in lesser Judaea, some Jews established an exclusive hierarchical society with its own laws, courts, and ritual standards. Valuing the sanctity of the Temple, they challenged the legitimacy of its priestly management. They envisioned a Messiah and a divine intervention that would restore the governance of Israel and its Temple to them. Intriguingly, John the Baptizer and Jesus of Nazareth similarly anticipated that God would intervene and reverse the present ordering of authority, privilege, and wealth.

Being generally distinct, military insurgents and charismatic preachers both posed problems for Roman and Herodian authorities. These cracked down hard on people who stoked insurrection or brigandage. They often could do it without attracting blame for tyrannical, excessive violence or alienating local populations. But how they dealt with popular, charismatic dissenting preachers invited complications and uncertainty. Violence could poison their reputations among local populations, who could escalate their dissenting behavior. It could attract criticism from their peers or municipal elites, sometimes with serious consequences for governors. But whether or not such dissenting preachers were engaging in seditious behavior was often unclear in both a legal and practical sense. The legal justifications for repressive violence could be murky. To some extent, different Roman authorities dealt with such preachers violently or not, according to different rationales. This was the world into which Jesus of Nazareth was born.

2

The Governing Order

Valerius Gratus put an end to Ananus' being high priest.... Joseph, also Caiaphas, was Simon's successor. Accomplishing these feats, Gratus returned to Rome after spending 11 years in Judaea. Pontius Pilate arrived as his successor.

—JOSEPHUS, *Ant.* 18.34–35

Woe to me from the house of Boethus, woe to me from its rods. Woe to me from the house of Qadros, woe to me from its pens. Woe to me from the house of Elhanan, woe to me from the home of their whispers.

—*T. MENAH.* 13.21, a rabbinic tradition on priestly families of the first century

IN JESUS' LIFETIME, greater Judaea harbored a host of social tensions. Roman imperialism had not quelled them (Chapter 1). It even made some worse. The people who embodied these tensions acted from political and personal motives. But they also acted to fulfill serious social and moral obligations. Their motives and obligations positioned them in debate and even conflict. Understanding them helps us understand Jesus' trial and death.

All figures of authority involved in governance in greater Judaea had reasons to want Jesus dead. Along with Pontius Pilate, these included the Herodian dynasts, the chief priests, and some allied scribes, especially among the Sadducees and Pharisees. They all were pitted against dissenting figures who challenged their governing legitimacy, their politics, their ethics, or their economic interests. Dissenters also could create social disturbances that the Herodians or chief priests had to resolve. Sometimes their actions could even get innocent people hurt or killed, especially at the Temple precinct. Some dissenters advocated for insurgency. Others preached an imminent intervention of God or a Messianic figure who would introduce it. We can place John the Baptizer, the Jewish community that inhabited the site of Qumran on the

Dead Sea, and Jesus of Nazareth in this spectrum of dissent. The conflicting motives at hand inspired Jesus' fateful pilgrimage to Jerusalem and his arrest. They shaped how Pilate handled Jesus' trial. But what were the motives of the people who governed Judaea? What were those of the dissenters?

The Jewish Leadership, Roman Authority, and the Historian Josephus

In Jesus' Judaea, some people coordinated with Roman authorities to maintain the present order of governance and wealth. Others tolerated it. Some preached military resistance. Others predicted its pending destruction. But what distinguishes governing authorities from dissenters? After all, the chief priests of Jerusalem and allied scribes sometimes criticized Roman or Herodian governance while benefiting from it. Some may well have anticipated its divine-mandated end. Some such figures fought against Roman rule during Jesus' lifetime. Some helped launch the revolt that erupted in 66. Dissenters similarly envisioned a divine destruction of the governing order. But many of them still lived their lives without fighting against it. The Jews of Jesus' Judaea overwhelmingly treasured the sanctity of the Temple. But they had different views on politics, morality, purity, and divine intervention. They also had different positions in the ordering of power and wealth.[1]

Even so, we can identify people who helped facilitate Roman governance and benefited from it. Most premodern empires were structured by webs of regional and municipal elites who worked with imperial power holders. The Roman Empire was no exception. We have seen how the chief priests and client dynasts of Judaea maintained their stature by coordinating with Roman authorities (Chapter 1). But they also had to act somewhat autonomously to be credible. This meant that they negotiated or even criticized Roman authority to improve the situation of their compatriots. It makes them distinct from military insurgents who fought to create an autonomous Israel, one without the Romans, Herodians, or even the current chief priests. It also distinguishes them from people who envisioned a divine reversal of the governing order and its wealth, lived in communities that anticipated it, or even proclaimed it publicly, especially at the Temple precinct. Despite their differences, the Jews of Qumran, John the Baptizer, and Jesus occupied this spectrum of behavior.

During the First Jewish Revolt (66–74), the priestly elite reached a point of no return. Some priests fought against Rome and tried to build an autonomous state. But the revolt is the exception, not part of a pattern. The priests were split about what their conduct should be. A son of a chief priest inspired revolt by stopping the customary sacrifice for the Roman emperor's well-being. But his father, the former high priest Ananias, was killed by insurgents. According to Josephus, some priests who rebelled played the endgame of negotiating with Roman authorities, not breaking from the empire entirely. By fighting in the insurgency, they could win greater loyalty from compatriots frustrated with Roman governance. By negotiating its end, they could secure their positioning in the eyes of Roman magistrates. Another former high priest named Ananus was one of those. But other insurgents were bent on autonomy and aimed to establish a new succession of priestly families. Ananus died by the hands of such insurgents, not the Romans. Whatever their intentions, they failed to prevent the Temple's destruction in 70 or the massacre at Masada a few years later.[2]

Josephus' information could be critiqued as specious. In 68 Ananus and his followers may not have sought a rapport with Rome at all. Their bid for authority in the revolt arguably fed an irreparable breach with Rome. It at least reflected their recognition that such a breach had already happened. Even so, Josephus deemed it believable that Ananus intended to negotiate with Roman authorities. This is because the priestly elite of Jerusalem had done this in the past century. Josephus even claims he desired such an outcome. When the rebellion began, leaders at Jerusalem appointed him to command insurgents in Galilee. These had already rallied behind local Galilean dynasts, and Josephus largely failed to win them over. Afterward, in both his *Jewish War* (his account of the revolt) and his *Life* (his autobiography of sorts), he claimed to identify with the same "reasonable" insurgency as Ananus had. The two works have some discrepancies, and Josephus wrote them in part to justify his past deeds. For example, he envisioned how insurgent priestly elites could advocate for negotiating with Rome. He claims he had preferred an opportunistic, beneficial reconciliation to devastating defeat under new Jewish leadership. After surrendering to the Romans, he became their apologist and even allegedly tried to persuade the insurgents in Jerusalem to capitulate. We can doubt Josephus' description of his own conduct. But it reflects how priests at Jerusalem coordinated with Roman authorities to provide stable governance and replicate the present order of authority and wealth.[3]

Writing in the later first century, Josephus created the only surviving narrative histories of greater Judaea for periods surrounding Jesus' lifetime. His testimony is important for how we understand the people who lived and acted then. It enables us to see the various governing authorities and dissenters of Judaea from vantage points that the New Testament Gospels do not offer. But Josephus has his limitations too. His historical vision usually favors the same governing priestly elite to which he belonged (though he sometimes criticizes powerful priests for misconduct). He also makes errors and misleading moral judgments. We cannot assume Josephus is always providing an accurate, neutral vision of Jesus' Judaea or its people. Even so, Josephus sometimes helps us gauge where the New Testament Gospels may be misleading, or vice versa. When we cast a critical eye, we can build a picture of Jesus' world, along with the motives and obligations of its actors.[4]

Josephus enables us to glimpse how the chief priests and allied scribes at Jerusalem sometimes leveraged dissent and potential insurgency for better imperial accommodation, not separatism, before the First Jewish Revolt. Not long after Jesus died, the disturbed emperor Caligula ordered a statue of himself placed in the Temple. The response was tumultuous, and we know about it from Josephus and Philo, a prolific Jew of Egyptian Alexandria who was Jesus' contemporary. When news of Caligula's intentions reached Judaea, mass demonstrations of Jews from city and countryside reportedly confronted Petronius, governor of Syria, at Akko in coastal Palestine and then at Tiberias in Galilee. The crowds proclaimed their desire to die before suffering such a sacrilegious act, and the negotiations with Petronius bought some time. Philo and Josephus portray the crowds as assembling on their own. But they tend to represent mass demonstrations as guided by divine intervention, not political leaders. Still, they mention that Herodian dynasts and established elites (*protoi*) were active in negotiating too. They may very well have circulated information and organized crowd demonstrations. Or they at least used their status to prevent repressive violence against the compatriots who had assembled. Caligula apparently died before fulfilling his desires. We cannot know whether the chief priests would have mounted an insurgency or accepted death if the statue was erected. Even so, the Herodian dynasts and the chief priests had criticized the current terms of Roman governance without triggering an irreparable breach. When Caligula's mandate was rescinded, they coordinated with Roman authorities as before. Yet in the prior decade people like John the Baptizer and Jesus of Nazareth were apparently prophesying a divine end to governance by the Romans and chief priests. They died violently while doing it.[5]

Indeed, in the decade before Caligula's inflammatory decision, Roman magistrates were cultivating a rapport with Herod Antipas and the chief priests of Jerusalem. This relationship killed Jesus (Chapters 5–10). Herod Antipas tried to have Jesus arrested while he preached in Galilee. In Jerusalem, the chief priests and their allies arrested Jesus when he made his final pilgrimage there. This probably was not the first time they had tried. Ultimately,

Pontius Pilate had him crucified. In other words, Pilate, Antipas, and the chief priests all had reasons to want Jesus' death. They probably believed they had a social obligation to kill him. But their motives and timing differed somewhat. They were to some degree communicating and sharing information throughout Jesus' itinerant preaching.[6] But as competitors, they also limited their coordination. They sought his death (and credit for it) as necessary or expedient. Jesus' final pilgrimage provided Pilate and the chief priests with an opportunity and a necessity that had eluded Antipas. But what were their motivations and obligations?

Herod Antipas

A key protagonist in the life of Jesus of Nazareth was Herod Antipas. The Gospels variously call him "Herod" or "Antipas." He governed Galilee and Peraea for much of Jesus' life. Jesus was subject to his authority. When Jesus preached in Galilee, he risked trial and execution by him. Antipas notoriously judged and executed Jesus' fellow traveler, John the Baptizer. We will examine why Antipas never arrested and executed Jesus (Chapter 5). After all, he had motives for having him killed. Some passages from the Gospel of Mark suggest he tried.

Herod Antipas was recognized by the Roman emperor as the ruler of Galilee and Peraea in 4 BCE or so. He was one of Herod I's surviving sons. His reign is notable for various reasons. One involves his building projects. We know of building and fortification at Betharanphtha and a fortress and palace at Machaerus in Peraea. Yet Antipas' main work was in Galilee. There he established the city of Tiberias and enlarged Sepphoris. Their surviving remains mostly date to after Antipas' reign. The cities he governed were more modest. Antipas' work mostly focused on fortifying them with circuit walls. These were his largest urban areas and palace sites. Like his father, Herod, Antipas did not undermine the existing villages of Galilee. They perhaps increased in size and wealth. The Romans backed him for several decades. Antipas' record was not conspicuous, and he never held the title of king like his father. But it was enough to keep him in power. If not for Jesus and John the Baptizer, he would be an obscure man indeed.[7]

Still, there was serious discontent in Antipas' Galilee. Antipas was an upstart Herodian. Roman support ensured his rule. Though an observant Jew, Antipas' conduct sometimes exposed him to critique from compatriots and subjects. Josephus claims his foundation of Tiberias encroached upon burial sites in ways that exposed Jews to the impurity of corpses (Num

19:11, 16). The critique seems exaggerated. Tiberian Jews could still travel to Jerusalem, purify, and engage in Temple rituals. Antipas' marriage to Herodias, the wife of his half-brother, perhaps violated prohibitions against marrying a brother's wife (Lev 18:16, 20:21). Or so claimed dissidents like John the Baptizer. Antipas undoubtedly promoted the interests of his courtiers and clients, allotting land to them. But economic and social resources were not distributed evenly. Antipas and those he favored benefited the most from land tenure. The working poor struggled as they had in prior generations. This exposed him to animus. When Antipas suppressed dissenting preachers and insurrectionists, he was defending a governing order and landed interests that he embodied.

While Antipas ruled Galilee and Peraea, his half-brother Philip had authority over territories east of the Sea of Galilee, especially Golan. These were populated mostly by non-Jews. Philip's reign was stable enough for the Romans to support it for several decades. During that interval, he founded Caesarea Philippi at Panias. Josephus' testimony places Philip's death in about 34. The episode most responsible for Philip's fame reportedly involved his wife Salome and her mother, Herodias, Antipas' wife. It hastened John the Baptizer's death (Chapter 5).

Josephus identifies other critics of Antipas' rule. A man named Judas, to be distinguished from Jesus' follower with that name, publicly maligned and resisted Roman intervention when prefects started governing lesser Judaea in 6 CE. Originating from either Galilee or Golan, Judas had been subject to Antipas or Philip. The same or a different man named Judas emulated his father, Hezekiah, by mounting an insurgency against the Herodians in Galilee before Antipas had even begun governing. This would mean that insurgents were pitted against both Herodian dynasts and Roman prefects in the years after Herod I's death in 4 BCE or so. More famous as a critic is John the Baptizer, the charismatic preacher in Antipas' Transjordan territories.[8]

Even so, Herod I and his successors evidently had a broad base of support among the chief priests and allied scribes, including the Sadducees and Pharisees. Antipas enjoyed it too. This would explain various passages from the Gospel of Mark that represent Pharisees as aligned with Antipas or so-called Herodians. In Mark 3:6, these "Herodians" mount opposition to Jesus while he preaches in synagogues of Galilee. While doing so, they accompany Pharisees and take a kindred interest on matters of law. Mark does not define who the Herodians are. We should accept that they were Antipas' officials and clients (Chapter 5). They were aware of scribal debates and had concerns about Jesus' preaching.[9]

In 39 or so, after a long reign, Antipas was deposed by the emperor Caligula for allegedly conspiring with the Parthians against Roman interests. The greed of Herodias proved pivotal in alienating Antipas' nephew Agrippa I, who made the accusation to the imperial court. An unsuccessful war Antipas waged against the Nabataean king Aretas did not help his standing either. Agrippa I received his territories shortly afterward, and Antipas died around that time.

Antipas did not execute Jesus. But he had motive and authority to do so (Chapter 5). His execution of the dissident preacher John the Baptizer shows as much. Antipas embodied Roman governance and Herodian dynastic rule in Galilee and Transjordan, and he defended landed interests there. Antipas had the legal means and obligation (so he believed) to classify John's activity as seditious and have him executed. But as a client dynast, he was also safeguarding himself and his allies. Jesus knew he could suffer a fate like John's. But he evaded arrest by Antipas. His path ended in Jerusalem, with Pilate.

Chief Priests and Scribes

The Gospels claim the chief priests played a key part in Jesus' death in Jerusalem. When Jesus preached at the Temple precinct in his final days, the chief priests sought grounds for having him executed. They arrested him, convened a council, and had him tried by Pilate. The Gospels shift responsibility from Pilate to the chief priests (Chapters 6–10). Yet they also identify other types of adversaries to Jesus and his message. They assert that Sadducees, Pharisees, and scribes sought to embarrass Jesus in public and collect information on him in Galilee and Jerusalem. Who were these people? Why were they reportedly hostile to Jesus?

Before confronting such questions, we should return to the role local municipal elites played in Roman imperialism (Chapter 1). These often criticized imperial authorities to create better conditions and maintain loyalty among compatriots. But they coordinated with Roman authorities too. Benefiting from this relationship, they rarely promoted acts of resistance that marked an irreparable breach with Roman authority or its ordering of wealth. If anything, they cooperated with imperial powers to suppress incendiary dissenting movements. Such dissidents could be hostile to their authority. They could also incite forms of social instability or violence governing elites had an obligation to neutralize.

The chief priests, scribes, and judges populating *synhedria* (councils) at Jerusalem, often being the same people, tended to coordinate with Roman and Herodian authorities to provide governance and maintain the present order of authority and wealth. Their families had profited from Herodian-Roman land tenure. They managed tithes and temple taxes. Many of them also collected taxes for the Romans and kept some of the profits. They had key exemptions too. Their wealth isolated them from the strain of subsistence labor. It afforded them the leisure to study the Torah, to manage Temple affairs and revenues for their compatriots, or to undergo commercial ventures generated by access to the Temple's sacred economy. Of course, priests and scribes were not always wealthy. Many affluent Jews were not priests or scribes. Priests, scribal experts, and council judges were not always the same people, but often they were. Wealth was concentrated in their hands, and they either managed the Temple or maintained social proximity to those who did. When Galilean laborers like Jesus of Nazareth claimed to be scribal experts in public, they did so as outsiders. They challenged whether the chief priests and allied scribes like the Sadducees and Pharisees understood the Torah properly. Such outsiders also sometimes classified the wealth of these priests and scribes as corrupt.[10]

Ultimately, the privileged positions that the chief priests and allied scribes had carved out in the Roman imperial context attracted some serious criticism from dissenters like Jesus of Nazareth. In turn, the advisory councils or courts (*synhedria*) that they convened at Jerusalem could intervene in the activity of dissenters there (Chapter 8). Their participants overwhelmingly consisted of the Temple's priests and allied scribes among the Sadducees and Pharisees. As such, the Gospels report that the judges at Jesus' hearing before a *synhedrion* had self-serving motives for seeking his execution. But they arguably were fulfilling serious social obligations by doing so. We now turn to what these were.

Annas and Caiaphas, High Priests of Jerusalem

During Jesus' lifetime, the Temple precinct at Jerusalem was managed by its priests. But the Gospels are somewhat confusing. They often refer to Jesus' encounter with many "high priests" or "chief priests" (*archiereis*) at Jerusalem. But in other instances they mention a single "high priest" (*archiereus*). Who were these people, and what did they do? Why did Jesus reportedly pose such a threat to them?

The Temple of Jerusalem was a vital sacred center. But it was also a robust socioeconomic and political institution managed by its priestly families (Chapter 1). The Temple's high priest played the most visible sacrificial role, but he worked closely with other senior priests from prominent households.

These are the people the Gospels call "the chief priests" (*archiereis*). Some of these undoubtedly had been high priest before. The priests were recruited from a select cluster of families. Their positions were in principle hereditary and held for life. All priests claimed descent from Aaron, the priestly brother of the prophet Moses. During Jesus' lifetime, members of priestly families served the Temple in a weekly rotation. They assembled in Jerusalem for the major festivals. Whoever their ancient ancestors were, many high priests originated from families of the Jewish Diaspora who had settled in Judaea under Herod I. At Jerusalem, their courtyard houses were usually located in the Upper City. By Jesus' lifetime, two men were typically described as high priest by Jews. One was Annas, a former high priest who remained a political force in Jerusalem. The other was Caiaphas, Annas' son-in-law and the incumbent high priest. The Gospels report that the council had assembled at one of their houses to determine Jesus' criminal liability (Chapter 8). It was there his apostle Simon Peter reportedly several times denied knowing him.[11]

In many respects, high priests like Annas and Caiaphas coordinated with Roman imperial authorities to maintain peace and stability in Jerusalem. They had a serious responsibility to ensure their compatriots were not endangered by outbreaks of violence, especially during major festivals. But they also benefited materially from this role. This attracted criticism, especially from dissenters. During Jesus' lifetime, the Roman prefect of Judaea selected them. After his death, the Roman governors of Syria and then the Herodian dynasts would do so. This dynamic had a visible impact. Like Herod Antipas, Annas and Caiaphas had to coordinate with Roman authorities. But they also had to act with enough autonomy and effectiveness to be useful for prefects like Pilate. This in part explains why the chief priests reportedly gathered information on Jesus' activity in Jerusalem and organized his arrest (Chapters 7 and 8). Their success at such endeavors and their support by Rome were vital to their political placement. By Jesus' lifetime, the high priest could no longer claim significant descent from the Hasmonaean priestly line. This line had claimed legitimacy because it freed Judaea from Seleucid rule and had annexed and settled Idumaea and Galilee, whose populations consequently became Jewish (Chapter 1). The Hasmonaean dynasts had displaced the most long-standing high priestly families. But their preservation of Israel's autonomy, military victories, and capacity for violence had initially stabilized their rule. After Herod I had eradicated most traces of their descent lines, his priestly appointees did not enjoy the same stature. But they staked positions of wealth and privilege in Jewish society. Under the Romans, they continued to benefit from the favorable land tenure and tax situation that the Herodians had sustained for

The Governing Order   45

their closest clients. They also managed the robust wealth the Temple required for its needs and benefited from commercial opportunities that management afforded. Their economic means typified those of landed elites throughout Roman territory. But how they handled wealth for the Temple or their own maintenance attracted criticisms. These leave traces in the caches of texts discovered in the caves of Qumran (otherwise known as the Dead Sea Scrolls) and later rabbinic sources. These are also featured in the Gospels' accounts of Jesus of Nazareth (Chapters 4 and 6).[12]

Despite their status, wealth, and detractors, the high priests were devout men who had serious responsibilities in managing the Temple and ensuring the safety of devout pilgrims. As such, they had ethical motives for opposing dissenters who could create social disturbance or even violence at the Temple precinct. They had to ensure the vastly amplified Temple institution followed proper ritual protocols, and in a peaceful way. They presided over celebrations, offerings, and sacrifices that happened on the Sabbath, key points in the lunar calendar, and during major observances. One major observance was Yom Kippur, when the high priest entered the inner sanctum and wore the most splendid, sacred vestments, which were kept under guard by the Roman garrison in the Antonia. Another was Passover week. By Jesus' lifetime, it involved two observances that had been combined into a single festival: the feasts of Passover ("Pesach" in Hebrew) and of Unleavened Bread. Passover week attracted pilgrims from throughout Judaea, Galilee, and the Diaspora to Jerusalem itself. During this time, the high priest oversaw rituals that purified the pilgrims of pollution incurred in various ways, like contact with corpses. Once cleansed, Jewish pilgrims entered the inner courtyard and slaughtered lambs by the thousands, and the priests would bring their blood and innards to the altar. We can envision a host of pilgrims and their sacrifices. Even so, Josephus' calculations that 250,000 animals were sacrificed to accommodate roughly 3 million people are exaggerated. By ancient standards, Jerusalem was a fairly large city, but not an enormous one. It could not sustain millions of people even for a short period. The day of preparation for Passover started on the 14th of Nisan (a Jewish month corresponding roughly to April), at sundown. After daylight returned, worshipers slaughtered their Passover lambs. When the next sundown ushered in the following day (the 15th of Nisan), the Passover festival and the Feast of Unleavened Bread began. On the first day, the pilgrims dined on the Passover lamb meal, and they then ate unleavened bread for the following week. The Synoptic Gospels claim Jesus' final meal was such a Passover feast.[13]

Before the Romans conquered Judaea, high priests normally held their position for life. Herodian-Roman governors departed from this precedent.

They intervened in priestly appointments often, just as the notorious Seleucid king Antiochus IV had done. In response, many Jews conceived of high priests as retaining their status for as long as they lived. Naturally, such former high priests would be among the "chief priests" (*archiereis*) that the Gospels describe. By all appearances the chief priests were responsible for municipal governance at Jerusalem and understood by Roman authorities as its civic council or senate (*boule*).[14]

The powerful high priest Annas is called Ananus by Josephus. These are Greek variations of the Hebrew name Hanan. Ananus held the high priesthood in 6–15 CE, a term that spanned the arrival of the first Roman prefect to the death of the emperor Augustus. After being deposed by the prefect Gratus, Ananus continued to be an influential priest and a key player in governance at Jerusalem as high priest. Besides his son-in-law Caiaphas, many subsequent high priests were his sons. With wealth and power came accusations of gain and political ruthlessness. At the beginning of the chapter, we quoted a passage from the Tosefta that impugns his house ("the House of Elhanan") for plotting against others. Ananus reportedly played a key role in arresting Jesus and evaluating his liability for a capital charge (John 18:12–24; Chapters 7 and 8).

A key member of Ananus' house, if by marriage, was Caiaphas ("Qaifa" in Hebrew). He was reportedly the last high priest (18–36/37) appointed by the prefect Gratus, who probably governed until c. 26. That makes him the last high priest appointed by a Roman prefect of Judaea. After that they all were appointed by the governor of Syria or a Herodian dynast. The political success of Caiaphas' priesthood is demonstrated by its length. Pilate never removed him during his many years of governing Judaea.[15]

By all appearances Caiaphas and Ananus were allies. But as the active high priest, Caiaphas ensured proper sacrificial rites at Jesus' final festival in Jerusalem. His deposition shortly after Pilate was dismissed accompanied the arrival of a new Roman governor in Syria. It also plausibly determined the governor's desire for shorter terms for high priesthoods, which became more typical. This pattern may have shaped how the Gospel of John (11:49, 18:13) describes Caiaphas as high priest for the year Jesus died.

Ananus' heirs were political forces at Jerusalem for 50 years after his demotion. Many of his sons became high priests. One of them, named Jonathan, was priest in 36–37. Like his father, he remained so influential as high priest that certain dissenters, called the *sicarii*, assassinated him sometime in the 50s. Another, also named Ananus, was high priest briefly in 62, when he orchestrated the death of Jesus' brother James. He later joined the insurgency in the First Jewish Revolt. We have seen how Josephus portrays him (perhaps misleadingly) as advocating for a negotiation with Roman authorities for a better position in the empire. The Acts of the Apostles (4:6) reports that Ananus, Caiaphas, and Ananus' children arrested Jesus' follower Peter, tried him before a council at Jerusalem, and had him lashed. It identifies Ananus as "high priest" and his relatives as "of the high priestly family."

The lives and careers of Ananus and Caiaphas have a coda. Their burial places may be known to us. Josephus locates the tomb of Ananus just south of the city. This seems to correspond with the location of numerous tombs, one of which has an impressive triple entrance. His son Theophilus and his high priestly title are celebrated on the ossuary of Theophilos' granddaughter, buried outside Jerusalem. In a burial cave north of Jerusalem, the ossuary of a person named Yehosef appears to identify his father as Caiaphas (*qyp'* and *qp'*), but without mentioning a priestly title. The remains of a man in his 60s, as well as those of people who died younger, were found there. Are these the burial places or even remains of the high priests who reportedly had Jesus arrested and tried? This is debatable. An unprovenanced ossuary, reportedly found in the Elah Valley, is inscribed with the name "Miriam, daughter of Yeshua, son of Qaifa," who is explicitly identified as priest. If authentic, it perhaps suggests Caiaphas' family had a burial plot in the countryside. Yet if any of these ossuaries do refer to the high priest Caiaphas, they also suggest he had sons who did not become high priests. This would be somewhat surprising in light of Caiaphas' own stature and long tenure.[16]

Despite their hostile portraits in the Gospels, Ananus and Caiaphas were devout men who had ethical motives for moving against Jesus. They took their oversight of the Temple's sacrificial rites and festivals very seriously. They were responsible for ensuring proper rites were done without Jesus' compatriots being harmed. They may have believed (or not) that a Messiah from the line of David would someday usher in an era of God's intervention. But they dismissed the claim that Jesus was a Messiah or a prophet and believed his preaching an affront to the divine order. At the same time, Ananus and Caiaphas were political players harboring some of the standard socioeconomic interests and worldviews of municipal elites throughout the Roman Empire. They did benefit from the popularity and grandeur of the Temple institution and its sacred festivals. Dissident preachers like Jesus, if successful, did pose serious challenges to their prestige, influence, and authority and could inspire social instability at the Temple the chief priests were obligated to prevent. If the chief priests failed to do so, their compatriots could get hurt or killed. Then the chief priests could lose status among Roman authorities and in their communities, who may want them replaced. The chief priests had serious ethical and political motivations. So did Jesus. Their differing aspirations pitted them against one another whenever the upstart Galilean preached in the Temple precinct of Jerusalem.

Scribes, Sadducees, and Pharisees

In many Gospel passages, scribes inquire into Jesus' message, pose questions to him, try to expose him as a fraud, or even plot his downfall (Chapters 5 and 6). But who were the scribes? These were any Jews deemed literate in the Torah and other sacred writings. Some professional scribes wrote official documents for the Temple. But the "scribes" of the Gospels were people who claimed authority in reading Jewish Scriptures, memorizing them, and communicating authoritative interpretations of them. They could be Temple priests or wealthy Jews who could afford formal education. Some were aspirational figures with middling or poorer backgrounds, like Jesus of Nazareth. But claiming scribal expertise elicited fierce competition. In the Gospels, the scribes seek to expose Jesus as a fraud. His origins as a Galilean craftsman were a factor. So was his preaching, which reportedly criticized them. The scribes occupied a vast spectrum of interpretation. But though some were dissenters, they were usually aligned with the Temple's management. In the Gospels and Josephus, two intellectual communities stand out. These are the Sadducees and the Pharisees.[17]

The Sadducees were Jews who dismissed the concept of resurrection of the dead and the validity of oral traditions for interpreting the Torah. They rigorously upheld the Torah's purity mandates as law in matters of Temple cult, and to some degree elsewhere. Families with such philosophical inclinations had found favor with the Hasmonaeans and the Herodians and had acquired priesthoods. Many priests thereafter embraced the philosophy, including those who reportedly confronted Jesus during his preaching in Jerusalem (Mark 12:18). A unique opposition to the concept of a Messiah perhaps played a role in Jesus' death. Even so, the Synoptic Gospels overstate the Sadducees' pursuit of Jesus, especially during his Galilean ministry. This is because Matthew and Luke sometimes rework Mark's references to the Herodians as Sadducees. By doing this, they emphasize or even exaggerate the hostility of scribal competitors and minimize that of Antipas' court (Chapter 5).[18]

Of all people, the Gospels most often cite the Pharisees as critics of Jesus who sought to expose him as a fraud and gathered information on him. As Josephus reports, they believed the soul survived the body's death and received rewards or punishment based on moral conduct. They espoused oral traditions for interpreting the Torah. They adhered rigorously to laws of purity that (in their view) extended beyond the Temple to the wider holy city of Jerusalem, if at a lesser scale. As such, they criticized the views and practices of the Sadducees. They could pose challenges to the leadership of the Herodians and chief priests, and some even became hostile. But they were generally aligned with the governing order. They conceivably served as forerunners for the rabbis later responsible for the Mishnah and Talmud. Even so, their precise relationship remains undetermined. Various elite and middling sorts inclined toward their philosophy, and they were clearly a presence in contemporary synagogue life. Many literate scribes disparaged by the New Testament Gospels are portrayed as adhering to their teachings. In the Gospels, Pharisees from the local communities of Galilee and from Jerusalem are concerned about Jesus' preaching (Chapter 5). These may be exaggerating. After 70, the priestly elite had been dispersed, and Pharisees became even more prominent. The Gospel accounts may reflect that contemporary situation. Little evidence places Pharisees in Galilee during Jesus' lifetime, and any who were had more in common with Jesus than the Gospels allow. They probably agreed that *qorban* should not keep wealth from parents (despite Mark 7:9–13), and they believed in the resurrection of the dead. The Gospels have an obvious goal in portraying consistent, enduring antagonism. Even so, the activity of Judas the Galilean at the time of Jesus' birth points to the presence of Pharisees there. Galilee's material culture also shows that its residents had concerns about purity at home among scribes in Judaea. Some Pharisaic opposition to Jesus in Galilee is plausible.[19]

Many scribes saw Jesus not merely as a rival. They saw him as an outsider, not one of them. A Galilean craftsman was not supposed to have the literacy and knowledge of Hebrew Scriptures to compete with them for authority over their interpretation. Moreover, his message was incendiary. It predicted a reversal of the governing order that privileged many of them. Scribes in Galilee may have collected information on Jesus for Herod Antipas. In Jerusalem, some were reportedly aligned with the chief priests in their desire for Jesus' arrest and execution. Enter Pontius Pilate.

Pontius Pilate

If the chief priests coordinated with Pilate, Pilate needed them just to govern Judaea. The Herodians and the Jewish priestly elite were vital vectors of Roman imperialism. The ancestral face of local and regional governance, they played key roles in negotiating the relationship between Roman authority and their compatriots. In return, Roman authorities reinforced their political authority and economic privileges, provided that the chief priests met their expectations. In modern literature, Pilate has variously appeared as vicious and cruel, unrelentingly hostile to Jews, weak and easily pliable, and an insensitive, sacrilegious stalwart of Roman power. All these conflicting representations oversimplify. But while contradictory, they give partial insights into Pilate's disposition as prefect. Pilate surely had a legal path to crucifying Jesus (Chapters 9 and 10). But what were his motives? What were his social obligations?[20]

Nowadays Pilate is the most notorious governor in the Roman world. But his fame is at odds with the traces he left. His precise origins and career in Italy, while often theorized, are obscure. Even the dates of his governance of Judaea and how to understand Josephus' testimony on it are uncertain. The conventional view is that his term as prefect was 26–36. But some theorize that it nearly paralleled Caiaphas' long tenure as chief priest (18–36). Pilate figures prominently in all the Gospel accounts of Jesus' crucifixion and in Josephus' description of Roman governance in Judaea (Chapter 9). Beyond that, a few objects corroborate his activity in Judaea. He (re)established what was probably a lighthouse honoring the emperor Tiberius at Caesarea. The foundation inscription for it partially survives. A copper alloy ring found at Herodeion might bear Pilate's name in Greek. This is debated. Remains of a long-known ancient road running from Jerusalem's southern gate to the Temple Mount, as well as those of an aqueduct, may be Pilate's doing. He also minted some anonymous bronze coins as prefect. As we have seen (Chapter 1), he occupied Herod's palace when governing from his headquarters at Caesarea (Figure 1.2). When visiting Jerusalem during Passover and other festivals, his *praetorium* was Herod's palace at the western end of the Upper City (Figures 10.1 and 10.2; Map 6.1).[21]

When Jesus was tried by Pontius Pilate, he encountered the embodiment of the Roman emperor's authority in Judaea. Pilate's main purpose was to stabilize its present order of governance and wealth. To this end he could virtually define what sedition and its punishment were (Chapter 9). But as prefect, Pilate faced many challenges. His goal was to provide peace and justice, as largely defined by landed elites, without compromising his career. He had to appear responsive to the people he governed. But he also encountered a mesh of competing interests. After all, Judaea was a district of the Syrian province. Its governor was Pilate's superior, and some disagree that subordinate prefects like Pilate were really "governors." Meanwhile Pilate had to coordinate with Antipas and the chief priests and take seriously what they communicated to him about local politics in Judaea. But these uneasy allies had to act on their own initiative and select what information they shared. By doing so, they made their roles seem essential. Although Pilate, Antipas, and the chief priests coordinated with each other, their relationship was tense. They had to work with one another, but not too much or too little.[22]

These challenges were amplified by the competing interests of Jews, Samaritans, and polytheists in greater Judaea. But Jews were also navigating some serious internal differences. In city and countryside, some even questioned the legitimacy of their landowning, priestly elite. By Pilate's lifetime, the Temple precinct had been attracting incendiary preachers, insurrectionists, and social unrest. Pilate had to be alert to these during major festivals. He also had to value what the chief priests communicated to him about the volatile activity of others. Pilate sometimes managed these competing interests with massacres and executions.

Yet Pilate could not inflict indiscriminate violence. Magistrates like Pilate did often abuse their power, but they faced serious consequences for doing so. Pilate's decade in office suggests he normally grasped when repressive violence was politically expedient. It followed a predictable logic (Chapter 9). Nothing indicates the chief priests or their core clients suffered from his brutality. His desire to maintain stability and promote his own career meant he had to coordinate with the chief priests in suppressing challenges to their authority. This made him partial to the information the chief priests provided about the political situation in Judaea. It also encouraged him to suspect their more hostile critics of criminal activity. Pilate's conduct was tolerable enough to his superiors and the chief priests for much of his term. If he had not crucified Jesus, would we even remember him?

3

Dissenters

Judaea was filled with brigandage, and whoever happened to be among some people willing to engage in sedition was promoted as king and hastened to destroy the common good.

—JOSEPHUS, *Ant.* 17.285 (on Judaea after the death of Herod I)

Its interpretation concerns the final priests of Jerusalem, who gather wealth and ill-gotten gains from the spoils of the Nations. . . . Its interpretation: the town is Jerusalem, in which the Wicked Priest committed abominations and polluted the sanctuary of God. Violence of the land is the cities of Judaea, where he stole the wealth of the poor.

—1QpHab 9.4–5, 12.7–10 (from Qumran)

IF SOME OF Jesus' compatriots coordinated with Roman authority, other Jews envisioned its end. Some of these built charismatic reputations by criticizing the governing order, including the Romans, Herodians, and chief priests. These often conceived of it as illegitimate and a temporary consequence of a failure to observe the Torah in Israel. Some such dissenters, including the Essenes and Jews at Qumran (these likely being the same people), were serious competitors as scribal elites. Some dissenters were insurgents, people who fought to free Israel from the Romans and restore autonomous rule by Jews. The revolts that erupted in Judaea in 66 and 132 arguably reflect this vision. But not everyone who anticipated the pending end of the established order was planning armed insurrections or rebellions. Many did not. The God of Israel would do that work for them.[1]

Some dissenters, like the Jews of Qumran, foresaw a divine reign over Israel. They believed the present governing order would be finished. A day of judgment would occur, and the just would flourish and rule. Such dissenters could be partial to figures who imitated prophets from Jewish Scriptures. Or they could imitate the prophets themselves. In the meantime, they were supposed to live righteously. But how they envisioned this divine reversal varied. The surviving documents rarely communicate their beliefs with clarity. Debates about how the Jews at Qumran, John the Baptizer, or Jesus understood it persist. But they plausibly anticipated that divine intervention would reverse the ordering of wealth and elevate the lowly and pious to leadership. Some dissenters may also have believed the existing world would end and that God would judge the righteous and unrighteous in a new cosmic realm. Whatever they envisioned, they knew they had to prepare for God's rule, or even announce it. Such a viewpoint would put Jesus on a collision course with Pilate.

Dissenters and God's Reign

When Jesus lived, ideas about the divine reversal of the governing order had found expression in modes of thinking scholars describe as eschatological or millenarian (promising a divine end) or apocalyptic (promising a divine revelation). The Seleucid kings had implemented a dating system that began in the year 311 BCE throughout their vast territories, spanning from Anatolia and the Levant to central Asia. Various Middle Eastern populations responded by imagining how divine revelation would end such absolute imperial time. Jews gravitated toward such thinking, especially after the desecration of the Temple of Jerusalem by Antiochus IV (reigned 175–164 BCE). This elicited the famous prophecies of the Book of Daniel. It predicted the destruction of all earthly empires by God's hand. One such prophecy claimed a king would come from heaven (7:13). In the Gospel of Mark, Jesus quotes this passage when questioned by the high priest at Jerusalem.[2]

We often cannot ascertain how dissenters in Roman Judaea envisioned God's intervention in Israel. They probably did it with some variety. What they shared is that they desired the end of the current, illegitimate ruling order. They also believed it was near or happening at any moment through divine action. Dissenters sometimes believed a Messiah, "the anointed one," would announce or even initiate God's reign. They sometimes envisioned him as a priest or prophet. Most often, they thought he would be a regal figure descended from king David who would liberate Judaea through armed resistance. A century after Jesus lived, the leader of the bloody Bar Kochba Revolt possibly posed as one, though this is debated. Yet some dissenters believed a divinely appointed Messiah would herald God's reign over Israel. One way or another, Jewish beliefs tended to associate the Messiah with the end of the governing order in Israel and the divine judgment of its population. Perhaps a God-governed kingdom on earth would follow. Or maybe people would witness the arrival of a heavenly kingdom. Either way, Roman rule over Israel would end. Its righteous would be freed from it. The lowly and just of Israel would become powerful, the powerful laid low.[3]

For such reasons we can conceive of prophetic dissenters as pitted against Roman and Herodian authority, even if they tolerated it for the present. This distinguishes them from the chief priests and allied scribes who coordinated with it and controlled vast resources by doing so. Their relationship with wealth, social status, and governance sometimes even attracted scathing criticisms from dissenters. After all, the Jews who inhabited Qumran and left caches of remarkable texts there disdained the wealth and status of the governing order and envisioned how divine intervention would invert it. John the Baptizer, Jesus of Nazareth, and various others did too. Some dissenters clearly envisioned that the current chief priests would no longer manage the Temple when heavenly judgment came. Of course, beliefs in Israel's revival by God could circulate among the priests and scribes who coordinated with Roman rule. But they often situated it in the remote future while accommodating Roman governance. They also could deem dissenting, prophetic preachers who predicted an imminent reckoning to be wrong or even subversive. If such preachers stirred violence at the Temple precinct and endangered their compatriots, the chief priests had to act.

In preparation for God's intervention in Israel, dissenters often promoted regimens of readiness and renewed commitment to their interpretations of the Torah. But how they did so varied. Some vaunted routine rituals of purity consistent with those required for periodic sacrifices at the Temple. Some advocated for celibate ideals or for sex strictly regulated for purity and procreation. Many disdained the accumulation of wealth, being perishable and corrupting. They celebrated communal living and sharing or household donations to priests, celibates, or the poor. Virtually all of them preached atonement and moral righteousness in anticipation of judgment, along with purifying ritual practices. Despite variations, such patterns defined the activity of the Jews of Qumran, John the Baptizer, and Jesus. They provided Jesus with motives for his final pilgrimage.

Jews of Qumran (Essenes)

The Jews of Qumran dissented from the governing order. Members of their movement inhabited many different residential communities. But they get their modern name from the site of Qumran, located southeast of Jerusalem, on the northwest shore of the Dead Sea. Their complex at Qumran, now excavated, was located near many caves. In them was discovered an array of documents now known as the Dead Sea Scrolls, or the Qumran texts. The relationship between the complex at Qumran and the texts found in the caves continues to be debated. But the people who inhabited the site apparently maintained them as part of "a scribal library with a sectarian component." They were Jews whose practices distinguished them from many compatriots. The documents say much about the rules, practices, and expectations of those who lived there. Among the most informative is *The Community Rule*, which was discovered in one well-preserved copy and 10 partial ones. Another important text is the *Damascus Document*, found in fragments at Qumran but known from surviving manuscripts elsewhere. The *Damascus Document* outlines rules for peers who live in towns or camps and maintain a regimen of work and charitable distribution of wealth. *The Community Rule* contains precepts for male celibates inhabiting different camps in the Judaean wilderness. By all appearances the stewards of the texts belonged to an exclusive, voluntary movement with rigorous standards for admission and membership, or in other words a sect. We will call its members "Qumran sectarians" or simply "Qumran Jews." With all their challenges, the documents and material culture of Qumran continue to fascinate. Their impact on how we place Jesus of Nazareth in historical context as a dissenting Jew is immense. From such sources, we learn that the Qumran Jews were prophetic dissenters.[4]

Qumran was only one residence of the Qumran Jews. The *Damascus Document* refers to men and women dwelling in towns and camps and practicing wealth redistribution. These were apparently living in various parts of lesser Judaea. Nothing in *The Community Rule* precludes a similar geographic distribution for the communal celibates. These documents suggest the practices of the Qumran Jews varied somewhat. Some were celibate men who disdained property and maintained a high level of purity while inhabiting camps in the Judaean wilderness. Others, both men and women, were married, had children, and could populate cities or towns. Even then, they apparently lived in communes, not traditional households. They also generated revenue for their priests and peers by working and adhered to strict rules for procreative marital intercourse. Whether celibate or married, the Qumran Jews maintained a strong collective consciousness. They were devoted to ritual bathing, prayer, and supporting their community through work and donations. They conceived of themselves as the true children of Israel and envisioned an imminent divine intervention. It involved a Messiah variously understood as a priest or a Davidic king who would judge between the righteous and unrighteous. They had their own priests, who ensured ritual purity before eating daily communal meals and various quotidian acts. They also had non-priestly leaders who oversaw the moral rectitude of members and, if necessary, arranged their expulsion through courts of communal judges. They apparently emulated the camp lifestyle of the Israelites in the Torah and conceived of themselves as being in the presence of God even while absent from the Temple precinct. This spelled a daily regimen of purification rituals, communal dining, and prayer. It also meant avoiding acts of impurity that generally prohibited Jews from eating or from worship at the Temple until they (re)purified. Such impurity would have disrupted their rigorous daily standards and communal dining. Yet, even despite their strong communal bonds and strict regimens, some lived in towns or villages of Judaea, where they interacted with others within ethical guidelines.[5]

Were the Qumran Jews the Essenes, a society of Jews described by Josephus, Philo, and various Roman authors? None of these had serious firsthand experience with them. But some Essenes practiced celibacy and lived in gendered communes. Others engaged in marriage solely to produce children, though they may not have lived as household units. They maintained possessions in common, avoided using clothing and oil for display or comfort, and dwelled in most cities and villages of Judaea. They embraced ritual bathing for purification before common meals and may have thought it could remit spiritual faults. They elected their own priests, appointed supervisors (*epimeletai*) of their conduct, and had their own courts. Though their rigor attracted admiration and fame, they tended not to preach in public or seek converts. They focused on maintaining purity and spiritual righteousness. The Essenes were a closed society that admitted novices for trial periods. Members could be expelled for moral violations, and supervising leaders ensured compliance. The Essenes earned their living by being craftsmen or farmers. They did not engage in commerce for profit, amass landed resources for gain, or benefit from the land tenure or revenues from taxes, tithes, and offerings enjoyed by many Temple priests and allied scribes. Even Essenes who had wives or children donated their earnings to a common fund, which in turn provided for the needs of other members, including their priests. They rigorously observed the Sabbath and prayed in synagogues. They had their own rituals of purification and communal meals. They made periodic ritual offerings at the Temple with their own priests (but not in the forecourt common to all Israelites). Even in commercial contexts, they interacted carefully with outsiders, who could introduce impurity or unrighteousness. They embraced the immortality of the soul and punishment after death.[6]

Dissenters 57

As known, the Essenes and the Qumran Jews bear many similarities. Despite some ostensible discrepancies, certain factors indicate they represent the same people. Qumran's location is in the Essenes' zone of known habitation. The Qumran documents clarify that the Qumran Jews lived in various camps and towns, just like the Essenes. The variations in the Essenes' daily lives and practices are consistent with what is outlined by the Qumran texts, especially *The Community Rule* and the *Damascus Document*. Whether celibate or married, the Essenes and the Qumran Jews had a strong collective identification, a high threshold for membership, and priests who oversaw their rituals and common meals. They valued communal living and support, the rejection of personal wealth, ritual bathing, and rigorous standards for purity in body and spirit. Most serious contradictions between the Essenes and the Qumran Jews are explainable.[7]

If we can identify the Qumran Jews as Essenes, their relationship with the Temple of Jerusalem, the chief priests, animal sacrificing, and the Herodians is more complicated to define. Some conceive of the Qumran Jews as rejecting the Temple at Jerusalem and opting for lives of righteousness in the Judaean desert. They criticized its current operations and may have compensated by conducting sacrifices at their own residential locations, including Qumran, where animal bones may reflect such activity. They apparently maintained a festival calendar not used by the Temple priests. Even so, certain factors suggest that they valued the sanctity of the Temple but had a tense relationship with its management. The Essenes had a reputation for ritual purity, for hostility toward the Hasmonaean dynasty, and for refraining from large-scale insurgency against the established order, presumably because their prophetic beliefs envisioned its divine end. Because of their reputation for virtue (and willingness to accommodate governing authority), the Herodians apparently conferred various privileges upon them. The Essenes were exempted from an oath of loyalty that Herod I had his subjects take. One Essene even allegedly predicted Herod's rise to power, and another foresaw the end of his dynasty's rule. Josephus states that the Essenes made offerings at the Temple. But due to their high standards of purity, they did not mingle with compatriots in its forecourt or make sacrifices with them there. They instead conducted sacrifices among themselves through their own priests. One Qumran text ostensibly mentions these and identifies the people who managed the Temple or made offerings there as corrupt. Because of their special dispensations granted by the Herodian dynasty and the Temple, some claim that the Essenes are the Herodians of the Gospel of Mark (Chapter 5).[8]

Even if they valued the Temple's sanctity and tolerated the ruling order, we should not see the Essenes as aligned with the Herodians or its priests. The Essenes had their own priests who oversaw rituals, offerings, standards of purity, and perhaps animal sacrifices, whether at the Temple or elsewhere. This suggests the Essenes did not embrace the legitimacy of the priestly elite created by the Herodians (or preceding them, the Hasmonaeans), despite the favors and admiration that they attracted. Their exemption from the loyalty oath to Herod shows the special favor they had earned. But it also highlights their ambivalence or even antagonism to Herodian rule. The Qumran documents support that the sectarians envisioned a divine end to governance by the Herodians (or Romans) and the chief priests. One of them may refer to Herod as a prophesied "gentile" king, but it still anticipates his dynasty's end. If the Essenes predicted the rise and fall of the Herodians, we can reconcile that with how Qumran Jews tolerated the present leadership. They thought a pending divine reversal would deliver them from it.[9]

In other words, while embracing the Temple's sanctity and tolerating the present governing order, the Qumran Jews or Essenes rejected the legitimacy of the current priests or the Herodian dynasty. They envisioned the end of such governance, and they may have conducted sacrifices at their residential locations, not (just) at the Temple. They also interpreted the Torah and rules of ritual purity in ways that distinguished them from many other Jews and in theory enabled their claims of unique righteousness. While doing so, they questioned the legitimacy of the current Temple's priestly order, its accumulation of wealth, and the ritual purity of its activities. Some texts from Qumran show that they disapproved of the half-shekel tax collected annually by the chief priests and instead envisioned one per lifetime. Others pointedly criticize how the Temple's priests collected wealth. At least one even describes the Hasmonaean priests-kings as imposters, which presumptively is how the Qumran Jews understood contemporary chief priests supported by Herodian-Roman authority. Ultimately the Qumran Jews gave tithes to their own landless priests, not the landowning priests of the Temple. In this vein *The Temple Scroll*, yet another text found at Qumran, formulates what the proper maintenance and proportions of the Temple should be based on the Torah. It also seems to envision that there would be a new Temple when God restored Israel to the righteous and enacted judgment. Claiming to embody Israel and the sanctity of the Temple wherever they lived, ritually bathed, and prayed, the Qumran Jews believed compatriots who engaged in festivals at the Temple did so in a state of impurity. If they did make offerings at the Temple or at their residential locations, their own priests oversaw any rituals of purity or blessings conferred. Otherwise, they conceived of their righteous way of life and ritual purity as offerings to God. By all appearances, the Temple at Jerusalem was an important structuring principle of their worldview just as it was for other Jews of the time. But they were disassociated from its current management. They even envisioned a priestly Messianic figure and a divine intervention that would terminate it and confer blessings on them.[10]

The Qumran Jews, or Essenes, were prophetic dissenters. They tolerated the governance of the Romans, Herodians, and chief priests. Refraining from public disputation, they did not preach openly against it. Even so, they anticipated its imminent and divine-imposed end. They did so while maintaining their strict regimen of ritual bathing, communal banqueting, and isolation from most forms of sex. They may have been patronized by the Herodians. They may have generally refrained from incendiary public criticism and insurgency. But in their practices, they took measures to minimize their complicity and the fruits of compliance. Emphasizing communal sharing and condemning excess wealth, they did not benefit from land tenure and revenues from taxes, tithes, and offerings in ways that the chief priests and allied scribes did. For them, God would end such accumulation of wealth and the Herodian and Roman rule that enabled it.

John the Baptizer

Because of his presence in all New Testament Gospels, John the Baptizer is very famous. With his camel tunic, diet of locusts, and prophecies of God's intervention, he cuts a striking feature. His grisly death at the order of Antipas betrays his influence as a charismatic preacher. We should deem John a dissenting figure. But what sort was he?

We can communicate certain premises, even if debates persist. Unlike Jesus, John apparently did not originate from Galilee or spend much time there. Luke (1:39) states that his father was a priest at Jerusalem and that John's home city (called "Iouda") was nearby. These specifics may not be accurate. Even so, John's known activity places him in the Judaean wilderness at the Jordan River, near the Dead Sea. He probably came from the area. Josephus indicates that when John was arrested, he was active in parts of Transjordan that Antipas governed. This places him across the Jordan from lesser Judaea.[11]

The Gospels represent John as advocating for acts of ritual baptism that brought or helped bring spiritual rectitude. Josephus corroborates it in a passage we should accept as authentic. Josephus states that John believed the ritual would purify the body and righteousness would cleanse the soul, though presumably in tandem with baptism. Even though the Gospels portray Jesus as baptized by John, they rarely suggest Jesus baptized others. We can accept that ritual baptism was a core aspect of John's preaching. He also maintained ritual purity very strictly. His isolation, his diet of wild locusts and honey, and his camel attire were presumably tied to this. John's diet ensured he did not consume unclean products. A garment of camel hair put his skin in contact with water during immersion, even if Jews debated whether camel skin and hair were unclean. He emulated the prophets from Jewish sacred writings, especially Elijah, by criticizing the governing order. He advocated for shedding wealth and circulating it to the poor. He preached that God would intervene to judge between the righteous and unrighteous. We do not know whether he claimed to be the Messiah, though his message had Messianic overtones and perhaps anticipated one. John primarily operated in Transjordan (ancient Peraea) and along the Jordan River, where he baptized and preached to those who gathered. Located east of the district of Judaea, Peraea was a territory governed by Antipas. John's activity there kept him out of the reach of Pontius Pilate, who massacred unarmed dissenters in Jerusalem roughly when John was active (Chapter 9). But he was not beyond the reach of Antipas.[12]

Very few aspects of John the Baptizer's career are uncontroversial. His views on bathing and ritual share some affinities with the beliefs of Qumran Jews. But what was John's relationship to them, and to Jesus? Some inferences can be made. John was a popular prophetic preacher. At the peak of his career, he attracted many sympathetic listeners and some ardent supporters who sought to be baptized and so purified. Jesus was reportedly one such person, and his message about imminent divine intervention owed many debts to John's. In fact, all the Gospel authors took pains to explain why Jesus was baptized by John despite Jesus being the true Messiah. The New Testament Gospels treat John as embracing Jesus as the Messiah or as a prophet who supersedes him. Yet we know the Gospels also have every reason to promote John as embracing Jesus' Messianic stature. Jesus may even have posed as a Messianic figure recognized by John without John's acknowledgment. After his death, John's supporters probably competed with Jesus for authority among Jews.[13]

John the Baptizer's origins are obscure. But his worldview suggests contact with the Qumran Jews or shared beliefs they had autonomously acquired. Like John, they advocated for repentance combined with rites of water immersion that were to accompany the remission of spiritual faults, not just ritual purity. They also envisioned that God would intervene in Israel, overturn the established order, and judge the righteous and unrighteous. They may even have envisioned the end of the world and an encompassing fire. John was active in Peraea, which was east of the Jorden River but still somewhat close to Qumran and adjacent parts of lesser Judaea. Qumran is at the northwest edge of the Dead Sea, and John did his work on its northern and northeastern edges. The meager sources record no statements made by John against the chief priests. He accepted the sanctity of the Temple and its sacrifices. But his advocacy of baptism to remove spiritual faults implicitly challenged the centrality of their sacrificial activity. Of course, these practices and perspectives were not unique to the Qumran Jews. They circulated among various Jews of the period. Whether John advocated for one or many baptisms remains unknown.[14]

What distinguishes John the Baptizer is that he advocated for repentance and ritual immersion at various locations along the Jordan River and in the Judaean wilderness. He did not practice close-knit communal living like many Qumran Jews. Instead, he leveraged his charisma, preaching, and ascetic reputation to attract followers and sympathizers seeking baptism from him. It is uncertain whether he gathered core followers or just attracted people who believed his message. Either way, he was influential. He did not engage in itinerant preaching at cities and towns as Jesus did. But we can describe John as a publicly prophetic preacher who sometimes shifted his wilderness locations, presumably in part because Antipas wanted to arrest him. Luke (3:1–3) places the beginning of John's ministry in the 15th year of Tiberius' reign, or 29 CE. It adds other chronological markers provided by Pilate and various dynasts and chief priests mentioned by Josephus. The Lukan author may have even attached the lives of John and Jesus to fixed points from Josephus' *Antiquities* (Appendix 1). Even so, Josephus' testimony does support that John, whatever his origins, had established his own prophetic stature among followers and sympathizers by around this time. Jesus may well have met him. Baptized by John, he too reportedly performed baptisms (John 3:22–4:3). Yet, if so, Jesus eventually initiated his own movement. Whatever their rapport, John and Jesus were making their own prophetic claims that their respective sympathizers believed. Despite what the Gospels say, John did not necessarily proclaim Jesus as a figure superior to him. John's followers probably deemed John, not Jesus, a Messiah.

The Gospels and Josephus blame Antipas for John's death. But when did he kill John? A few observations here should provide some clarification. As widely observed, the Gospels of Mark and Matthew link John's death to his criticisms of Antipas for taking Herodias as his wife after she had been married to his half-brother. Josephus does not draw a link between the marriage and

John's execution, but he locates John's death in events set in motion by it. As Josephus narrates, Antipas was in Rome when he met Herodias, wife of his half-brother Herod. This Herod is often confused with the tetrarch Philip, who died in 34, because Mark mistakenly calls him Philip. Herodias' husband Herod had in fact been passed over for rule by Herod I in his final years and had lived at Rome as a result. Yet for Antipas to marry Herodias, he had to divorce his current wife, the daughter of the Nabataean king Aretas IV.[15]

According to Josephus, hostilities between Antipas and Aretas boiled over after the divorce, and Antipas suffered a humiliating defeat at Gamala, in Philip's territory. This supports that Antipas and Aretas were contesting Philip's territories after his death in 34, when no consular governor of Syria could intervene. The governor Flaccus had died in 33; Vitellius did not arrive in Syria until 35, and he came to Jerusalem in 37 in response to Antipas' failure. Meanwhile Aretas apparently maintained a military presence in Philip's former territories until his death in 40 (Chapter 11).

Altogether we can date Aretas' victory over Antipas to 36 or so. Josephus in turn claims that many Jews deemed Antipas' defeat divine retribution for the murder of John the Baptizer. This establishes that John's death preceded that defeat. It also supports that Antipas and Herodias were married as early as the late 20s or early 30s. If we accept the Gospels' claim that John died before Jesus, we can place John's death in 30, more or less.

John the Baptizer was like many dissenters in a key respect: he envisioned God's pending intervention in the established order. But some dissenters who opposed the Romans, Herodians, or chief priests did not wait for God's intervention and judgment. They mounted an insurgency in the present.

Insurgent Leaders and Prophetic Preachers

In Jesus' Judaea, certain people resisted Roman governance through military insurgency. In some cases, they had prophetic views about Messianic figures and God's intervention in Israel. In others, they perhaps did not. But whatever they believed, they aimed to create an autonomous Israel in the present through organized, armed activity. They opposed the chief priests' coordination with the Romans and Herodians by violent means. We can place their aspirations on a continuum with those of other dissenters. But their actions set them apart.[16]

Some people in Judaea advocated for armed uprising against the Romans. When Herod died in 4 BCE, various people staged revolts and communicated royal and seemingly Messianic aspirations in different parts of greater Judaea.

These include Judas, son of Hezekiah in Galilee; Simon in Transjordan; and Athronges in lesser Judaea. According to Josephus, a man named Judas, perhaps identical to the Judas just mentioned (but distinct from Jesus' follower with the name!), was a Pharisee who opposed Rome and encouraged revolt. Josephus variously places his origins in Galilee and Golan. He was hostile to the census and taxes assessed by Quirinius, the governor of Syria, in 6 CE. Josephus claims he founded one of the Jews' four major philosophical traditions. He was probably a Pharisee with an anti-Roman bent. Josephus states that Judas and his followers engaged in insurrection and assassinations for a long time. Judas' sons apparently persisted in revolt after his death. Two of them, named James and Simon, were executed c. 46–48 by the governor Tiberius Alexander.[17]

One son of Judas, named Menahem, reportedly played a role in the outbreak of the Jewish Revolt in 66. He organized a band of insurgents in Jerusalem, but his capacity for violence and royal pretense alienated other leaders. He had the chief priest Ananias killed for his willingness to negotiate with Rome. He then worshiped at the Temple wearing regal garments. Ananias' son Eleazer, another insurgent leader, took vengeance by having him killed. Even so, a man who was reportedly descended from Judas, also named Eleazer, organized an insurgency at the fortress of Masada. Josephus claims the insurgents engaged in mass suicide after a siege by the Romans. Archaeological finds have not confirmed this unambiguously. We can wonder whether such military leaders were Judas' actual descendants. But they were surely among the people who resisted Roman (and Herodian) rule.[18]

Some insurgents Josephus calls *sicarii* were reportedly followers of Judas' descendants Menahem and Eleazer. They carried daggers under their tunics and assassinated members of the Jewish leadership at Jerusalem immediately before the First Jewish Revolt. They even murdered the former high priest Jonathan in the 50s. Josephus treats this act as initiating a pattern of targeting priestly and scribal elites. His *Antiquities* even alleges that the governor Felix paid them to kill Jonathan during a dispute. Josephus ostensibly suggests the so-called *sicarii* were an actual political faction that joined the insurgencies at Jerusalem and Masada. But he uses the term for anyone who attacked the Jewish leadership or acted as hired assassins. It referred to their mode of attack and not to a movement, even if they often targeted ruling elites. We should envision various charismatic leaders with their own armed followers and with similar agendas.[19]

In Josephus' narrative, the *sicarii* are distinct from Zealots. Josephus mockingly uses this Greek term (meaning "disciples") for members of an insurgent faction (or factions) active at Jerusalem in 68–69 behind various leaders.

These sought to establish their own priestly lineage and, while fighting one another, also fought those who supported priestly continuity or negotiation with Rome. Since Josephus advocates for rapport with Rome and traditional priestly continuity, we can expect him to criticize such insurgents. He even claims that after the Romans had captured him, he tried to persuade Zealots to negotiate with the Roman army besieging Jerusalem. He celebrates a former high priest named Ananus for getting killed while doing so.[20]

The testimony of Josephus tends to lump the people who resisted Roman rule during the first century into cohesive movements or political factions. But as we have seen, opposition to Rome between 6 and 66 largely involved disparate groups organized around their own individual leaders with similar worldviews. Such groups and their leaders competed for authority at every stage of the Jewish Revolt, and they even warred with one another to that end. We can surmise that many different Jews (including some priests) advocated for revolt against Rome, with various degrees of organization. Other Jews, particularly the Herodians and some influential priests, opposed the revolt or participated reluctantly.[21]

In some instances, armed uprising and Messianic or prophetic preaching were intertwined. The followers of some insurgent leaders, like Judas the Galilean or his son Menahem, conceivably believed that divine intervention was imminent. They plausibly thought a Messiah lived among them, and they framed their insurgency as part of a greater cosmic drama. But many prophetic movements were not armed uprisings. They instead involved incendiary preaching about how God would reign in Israel. Josephus observes that preceding the First Jewish Revolt, certain men proclaimed God would reverse the governing order through their activity. In the 50s, a Jew from Egypt posed as a prophet, gathered a crowd at the Mount of Olives, and asserted that God would make the walls of Jerusalem collapse. The governor Felix massacred them. Around 45, the followers of Theudas were slaughtered by the governor Fadus while they marched to the Jordan River, which Theudas claimed God would part. Such repression points to challenges faced by governors when determining whether unarmed preachers and their followers were insurgent or seditious. After all, these could potentially shift to inflicting violence or inspire it in others.[22]

Some dissidents preached armed insurrection. Others preached imminent divine intervention without calling for military activity. Roman authorities did not always distinguish between them. Difficulties in doing so plausibly had bearing on Pilate's decision to execute Jesus. All Roman authorities deemed figures engaged in armed insurrection worthy of repressive violence (Chapter 9). They also thought mass movements organized by prophetic preachers were criminally seditious. Their justification, apparently, was that such activity *could* breed acts of insurrection or civil disorder. It authorized Fadus' massacre of Theudas' followers and Felix's slaughtering of people marching on Jerusalem's walls. Perhaps similar factors motivated Pilate to crucify Jesus. But what brought Jesus into Pilate's path in the first place?

Jesus of Nazareth

Jesus of Nazareth is nowadays the most famous Jewish dissenter of first-century Judaea. But when he lived, he had competition. He may not have been altogether unique from other charismatic preachers. Even so, his mission and death inspired a Jewish movement that set the stage for the second-century Christians who treasured his memory (Chapter 4). It led to his common recognition as the Christ (the Greek translation of "Messiah") and the Son of God. Billions of people have embraced him as their savior over the course of world history.

Jesus' fame and the movement he inspired in the generations, centuries, and millennia after his death can easily obscure his motivations and contexts for preaching, as scholars overwhelmingly recognize. But we can make some widely accepted observations about Jesus and his context. No doubt, Jesus' agency as a prophetic or Messianic preacher was a key factor in the birth of the Jewish sectarian Christ movement and, eventually, Christianity. But Jesus was first and foremost a Galilean Jew. His concerns were firmly at home in Antipas' Galilee and Roman Judaea. They fall within a range of debates and reflections people were having about how to be righteous, devout Jews. These debates centered on many issues. Some prevalent ones involved how to observe the Torah, practice ritual purity, manage the Temple, handle wealth, and have sex (or not). Others focused on the soul and what happens after death. People were also debating whether divine intervention was near, what form it would take, and what it would bring. With this in mind, we can place Jesus and his followers among the dissenters of the period. But what sort of dissenter was he? When did he begin behaving publicly as one?[23]

During the formative periods of Jesus' life, Antipas ruled Galilee and Roman prefects governed Judaea. But controversies plague any attempt at specific dates. Jesus' birthdate is an irresolvable knot. We have better signposting for his death, which happened by 36. Josephus' testimony is pivotal once again. We know Tiberius was emperor and Pilate prefect when Jesus was crucified. When the governor of Syria Vitellius (active 35–39) dismissed Pilate, the chastened prefect returned to Rome, but Tiberius had already died

66   KILLING THE MESSIAH

by that time. This means Pilate was dismissed around the end of 36. Jesus died some time before that. But how long before?[24]

We have already noted that John the Baptizer was most probably arrested and executed in 30 or so. The Synoptic Gospels agree that Jesus began his ministry in earnest after that. They all support that Pilate crucified Jesus sometime after John's death. The Gospel of Luke (3:1–3) states that John began his ministry in the 15th year of the Tiberius' reign (14–37). Even if engaging with Josephus' *Antiquities*, the testimony most probably places John's work in 29 CE. Luke also says Jesus started preaching sometime later, when he was roughly 30 years old (3:23). This passage ostensibly conflicts with the Gospel of John (2:20), which claims Jesus began preaching publicly when Herod's Temple had been under construction for 46 years, in 28. Even so, it supports that Jesus died between 30 and 36. If John correctly portrays Jesus as preaching over the span of three Passovers, we should place his crucifixion in Passover week of 33. The Synoptics seem to depict a shorter public ministry and place the crucifixion earlier. The death date may never be fixed. But Pilate probably had Jesus crucified in Passover week (April) of 33 or so.[25]

When Jesus began to preach his message, he did so in his home region of Galilee. His upbringing among laborers who endured the ordering of landed wealth in Antipas' Galilee surely shaped his worldview and convictions (Chapter 1). Originating from the town of Nazareth, his preaching embodied the concerns of Galilean townspeople and villagers who were devout Jews but did not study the Torah and other Jewish Scriptures as the priests or scribes did. Jesus' itinerary focused foremost on communities near the Sea of Galilee. For the next several years, he built a core following among Galileans. He also attracted Galilean and Judaean sympathizers who listened to him preach or solicited his intervention, especially as he built a reputation for performing miracles. His message and emulation of the prophets were like John the Baptizer's. But his approach to circulating his message was different. The Qumran Jews (or Essenes) attracted followers based on their reputation for strict ritual observance and moral rectitude. They perhaps preached publicly at times, but they were not itinerant proselytizers. John the Baptizer camped along the Jordan River and attracted people who sought purification from him. He was not quite as itinerant as Jesus, who frequented cities, towns, villages, and wilderness locations. John's reputation instead attracted sympathizers into the Judaean desert to be baptized and hear him preach. While Jesus was apparently celibate, he did not adopt the ascetic behaviors or isolation of John the Baptizer. He also perhaps did not baptize others as John and subsequent Christians did. Only the Gospel of John mentions this. Despite observing general rules of purity, Jesus did not cultivate the regimen of the Qumran Jews. Altogether, his views on the Torah and purity shared affinities with the Pharisees, despite what the Gospels claim.[26]

Even if his methods were different, Jesus resembled John the Baptizer in many ways. Jesus' reputation owed a great debt to his reported affiliation with John. The two men also bore some striking resemblances to the Qumran Jews. Sharing in the general context of first-century Judaea, they all were involved in debates happening among contemporaries there. Like virtually all Jews, they treasured the Temple's sacrifices, the Torah, and what they deemed the appropriate rules of ritual purity. They also envisioned a divine intervention in Israel's order of governance and wealth. The Gospels portray Jesus asserting that the "Kingdom of God" (*basileia Theou*) was imminent. But what did he mean? What did it mean for contemporary Jews? Interpretations vary. Jewish sacred writings often celebrated God's dominion over Israel, usually without the phrase "Kingdom of God." In some reckonings, this spelled God's revived governance of Israel with (or through) the righteous. In others, it meant an apocalyptic revelation and an eschatological end to the world that had existed. But either way, it involved reversing the imperial governing order in Judaea and establishing a divine order that resembled it in form. Because of this some describe a "reign," "empire," or even "dictatorship" of God that Jesus and his followers were to spearhead. We will refer to a "reign of God."[27]

The consistency with which Jesus calls himself "Son of Man" in the Gospels is perplexing. The term could simply refer to a human, but in Jewish writings it also denoted a divinely inspired prophet who spoke with the voice of God. This is frequently its meaning in Ezekiel, for example, and suggests Jesus' emulation of prophets like Elijah and Moses. The "Son of Man" also could describe a divinely appointed figure who announced God's end to earthly kingdoms and his restoration of Israel, as in Daniel 7:13. But did "Son of Man" entail a claim to Messianic stature, which itself often bore connotations of Davidic warrior kingship? It is hard to tell. In the Gospel of Mark, Jesus calls himself "Son of Man" and only rarely associates himself with the term "Messiah"; most often that term is ascribed to him by others. The remaining Gospels stress his Messianic stature more overtly, but he mostly calls himself "the Son of Man" in these too. Scholars debate whether Jesus identified himself publicly as the Messiah or whether the Gospels, written at least decades after his death, just claimed that he did. After all, Jesus apparently did not behave as a warrior king or call himself Messiah in his preaching, and the Gospels could have simply portrayed him as the Messiah. Even so, in Jewish traditions references to the "Son of Man," "Son of God," and the

"Messiah" had overlapping meanings. For some Jews the Messiah was a prophetic agent who would announce the imminent reign of God and perhaps even ascend to heaven and return when it arrived. When Jesus called himself "Son of Man," he could have been communicating, if ambiguously, his divinely appointed Messianic agency. Or at least this is how some members of his audience might have understood him.[28]

The debate about Jesus' core message and the Gospel accounts will continue. But while we accept that Jesus was a Messianic, eschatological prophet, our understanding of his trial and execution does not rely on a particular interpretation. Roman authorities and the chief priests could have responded repressively to many different possible iterations. Even so, we can define some general premises. After all, Jesus' trial and execution stemmed from his preaching or actions he undertook while doing it. The Gospels agree that Jesus imitated the prophets of Jewish Scriptures. Like them, he preached God's imminent reign over Israel and punishment of the unrighteous. He also frequently called himself the "Son of Man" while doing so. These themes were familiar to the villagers of Galilee who could be persuaded by charismatic preachers that governance by Antipas was oppressive and illegitimate. They support that Jesus envisioned that God would rule Israel with (or through) the righteous and reverse the governing order. In this vein Jesus' claims of being the "Son of Man" could have appeared Messianic to people who witnessed him preach or act out biblical templates. The Gospels' agreement that Pilate labeled him "King of the Jews" during his trial and execution points to such a regal, Messianic understanding of Jesus' preaching and behavior. Yet Jesus may very well have conceived of the reign of God in eschatological terms. He may have anticipated that the material world would cease and a heavenly redemption would ensue for the righteous and just. If so, it would still end Herodian-Roman rule in Judaea and elevate the devout poor, especially Jesus' followers. Whether Jesus was preaching an earthly or heavenly reign of God over Israel, his message prophesied the end of present governance and Temple management. He also claimed to be playing a pivotal prophetic or Messianic role in the drama.[29]

Despite ambiguities, Jesus envisioned a divine intervention that would restore Israel to rule by God. A day of judgment would ensue, and it would reverse Roman Judaea's ordering of governance and wealth. The Romans, the Herodians, and the Temple's priests would rule no more. Their accumulation of wealth would end. The righteous poor would be relieved of their suffering. His preaching brought him into conflict with Antipas and then the chief priests and Pontius Pilate. His crucifixion would follow. How these played out is the focus of Part II.

PART II

Jesus of Nazareth and the Gospels

4

The New Testament Gospels and Jesus

Many of the first will be last, and the last will be first.
—MARK 10:31.

Blessed are you who are poor, because the reign of God is yours... [B]ut woe to you who are wealthy, because you are having your consolation now.
—LUKE 6:20, 24.

WAS JESUS A seditionist? The Gospels say no. In their accounts, the chief priests of Jerusalem and allied scribes worry about Jesus' popularity and influence. They chafe at his Messianic pretentions. They arrest Jesus. They summon a council that declares him worthy of death. They then petition Pontius Pilate to judge capital charges against him. Pilate believes Jesus is innocent. But he puts him to death anyway, to placate the chief priests and attending crowd. Their hostility, not so much Roman authorities, kills Jesus. So the Gospels assert.

The Gospels by all appearances shift responsibility for Jesus' death from Roman authorities to the chief priests. But people interpret their reports in different ways. One perspective takes the Gospels mostly at face value: Pilate acted on Jesus' sentencing by a *synhedrion* (council) at Jerusalem or was cowed by the chief priests into execution. Another, its opposite, identifies Jesus and his followers as armed insurrectionists. The Gospels negated earlier traditions to this effect, though they still retain traces. Between these poles, almost every conceivable position has been staked. Some believe Pilate convicted and executed Jesus for sedition, but without deeming him guilty of criminal behavior, because he feared Jesus' inflammatory influence on the crowds at Passover. Others think Pilate, though doubting his guilt, convicted Jesus to accommodate the chief priests and his own interests,. But could Jesus' activity have met Pilate's criteria for sedition, even if he was not an armed insurrectionist or planning social disturbance? Could Pilate have thought that Jesus' preaching at the Temple precinct was criminal behavior that warranted crucifixion?

To address these questions, we must understand the New Testament Gospels as historical sources. But to do that, we must understand them as literary and theological texts. What are the New Testament Gospels? How do we read them to understand Jesus' message? Do they betray traces of a seditionist Jesus?

The Gospel Accounts and Jesus

As already discussed, Jesus was a prophetic preacher who envisioned the pending restoration of God's rule over Israel, the judging of the righteous and unrighteous, and a reversal of the current governing structure. He probably anticipated an end to the perceptible world and the rise of a heavenly order. He may have posed as their Messianic forerunner. In Mark and Luke (and in John 3:3–5), Jesus continually refers to a reign of God, which Matthew interprets as a "reign of Heaven." But was Jesus' message seditious as far as Roman authorities were concerned?

The answer is much more complicated than a simple yes or no. Different figures of Roman authority had different definitions of seditious behavior (Chapter 9). They had different legal and moral justifications for responding with violence and different motives for doing so. But the New Testament Gospels consistently depict Jesus' trial and execution as manufactured by the distortions of the chief priests and Pilate's lack of moral fortitude. One modern tendency takes the Gospels at their word. The chief priests of Jerusalem foremost desired Jesus' elimination and suborned an amoral, weak, or self-interested Pilate to this purpose. But what if Jesus' preaching anticipated the end of the present order of governance and wealth in Judaea? What if it could stir serious crowd violence at the Temple precinct? What if Jesus was indifferent to such a foreseeable outcome, or even using it as leverage? What if Pilate simply believed Jesus had committed a dangerously criminal act?

The four Gospels included in the Christian New Testament that church authorities defined in the fourth century remain our main sources for Jesus' final Passover week in Jerusalem. No surviving apocryphal Gospels or other early Christian works offer historical commentary independently of them or their sources, despite occasional claims otherwise. Nowadays we know the New Testament Gospels by the names of the people that early Christians believed wrote them. We describe them as the Gospels according to Mark, Matthew, Luke, and John. Their authorship remains debated, however, and scholars mostly treat them as anonymous works. For clarity, when we refer to these texts, we will identify them by their traditional names. We will note, for instance, what Mark says and what Luke describes. But when we mention the people that wrote them, we will refer to a Markan author, a Lukan author (who also wrote Acts of the Apostles), and so forth.[1]

Mark, Matthew, and Luke are often called the Synoptic Gospels in modern scholarship. This is because they obviously share much material. At times Matthew and Luke share material not in Mark. But what is their relationship? Many accept that Mark is the earliest surviving Gospel. Matthew and Luke, written later, derived much material from it. Independently of one another, Matthew and Luke also used a source that is now lost (called "Q"). Based on what they share (along with the apocryphal Gospel of Thomas), this common source largely consisted of sayings attributed to Jesus. Some surmise that the Lukan author had access to Mark and Matthew, which mostly explains the shared material and divergences. Other perspectives on "the Synoptic Problem" are legion. John is the latest Gospel. Even so, it apparently reworks material from the Synoptic Gospels or common sources while integrating some independent traditions.[2]

An additional layer is presented by a controversial figure named Marcion, the focus of much recent scholarship. In the 130s–140s, Marcion wrote (or obtained) a Gospel that can be theoretically reconstructed, in part, from its citations by Tertullian and other later Christians who pilloried him as a heretic. This work was closely related to Luke and conceivably reflects an older form of its existing text. The Lukan author may even have composed Luke and Acts in response to it. A few scholars now believe it even preceded all the New Testament Gospels, which ultimately would reflect responses to Marcion's activity and bear witness to Christian concerns after the Bar Kochba Revolt (132–135). If correct, the theory means that the Gospels' relationship to the activity of Jesus or his first-century believers is even more tenuous.[3]

In this book we accept the dating of the Synoptic Gospels to various points from the late first to the mid-second century. We also believe the Lukan author engaged with Mark and Matthew, though Luke and Matthew probably benefited from a basic "Q" source too (Appendix 1). Even so, we must stress that this hypothesis, while fairly conventional, is just a hypothesis, and one vulnerable to revision. At the very least, second-century Christians heavily intervened in the Gospels to create the surviving forms and to define an increasingly non-Jewish (and anti-Jewish) Christianity. Their relationship to first-century people of both Jewish and non-Jewish origins who embraced Jesus as Messiah or divine is a vital scholarly issue, one that will continue to

74

KILLING THE MESSIAH

attract serious debate. In this book we distinguish between first-century Jesus Christ believers and second-century Christians on this basis. But our goal here is simply to understand what made Jesus ultimately cross paths with Pilate. Is that even possible?[4]

The Gospels pose serious complications. As Jews of Judaea, Jesus and his compatriots spoke Aramaic and quoted Hebrew Scriptures. But the Gospels, composed in Greek, put into their mouths what are in theory translations of their statements, if not distortions or inventions. When such figures quote Greek translations of Hebrew Scriptures, skepticism is especially warranted. Also important is that the Gospels were written *after* Jesus Christ believers had been defining what made them distinct from other Jews for decades. We now understand Jesus was foremost debating with his compatriots about how to be righteous Jews. Yet the Gospels in various ways seem to pit him against Jews or the Temple at Jerusalem altogether. Moreover, most or even all the Gospel accounts were written after the outbreak of the First Jewish Revolt, the destruction of the Temple in 70, the dispersal of the chief priests, and the imposition of a penalty tax on Jews by the Romans. For scholars who date them after Marcion's Gospel, the tragic Bar Kochba Revolt and the dispersal of Jews from Jerusalem also had a serious impact. As believers in Jesus Christ made their homes in the Roman Mediterranean, they distanced themselves from such insurgency (or insurgencies) and portrayed Jesus and his followers as acceptable to Roman authority. They were also hostile to scribal elites who were displacing the chief priests as authorities in Judaea and rejected that Jesus was the Messiah. These are reasons why the Gospels minimize the hostility of Roman authorities like Pilate toward Jesus. They are also why the Gospels exaggerate Jesus' conflict with Jewish scribes like the Pharisees.[5]

In posing such problems, the Gospels thus raise an important question: How are we to understand Jesus in historical terms? Nowadays many scholars distinguish between the theological and historical value of the Gospels. One can believe they communicate a cosmic truth about Jesus even if they are not accurate historically. But how we read the Gospels to understand what scholars have often called "the historical Jesus" is intensely debated. Throughout the 20th century, scholars vaunted various "criteria of authenticity." In theory these enabled people to distinguish the words and deeds of Jesus from the contrivances of later Jesus Christ believers or the Gospels. After all, the Gospels had an obvious goal in promoting Jesus as a Messianic or even divine figure whose eschatological worldview superseded Jerusalem's Temple. Through such criteria, some frame Jesus as a peasant sage or prophet concerned with ethics or justice in contemporary Israel. Others criticize that approach because it almost invariably reflects arbitrary or circular reasoning about what material originates with Jesus. The priority of Marcion's Gospel, if accepted, invalidates the approach even more. It would place the writing of all New Testament Gospels over a century after Jesus died. But without such an approach, what can we know about Jesus as a historical person? Can we know anything at all?[6]

The challenges are immense. But we can still identify general features of Jesus' activity and message and the debts they owed to his contemporary Jewish context and social underpinnings. In broad outline, we can surmise basic continuity rather than total discontinuity between Jesus' message and how later generations remembered him. After all, the Gospels reflect the impact Jesus' words and deeds had on his followers' memories. A Messianic worldview that envisioned a divine reversal of the Temple's management is consistent with views expressed by Jews preceding and contemporary to Jesus. It is compatible with how some Galilean laborers like Jesus viewed society and the governing order in greater Judaea. It is also a recognizable if distinct precursor for the shifts in how Jesus Christ believers, and subsequently Christians, understood his death, resurrection, and relationship with Jerusalem's Temple both before and after its destruction in 70 and the ultimate failure of the Bar Kochba Revolt in 135. In fact, some evidence points to a basic tradition or overlapping traditions about Jesus' words and deeds that were preserved and transmitted by his followers after his crucifixion. Both Paul and the Gospel of Mark ostensibly call this information "the Gospel" (*to euangelion*), and its existence conceivably shaped how the New Testament Gospels retain variations on the same basic, fixed framework for narrating Jesus' life. All these factors mean that Jesus is knowable in general historical terms from the Gospels, even if precision fails. Because of them narratives of a Messianic Jesus who preached an apocalyptic message continue to compel. This is arguably so even if people continue to debate the date of the Gospels, the nature of first-century Jesus Christ believers, and how second-century Christians impacted prior textual and oral traditions (or created new ones).[7]

The letters of the Jesus Christ believer and preacher Paul contain traces of Jesus' eschatological perspective and of a basic gospel tradition about Jesus' career, teaching, and life. No doubt the letters raise their own challenges, not least because second-century Christians reworked Paul's existing letters or associated new ones with his name. In the 130s–140s, Marcion conceivably handled earlier forms than the ones that survive. But despite the challenges, we can surmise that Paul's surviving letters generally reflect his orientation as a

Jesus Christ believer of the first century, one who deemed Jesus the fulfillment of Messianic expectations that had circulated among Jews. As early as 1 Thessalonians (c. 50), Paul communicates eschatological views that parallel those from the Gospels. Familiar with some of Jesus' core followers, Paul refers to statements and teachings of Jesus later recorded by the Gospels, including Jesus' prohibitions against divorce and words spoken at the Last Supper enshrined in eucharistic celebration. This testimony supports that variations on a basic gospel tradition for Jesus' ministry were preserved by his core followers and eyewitnesses after his death. This basic tradition is what Paul and Mark call "the Gospel" (*to euangelion*), a term that Christians would only later recast as "Gospels" (*euangelia*). The general view of Papias (early second century) that Jesus' followers stewarded details about his life is plausible, even if we can doubt specific claims about witnesses and authorship. In fact, Mark arguably prioritizes the agency of Jesus' core follower Peter because it filters what a subsequent generation preserved from his eyewitness testimony of Jesus' preaching and arrest. No doubt the basic gospel tradition was shaped by the partisan subjectivities of his core followers. It was somewhat fluid and reworked by Jesus Christ believers in the first century. Christians intervened in it heavily in the second century. We cannot assume flawless reliability and precision in its particulars. But the tradition was also somewhat fixed and contains a basic historical outline for how Jesus affected his followers.[8]

These factors have a bearing on how we understand the final week of Jesus' life and Antipas' prior hostility to him in Galilee (Chapters 5–10). Scholars challenge the historical basis of many episodes recorded by the Gospels for Jesus' activity in Jerusalem. Prominent among them are Jesus' regal entry into the city, his prediction of the Temple's destruction, "the Sanhedrin's" hearing against him, and even a trial by Pilate. Yet the statements about Jesus' death made by Paul's letters support that a basic gospel tradition for his death had been established by the 50s. It describes the cross and crucifixion in ways that point to the intervention of Roman authorities. Paul also ascribes some responsibility to the chief priests, though he misleadingly universalizes it to "the Jews/Judaeans" (1 Thess 2:14–16). He indicates that Jesus was handed over at night (1 Cor 11:23) without resisting (Gal 1:4, 2:20; Phil 2:8). In other words, such a tradition for Jesus' death was circulating among his believers when the Gospels' authors were active. This plausibly explains why Mark's account of Jesus' final Passover week is a continuous narrative signposted by daily intervals, not the standard self-contained pericopes. Scholars naturally debate whether Mark's account is indebted to a single Passion narrative that circulated broadly among Jesus' followers or to assorted episodes on which

The New Testament Gospels and Jesus   77

Mark imposes temporal signs. Mark's source(s) also probably shifted responsibility for Jesus' death from Roman authority to the chief priests. Its accuracy and that of its source traditions remain contested. Some elements of it raise doubts that Jesus even died during Passover week (Chapter 7). Even so, Mark's narrative and its source (or sources) reflect how Jesus' followers understood his message and crucifixion as part of their gospel tradition. It offers a basic outline for the impact that Jesus' final week had on their memories.[9]

In this sense, we can theorize that the Gospel narratives retain aspects of Jesus' final Passover week in Jerusalem that were preserved by his followers after his death. Yet they do not capture past events with the same aspirations or precision as modern historical compositions. Their goal of communicating a theological truth often compromises their historical accuracy. But even then, their framework was not necessarily alien to Jesus himself. For example, Mark and the other Gospels treat Jesus' words and deeds in Jerusalem as fulfilling prophecies from Hebrew Scriptures (if mediated by Greek translations). A good example is his "regal" entry into Jerusalem on a colt. In Mark, it echoes a prophecy from Zechariah (9:9) that a Messiah would ride a donkey's colt into the city. Matthew and Luke tighten this episode's relationships to the prophecy more explicitly. This could point to invention by the Gospels, not Jesus' historical activity. But this could also mean that the Gospels' theological orientation reflects how Jesus viewed his activity. He conceivably saw it as a Messianic fulfillment of Jewish Scriptures in ways that affected how his followers and subsequent generations of Jesus Christ believers represented him and his life. On a case-by-case basis, it is often hard, even impossible to tell whether statements of the Gospels are accurate. But when Mark treats Jesus' final Passover in general as fulfilling scriptural prophecies, this is not entirely arbitrary. To a certain extent it represents how Jesus portrayed himself in his own public ministry: as a prophet, and perhaps even a Messiah, anticipating a divine intervention predicted by texts known to Jewish scribes. Subsequent believers in Jesus Christ amplified this aspect of his ministry in the generations after his death.[10]

The Gospels and a Seditionist Jesus

We can surmise that the Gospels capture what Jesus was basically like. But was this Jesus seditionist? The Gospels of Matthew, Luke, and John were composed after the Temple was destroyed in 70. Yet Mark, the earliest, was written immediately before or after. Some of the passages ostensibly reflect the Temple's destruction, and it reconfigures the basic gospel tradition for Jesus to align with its own theological purposes and contemporary perceptions. But the basic tradition preceded the Temple's destruction. The remaining Gospels, in turn, often depend on Mark (or common source traditions) and were composed significantly later.[11]

The relationships among the Gospels are important to keep in mind when analyzing Jesus' execution. It is tempting to interpret Mark's portrayals of Jesus in light of what other Gospels say. But the other Gospels altered elements of Mark's narrative or a common source whenever these portrayed Pilate as hostile to Jesus. Mark retains various traces for how Antipas was hostile to Jesus' preaching during his ministry in Galilee (Chapter 5). It also points to how Pilate deemed Jesus' activity in Jerusalem to be criminal. To some degree, the Markan author took measures to negate the connotations of these traces, but without occluding them entirely.[12]

The writers of Matthew and Luke (not to mention John) took even greater measures, sometimes quite elaborately, to shift the blame for Jesus' death to the chief priests or other contemporary Jews. They portray an innocent Jesus, a sympathetic Pilate, and a hostile Jewish leadership. Luke's version of Jesus' trial does this emphatically for apologetic purposes while affecting verisimilitude to judicial procedures (at least in form). The goals of these Gospels often make it hard to know whether they are reliably using earlier source traditions. But even they arguably bear traces of a Jesus that Pilate classified as seditionist.

If certain traditions do point to Herodian and Roman hostility in the Gospels, how do we identify them? After all, the Gospels consistently depict Jesus as an innocent man targeted by the chief priests and scribes. Even so, words or deeds ascribed to Jesus, the chief priests, or Pilate sometimes defy plausibility or bear obvious anachronisms (though what is anachronistic can often be debated). Jesus and scribal competitors spoke Aramaic and debated Hebrew Scriptures. Yet the Gospels sometimes portray Jesus and his contemporaries as quoting translations from the Septuagint, the Greek translation of Hebrew Scriptures, or as using phrases that made sense only among later generations of Jesus' followers. A well-known example occurs in Mark (14:61–62) when the high priest asks Jesus whether he is the "son of the Blessed One." The phrasing is unattested among Jews before Jesus' lifetime. The Markan author, in Greek, is perhaps representing the high priest as not invoking the four-letter name of God (the tetragrammaton) in Aramaic/ Hebrew. But Mark is also clearly putting words into the high priest's mouth to set up Jesus' explicit disclosure that he is the Messiah and Son of God. From there, scholars differ on the implications. Does it mean the high priest said something slightly different? Is the entire exchange scripted by Mark? Did the chief priests actually arrest Jesus and question him before a council at all? Or

The New Testament Gospels and Jesus

was the sequence contrived by Mark or earlier Passion traditions to make the chief priests appear more culpable?[13]

Otherwise, some words and deeds of Jesus disrupt the Gospels' main narrative goals. They point to a hostility toward Jesus harbored by Pilate and Antipas on which the Gospels do not elaborate in the manner that they do for the chief priests and scribes. We can suspect these are based on an earlier tradition (or traditions) in which Pilate deemed Jesus guilty of a crime. The Gospel authors embedded these traces in their accounts anyway. We can only theorize why they were not excluded. But the Gospels' authors were not flawless as redactors and writers. When the Gospels were written, certain traditions about Jesus' death were also so well established they could not be easily altered.[14]

Some good examples are Jesus' death by crucifixion and the sign (*titulus*) fixed to his cross that mocked him as "King of the Jews." The Gospels agree about these aspects of Jesus' death (Chapters 9 and 10), and they support that he was executed by Roman authorities as a seditionist. Yet the Gospels' authors apparently had to include these in their accounts even as they blamed the chief priests and allied scribes foremost. As far as crucifixion is concerned, this is also Paul's position: he emphasized Jesus' death by crucifixion in the decades preceding the Gospels' composition, but despite this, he argued that Jews/Judaeans had killed Jesus (1 Thess 2:14–16). In the decades after Jesus' death, his crucifixion had clearly been established among Jesus Christ believers. But some, like Paul, soon focused the blame on the Jewish elite. Their perceptions were plausibly linked to a role played by the chief priests and allied scribes in Jesus' arrest. But they exaggerated it to portray Jesus as not inimical to Roman authority, even if they believed his return would end it. The First Jewish Revolt and destruction of the Jewish Temple in 70 (if not the Bar Kochba Revolt) amplified such tendencies even more. But the Gospels otherwise could not negate the widely accepted understanding that Jesus was crucified by Pilate.[15]

The Gospels claim that Pilate believed in Jesus' innocence. But they still retain traces of a tradition pointing to his animus. A case in point is the controversial release of a convict named Barabbas. According to all the Gospels, Pilate decided to release Barabbas and to execute Jesus at the request of the crowd witnessing his trial. This episode ostensibly points to Pilate's sympathetic attitude toward Jesus. After all, the Gospels in general claim Pilate tried to persuade the crowd to seek Jesus' release. Yet their accounts exhibit signs that Pilate was, if anything, hostile to Jesus. As Mark (15:8–11) reports, "The crowd came up and began to ask of him what he customarily did for them. Pilate responded to them by saying 'do you want me to release the "King of the Jews"'? For he knew that the chief priests had handed over Jesus because of their envy." In isolation, Pilate's statement does not communicate any expectation that the audience would select Jesus for release. If anything, Pilate was mocking him when he called him "King of the Jews" instead of his actual name. The passage reflects a tradition in which Pilate was not sympathetic to Jesus at all and was convinced of his criminal guilt. Mark ostensibly asserts otherwise by adding that Pilate believed Jesus was innocent, supported his release, and thought the crowd would agree ("For he knew that the chief priests had handed over Jesus because of their envy"). But this makes no sense. If Pilate perceived Jesus was being treated unfairly and desired to pardon him, he would have identified Jesus by his actual name. Instead, he invoked the derisive title attached to Jesus by his opponents and associated with the charges of which he stood accused. Another possibility is that Mark portrays Pilate as knowing Jesus was innocent but manipulating the crowd into executing him for Pilate's own expediency. Either way, the sequence bears signs that Mark engages with a tradition in which Pilate believes Jesus is guilty. But the Markan author reworked it to make him appear either sympathetic or scheming Jesus' execution despite believing in his innocence.[16]

Intriguingly, the authors of Matthew and Luke apparently did not think Mark's treatment of Pilate's conduct made much sense. They expand on Mark's material by attributing to Pilate explicit statements about Jesus' innocence (Chapter 10). Having Pilate refer to Jesus by his actual name, they also specify that Pilate's purpose was Jesus' release. Likewise, John independently has Pilate recognize Jesus' innocence and advocate for him. Even so, John (18:39) apparently integrates material from the same basic tradition as Mark and reports that Pilate called Jesus the "King of the Jews" (not Jesus) when addressing the crowd. Pilate then has his soldiers mockingly dress him in a parody of royal attire and flog him. Oddly enough, he does so immediately before once again proclaiming Jesus' innocence. Altogether, what plausibly explains such inconsistencies is that an early gospel tradition portrayed Pilate as convinced of Jesus' guilt on a serious capital charge. He had convicted Jesus and sentenced him to death by crucifixion. He had him mocked, tortured, and executed. He may have made him eligible for pardon, but without advocating for it to the attending crowd. In their own ways, the Gospels all reworked this basic tradition to make Pilate appear a sympathetic, unwilling executioner. Yet traces of a hostile, willing Pilate still persist.

Jesus' Message and Its Incendiary Nature

What Jesus preached has long been debated, and we do not pretend to resolve this debate here. Even so, the Gospels assure us Jesus posed as a prophet or even a Messiah while emulating biblical exemplars. He predicted an imminent change to the governing order, if not the end of the world as everyone knew it. The message was abrasive to Herodian and Roman authority. Even so, it did not make his arrest and execution by Pilate inevitable. Roman governors spared or ignored people who made similar predictions (Chapters 9 and 10). But the activity of Jesus in Jerusalem that precipitated his death unfolded within the general framework of his message and its implications.

We have seen how the reign of God that Jesus envisioned may have been an earthly ruling order. It more probably referred to a heavenly, eschatological one (the "reign of Heaven" in Matthew). Either way, his message was Messianic, even if this reflects the Gospels' overall theological agenda. True, the Gospels rarely communicate that Jesus explicitly referred to himself as Messiah. They instead portray him as not denying it when asked by others. But whatever Jesus meant when he called himself the "Son of Man," his followers and sympathizers plausibly believed he was a divinely appointed Messiah. The Gospels engage with Jewish traditions that frame such a person as a regal figure sent by God to revive the kingdom of David or even announce a heavenly day of judgment. They make various assertions about whether Jesus was descended from King David or whether the Messiah had to be. They portray him as emulating biblical prophecies of Messiahs and imminent divine intervention. Jesus' reign of God was clearly to reward the righteous and punish their oppressors. It would end the ordering of wealth and governance that the Romans underpinned in Judaea.[17]

Jesus had more in common with the Pharisees and other scribes on Torah interpretation than the Gospels assert (Chapter 3). But his ostensibly eschatological worldview aligns with what John the Baptizer and the Qumran Jews envisioned. Jesus' views on the present order of governance and wealth apparently did too. We can dispute any individual passage. But in composite the Gospels support that Jesus expected his core followers to have no possessions. He believed Jews, but especially the rich, should distribute their wealth to the poor, who could use it for personal needs and piety toward the Temple. When he notoriously recruited tax collectors, wealthy "sinners," or their more middling clients, he expected them to distribute their ill-gotten resources. His views were grounded in how the Torah (especially Leviticus 19) and Jewish traditions mandated Israelites treat their neighbors and community members. How municipal elites of the Roman Empire normally accumulated wealth was immoral. The reign of God would reverse the present ordering of wealth and status: the poor and righteous would rule, the wealthy and powerful would be laid low. Naturally, Jesus' viewpoint was hostile to Roman-Herodian power. But it also pitted him against the Temple's current priestly management when he made pilgrimages to Jerusalem and preached. The Synoptics' Greek iteration of a statement attributed to Jesus (Mark 10:31), "many of the first will be last, and the last first," uses a term that Josephus often ascribes to the chief priests and allied scribes (*protoi*: the first, foremost, leaders).[18] The following passages attributed to Jesus cast him in such a light:

Mark 4:19: "The concerns of the world, and the deceit of wealth, and desires for everything else come in to choke the word."

Mark 10:21–25: "Go, sell what you have and give it to the poor.... [H]ow hard will those who have wealth enter into the reign of God?... It is easier for a camel to go through the eye of a needle than for a rich man to enter into the reign of God."

Mark 10:31: "Many of the first will be last, and the last will be first."

Mark 12:9–10: "What will the master of the vineyard do? He will come and kill the farmers and give the vineyard to others."

Mark 12:38: "Look away from the scribes.... [T]hey eat up the houses of widows.... [T]hey will receive harsher judgement."

Mark 12:43–44: "Amen, I say to you that this poor widow contributed more than all the contributors to the treasury. For they all contributed from their excess, but from her lack she contributed all that she had, all her means."

Luke 6:20 (Matt 5:3), 24: "Blessed are you who are poor, because the reign of God is yours... [B]ut woe to you who are wealthy, because you are having your consolation now."

Luke: 6:30: "Give to all who ask you, and do not seek back what is yours from someone who takes it."

Luke 12:33 (Matt 6:19): "Sell your property and give charity."

Matthew 6:11–12 (Luke 11:3–4): "Give us today our daily bread, and release our debts, just as we have released our debtors."

Matthew 6:24 (Luke 16:13): "You cannot be a slave to God and mammon."

For such reasons, Jesus' prophetic preaching and ostensible Messianic claims potentially raised serious concerns for the people who governed in greater Judaea, even if they had only a basic understanding of his message. Some number of people, especially Galileans, deemed him a miracle worker and a scriptural authority. If crowds sometimes sympathized with his message, it could sow or worsen social division. This is why the Herodians, chief priests, and allied scribes saw him as a rival when they encountered him. His message denied the legitimacy of their governance, which was backed by Roman rule. It also anticipated its sudden end. He may have made coded statements when he faced off against figures of authority. The Synoptics sometimes maintain he did so during his final days and hours in Jerusalem. When confronted by competitors about his views on Roman rule, Jesus reportedly communicated his message with a touch of ambiguity. His famous statement "give unto Caesar what is Caesar's" was, in its narrative context, not really a concrete answer to a question posed by scribes about paying taxes. When Pilate reportedly inquired whether he was the "King of the Jews," his response was not very explicit either ("you are saying it"). But even if Jesus made the ambiguous statements the Gospels attribute to him, certain aspects of his message were plausibly clear enough to the chief priests and allied scribes when he preached at the Temple precinct in his final days. Jesus described them as among the wealthy, powerful, and unrighteous who would be judged and punished by the reign of God (Chapters 6 and 8). The chief priests did not see themselves that way, and they thought Jesus was making irresponsible Messianic claims that could incite serious violence. In this light, Jesus' reputation as a miracle-worker and a scriptural authority among at least some Jewish pilgrims in Jerusalem raised alarms.[19]

The Gospels sometimes point to conceptions of Roman governance as a corrupting, illegitimate force, even if it had to be accommodated in the present. In certain respects, the structures of Roman governance were exploited successfully by Jesus and his followers. The Gospels represent Jesus as sometimes sojourning to the Greek cities embedded in the Roman province of Syria. This enabled Jesus to escape the clutches of Herod Antipas in Galilee (Chapter 5). But in one such instance, the Synoptic Gospels communicate a serious critique of how Roman imperial intervention patronized the Greek city-states surrounding Judaea. According to them, Jesus banished an impure spirit from a man (or two men) into a herd of pigs, who then ran off a cliff into the sea. Mark and Luke place this episode at a necropolis in the hinterland of Gerasa. Matthew situates it at Gadara.[20]

In either case, the Gospels represent Jesus leaving what Romans defined as the land of the Jews and entering territory in which Greeks were the dominant civic population. This figures into the Synoptic Gospels' accounts in various ways. First, Jesus encounters a herd of pigs, a reflection of the local inhabitants' dietary patterns. Second, in the account of Mark (5:9), the impure spirit that Jesus casts into the pigs describes himself as named Legion, because "we are many." The Latin naming of a demon after a tool of Roman military domination and its banishment into swine implies an unfavorable view of Roman governance. Matthew apparently reworked the tradition to minimize its anti-Roman connotations. Claiming that Jesus encountered two men possessed by different demons, it omits the name Legion.[21]

The Roman legionary presence in greater Judaea was low during Jesus' lifetime. Most auxiliary soldiers were stationed at Caesarea, the prefect's headquarters. A cohort manned the Antonia fortress at the Temple of Jerusalem. Legions were concentrated in the Syrian province, but not Judaea itself. The routine stationing of legions in greater Judaea happened only during and after the First Jewish Revolt (66–74). The Gospels recounting Jesus' encounter with Legion were probably informed by that fact. Even so, during Jesus' lifetime Roman legionaries sometimes engaged in serious sacrilegious behavior and violence in Judaean territory (Chapter 1). Around the time Jesus was born, a legion commanded by the procurator Sabinus had massacred thousands of Jews who had staged an insurrection in Jerusalem during Pentecost, set fire to the porticoes surrounding the Temple precinct, and plundered the Temple. Just a few years after Jesus' execution, the chief priests had to petition the governor of Syria not to march through Judaea with legionary standards. The potential for the legions of Syria to massacre and plunder in Judaea was real.

In the Legion episode, the Synoptic Gospels are celebrating Jesus' preaching and miracles near a Greek city outside Judaea. Yet their narrative does reflect an anti-imperial bent consistent with Jesus' core message. It likens Roman legions to swine and points to the impurity of swine consumption and cultivation, a hallmark of Roman authorities and the Greek communities they patronized. Given the previous century of violence and sacrilege committed by Rome's legions, such a characterization is not surprising. The narrative may very well reflect how Roman legions invaded Judaea and patronized the needs of the Greek polities surrounding it during the First Jewish Revolt. We cannot know whether it happened. But it coheres with Jesus' message that the imminent reign of God would subject the unrighteous governing Judaea to judgment. In his view, righteous ones who believed in the reign he prophesied would be rewarded. The landed and wealthy who profited from the Roman governing order would not.[22]

Ultimately, the Gospels hint that Jesus' arrest was desirable to Antipas. He reportedly understood that Jesus resembled John the Baptizer in reputation and message. This explains various indications that he sought Jesus' arrest

The New Testament Gospels and Jesus

while Jesus preached in Galilee (Chapter 5). He did not succeed. Likewise, during his final pilgrimage to Jerusalem, Jesus and his followers engaged in Messianic preaching and aggressive activity in the Temple precinct. While small-scale, it had a recognizable potential to trigger serious crowd disturbance and elicited a confrontation with the chief priests (Chapter 6). These had an obligation to protect innocent pilgrims at the Temple from such danger, and they organized his arrest. Once that happened, Jesus' activity at the Temple was volatile enough for Pilate to classify it as sedition. It was enough for Pilate to have him crucified.

5

Jesus, Herod Antipas, and Galilee

Jesus' name had become famous....Hearing about it, Herod said, "The one I beheaded, John [the Baptizer], has been raised."

—MARK 6:16

Jesus warned his followers while saying, "Watch out!—look away from the leaven of the Pharisees and the leaven of Herod."

—MARK 8:15

IN THE GOSPELS, Jesus does not say much about Herod Antipas. His harshest rebukes target the chief priests, scribes, and Pharisees, who oppose him wherever he goes. The Gospels also do not depict Antipas as pursuing Jesus consistently. Even so, Jesus' message did pose a challenge to the Herodian dynasts, and Antipas' hostility leaves its mark on the Gospels. If they do not focus consistently on Antipas' pursuit of Jesus, it is because they have other priorities.

Various Gospel passages suggest hostility between Jesus and Antipas. Yet the Gospels do not consistently trace it. Even so, we can surmise that Antipas sought to arrest and execute Jesus. The Gospels all highlight Jesus' rivalry with Pharisees and scribal elites. They mostly sidestep his relationship with Antipas. But Mark bears traces of hostility, which the other Synoptics sometimes negate. What are these signs? Why did Antipas deem Jesus a criminal threat?

Client Ruler as Judge: Antipas' Execution of John the Baptizer

As client ruler of Galilee, Antipas was a figure of Roman governance. He had vast scope for identifying and suppressing seditious behavior. He also had an interest in doing so. A devout Jew embodying Herodian-Roman governance, he managed and benefited from the order of authority and wealth that dissenting preachers, insurrectionists, and laborers opposed. To see his powers in

Jesus, Herod Antipas, and Galilee

action, we need look no farther than his execution of John the Baptizer. Antipas had personal motives for eliminating John. But he also had legal justifications for classifying John as seditious.

As tetrarch (but not formally "king"), Antipas was authorized by Rome to exercise regal powers in his realm. He could also act by the legal precedents traditional to his dynasty's rule. To prove his worth, he had to coordinate with Roman governors like Pilate, but not too much. Excess help from them could overshadow his achievements and make his governance look toothless. If Antipas' actions were counterproductive, the Roman government could intercede in his affairs (Chapter 11). But it recognized him as the senior figure of Roman authority in Galilee. It acknowledged his legal autonomy in executing his subjects, especially if doing so brought stability. Antipas' father, Herod, made such decisions with near complete license. In fact, Antipas came to power because his father prosecuted several of his brothers on capital charges. Whenever Herod appealed to the Roman emperor or judges from outside his kingdom, it was at his discretion. Such favors enabled Antipas to have even greater scope than Pilate to identify criminal behavior and respond violently. John the Baptizer apparently had not organized any cohesive movement. But his popularity and antagonistic message were enough for Antipas to kill him, ostensibly without Pilate's involvement.[1]

In 30 or so, Antipas' vast scope for violence came crashing down on John the Baptizer. Mark (6:17–29) and Matthew (14:3–12) claim John was admired and feared by him. His motive for the arrest was reportedly that his wife, Herodias, was angry that John had disparaged his marriage to her. At Herodias' behest, her daughter demanded John's head in exchange for her dancing at a banquet that Antipas threw for the notables of Galilee. Antipas thus had John beheaded, reluctantly.

John the Baptizer may well have criticized Herodias' marriage to Antipas. It was probably a factor in his arrest and death. Herodias had been married to Antipas' half-brother previously. Apparently, the Herodians did not believe such a marriage violated the biblical prohibition against marrying a brother's wife (Lev 18:16, 20:21). John reportedly believed it did. But we can question whether Antipas had John the Baptizer executed simply because the women in his life wanted it. Mark's account gets some basic facts wrong, which Matthew and Luke largely fix or omit. Its information on Antipas' familial relationships differs from what Josephus describes with ostensibly greater accuracy. Mark states Herodias had been married to Antipas' brother Philip (the Tetrarch). In truth, Herodias' husband was Antipas' brother Herod, and her daughter was Philip's wife. The Markan author calls this daughter Herodias even though her name was Salome. Being married to Philip, she was

88 KILLING THE MESSIAH

presumably at his court when John was executed. The fact that dancing for audiences was normally the work of enslaved people, not wealthy daughters, casts further doubt on how reliable Mark is.[2]

Josephus adds another key detail. He locates John's imprisonment at Machaerus, a fortress in Transjordan. Excavators at Antipas' palace there claim to have identified the courtroom floor where the lethal dance occurred. The location was close to where John preached (Map 1.1). But it was much farther from Galilee, where Mark and Matthew place John's death. It is doubtful that John was imprisoned in Galilee and could be executed for his head's immediate display there. The Markan author surely included the dance episode because it disparaged Antipas and portrayed John as an innocent man. Yet Luke omits the episode altogether. The Lukan author apparently had more accurate knowledge of the Herodians, perhaps due to Josephus' account of John's death.[3]

Despite the tale's fame, we should accept Antipas had John executed primarily because he had classified his activity as seditious. Josephus and Luke (3:18–20) communicate that John's criticisms of Antipas were wide-ranging and aroused fears of insurrection or revolt. Josephus does not mention Herodias at all. Ultimately, John's baptizing attracted throngs of people to his location in the Judaean desert, along the Jordan River. He also preached a message that challenged Antipas' ruling legitimacy. Under Roman governance, Antipas could forge his own legal pathway for identifying and eliminating threats to the order of authority and wealth in Galilee and Transjordan. He had an even larger remit than Pilate. John had not organized a cohesive rebellion, but his preaching and popularity were enough for Antipas to see him as seditious. The same was true of Jesus.

The legal basis for Antipas' repressive violence was somewhat different from Pilate's. The Roman emperor recognized Antipas as the rightful dynastic ruler of Galilee. He could largely identify and respond to criminal matters as he saw fit. As an ancestral ruler of Jewish subjects, he also had a unique interest in suppressing hostile critics. Even so, he had the same legal justification as Pilate and other Roman governors when they executed popular, dissenting preachers or even massacred their followers. John the Baptizer's incendiary message had attracted a vast audience. It apparently had not incited violence, insurrection, or a cohesive movement. But its potential to do so prompted Antipas to execute him for sedition.

Antipas, Jesus, and John the Baptizer

Of all the Gospels, Mark features the most trace evidence of Antipas' desire to arrest Jesus. Despite this, a main concern of Mark in portraying Jesus' Galilean ministry is to highlight his conflict with the Pharisees. It refers to Antipas' hostility sporadically and inconsistently. Even so, Mark's narrative bears various signs of a tradition that Antipas deemed Jesus a threat. Matthew and Luke intriguingly took some measures to erase these.[4]

Various Markan passages point to Antipas' hostility. Any of them could be challenged in isolation, but in aggregate they support such an outlook. The Synoptic Gospels state the beginning of Jesus' ministry was intimately tied to the arrest of John the Baptizer. After John was seized by Antipas, Jesus began preaching throughout Galilee and made Capernaum his base of operation (Mark 1:14, 2:1, 9:33). His prophetic message resembled John's. Some passages of Mark suggest Jesus intermittently feared arrest by Antipas after John's execution. In these passages, Jesus evades the main Herodian cities of Sepphoris and Tiberias and frequents places along the Sea of Galilee (Capernaum, Gennesaret, and Bethsaida) where he could easily leave Antipas' realm. He even travels continuously outside Galilee, preaches in ambiguous parables, and tells his apostles to conceal his deeds and identity. Mark's testimony supports that Jesus aimed to attract an audience for his prophetic message after Antipas had eliminated John the Baptizer. But he had to be careful. Jesus did not necessarily have a robust personal following. But Antipas clearly would arrest and kill popular, charismatic preachers who challenged his ruling legitimacy.[5]

When Jesus traveled into the realm of Philip the Tetrarch or the province of Syria, he was exploiting the territorial limits of different Roman governors. These coordinated with one another to some extent, but not consistently. They were also competing for approval from the Roman emperor, which limited close cooperation. Antipas had an incentive to eliminate Jesus without too much support from Philip or Roman governors. True, he was a figure of Roman governance just as they were. He was a half-brother of Philip. But he was also their political rival in seeking favor from the imperial dynasty. He had to demonstrate an autonomous competency and initiative. This meant he ideally would arrest Jesus inside his realm. Also, Antipas may not always have known Jesus' whereabouts while Jesus was keeping a low profile. Evading Antipas was surely a factor that encouraged Jesus' activity in Philip's realm and nearby in parts of the Syrian province. The Gospels agree the main audience for Jesus' preaching was the people of Israel governed by Pilate or Antipas, not polytheists in Syria. Mark (8:27–30) even says Jesus forbade his followers to disclose his identity to others while he was near Caesarea Philippi, Philip's palace center. One reason for his being there must have been concealment.[6]

Before Jesus' ministry, Antipas had been hostile to John the Baptizer for similar reasons. But the Synoptics did not give this hostility consistent treatment either. They instead include a tradition that Antipas killed John for reasons other than his seditionist potential. The passages associating John's death with the hostility of Antipas' wife and daughter are worth revisiting here. In the Synoptics, John's death is introduced by brief, laconic passages (Mark 6:14–16; Matt 14:1–2; Luke 9:7–9). These state that Antipas, upon hearing about Jesus, thought of him as John the Baptizer resurrected. In isolation, they imply Antipas had arrested and executed John because of his prophetic message and that he feared Jesus for similar reasons. In both Matthew and Mark, this brief testimony awkwardly marks a transition to an elaborate flashback about John's death. As such, it arguably represents the trace of an earlier tradition for Antipas' hostility to John and Jesus. Josephus corroborates this premise. He says Antipas had John arrested and murdered because he feared the charismatic leader could inspire insurrection (*apostasis*).

Immediately after this passage, Mark (6:17–29) and Matthew (14:3–12), but not Luke, describe how Herod Antipas had John the Baptizer imprisoned and executed in a much more elaborate narrative. They ascribe the motivation for John's death to women in Antipas' household. John was reportedly arrested by Antipas for condemning his marriage to Herodias, the former wife of his brother. Mark even indicates Herodias had pressured Antipas to have him imprisoned and killed. Mark's narrative maintains that Antipas was so overwhelmed by fear or admiration for the charismatic preacher that he did not want to execute him. Thereafter, however, Antipas had John executed at the request of his stepdaughter, who had danced at a banquet Antipas hosted for various courtiers in Galilee. He had John's head placed on a platter and given to her, apparently as his dinner guests watched.[7]

In Mark, the elaborate narrative explains why Antipas had described Jesus as John the Baptizer resurrected (6:17: "for Herod himself sent people to seize John"). Its reliability is suspect, so why did the Markan author include it? No doubt it portrays Antipas as an incompetent, weak, and unjust ruler governed by women at his court. It frames him as an illegitimate ruler, a complete foil to Messianic Jesus. It also distances John from political wrongdoing. Even so, Mark mostly establishes a continuum of hostile behavior for Pharisees and scribes during Jesus' preaching in Galilee. While not omitting Antipas' hostility altogether, neither does it establish a continuum for it. This explains why its traces have random placements in Mark's narrative. It also explains why, at times, Mark portrays Antipas as somewhat favorably disposed toward John and motivated to kill him only when instigated by women. Otherwise, the author was unaware or less interested in the tradition for John the Baptizer's death retained by Josephus.

Jesus, Herod Antipas, and Galilee

In this respect, Mark differs significantly from Luke. Luke claims Antipas arrested and executed John because he had criticized him for both his marriage to Herodias and other misdeeds (*ponera*) he committed (3:18–20). The narrative omits the activity of women at court. Its statements align with how Josephus' account attributes the death of John the Baptizer explicitly to Antipas' fear that he could inspire sedition. In fact, the Lukan author probably knew of the problems posed by Mark's treatment by consulting Josephus' account of John's death.[8]

Mark's first mention of animosity between Jesus and Antipas by name links it to Jesus' preaching near the Sea of Galilee. According to Mark (8:15–16), Jesus warned his followers to avoid the leaven of the Pharisees and of "Herod." He was responding to his followers' having no bread, but his meaning was metaphorical. In the ancient world, dough from a prior batch of bread was preserved and mixed with dough made for the next batch. Jesus is exhorting his followers to break entirely from the teaching of the Pharisees or Antipas while they receive his message. As noted, Mark probably exaggerates Jesus' rivalry with the Pharisees while mostly sidestepping his relationship with Antipas. But we can surmise that in a tradition retained by Mark, Jesus had been criticizing Antipas. Matthew noticeably reworks this episode to portray Jesus as warning against the leaven of the Pharisees and Sadducees. Luke omits mention of Antipas altogether.[9]

Intriguingly, in a sequence Mark places just after the leaven episode, all the Gospels portray Jesus as shifting his activity outside Galilee and beyond Antipas' direct control. The Synoptic Gospels claim Jesus was in the hinterland of Caesarea Philippi, the palace city of Philip the Tetrarch, when he petitioned his followers not to tell others he was the Messiah. Jesus' movement outside Antipas' territory and desire to keep secret his identity suggest he was keeping a low profile in Philip's territory. Mark reworks this episode into a portrayal of Jesus as keeping his Messianic stature secret from everyone but his closest followers.[10]

Luke's account also provides an independent statement about Antipas' hostility to Jesus. It claims that during his itinerary to Jerusalem, Pharisees warned Jesus that "Herod" wanted to kill him (13:31–33). This statement is not attested by the other Gospels. Its origins are hard to trace. It perhaps represents an independent tradition. Or maybe the Lukan author included this passage to highlight the paradox of Jesus' later acquittal by Antipas in Jerusalem (23:6–12), an acquittal that, suspiciously, Luke alone reports (Chapter 10). The Herodian dynast who had wanted Jesus dead ultimately recognized his innocence.

According to Mark, so-called Herodians took an interest in Jesus during his preaching in Galilee. They plotted against Jesus along with certain Pharisees who resided in Galilee or Judaea. These had encountered Jesus' preaching at synagogues and had alerted the Herodians to them. But who are these "Herodians"? Is Mark's portrayal of them reliable?

In Mark, "Herodians" probably refers to courtiers, administrators, or clients of Herod Antipas. Their first mention by Mark (3:1–6) occurs in its report of how Jesus healed a man's withered hand in the synagogue of Capernaum. All the Synoptics claim that local Pharisees opposed his doing it on the Sabbath. According to Mark, the Pharisees started plotting with the Herodians to kill Jesus. This suggests the Pharisees were coordinating with Antipas' clients. But to make Jesus appear less antagonistic to Herodian-Roman authority, Matthew (12:9–14) and Luke (6:6–10) both alter the passage to omit the Herodians. Matthew and Luke simply describe the Pharisees alone as conspiring against Jesus.[11]

Mark's reference to "Herodians" here attracts suspicion. The term is unknown elsewhere. "Herodians" play no role in the sequence until the end. The same could be said for Mark's claim (12:13, replicated by Matt 22:16) that Pharisees and "Herodians" questioned Jesus in his final days at Jerusalem about paying taxes to the Romans. Even so, this does not mean Mark invented the hostility of Antipas' clients out of whole cloth. After all, Mark's narrative otherwise bears traces of Antipas' hostility to Jesus.[12]

In fact, Mark (3:6) plausibly retains traces for how Antipas' clients and Pharisees in Galilee were hostile to Jesus. After all, Mark exhibits no consistent purpose in establishing or exaggerating Antipas' hostility. The Markan author may have just coined the term "Herodians" to describe Antipas' clients or supporters. Material culture suggests Galileans were concerned with the same issues of purity as Judaeans, including priests and scribes at Jerusalem. Some Galileans, including Antipas' clients, were involved in interpreting the Torah. But when reworking Mark's accounts, Matthew and Luke omit any mention of Herodians.[13]

Jesus' antagonism toward Antipas is consistent with his reported conflicts with the chief priests and scribal elites. Despite their distinct motives, they were aligned with Herodian and Roman governance. Their ruling legitimacy and their accumulation of wealth attracted similar criticisms from him. They also had the same obligation to neutralize social disturbances. The difference is that Jesus' hostile relationship with Antipas occurred primarily during his preaching in Galilee. If the chief priests and scribal elite were concerned about Jesus, it was primarily when he preached in Jerusalem and at the Temple.

Antipas at Jesus' Trial, Herod at Jesus' Birth

As discussed so far, all the Synoptic Gospels bear traces of Antipas' hostility to Jesus. These are most prominent in Mark. Matthew and Luke are more consistent in minimizing them. Even so, the later Synoptics sometimes portray a (relatively) sympathetic Antipas or shift his hostility to Herod I. A key example is Jesus' trial. Luke alone reports that Pilate sent Jesus to Antipas to be judged. It claims Antipas found Jesus faultless but had him humiliated and dressed him in ironically elegant attire anyway (Luke 23:6–12). This testimony does not make much sense. If anything, Antipas' treatment of Jesus suggests he found merit in the accusation that Jesus claimed to be King of the Jews. He had him mocked before returning him to Pilate for execution. But to make Jesus appear faultless before Roman authorities, Luke communicates that Antipas (like Pilate) acquitted Jesus, despite chastening him. Of course, the Lukan author is this episode's only witness and tends to portray Jesus' followers as innocuous to Roman authorities. This casts doubt on whether it happened at all (Chapters 10 and 11). For now, we can note Luke portrays Antipas as not hostile to Jesus hours before his execution in Jerusalem. Elsewhere, it retains traces that portray him as the opposite.[14]

Likewise, the other New Testament work of the Lukan author exhibits signs of a hostility borne by Antipas and other Herodian dynasts. In Acts of the Apostles, Antipas and his successor, Agrippa I, are hostile to Jesus and his followers, while Agrippa II is well-disposed (Chapter 11). In one passage (4:27), Acts depicts "Herod" (Antipas) and Pilate as the foremost agents in Jesus' death. Its treatment of Agrippa I is consistent with that. After Antipas' deposition, the emperor Claudius made Agrippa I king of all greater Judaea. This brought a brief interruption to the governance of a Roman prefect over Jerusalem and its environs. Significantly, Acts claims Agrippa I was hostile to leaders in Jesus' movement. It states he had James, the brother of John, executed and had Peter arrested during Passover week (12:2–19). Acts also depicts Agrippa as dying because of his willingness to accept divine honors (12:20–23). In other words, Acts portrays both Antipas and Agrippa I as embodying Herodian-Roman authority. The Lukan author was obviously engaging with traditions that the Herodians were hostile to Jesus, despite sometimes portraying Antipas and Agrippa II otherwise.

As noted, Matthew does not place Antipas' hostility toward Jesus at center stage. At times it even negates references to such hostility in Mark. But it asserts that his father, Herod I, was hostile to Jesus' Messianic reputation from the moment of his birth (Matt 2 generally). It narrates the tale, uncorroborated by Josephus or other Gospels, that he had Jesus pursued and had babies in Bethlehem murdered to prevent a royal challenger. The passage points to an inconsistency in Matthew. It treats Herod I as murderously concerned with Jesus' Messianic reputation long *before* he begins preaching. Yet it minimizes Antipas' hostility toward Jesus' Messianic message *during* his actual preaching. Through such portrayals, Matthew's narrative depicts Jesus as a new Moses pursued by a pharaonic figure. Here Matthew exhibits some awareness of earlier source traditions for Herodian hostility to Jesus, especially from Mark. But it emphasizes the hostility of Herod I and scribes. The traces of Antipas' hostility never receive a consistent thread.[15]

A Hostile Antipas

The Synoptic Gospels, especially Mark, bear signs that Antipas was hostile to Jesus during his preaching in Galilee. But they do not do this consistently. This is in part because they focus on and even exaggerate the acrimony of scribes. Matthew and Luke negate some traces of Antipas' hostility retained by Mark. This helped them emphasize Jesus' innocence for wrongdoing in the eyes of Roman authority. But in a source tradition retained by the Synoptic authors, Antipas had John the Baptizer arrested and executed in part due to his prophetic message and its political implications. On similar grounds Antipas had motive to arrest and execute Jesus, who anticipated this and took steps against it. His movements outside Galilee were among them.

If Antipas never arrested and executed Jesus, it was not from lack of trying. He had many of the same motives and justifications for eliminating Jesus as he had for John the Baptizer. But Jesus took precautions and evaded arrest. He took similar measures when visiting Jerusalem to preach. But the counter-moves of the chief priests accomplished what Antipas did not.

PART III

Arresting Jesus

6

Jesus, the Temple, and the Chief Priests

[The chief priests] began seeking to seize him, and they feared the crowd. For they knew that Jesus said the parable against them. Letting him go, they went away.

—MARK 12:12

The chief priests and scribes began seeking how they could seize him by deception and kill him. For they were saying, "Not during the festival, so there will not be a riot of the people."

—MARK 14:1–2

IN SOME GOSPEL accounts, Jesus predicts his death in Jerusalem (Matt 16:21; Luke 13:33–34). These statements attributed to him point to an obvious fact: Jesus did die in Jerusalem, not Galilee. His judge was Pilate, not Herod Antipas. True, Jesus' prophetic message antagonized Rome's client dynast in Galilee. Antipas did pose a threat. Even so, Antipas did not arrest Jesus in his territory. Pilate crucified him in Jerusalem. This is one rare aspect of Jesus' death on which scholars agree. The rest is disputed.

Even Mark does not escape such scrutiny. Despite being the earliest Gospel, its reliability is open to debate. We have noted how its narrative for Jesus' final week alive provides a day-to-day account, not the usual unconnected episodes. It plausibly reflects basic gospel traditions that were established shortly after Jesus' death. But it also reflects the filtering of Jesus' followers and the Markan author. We cannot trust without reservation much of what it reports. Its temporal markers for Jesus' final week often inspire debate or confusion. But we can still establish a plausible outline of Jesus' activity from Mark's account.[1]

In the days preceding his death, Jesus engaged in activity at Jerusalem that some Roman authorities, including Pilate, believed criminal. He preached an incendiary message at the Temple precinct, a turbulent space, during Passover week, a time of peak crowd presence and volatile emotions (Figures 6.1 and 6.2;

FIGURE 6.1 View of Temple Mount from the Mount of Olives. Photo by N. Andrade.

FIGURE 6.2 Temple Complex, model of Jerusalem in the Second Temple period. Photo by N. Andrade. © Holyland Tourism 1992, Ltd. Courtesy of The Israel Museum, Jerusalem, at the Israel National Museum.

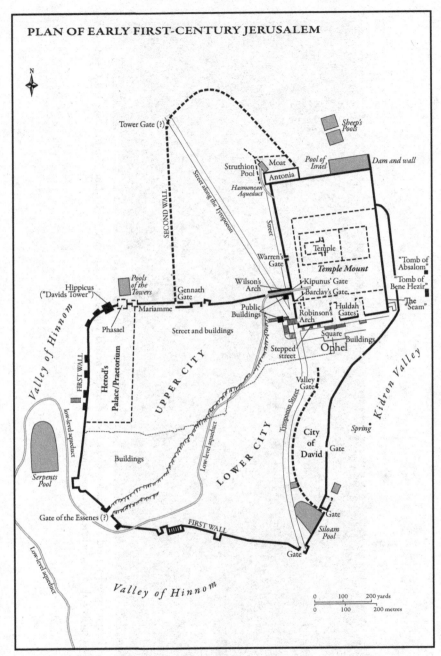

MAP 6.1 Plan of early first-century Jerusalem.
After E. Stern (ed.), *The New Encyclopedia of Archaeological Excavations in the Holy Land*, New York: Simon and Schuster, 1993, vol. 2, p. 718. © Carta Jerusalem

Map 6.1). He and his core followers engaged in confrontational, aggressive activity. Where, when, and how Jesus preached contributed to his death by Pilate's orders. But what exactly made Jesus' conduct during his final Passover so seditious? What did his followers do that was so volatile? What traces do they leave in the Gospel narratives?

Jesus and Jerusalem

During his last Passover week, Jesus' activity at the Temple precinct involved some public, incendiary preaching, but otherwise he kept a low profile. Jesus and his followers preached their message at the Temple precinct over only two days. They engaged in seriously confrontational behavior there. But they apparently anticipated that the chief priests or Roman authorities would seek to make arrests or that they could die if crowd violence broke out. When absent from the Temple precinct, they took measures to avoid detection. While there, they exploited the hesitation of the chief priests to risk serious chaos and bloodshed by attempting an arrest or summoning Roman troops. In such a confrontation, the core followers of Jesus and the chief priests could potentially incite or motivate crowd behavior. But crowds could also act beyond anyone's control. Along with his core followers (mostly Galileans), Jesus had sympathizers in Jerusalem which made confrontation and arrest at the Temple even more difficult. Paul (1 Cor 15:5–6) claims Jesus' broader following numbered about 500 at the time of his death. But he had only one or two dozen of his core followers at the Temple precinct when he preached. Only this number would be with him where he lodged or camped.[2]

These aspects of Jesus' activity suggest he had made pilgrimages to Jerusalem before and expected the chief priests to seek his whereabouts. Luke refers to a pilgrimage Jesus made with his parents when he was a youth. But the Synoptics describe only one pilgrimage Jesus made as an adult: during his final Passover week. Even so, the Synoptics hint that Jesus had been at Jerusalem several times to preach. When Jesus arrived for his final Passover, he was reportedly met with great acclaim. He apparently had built a reputation among Jerusalem's inhabitants and pilgrims. This also is what John suggests. It narrates that Jesus visited Jerusalem for many different festivals before his final pilgrimage.[3]

A key problem is that John places in Jesus' prior visits to Jerusalem many deeds that the Synoptics situate in his final, fatal pilgrimage. These include his famous confrontation with the moneychangers and merchants at the Temple precinct. John never even specifies that Jesus went to the Temple during

KILLING THE MESSIAH

his final pilgrimage. What explains the discrepancies? Most probably, John distributed the events that happened during Jesus' final pilgrimage to Jerusalem among several prior trips. After all, the Synoptic Gospels do not say Jesus had never traveled to Jerusalem before his final trip there. They merely recount his final, pivotal pilgrimage. The Synoptics also report that Jesus' movements in Jerusalem were clandestine. He used secret messages to acquire a colt to ride into the city and a house for his Passover meal. Jesus aimed to move about undetected whenever he was not actually at the Temple precinct or among crowds. He also anticipated the chief priests or Pilate would want to know his whereabouts. He must have preached in Jerusalem before. Many now surmise that John used and re-sequenced Mark, the Synoptics, or a common source for its own theological purposes. In this case, John shifts various deeds of Jesus from his final pilgrimage to prior trips to Jerusalem.[4]

The Synoptics and John provide another clue that Jesus had made pilgrimages to Jerusalem in the years preceding his death: his known contact with John the Baptizer. Both John and Jesus were subjects of Herod Antipas. But they preached in different places. Jesus was active in Galilee. John worked along the Jordan River, in the wilderness of eastern Judaea and Peraea. All the Gospels agree Jesus was baptized by John (Chapter 3). This places him near Jerusalem in his adult life. Jesus' message was for all Jews of Judaea, not just Galileans. We could expect him to frequent Jerusalem during festivals, circulate his message, and recruit followers there.

Jesus' earlier pilgrimages to Jerusalem are difficult to reconstruct. Even so, John provides plausible sketches of what could have happened. Attending major festivals, his preaching apparently did not attract the attention of Roman authorities. Or at least they did not have him arrested or executed. But he surely preached God's coming reign. If his activity was incendiary enough to inspire crowd disturbance, the chief priests would have considered arresting him. Otherwise, the activity that John associates with Jesus' earlier pilgrimages happened during his final Passover week, as the Synoptics report.[5]

Jesus' earlier pilgrimages conceivably motivated the chief priests against him. But Jesus did not suffer arrest and execution then. Why is this? Perhaps John's testimony is wrong, and the priests did not try to arrest him at all. Or maybe they made a failed attempt that prompted Jesus to leave the city. Once Jesus returned to Galilee and did not threaten public order at Jerusalem, he was beyond their reach and responsibility. They would have sought to arrest him only if he returned to Jerusalem and preached at the Temple precinct again. If so, they would have wanted to detain him without help from Pilate or his soldiers. This would bolster their stature as loyal, effective municipal

Jesus, the Temple, and the Chief Priests

elites. It would also minimize the risk of violence occurring beyond their control, which could happen once Roman soldiers were involved (Chapters 1, 2, and 9). Altogether, Jesus was familiar to the chief priests of Jerusalem by his final pilgrimage and anticipated their attempts to arrest him there. Whether Jesus had become known to Pilate during these earlier pilgrimages remains unclear. The Gospels' testimony, if anything, suggests Jesus' preaching at the Temple attracted concerns from the chief priests, who sought to neutralize him without involving Pilate too much. Otherwise, no serious disturbance arose from Jesus' preaching that attracted the attention of Pilate or the Roman garrison at the Antonia (Chapter 1). The chief priests were surely concerned about the incendiary nature of Jesus' preaching at the Temple. They had a moral obligation to protect their compatriots from outbreaks of violence. But they credibly believed the best solution was to arrest and bring him to Pilate themselves.

Altogether, Jesus' clandestine movements in his final pilgrimage, as reported by the Synoptics, support that his prior trips to Jerusalem played out like his final one, short of his actual arrest, trial, and execution. In the Temple precinct, Jesus made incendiary prophecies about the reign of God over Israel. But since no seriously violent uprising or altercation occurred, the Roman garrison at the Antonia had not intervened. The chief priests also hesitated to arrest him publicly at the Temple precinct, where his dozens of followers created a real potential for mass violence or crowd disturbance. If they sought to subdue Jesus at his lodgings instead, they failed to locate them. Through such experiences, Jesus apparently surmised that arrest attempts would occur during future trips to Jerusalem. In his final pilgrimage, his response was to remain hidden except for when he preached in public and could leverage volatile crowds. He wagered that the chief priests would avoid serious confrontation at the Temple precinct but would try to seize him elsewhere. He and his followers otherwise had to keep their whereabouts secret.

Despite his clandestine movements, Jesus made a conspicuous impact at key moments. He had, after all, traveled to Jerusalem to preach his message to pilgrims at the Temple precinct. All the Gospels agree Jesus' initial entry into Jerusalem was impressive. It emulated the conduct of kings and governors and may even have mirrored Pilate's own public entry into Jerusalem. This and what the crowd reportedly chanted may have hastened his trial and execution days later. Echoing a prophecy from Zechariah (9:9), Mark claims Jesus arrived mounted on a donkey's colt while jubilant followers, residents, and pilgrims announced the kingdom of David and Jesus' role in its imminent arrival. The other Gospels introduce elements that tighten the link with Zechariah's prophecy but are basically consistent. Jesus' core followers and sympathizers were celebrating a reign of God that would overturn the governing order and punish the unrighteous. Jesus' entry was a public one, with regal, Messianic overtones. Why did it not invite immediate repression by Pilate or the chief priests? Of course, we can doubt how many people were present at Jesus' arrival, how conspicuously "regal" it was, how much attention it attracted, whether Jesus rode a colt, even whether it happened at all. Mark's passage could have been inspired by Zechariah 9:9 and its portrayal of a Messianic figure who rides a donkey's colt. But we can surmise that the volatility of crowds offered protection from arrest, and we cannot determine whether Jesus' entry was as prominent and visible as the Gospels claim. Jesus may have ridden a colt in emulation of a grand regal entry, but with a modest following and an audience that was large but not massive. In a Jerusalem teeming with pilgrims, crowds, and other charismatic preachers, his entry at its eastern end was probably inconspicuous to the garrison at the Antonia. For Pilate's troops concentrated at the *praetorium* on the city's western end, it simply may not have been noticeable at all.[6]

Even so, the Synoptic Gospels also support that Jesus operated largely in secret during his final pilgrimage. He constantly shifted residences in Jerusalem, adjacent towns, or various camping locations. It could be difficult to find places to stay or eat the Passover feast as pilgrims thronged to Jerusalem. But Jesus also wanted to prevent the chief priests and Pilate from knowing where he was staying. His followers apparently communicated with sympathetic residents through secret phrases. The Gospels state that upon approaching Jerusalem Jesus commanded his followers to go ahead of him. Upon finding a bound colt (Matthew unrealistically states that Jesus found and rode both a colt and a donkey), they were to claim it and to say to anyone confronting them (11:3), "Its master needs it, and he is sending it back here right away." A few days later, Jesus reportedly executed similar arrangements for his final Passover meal. From Bethany, he had his disciples entered the city from the east, where a man with a water jug was to lead them to a house whose owner they were to greet thus (14:14): "The Teacher asks, where is my lodging where I may eat the Passover with my disciples?" The Gospels' report that Jesus evaded detection from authorities through such mechanisms. Or at least he did until the chief priests learned his final campsite.[7]

Jesus and the Temple Precinct

Despite his precautions, Jesus made some public appearances in the Temple precinct in his final pilgrimage. Mark (11:11) reports that this first happened

Jesus did not preach, but instead "looked around at everything" before departing to nearby Bethany. The next morning, he and his followers traveled back to the Temple precinct. There they intimidated and suppressed the activity of some merchants and moneychangers. The Gospels say that Jesus and, presumably, his followers expelled from the Temple precinct "people who were buying and selling" there. He overturned the tables of those who collected commissions on the Temple tax or monetary exchanges (*kollubistai*, "small change collectors") and the chairs of dove sellers. He also prevented people from carrying vessels, which probably held commercial wares or priestly tithes that pilgrims paid. Jesus reportedly claimed that the collectors and commercial players had made the Temple a "hideout of brigands." The statement invokes a passage of Jeremiah (7:3–20) in which God threatens the Temple's destruction due to corrupt behavior. Whether he made the statement as Mark reports often attracts doubt. It seems too conveniently to reflect the attitudes of the Markan author and Jesus Christ believers after the Temple's destruction in 70.[8]

The Gospels do not specify the scope of Jesus' activity, but they imply it covered the entire Temple precinct. Some even see it as serious insurrectionist activity, which may have involved an attempt to occupy the Temple precinct with weapons. Others surmise a collective effort to incite a disturbance. For them, the Gospel accounts all minimize what Jesus was doing. But if the activity of Jesus and his followers was so large-scale or even violent, why did the Temple guards or the Roman soldiers at the Antonia not respond? The Gospels may be exaggerating its scope. It may have been restricted to a part of the Temple's external courtyard and seen or heard only by people immediately surrounding his followers. The courtyard was massive, crowded, and loud. Commotion and heated confrontations there were probably commonplace and, if kept within certain limits, ignored or unknown to authorities. The chief priests were also focusing their sacrificial activity on the Temple's inner courtyard. The Gospels do nothing to indicate that the chief priests, any guards, or the Roman garrison at the Antonia intervened in his disruption. They apparently did not notice it. Maybe the Gospels made activity that was unnoticeable to authorities appear to be serious events.[9]

Even so, the Gospels' report that Jesus' activity did not invite an immediate response is a serious problem. For some scholars, it casts doubt on whether this episode happened at all and raises the possibility that Jesus was not hostile to the moneychangers or merchants who enabled the payment of the Temple tax and provided animals for the Temple's sacrifices. After all, Jesus was an observant Jew who valued the Temple's rituals and sanctity. Perhaps the Gospels or their sources generated the episode. This would have made Jesus' movement appear hostile to the Temple and to shift responsibility for his death from Pilate to the chief priests.[10]

A strength of this perspective is that it can explain why no one tried to arrest Jesus immediately. If the Roman soldiers at the Antonia, the chief priests, or the Temple guards had noticed disruptive or volatile activity, they would have intervened. Even so, Jesus was plausibly hostile to the chief priests. True, he deemed the Temple a sacred institution and the sacrifices important. But he still might have believed that the Temple's stewards were accumulating unwarranted wealth, for the Temple or even themselves. The Qumran Jews and other Jewish witnesses clearly thought of the chief priests in this way (Chapter 3). Also, even if small in scale and initially unnoticed, Jesus' activity could have posed serious problems for the chief priests and their obligation to protect pilgrims from outbreaks of violence. If it continued, Jesus' activity could have galvanized or aggrieved people until it cascaded into serious crowd disturbance. Yet any attempt to detain Jesus at the Temple precinct in the presence of potentially sympathetic crowds and his confrontational followers could incite serious violence too. The chief priests and allied scribes faced a serious quandary. They had valid reasons to deem Jesus' activity incendiary and dangerous for worshipers. They knew that it could stimulate crowd violence or even invite repression from the Antonia garrison. They were obligated to ensure the safety of the Temple's pilgrims. Yet they also knew that an arrest attempt could make the problem worse. For such reasons, we should not dismiss the Gospel accounts altogether. Their portrayal of Jesus' activity as posing serious problems for the chief priests is plausible, even if they exaggerate its impact and visibility. We should accept that Jesus and his followers engaged in confrontational and aggressive activity at the Temple. But its purpose was not to undermine the status of the Temple's sacrifices or their financial basis. It instead challenged the legitimacy of the Temple's current priestly management. Small in scale, it did not attract notice or concern from the Antonia garrison. It was also initially unknown to the chief priests. Not being in the external courtyard where Jesus was preaching and intimidating others, they did not find out what Jesus had done and begin planning countermeasures until it was reported to them later (Mark 11:18).[11]

But what was Jesus' goal? The Gospels all agree that Jesus was suppressing activity he defined as corrupt, but they do not clarify why he deemed it so. Like most observant Jews, Jesus probably thought it appropriate for people in the vast courtyard of the Temple to sell animals for sacrifices or exchange money to keep the Temple's rituals intact. He may not have opposed the

Jesus, the Temple, and the Chief Priests

Temple tax or commercial activity at the Temple in general. This has given rise to a theory that Jesus' recorded activity at the Temple, if it even happened at all, symbolically staged an imminent eschatological moment at which the destruction or restoration of the Temple was at the center. Even so, there are other widely noted considerations related to Jesus' views on wealth and its distribution, ones he shared with the Qumran Jews (Chapter 4). Jesus conceivably objected to how the priests were regulating the Temple's sacred economy to exploit personal commercial ventures that could have burdened the poor who sought to lead devout lives. By Jesus' lifetime the chief priests expected all Jews to make an annual payment for the Temple's sacrifices, and the activity of collectors or moneychangers enabled this. But Exodus (30:13) established that adult Jews were to make only one half-shekel payment in their lifetime. While perhaps necessary for the Temple's maintenance, the annual payment could burden the poor, and Jesus conceivably confronted the moneychangers to disparage this annual collection or the charging of commissions from which priests or their clients profited.[12]

Likewise, Jesus' confrontation of people selling doves or carrying vessels of tithes or commodities plausibly involved similar criticisms of how the priests were accumulating personal wealth. Doves were mostly sacrificed by the poor, but their sellers at the Temple precinct were plausibly the clients or dependents of priests. The Mishnah suggests that the chief priests or the traders regulated by them were providing unblemished animals and grain, wine, or oil being sold for sacrifice at the Temple. If so, Jesus' activity implicated the chief priests, who in his view were organizing the sacred economy for profit instead of alleviating the burdens of poor Jews participating in Temple rituals. Jesus may have accepted the validity of money exchanges and animal sales necessary for sacrifices. But he still might have decided that their impact on the devout poor or the derivative commercial ventures of priests violated his ethos for how Jews should manage wealth. This does not mean that the chief priests or the Temple were intrinsically corrupt and that Jesus was simply right (or vice versa). The chief priests managed a vastly expanded Temple and numbers of pilgrims. Their means of acquiring wealth at the Temple or benefiting from its sacred economy typified that of landed elites in the Roman Empire. But this does mean that Jesus and the chief priests were at odds about what the relationship should be between maintaining the Temple's sacred rituals and the circulation of wealth at the Temple, and among the priests and the poor. It was a locus of conflict among Jews of Judaea with different moral visions. While fulfilling obligations to the Temple and its pilgrims, the chief priests occupied a privileged place in Roman Judaea's ordering of wealth. Jesus and his followers believed that rich, powerful people like them should distribute their resources to devout, poor Jews who bore most of the hardships. Otherwise, God's imminent reign would lay the powerful low.[13]

When Jesus and his followers aggressively confronted some collectors and merchants, their activity had the potential to inspire an outbreak of crowd violence. But some surmise that they were armed with weapons, including swords. Luke (22:35–38) suggests that Jesus' followers were armed with *machairai* during their activity in Jerusalem's vicinity. In the New Testament, the term *machaira* often refers to a curved, cutting sword (analogous to *hereb* in Hebrew), but it could also refer to a large knife or dagger. Luke describes Jesus telling his followers that if they have a purse or a wallet, they should purchase a *machaira*; otherwise, they should sell their cloak and purchase one. His followers responded, "Look, master: here are two *machairai*." Yet, if so, nothing indicates that they brandished *machairai* inside Jerusalem's walls or at the Temple precinct, which the Roman garrison would have deemed a sure sign of armed insurrection. The Gospels only point to Jesus' followers as having swords for protection from robbers, hostile opponents, or arrest attempts while traveling or camping outside the city. Also possible is that *machaira* here represents the Greek translation of the Hebrew *makelet*, which refers to the sacrificial knife that many pilgrims would have had. On this basis, it does seem that Jesus' confrontational activity at the Temple was small-scale and not involving swords or clubs. Moreover, if Jesus and his followers were brandishing weapons like these in Jerusalem, it becomes much harder to explain why the Antonia garrison or, if necessary, Pilate did not respond immediately. Their *machairai* must have been sacrificial knives or swords that they carried outside Jerusalem to deal with adversaries (or perhaps both).[14]

In other words, the confrontational activity of Jesus and his followers was fairly modest in scope and initially went unnoticed by the chief priests and Roman troops in the huge, busy, and loud Temple precinct. He and his followers engaged in aggressive and perhaps even violent activity against some people in a small part of it. But a disturbance large enough to attract the immediate attention of authorities did not erupt. The chief priests did not make an immediate countermove or arrest attempt that halted Jesus' activity or, alternatively, escalated the situation. The Antonia garrison did not either. If Jesus' followers aimed to leverage the potential for crowd disturbance to deter an arrest attempt, that does not mean they wanted crowd violence to break out. Jesus also did not intend to be immediately noticeable to the Antonia garrison or Pilate. In truth, Jesus and the chief priests shared kindred interests in avoiding repressive violence from Roman soldiers. All the Synoptic

Gospels state that Jesus returned the following day to preach. Apparently no Jewish or Roman authorities had confronted him or tried to arrest him before then. The Roman garrison at the Antonia, by contrast, reportedly detained Paul during a social disturbance a couple decades later (Acts 21:32–33).

Jesus' confrontational behavior apparently escaped initial notice from the chief priests. Mark indicates (11:18) that they did not witness it but learned of it from others as the day closed. Only then did they begin to organize countermeasures. Reworking Mark, both Matthew and Luke make the chief priests appear to witness Jesus' activity more directly. But according to Mark, Jesus and his followers returned to the Temple precinct the day after their aggressive activity there. Now informed, the chief priests and allied scribes confronted him publicly and sought to ascertain whether Jesus claimed Messianic stature. Whether the Gospels accurately report the nature of their conversations will perhaps never be resolved. Even if statements attributed to Jesus are authentic, he could have made them earlier in his preaching and not during his final Passover week. According to Mark, when Jesus was moving about the Temple precinct, the priests asked him by which authority or power (*exousia*) he did "these deeds." Jesus reportedly evaded a direct, literal answer. He instead communicated the parable about the evil vine farmers who murdered the son of the vineyard owner. The message was that the chief priests would face punishment when God reigned and avenged Jesus' death, and it encouraged them to strategize all the more how to arrest Jesus. According to the Synoptics, some scribes then challenged Jesus about whether he should pay taxes to Caesar. Jesus once again answered evasively. When they displayed a coin with Caesar's likeness and inscription on it, he maintained that they should give to Caesar what was Caesar's and to God what was God's. He reportedly proclaimed to the crowd that the Messiah could not be descended from King David, as many believed. Here Jesus' citation of Psalms (110:1) from a Greek translation of the Hebrew original overwhelmingly suggests that the Markan author contrived the episode while engaging in a contemporary debate about Messianic lineage. Mark (13:2) also states that while leaving the precinct, Jesus asserted that not a single stone of the buildings in the Temple's vicinity would remain on one another. Some assert that the statement does not refer to the Temple itself, even if Matthew and Luke rework it so that it does. Jesus may have been predicting Jerusalem's destruction. But perhaps, not unlike the Qumran Jews, he was also envisioning the arrival of a heavenly Temple that would replace the present one being managed by the chief priests. As daylight ended, he and his followers left the city and went into hiding at the Mount of Olives.[15]

All the exchanges just described are open to scrutiny and create doubt among scholars. Most important for present purposes is whether Jesus made Messianic claims and predicted the destruction of Jerusalem or the Temple. Mark and the other Synoptic Gospels were written after the Temple's destruction in 70. By that time believers in Jesus as Christ thought of him as a Messiah. They were also increasingly envisioning a future without the Temple or its sacrifices, which they thought Jesus' death and resurrection had superseded. The Gospels have the goal of portraying him as a Messianic preacher who prophesied the Temple's destruction. This in theory would explain Mark's portrayal of a council at Jerusalem where Jesus is accused of predicting just that (14:58) and is treated as blasphemous for asserting a Messianic, divinely sent stature. Mark could have staged such statements and accusations to promote Jesus as a Messiah whose prophecies got him killed. Other Gospels then reworked the testimony of Mark (or a common source) to portray Jesus as specifically predicting the Temple's destruction (Matt 24:1–2; Luke 21:5–6). It remains possible that such portrayals of Jesus were contrived by the Gospels' authors after 70. This would explain why Paul's letters do not make any references to such a prediction, by Jesus or himself.[16]

Yet in his final days in Jerusalem, Jesus plausibly posed as a Messianic figure and prophesied the destruction of the Temple wrought by God's reign. Even if he did not call himself Messiah, his activity had recognizably Messianic connotations. Pilate's notorious mockery of Jesus as "King of the Jews" does not make much sense if it were otherwise. This carried clear regal implications among Jesus' compatriots. Josephus also describes how various popular leaders claimed the title of king after Herod died in 4 BCE. This undoubtedly reflects Messianic claims that Josephus was rephrasing for a Greek-reading audience. True, in his preaching Jesus emulated the prophets from the Hebrew Bible and not a warrior Davidic figure leading an army, a typical understanding of the Messiah. But his prophesied reign of God that would free Israel from illegitimate governance had militaristic overtones, and some Jews understood the Messiah to be a divinely sent prophet preceding God's intervention. Significantly, the Gospels agree that Jesus presented himself as a divinely sent agent who preached a reign of God that would end the contemporary order of governance. This would explain why his sympathizers and opponents alike associated him with Messianic claims. It clarifies why the Gospels agree that Pilate had him executed as "King of the Jews."[17]

The prophecies about the destruction of Jerusalem and the Temple that Jesus reportedly made are consistent with what other charismatic preachers of the period claimed. Josephus communicates that deceptive people were

Jesus, the Temple, and the Chief Priests

promoting themselves as prophets or predicting Jerusalem's destruction in the generation preceding the First Jewish Revolt. Whether Mark was written before or after 70, its sources and an established gospel tradition for Jesus almost certainly predated the destruction of Jerusalem and could be recording a claim that Jesus made. In his lifetime Jesus plausibly predicted how God's reign would overturn the governing order and ruin many buildings (and kill many people) at Jerusalem. He may have conceived of the Temple as being transferred intact to those who could govern it justly when God restored Israel to the righteous. Or he may very well have anticipated its destruction and replacement by another earthly Temple or even a heavenly one. The works maintained by the Qumran Jews prophesied their management of the Temple (or a new one) at a time of divine judgment. Predictions about the Temple's destruction or its heavenly (re)building, sometimes paired with a Messiah's coming, had appeared in various Jewish texts by Jesus' lifetime. Jesus credibly envisioned an eschatological moment when the first (like the chief priests) would be last and the righteous lowly would be elevated.[18]

For many particulars about Jesus' conduct at the Temple, we can suspect the exegetical intervention of Mark or the Synoptic Gospels. But the basic tradition consistently points to antagonism between Jesus and the chief priests and a real possibility for motivating crowd disturbance. They had a legal pathway and personal interest in seeking Jesus' arrest. But they also had a serious obligation to keep Jesus' compatriots safe from harm while they participated in sacrifices. Jesus' prophetic claims could have inspired crowd violence, rioting, or factional strife that could have hurt innocent people.

Mark and Matthew mention no more visits to the Temple precinct after Jesus' second day there. At this point, Jesus and his followers apparently moved about Jerusalem's environs in secret, without public preaching. They anticipated arrest if they returned to the Temple. We can dismiss Luke's claim that Jesus preached at the Temple during each day of Passover week (19:47, 20:1, 21:37). If anything, its account reworked Mark's material to make it seem that Jesus had not gone into hiding. A wanted man, Jesus mostly lurked outside the city. According to Mark and Matthew, he was staying in Bethany at the house of Simon the Leper two days before the Passover meal (Mark 14:3; Matt 26:6), where he apparently remained until celebrating it. Mark (14:12) suggests that his core followers sacrificed the Paschal lamb at the Temple and then found a house for the Passover meal without him: "On the first day of Unleavened Bread, when they customarily sacrificed the Paschal lamb [*to Pascha ethuon*], his disciples said to him, 'Where do you want us who are departing to prepare for you to eat the Paschal lamb [*to Pascha*]?'" John

(13–18 generally) places Jesus' arrest before the Passover meal takes place and right when the Passover lamb is slaughtered, but this is because it likens Jesus to the Passover lamb for exegetical purposes. For the Passover meal, which technically happened the day after the lambs were slaughtered and on the first day of the Feast of Unleavened Bread, Jesus' followers reportedly prepared a house in Jerusalem where they ate in secret (Mark 14:12–16). They then spent the evening at Gethsemane, on the Mount of Olives (14:32). But Jesus had run out of time at Jerusalem. The chief priests had determined Jesus' nocturnal whereabouts. In this remote place, where a confrontation would not escalate into serious social disturbance, they overwhelmed Jesus and a couple dozen or so core followers. The chief priests had negated an imminent threat to worshipers at the Temple.[19]

Jesus' Opposition at the Temple Precinct

The Synoptics make it look like Jesus' incendiary preaching at the Temple precinct did not lead to a serious arrest attempt or crowd disturbance there in his final days. They hint that the chief priests' fear of the crowd, which reportedly favored Jesus, was the reason why. In Mark (12:12) and Matthew (21:46), the chief priests ponder arresting Jesus after his parable about the vineyard owner predicts their judgment and demise. But they do not do it. The Synoptic Gospels agree that when Jesus was captured on the Mount of Olives (Mark 14:49; Matt 26:55; Luke 22:53), he even criticized the priests for not arresting him publicly at the Temple. They had instead opted for the middle of the night and outside the city walls, as though accosting bandits.

The Gospels are in certain ways misleading. They portray the crowds at the Temple precinct as enthralled by Jesus. For this reason, it is odd, if widely noted, that a similar crowd condemned him at his trial before Pilate shortly afterward. In truth, the crowds at the Temple precinct did not all support Jesus. Being residents and pilgrims with many different political alignments, they included Jesus' core followers, Galilean and Judaean sympathizers, supporters of the chief priests, scribes, and curious bystanders. Some may have been hostile to both Jesus and the chief priests. Most were presumably neutral, pious worshipers on pilgrimage at the Temple. A preacher and followers engaged in disruptive, prophetic behavior may not have been very endearing to them. But if serious violence broke out, their presence or attempts to flee would have added to the chaos. The chief priests were dealing with a volatile situation. If the supporters of Jesus or the chief priests resorted to violence, any crowd panic, rioting, or bloodshed could exceed anyone's control. They could motivate a crowd, but they could not control what it did in its collective autonomy. If the Roman garrison in the Antonia noticed, it could suppress the disturbance. It could also make the violence much worse. The chief priests had both an obligation and a real interest in avoiding a disturbance, whatever people's beliefs or intentions were.[20]

The crowd dynamic and the confrontational actions of Jesus' followers would have justifiably deterred the chief priests from an arrest attempt, as Matthew (21:46) states while reworking Mark (12:12). There are many reasons for this. First, the chief priests may not have believed that they could seize Jesus or overwhelm his followers without fomenting some social disturbance. Jesus' core followers numbered in the dozens. By themselves, they were not a massive threat or immediately visible to authorities. But when combined with sympathizers and opponents, their potential for inciting violence was great. This was especially so if they resisted a countermove with hostility. Second, any act that generated a popular disturbance or invited the intervention of the Roman garrison could escalate into unconstrained bloodletting. Once Roman troops were involved, the chief priests could not prevent even more innocent people from getting hurt. This had apparently happened in the recent past. Josephus reports that Pilate's troops slaughtered a demonstration at Jerusalem in excess of his orders. Luke (13:1–5) claims that while Jesus was preaching in Galilee, some people had announced to him how Pilate "mixed" the blood of Galileans with the sacrifices. If not replicating Josephus' testimony, this refers to how Pilate's soldiers had brutally suppressed a social disturbance at the Temple. Around the time Jesus was born, Herodian troops massacred a crowd at the Temple precinct during Passover when its ringleaders inspired it to violence, and not much later Roman soldiers slaughtered an insurrection there. If Jesus' activity had not yet created a disturbance that the Antonia garrison would notice, the priests may have opted not to confront Jesus aggressively or invite Roman military intervention. This would explain the failure to arrest Jesus while he was preaching at the Temple in his final Passover and perhaps during his previous pilgrimages.[21]

Even so, not arresting Jesus came with risks. If his activity went unchecked, it could have fomented a crowd disturbance that invited repression from Roman troops and highlighted the priestly leadership's failure to fulfill its obligations. The chief priests had ample scope and obligation for organizing arrests in the eyes of Roman authorities (Chapter 7). By completing an arrest without Pilate's help, the chief priests could demonstrate their value as an effective municipal leadership and negate any need for repressive violence by the Roman garrison. They could fulfill pilgrims' expectations of safety at the Temple.

Mark suggests that the chief priests harbored such concerns. It reports that the chief priests sought to arrest Jesus on his second day of preaching at the Temple *because* he was inciting the crowd against them. According to Mark (12:12), The chief priests "began seeking to seize him, and they feared the crowd. For they knew that Jesus said the parable [of the vineyard owner] against them. And letting him go, they went away." Luke (20:19) retains the implication of Mark's phrasing: "they began seeking to throw their hands upon him at that time, and they feared the people, for they knew that he said this parable against him." Matthew (21:46) reworks Mark's version so that the priests instead desist from arresting Jesus because they fear the crowd. Even so, Mark's phrasing hints at a tradition in which the priests began to detain Jesus because they were afraid of the crowd but let him go. Their fear of the crowd is implicitly the reason for releasing him. Mark (14:1–2) even reports that after they had failed in their arrest attempt at the Temple, the chief priests pondered how to capture Jesus without doing it "during the festival" because they feared that a crowd disturbance would erupt if people witnessed it. Mark's phrasing leaves ambiguous whether the priests feared arresting him in public at the Temple or just during Passover week generally. But it clearly specifies a desire for a strategic encounter not witnessed by crowds. It states that the chief priests began to ponder arresting Jesus by guile because they feared what detaining him visibly during Passover week could inspire. Seizing him at night and outside of town solved the problem.[22]

John (7:32, 40–47) potentially offers corroboration. It communicates that the priests had their subordinates or the Temple's guards make an attempt to arrest Jesus while he preached that the Messiah was not descended from David. Though John once again transfers this episode to an earlier pilgrimage, its account reflects a gospel tradition related to Jesus' final pilgrimage. We have already noted problems with the Synoptics' portrayal of Jesus as preaching that the Messiah was not descended from David. But even so, the Synoptics and John were apparently engaging and reworking a tradition in which an arrest attempt was made by the priests at the Temple precinct on his final day of preaching. But dissension (*schisma*) within the crowd prevented it. The implication was that the chief priests tried to arrest Jesus at the Temple precinct because they feared the effect that his preaching was having on the crowd. Yet they ceased because their attempt (paradoxically) was further inciting a disturbance.[23]

Other aspects of the Gospels raise the possibility that an arrest attempt by the chief priests inspired social disturbance or ensuing bloodshed, with the Roman garrison intervening and making arrests. The Gospels' treatments of

Jesus, the Temple, and the Chief Priests

the prisoner Barabbas and the two criminals executed with Jesus support that all their arrests pertained to the same general legal context, if not his activity. While describing Barabbas, Mark (15:7) arguably provides the earliest and most significant statement: "There was a man called Barabbas imprisoned with the seditionists who had committed murder during *the sedition*." Mark's phrasing "the sedition" is odd. It refers to a specific event as though the reader should be familiar with it. Yet the Gospel accounts otherwise never mention it. Mark's statement points to a source tradition that described what it was.[24]

Romans did not practice incarceration in the way that modern governments often do. Prisoners were usually detained only prior to their trials or executions. There are exceptions; for example, the prefect Felix reportedly imprisoned Paul for two years after being bribed. Even so, most trials and sentences were swift, and contemporaries thought of Felix as unusually corrupt. This sedition possibly corresponds to crowd turbulence known from Pilate's term as prefect (Chapter 9). It probably happened during Passover week, which often inspired instability. The other Gospels occlude this. Matthew (27:16) simply refers to Barabbas as a notable prisoner. Luke (23:19) reworks Mark's testimony to refer vaguely to "some sedition." Ultimately, Jesus' death by crucifixion supports that he was executed for seditious behavior. Mark's reference to "the sedition" and its fatal impact places them in proximity to Passover week. Jesus' preaching at the Temple happened at the same time. Is there a relationship?[25]

The Gospels' treatment of the two men killed with Jesus suggest other people were executed for deeds that coincided with his activity at the Temple precinct. Most Gospels refer to two *leistai* (brigands) or "others" who were crucified with Jesus. In general, their phrasing suggests no affiliation with Jesus. Luke describes these men as "evil-doers" (*kakourgoi*), and some manuscripts even describe them as "two other evil-doers." This implies that Jesus had been convicted of being an "evildoer" by Pilate's court in the same general legal context. Intriguingly, nearly identical language appears in John (18:30), where the petitioners insist before Pilate that Jesus is an "evil-doer" or "criminal" (*kakon poion*). In tandem, such statements point to a tradition in which the two persons crucified with Jesus had been tried and convicted by Pilate at roughly the same time, and for similar crimes. Even if they had no relationship with Jesus, they were convicted of seditious behavior in the context of Passover week.[26]

These ostensible traces of attempted arrest or crowd disturbance, dispersed throughout the Gospel narratives, do not enable any precise reconstruction of what happened during Jesus' preaching at the Temple precinct. Even so, a failed arrest attempt was probably threatened or made. In one possible (if unlikely) scenario, some sort of violence broke out as a result. Barabbas and the men executed with Jesus may have been involved in some way. Nothing suggests that they were Jesus' followers, but they were convicted of sedition in the same general context. At the least, they and Jesus were classified by Pilate as engaged in criminal behaviors in Jerusalem during Passover. If Jesus' incendiary preaching set in motion an arrest attempt and ensuing violence, it surely exposed him to capital charges.

In a more likely scenario, the chief priests desisted after making their failed arrest attempt, and no actual violence broke out. They had surmised that arresting Jesus could exacerbate the volatile situation and create an even greater capacity for crowd violence. In this case, the seditious activity of Barabbas and his colleagues was not related to Jesus' activity at the Temple precinct. Yet their happening at the same time and in the same general legal context tainted Jesus' activity in the eyes of Pontius Pilate. As for the chief priests, they shifted strategies. They sought to isolate Jesus from large crowds. They knew it would be safer for everyone worshiping at the Temple if they identified where Jesus was lodging and arrested him.

A Seditionist Jesus?

Did Roman authorities like Pilate conceive of Jesus' activity as seditionist? The traces of such a Jesus are scattered among the Gospel narratives. They usually have no obvious relationship to one another. They do not enable a coherent picture. Even so, they are also too many to be dismissed entirely or in generality. This does not mean that Jesus was an armed insurgent or preaching military resistance. But the confrontational behavior and incendiary preaching of Jesus and his followers at the Temple precinct exposed him to charges of sedition. It probably elicited an arrest attempt by the chief priests on his second and final day of preaching there. This attempt may even have escalated into a violent social disturbance. We will perhaps never know the specifics for sure, but that does not make much difference. The perception that Jesus' activity could have done so met some Roman authorities' criteria. Even if Jesus was not trying to incite crowd violence, he seemed wantonly indifferent to the fact that it could foreseeably result from his followers' activity. He may even have seemed to be leveraging the threat of crowd violence to evade arrest. Roman governors had vast leeway in defining criminal behavior (Chapter 9). They did not have consistent views on whether incendiary preaching in a volatile social space was seditious. They did not agree on whether it was a capital crime or on what factors made it so. Some believed it was, and others

Jesus, the Temple, and the Chief Priests 117

did not. Pilate's own understanding of sedition would reverberate through the course of human history.[27]

Jesus' preaching had great potential for Pilate and the chief priests to see it as inflammatory because he did it at the volatile social space of the Temple precinct. Yet to some degree it had this same potential because of its content, which could have stirred social disturbance because of the people it could attract, offend, or motivate. Though people will continue to debate the accuracy of the Gospel accounts in all their particulars, we can accept that basic elements of Jesus' preaching occurred as they report. Jesus was arguing that God's reign was imminent and that the unjust would receive judgment. Unraveling the established order of authority and wealth, God would govern through Jesus' followers and the righteous on behalf of poor, devout Jews. Through an array of words and actions Jesus or his followers communicated to Jerusalem's residents and pilgrims that he was the Messiah or "the Son of Man" sent by God. Couched in confrontational behavior and criticisms of the Temple's management, his message had serious potential to incite a disturbance that could get pilgrims hurt or killed. The chief priests had an obligation to act. Jesus' conduct and message enabled them to assert to Pilate, with some distortion, that he was claiming to be "King of the Jews" at the Temple precinct, and in ways that could incite serious unrest. But nothing occurred that attracted Pilate's immediate attention. It was up to the chief priests to make the arrest.

7

Jesus' Arrest

A crowd (ochlos) with swords and clubs from the chief priests, scribes, and elders arrived.

—MARK 14:43

Jesus said to them: "You came out with swords and clubs to seize me, as though against a brigand? I taught to you each day at the Temple, and you did not seize me."

—MARK 14:48

AT A FATEFUL moment of Passover week, Jesus was arrested. The Gospels claim the chief priests and allied scribes sent followers to confront him. They also specify that a man named Judas Iscariot disclosed his whereabouts. They say Judas was a core follower, but his status, role, identity, and existence often give people pause, and rightfully so. His betrayal of Jesus and suborning by the chief priests play an obviously convenient role in the Gospel accounts. But one way or another, the chief priests found out where Jesus was camping.[1]

The Gospels are at odds in various ways. One example is the dating for Jesus' arrest and execution. The nature of the arresting party is another. At one extreme, Mark and Matthew portray an arrest party the chief priests organized. It consisted of their clients and enslaved. At the other, John apparently places a military tribune and soldiers from a Roman cohort at Jesus' arrest site. What explains these discrepancies? What do they mean for Jesus' arrest?

Jesus' Arrest: Date and Mechanics

Exactly when Jesus was arrested is hard to determine. The Gospels vary about the timing. In the Synoptics, Jesus is arrested on the night that he celebrates the Passover meal. Passover (Pesach) commemorated the divine intervention that had released the Israelites from captivity in Egypt, according to the Hebrew Bible. It was in effect the first day of the Feast of Unleavened Bread, and on the night when it began, Jews at Jerusalem dined on the Passover lambs that they had sacrificed during daylight. Jesus' compatriots normally began new festival days at sundown. For this reason the Synoptics place Jesus' final meal, arrest, and death between the evening when the day of Passover started and the evening that came after. In John, the setting for Jesus' arrest is on the night when the day of preparation for Passover starts. John's theology likens Jesus to the sacrificed Passover lamb and shifts his crucifixion to the day when they are slaughtered. But the Synoptics too have theological reasons for making Jesus' final meal a Passover feast. Some suspect that Jesus' conduct at Jerusalem drew an immediate response, before the climactic day of Passover (or even a week earlier). The Synoptics then reworked their source traditions, if imperfectly, to shift Jesus' arrest to the night of the Passover meal, when the overworked chief priests were unlikely to gather at short notice. At times Mark appears to contradict how it otherwise dates Jesus' death to Passover, which provides ostensible evidence for this. It portrays the chief priests as opposed to arresting Jesus "during the festival" (that is, during Passover week) because they thought crowd violence would break out if they did (14:2). It also claims that people rushed to bury his body before the Sabbath and its labor prohibition, even though burying him on Passover posed the same problem (15:42–46).[2]

Even so, we should still prefer the timing the Synoptics report. An early gospel tradition apparently associated Jesus' final meal with the Passover feast. In 1 Corinthians (5:7, 11:23–25), Paul conceives of Jesus as a Passover lamb, but he imparts that Jesus took his last meal and was "handed over" after sundown. This would refer to the Passover feast, the first meal of Passover week required after sunset. During Jesus' lifetime, Jews normally ate their large daily meal in the afternoon. But the Passover lambs slaughtered at the Temple had to be eaten after sunset and in Jerusalem itself. Mark portrays Jesus as having his followers secure a house in Jerusalem, traveling there from the Mount of Olives and eating at night for that purpose. The chief priests then have him arrested on the Mount of Olives later that evening (Figure 7.1). After Jesus was dead, purchasing a cloak and burying him did not violate the Passover prohibition, which was more flexible than the prohibition on the Sabbath, the following day. It permitted necessary, nonoccupational tasks, which would logically include preparing and burying the dead (Lev 23:7–8). When Mark mentions that the chief priests feared arresting Jesus "during the festival," it is explaining why they resorted to a strategic arrest away from the Temple and its crowds.

Why would the chief priests organize Jesus' arrest? The basic answer is that it was their obligation to do so. Jesus' compatriots expected them to

FIGURE 7.1 View of the Mount of Olives from Jerusalem. Photo by N. Andrade.

Jesus' Arrest

ensure safety and protection when they worshiped at the Temple. So did the Roman authorities, who often charged municipal elites with such tasks. But the Gospels raise serious concerns by portraying the chief priests and allied scribes as organizing Jesus' arrest and inflicting violence upon him. Predictably, they assert that the chief priests acted on personal motives (and base, selfish ones) to remove a rival for authority. They shift responsibility for Jesus' death from Roman magistrates to people in Jewish society. Their portrayal has had profound implications for the global history of anti-Semitism. But is it even accurate? Could it have been contrived as a smear?

Many factors distinguish policing and arrests in the Roman Empire from modern practice. The police departments of modern cities did not exist. In Jesus' lifetime, local "civilian policing" was prevalent. Roman troops dealt with insurrections, serious social disturbances, and large-scale brigandage. But municipal leaders were responsible for organizing armed bands to respond to most other threats. According to Mark, the party that arrested Jesus was such an armed band. According to John, Roman troops were involved.[3]

In the first-century Roman provinces, municipal elites handled policing matters on a reactive basis. But they were the ones who addressed most local criminal matters. Some surviving municipal charters charge officials or town councilors with mustering armed bands in response to threats. Otherwise, unauthorized civilians could do it, with questionable legality. Mark and Matthew make it appear as if the chief priests exercised such extralegal or illegal means to muster an armed rabble (*ochlos*). They also ascribe personal, corrupt motives to them. But the chief priests plausibly had the authority and duty to organize armed bands and arrest people like Jesus. The high priest was the supreme municipal official at Jerusalem recognized by Roman authorities and Jesus' compatriots. The chief priests, in turn, were recognized by Roman authorities as Jerusalem's civic council (*boule*), which provided municipal governance and tended to policing matters. Sometimes they did so in tandem with allied scribes and other elites who participated on their advisory councils (*synhedria*). Jesus had been engaging in incendiary conduct at the Temple precinct that could foreseeably result in crowd disturbance or the death of innocent compatriots. The chief priests had an obligation to neutralize such a threat, in the eyes of Roman prefects and worshipers.[4]

In the decades after Jesus' death, "civilian policing" in the Roman Empire's local communities became increasingly formalized. Many cities established an official whose exclusive task was policing. The commander (*strategos*) of the Temple at Jerusalem, recorded by the Lukan author, worked in such a capacity. This figure apparently maintained clients, hirelings, or even the enslaved as "subordinates" or "servants" (*hyperetai*) who could assist in arrests. People sometimes call these figures the "temple police," but "retainers" is much more accurate. Even so, no evidence securely verifies that an appointed commander of the Temple existed before 50. The testimony of the Lukan author, who places several *strategoi* at Jesus' arrest, is arguably anachronistic and may reflect material from Josephus (Appendix 1).[5]

During Jesus' lifetime, municipal elites of the Roman Empire instead mustered groups of armed men when it was necessary to confront a band of potentially violent criminals. These groups could include free clients or the enslaved. By resolving such matters themselves, municipal elites could prove their worth to Roman authorities and avoid excess bloodshed that inviting Roman military intervention might attract. Being the municipal leaders at Jerusalem, the chief priests had such an incentive to arrest Jesus, even if they had to transfer him to Pilate. Their success would prove them capable allies of Roman authority. Pilate had troops, but he had an interest in not dispatching them unless the scale of any seditious or criminal behavior demanded it. Any policing organized by the chief priests would appear less invasive than the work of his soldiers. Also, various seditionists and brigands were at work in or near Jerusalem during Passover week, as pilgrims thronged to the city. The Gospels report these had been detained by Pilate, perhaps by his own troops. But Pilate's resources were stretched thin, and he relied on the chief priests for some policing.

Outside the Gospels, the chief priests reportedly organized policing and arrests to keep the peace, like many municipal elites in the Roman Empire. Josephus records moments when the chief priests organized armed bands and arrested ostensibly seditionist figures for capital judgment by the Roman prefect or, extralegally, by a *synhedrion*. In times of strife, the chief priests mobilized bands for conflicts with one another. In his letters, Paul describes how he had been arrested and lashed by the local Jewish leadership on five different occasions (2 Cor 11:24–25). His arrests were probably motivated by the potential for his public preaching to trigger social disturbance or violence (Chapter 11), just like Jesus' preaching at the Temple. When the Gospels describe the chief priests as key players in organizing Jesus' arrest, their portrayals are historically plausible.

The Gospels support the chief priests arrested Jesus, in keeping with contemporary practice in the Roman provinces. They all refer to a crowd sent by the chief priests and elders. Its members were armed with swords or clubs. Among them were allies, clients, or dependents of the chief priests. By organizing such an arrest, Jesus' opponents operated under the assumption or pretense that Jesus would not surrender willingly. In most Gospel accounts, Jesus reproaches them for treating him like a "brigand" (Mark 14:48; Matt 26:55; Luke 22:52).

Even so, the Gospels are notably inconsistent about who arrested Jesus. They agree the chief priests played a role. But John (18:2) claims that members of a cohort (*speire*) and tribune (*chiliarchos*) were involved. Scholars sometimes classify these as a local Jewish police force or Herodian troops. Yet in Greek texts from the Roman Empire, such terms overwhelmingly denote Roman military units and officers. John's account does refer to Roman soldiers. It perhaps engages a tradition in which Roman soldiers did arrest Jesus. The Gospel accounts or their sources may have doctored the narrative tradition to minimize the accountability of Roman authorities and ultimately Pilate. They may even have modeled their narrative anachronistically on known examples of chief priests organizing violent bands shortly before the First Jewish Revolt (66–74). But they did not necessarily tie up all loose ends, and John retains a reference to Roman soldiers at Jesus' arrest. Such involvement could conceivably happen. It is why Roman soldiers reportedly detained Paul at the Temple precinct (Acts 21:32–33). It is why Matthew claims that Pilate assigned soldiers to secure Jesus' tomb after his crucifixion (27:65–66). The fact that Jesus was crucified by Pilate offers ostensible support to the premise.[6]

There is an obvious problem, however. As noted, the Gospel accounts of Jesus' arrest intriguingly align with policing procedures current to their widely accepted times of composition. In Mark (14:43) and Matthew (26:47), an armed crowd (*ochlos*) organized by the chief priests makes the arrest. This approach was typically employed during Jesus' lifetime. Some chief priests may have attracted criticism for organizing armed bands for civil strife in the 50s and 60s, but this in itself probably did not shape Mark's narrative. Such forms of civilian policing for criminal arrests were common during the early and mid-first century. The variations in Luke (22:48–52) and John (18:3–12), in which policing officials of the Temple (*strategoi tou hierou*) or Roman soldiers are involved, can be explained by shifts in policing practices after the mid-first century. Formal municipal policing institutions became more robust, and Roman soldiers became more active in intervening in such matters. Luke and John alter a gospel tradition in which Jesus is arrested by an armed band organized by the chief priests to mirror trends in contemporary policing (Appendix 1). Some even suspect theological motives for John's report that Roman soldiers arrested him. Its claiming that they fell to the ground in reverence (18:6) elaborates on the theme that everyone in the world who should have venerated Jesus acted with hostility toward him. We should instead give Mark's version priority. Jesus' core followers were a couple dozen people. The chief priests opted to organize an arresting party of their own clients, followers, and retainers.[7]

Another factor supporting that the chief priests had assembled Jesus' arrest party is one on which all the Gospels agree: Jesus' brief detainment at the house of a chief priest and not at Pilate's headquarters. In the ancient world, governments did not routinely practice long-term mass incarceration. Imprisonment did not typify criminal convictions, either as a punishment or a form of rehabilitation. Execution or consignment to the mines was more common. (Elites could expect property confiscation or exile.) The main purpose of imprisonment was to ensure that defendants were at their criminal trials. Lengthy periods of imprisonment were a hallmark of corrupt magistrates or befell members of the laboring class who lacked proper patronage and resources to expedite a court date. When Acts of the Apostles (24:27) claims that the governor Felix detained Paul for two years to accommodate the chief priests, it does so to portray Felix as unusually immoral. Felix had a reputation for this. A good governor was supposed to provide a speedier trial for an imprisoned man.[8]

The agreement of the Gospels regarding the nature of Jesus' detainment, if anything, supports Mark's version of Jesus' actual arrest. All the Gospels state that on the night of his arrest, Jesus was not taken directly to Pilate's headquarters. Instead, he was kept at the house of a person who had served as high priest (Matt 26:57; Mark 14:53; Luke 22:54; John 18:13–24). Yet, the Gospels vary in their identifications. Mark and Luke do not name the high priest. John specifies Annas, the former high priest, whereas Matthew identifies Caiaphas, the incumbent high priest and Annas' son-in-law. John also identifies Annas' house as the location of Jesus' trial before a council (Chapter 8). This is probably the "high priest" to whom Mark and Luke were referring. Either way, after his arrest Jesus was taken to the house of a chief priest, probably in the Upper City, and kept under guard there. This makes sense only if we accept Mark's version of an impromptu arrest party organized by the chief priests. Roman soldiers would have detained Jesus at Pilate's *praetorium* or the Antonia fortress. Some suggest that Pilate had his soldiers bring Jesus to the chief priests for interrogation under the expectation that they return him to Pilate for trial. This is implausible. The chief priests had initiated the arrest and had imprisoned Jesus while he awaited his trial before Pilate. This procedure was normal in the Roman Empire at the time.

By all appearances, the testimony of Paul's letters supports this understanding of Jesus' arrest. We have already seen how they corroborate many aspects of Mark's narrative for Jesus' death. But Paul also asserts the involvement of "the Jews/Judaeans" (1 Thess 2:14–16) and that Jesus was handed over at night (1 Cor 11:23) without resisting (Gal 1:4, 2:20; Phil 2:8). Paul's statement from 1 Thessalonians has sometimes been deemed inauthentic. But this is in part because it contradicts his tendency to imply Roman agency and aligns with how the Gospels too shift responsibility to people in Jewish society, with all its malevolent consequences.[9]

The testimony of the Gospels and Paul supports that the chief priests orchestrated Jesus' arrest. But is there any other evidence for this? Here we introduce the controversial testimony of Josephus. That testimony is intensely debated, but it provides basic, if qualified, corroboration that the chief priests were responsible for arresting Jesus and bringing him to trial.

Josephus on Jesus' Trial

The so-called *Testimonium Flavianum*, the passage of Josephus' *Antiquities* (18.63–64) that famously describes Jesus, is notorious for its ambiguities. If authentic, it is the earliest passage outside the New Testament to mention Jesus as a historical figure. It is also the earliest surviving testimony of Jesus' activity not produced by a Jesus Christ believer. Yet the passage seems to acknowledge that Jesus is "the Christ" and more than a mere man. It refers to Jesus' resurrection, as understood by his followers. All this points to Christian doctoring. Does this mean that the passage is inauthentic? Nowadays the dominant opinion is that Josephus wrote the *Testimonium Flavianum* and that Christians later reworked it. But there is no consensus. Some scholars dismiss the passage entirely.

For various reasons, we can surmise that the core passage originates in Josephus even if his source remains an open question (Appendix 2). As such, Josephus' testimony imparts vital information, however brief, about the mechanisms that led to Jesus' death. It states he was convicted and executed by Pontius Pilate, but in response to "the *endeixis* of the foremost men (*protoi*) among us." What does this mean? An *endeixis* is an accusation or a formal charge brought to a judge. The "foremost men" of Jerusalem were the chief priests. In this sense, the passage supports the gist of the Gospel accounts: the chief priests brought legal action against Jesus before Pilate. It does not say much else, and we cannot assume it corroborates the Gospel narratives in their totality. But it does indicate that the chief priests charged Jesus with a crime before Pilate. And if they did that, they plausibly played a key role in his arrest and had deliberations of their own about how to proceed.[10]

We can surmise that Jesus' arrest by the chief priests is not the pure fabrication of the Gospels. We should be more suspicious of how they frame the motives of the chief priests as purely self-serving. Their own motivations aside, the chief priests were fulfilling an important obligation to Jesus' compatriots by arresting him. They were neutralizing an ostensible imposter whose actions could cause serious violence at the Temple precinct. They next had to decide whether Jesus' actions warranted a capital charge before Pilate.

The Arrest of Jesus

All the factors just described point to an arrest made by the chief priests with little to no involvement by Pilate. What exactly Pilate knew about Jesus or his activity is unclear. But the chief priests deemed it advantageous to gather information and make the arrest without involvement from him or his troops. By doing so, they demonstrated their value as municipal leaders without inviting the escalation and bloodletting that involving Roman troops could bring. Even so, none of this means Pilate would have dismissed Jesus' alleged crimes as negligible. He was also undoubtedly interested in whatever information the chief priests were sharing with him. When the chief priests sought Pilate's intervention the day after arresting Jesus, they were in fact accusing him of serious criminal behavior (Chapters 9 and 10). When they organized Jesus' arrest, they were performing the standard obligations of municipal elites throughout the early first-century Roman Empire. The Gospels and subsequent strands of anti-Semitism ascribe uniquely and exclusively corrupt, self-serving motives to them.

When the chief priests organized Jesus' arrest, they were taking normal measures against insurrectionists or brigands. Jesus apparently perceived this. All the Synoptic Gospels (Mark 14:48; Matt 26:55; Luke 22:52) portray him as protesting, "You came out with swords and clubs to seize me, as though against a brigand [*leistes*]?" He also disparages the chief priests for not arresting him publicly at the Temple precinct. In ancient Greek, *leistes* referred to any person who sowed social unrest, and its meanings ranged from robber or brigand to seditionist. In effect, the Gospels say that Jesus was being classified as a seditionist figure and arrested like a brigand. They claim that the chief priests were staging theatrics to this effect to tarnish his reputation and strengthen their accusations. As far as the Gospel authors are concerned, Jesus would have appeared before a court if summoned. But the chief priests were claiming otherwise. They also believed they needed to arrest Jesus where the crowds of the Temple precinct were not present.[11]

Once again we can doubt various details imparted by the Gospels while accepting, in general, that an arrest and brief conflict occurred. All of them record that some of Jesus' companions initially resisted. They also agree his companions were armed. One of them reportedly struck a blow that cut off the ear of a man enslaved to the high priest. As already mentioned, the offending weapon could have been a sacrificial knife or sword. Mark describes the assailant as "one of those standing beside Jesus" (14:47). This presumably refers to a companion of Jesus who was defending him, as the other Gospels state. They differ from Mark in portraying Jesus as opposed to the act. Matthew specifies that he was one of those "with Jesus" (26:51) and that Jesus reprimanded him at length for his action. In Luke (22:49–51), Jesus' followers surround him and ask, "Master, should we strike with the knife/sword?" One of them then proceeds to do so. Jesus tells them to stop and then heals the injured man. In John (18:10–11), it is Peter who commits the violent deed, and the enslaved is named Malchos. The reported conduct of Jesus' followers points to the challenges of arresting him among the throngs of the Temple precinct in prior days. This could easily have inspired much more serious violence. But in the dead of night and on the Mount of Olives, no such crowds were present to protect Jesus or deter arrest. Jesus lived or died by those of his companions who were there.

According to the Gospels, Jesus' core followers were outnumbered. After an initial confrontation, most fled, and he apparently submitted willingly. Even so, Jesus may not have been the only person the chief priests intended to arrest. They all report that Simon Peter denied knowing Jesus at the house of either Caiaphas or Annas. Jesus' followers apparently suspected that their leader was not the sole target. If possible, the person who harmed the enslaved of the chief priest would have been captured. On this issue, Mark (14:50–52) reports that while everyone else fled, a young man wrapped only in a linen cloak was following Jesus. The arresting party tried to detain him, but he escaped by discarding his garment and fleeing nude. If the arresting party apprehended only Jesus, it was because he was their main target and almost everyone had fled the scene after the initial confrontation. Whoever the arresting party could conveniently capture was apprehended. But Jesus was always the goal.

The Gospels agree that Jesus was the only person the arresting party detained. Some theorize that the two men executed with Jesus were members of his party. But the chief priests did not need to arrest anyone else, even if it was desirable. Eliminating Jesus, the leader, was enough to curb the threat of disturbance at the Temple precinct. His core followers did not necessarily know the chief priests' intentions and went into hiding to avoid arrest. The chief priests were now ready to have Jesus' criminal liability assessed by a *synhedrion* at Jerusalem.[12] Did he deserve to die?

PART IV

Jesus' Trial and Death

8

Jesus and "the Sanhedrin"

[The arresting party] led Jesus off to the house of the high priest, and all the chief priests, elders, and scribes were gathering.

—MARK 14:53

All of [the councilors] judged him to be liable for death..... Binding Jesus, the chief priests led him away and handed him over to Pilate.

—MARK 14:64, 15:1

JESUS' ORIGINS WERE humble. He was a Galilean laborer, a craftsman. He did not have easy access to the formal learning of scribes. But his preaching was profound. It was so potent the chief priests reportedly sought his death and a Roman prefect sentenced him to it. The Gospels claim that distinct legal machineries cooperated to kill Jesus. He is first interrogated by a *synhedrion* (council) at Jerusalem, which condemns him as blasphemous and worthy of a capital charge. But the council cannot put him to death. Its members must petition Pilate and bring the case before him. The reason why is implied by the Synoptics. But John (18:29–32) clarifies it. When the chief priests petition Pilate, he tells them to try Jesus themselves. When they respond that they do not have license to kill, he accepts their petition. Jesus' fatal trial begins.

We can now explore the intricacies of courts in the Roman Empire from the perspectives of judges and arbiters. These could be councils of municipal elites at Jerusalem or Roman magistrates like Pilate. When Jesus was preaching, what sort of courts existed in greater Judaea? What were their competencies? How were they related? Who were their judges? Answers provide context for what a *synhedrion* (council) at Jerusalem, often misleadingly labeled "the Sanhedrin," did with Jesus. They help cast light on his trial by Pilate.

The Gospels report that Jesus was interrogated by the chief priests after his arrest. The Synoptics state the priests convened a council to evaluate Jesus' criminality. But its competencies remain under debate, and the Gospels often inspire doubts. What happened when a *synhedrion* assembled to confront Jesus? Did one even assemble at all?

Courts of Roman Judaea and the Near East

The Gospel narratives point to a division of labor between the courts of Roman governors and courts, tribunals, and legal arbiters from local populations. Such legal machineries typified provincial life in the Roman Empire. We glimpse them, partially, a century after Jesus' trial through a woman named Babatha. A successful property owner, she was a Jewish commoner, much like Jesus. But unlike Jesus, she was apparently illiterate and originated south of the Dead Sea, not Galilee. She also did not stand accused of criminal behavior, as Jesus did. She instead immersed herself in civil disputes. Living at the village of Mahoza, she spent her early life as a subject of the Nabataean king. After 106, she was in the Roman province of Arabia. Even so, her village was virtually at Arabia's boundary with Judaea and enmeshed in its political situation. She died in a cave on the Dead Sea during the Bar Kochba Revolt (132–135). There she left behind a cache of legal documents she had assembled during her lifetime. Most were written in Greek, but some were in Nabataean Aramaic or Jewish Aramaic. These reflect the varying literacies and legal expertise of local scribes. They also suggest Babatha anticipated what languages and legal formulations would be most compelling to different legal authorities.[1]

Babatha's legal world can be reconstructed, in theory, from her documents and other testimonies for Roman Judaea and Arabia, including later rabbinic sources. These suggest that various forms of arbitration operated locally. Some would have consisted of assembled tribunals and court institutions with which Roman magistrates coordinated. Others would have involved local headmen or elders deemed worthy to adjudicate local matters. Roman authorities probably paid no notice to most local arbitration. They just selected their cases and left the rest for others. Some arbiters are specified by Babatha's documents. Others are implied by the language in which they are written. In a Greek text, the civic council (*boule*) of Petra, the nearest metropolis, appointed a guardian for Babatha's child in 124. Her marriage contract, written by her husband in Jewish Aramaic, foreshadows involvement by Jewish arbiters. Her early documents in Nabataean perhaps anticipated judgments from Nabataean kings before 106. Some Greek documents invoke Titus Haterius Nepos, the governor of Arabia in 130–31. Others refer to governors in general. Some of Babatha's copies were apparently Greek translations

Jesus and "the Sanhedrin"

of Latin originals. Babatha understood that courts judged by Roman magistrates preferred Greek or Latin documents. Yet she surmised that civil documents in Jewish or Nabataean Aramaic were actionable in Roman courts, and so she kept them. Roman jurists agreed. They recognized the legitimacy of wills in Aramaic, or "the Assyrian language" (*sermo Assyrius*).

Through materials like Babatha's, we can surmise that Roman provincials had access to different types of legal arbitration, even if they are poorly documented. Some were local. In cities with governments organized on contemporary Greek models, courts could consist of the municipal senates (*boulai*), institutions populated by council members, or tribunals manned by a city's magistrates. We have seen how the civic council of Petra, the nearest Greek *metropolis*, assigned a guardian to Babatha's son. Throughout the eastern provinces, Jews and ethnic communities in Greek cities and towns had their own courts, tribunals, or arbitration too. Local courts or arbiters were plausibly active in the cities, towns, and villages of Judaea, even if they scarcely leave traces. Villagers or townsfolk could approach respected locals, including sages and rabbis, to resolve disputes. The Qumran Jews organized their own courts to handle internal matters. Other courts had a regional remit. Roman governors held courts whose jurisdictions extended over entire provinces. While notionally serving Roman citizens, they received cases from people of varying status. In client kingdoms, kings were bearers of Roman *imperium* and maintained courts. When Jesus lived, Antipas was Galilee's most senior judge. Pilate was preeminent in Judaea. The proconsular governor of Syria was senior to them both.

The Roman Empire's most famous, and controversial, local courts are the *synhedria* at Jerusalem. These were ad hoc advisory councils that the rabbinic tradition misleadingly treats as an established court, "the Sanhedrin." The councils' capacities loom large in our understanding of Jesus' trial and death. After all, one reportedly deemed him worthy of a capital charge. Its members then petitioned Pilate to put him on trial. Jesus died as a result. But are the Gospels accurate? What was such a council, and what role did it play in local legal culture?

The Councils (Synhedria) of Jerusalem and Their Judges

Despite debates, we can infer the basic role of councils at Jerusalem. The Mishnah and other rabbinic texts describe "the Sanhedrin" as a stable court with great authority among Jews. But for present purposes, it is best to use the Greek term from the Gospels (*synhedrion*) and conceive of councils in the plural (*synhedria*). Mark (14:55, 15:1) refers to "the entire council" (*holon to synhedrion*) that evaluated Jesus to distinguish that specific council from the other ones that the chief priests assembled at Jerusalem. It is not describing "the Sanhedrin" or a standing court. Before Roman prefects began governing lesser Judaea in 6 CE, a *synhedrion* was an advisory council or court convened at Jerusalem by a Herodian dynast or high priest. It was populated by chief priests and allied elites, including scribes, but it was probably distinct from the collective of chief priests that Roman authorities recognized formally as Jerusalem's municipal council. We can doubt that *synhedria* met routinely as a formal institution with a regular schedule. They were assemblies of available elites that chief priests could quickly convene, as necessary, to deliberate on important matters in Jerusalem. They could also serve as courts. Being priests, scribes, and established elites, their participants sometimes criticized Roman authorities and Herodian rulers. But they also coordinated with them and benefited from Roman Judaea's ordering of authority and wealth.[2]

For serious matters at Jerusalem, the councils had a reputation for legitimate arbitration. Roman magistrates apparently accepted many of their decisions and competencies as valid. But they expected to intervene in certain matters. Various documents give us a sense of what they were. A statute issued by the emperor Augustus around the time of Jesus' birth outlines the competencies of local courts of Cyrene in North Africa. It indicates they could judge most cases not involving capital punishment. A Latin municipal charter from Spain is more restrictive. It mandates that municipal judges should handle only civil cases involving modest sums, provided these did not involve fraud, theft, or violence. They also were to follow directives from their governor's edicts and bring most serious affairs to his court (Chapter 9). Roman prefects of Judaea and the councils of Jerusalem generally interacted in similar ways.

The decree of Cyrene (in Libya), issued by Augustus in 6–7 CE, has long attracted attention for its potential to clarify the competencies of councils at Jerusalem. The decree prohibited the local court at Cyrene from handling capital charges. This court had harbored Roman jurors who were to ensure that local Greek jurors did not prosecute cases judged by their friends. But at Cyrene Roman jurors had been doing this too. Augustus advised the governor to ensure some Greeks served alongside Romans as jurors. But he was to judge capital cases himself. This in theory prevented conflicts of interest from determining mortal decisions. The Gospels portray such a conflict. When Jesus is questioned by a council at Jerusalem, his accusers are men closely connected to its judges. Though it deems Jesus "liable for death" (Mark 14:64), it cannot execute him. Roman governors like Pilate, notionally impartial, were to handle such affairs.[3]

Based on such information, we could expect Roman prefects to prohibit any council or court at Jerusalem from doling out capital punishment after 6 CE. Perhaps they had this authority before that. John (18:29–32) clarifies this prohibition for its audience. When the chief priests petition Pilate to judge Jesus for being a criminal, he exhorts them to try Jesus in their own court. But they respond, "we cannot kill anyone [*apokteinai*]." Some suggest this phrasing, distinct from "we cannot put anyone to death [*thanatoun*]," communicates that the chief priests could enact capital punishment but considered it morally wrong for them to do so. It more probably points to how Roman authorities prohibited local courts from inflicting capital punishment. To do so would be extralegal murder. *The Scroll of the Fasts*, produced not long after the First Jewish Revolt, bears witness to how Roman magistrates prevented executions by local courts. In the Qumran sect, judges apparently claimed discretion over even capital matters, and they in theory could execute members without others being aware. But nothing supports that Roman governors knowingly accepted this. Councils at Jerusalem could perhaps execute non-Jews for entering the inner court of the Temple. Josephus even claims Roman authorities allowed Jewish leaders to exercise power in this matter. If true, the prefect presumably needed to be notified and to affirm each individual case. A council reportedly played a role in stoning Jesus' disciple Stephen. This is dubious, however (Chapter 11).[4]

In truth, capital cases were supposed to be referred to a Roman magistrate. Roman authorities allegedly intervened when the chief priests sought Paul's execution in Jerusalem during the 50s. The governor Albinus deposed a chief priest responsible for executing James, identified as the brother of Jesus by the surviving text of Josephus, in 62; he thought the council overstepped. A Greek intellectual reportedly reminded fellow citizens in Asia Minor to take capital cases to their governor. His statement implied that sometimes municipal courts invited their governor's wrath by taking them. Roman soldiers who committed crimes against Jews may had been transferred by Roman magistrates to the chief priests or a council for execution, but they were sentenced by Roman judges. A remarkable case shows a council did not ordinarily execute the accused but petitioned governors to try them. The governor Albinus convicted a man of sedition after "notable community members" seized him and had him lashed. But the governor had him scourged and released, not executed.

Even the stoning of the protomartyr Stephen plausibly happened under unique "extralegal" circumstances, assuming it happened at all (Acts 6:8–8:1;

Chapter 11). According to one theory, a council at Jerusalem had Stephen stoned or authorized it during a transition between prefects of Judaea, and the governor of Syria deposed the high priest Jonathan in 37 because of it. As mentioned, the governor Albinus deposed the chief priest after a council executed Jesus' brother James in 62. After 6 CE, Roman authorities usually expected a council not to pursue capital cases without their permission (though it may have done so anyway on occasion). Later rabbinic memories that the Romans stripped "the Sanhedrin" of its powers 40 years before the outbreak of the First Jewish Revolt are in principle correct, if chronologically imprecise. This is presumably why the Synoptic Gospels provide no corroboration for John's claim that Jesus intervened in the stoning of a sex worker, if it is authentic. When Jesus lived, a council at Jerusalem could not execute offenders. When one such council decided Jesus was liable for a capital charge, it had to petition Pilate's court.[5]

Jesus before a Synhedrion *at Jerusalem*

Before proceeding to Jesus' treatment by a council at Jerusalem, we must confront a serious question: Did Jesus appear before it at all? John does not report a trial or formal hearing. It recounts an interrogation by the former high priest Annas. The Synoptics portray what appears to be a formal trial. Mark and Matthew even seem to depict two gatherings, one on the night of Jesus' arrest and another the following morning. Some scholars harmonize the accounts while generally prioritizing Mark and infer many meetings of a *synhedrion* or a single protracted one. Others favor John's version or challenge altogether what the Gospels report. Passover week was very hectic, and in the Synoptics the chief priests would have just overseen a vast amount of Passover lamb and related sacrifices. They still had to tend to the Temple and rituals for the first day of the Feast of Unleavened Bread. Why would a council judge a capital case against Jesus when it could not execute? Would the chief priests really assemble a council so late at night and after the Passover feast? Could the Synoptics have invented the whole sequence for the purpose of character assassination?[6]

Later rabbinic texts arguably pose problems for the Gospel accounts. These formulate many rules for how "the Sanhedrin" was supposed to work. Among these, the Mishnah prohibits "the Sanhedrin" from holding meetings at night, especially for capital charges, and from tendering capital convictions on the Sabbath or festival days. If these mandates were active during Jesus' lifetime, then the Gospels portray Jewish legal authorities as breaking their

Jesus and "the Sanhedrin" 137

own rules. It is also unclear how the Gospels or their sources were informed about a hearing in which Jesus' followers were not present. This poses a serious problem and governs suspicions that the *synhedrion*'s hearing is the Gospels' invention. Another problem is the ostensible parallels between Mark's account and Josephus' reports of arrests, trials, and punishments doled out by chief priests or *synhedria* in the 50–60s. When a man named Jesus bar Ananias publicly predicted the Temple's destruction, he was arrested by the chief priests ("notable community members"), lashed, and turned over to the Roman magistrate. Mark could be imposing on Jesus' lifetime the sorts of legal or extralegal actions initiated by the chief priests decades later.[7]

Finally, Mark and the Synoptics are clearly recounting the actions of a council in pursuit of their own literary goals. These texts promote Jesus as a Messiah who predicted the Temple's destruction. In Mark's portrayal, Jesus famously communicates his Messianic, heaven-sent stature explicitly to people outside his inner circle for the first time. The Gospels also are bent on making the chief priests bear responsibility for Jesus' death by portraying them as maliciously assembling a court intent on a predetermined outcome. Scholars can debate whether calling Mark's portrayal "anti-Jewish" is anachronistic. Many Jesus Christ believers were Jews before and after 70. But like the other Gospels and Acts of the Apostles, it is clearly hostile to Jews who deny Jesus' Messianic stature. Whatever we think may have happened, the literary and theological goals of Mark and the other Gospels are obvious.[8]

Ultimately we must treat the words and deeds that the Gospels ascribe to the council as suspect. But we can accept that one was assembled, for various reasons. First, Mark does not state the name of the chief priest who oversaw the proceedings. It does not explicitly place Caiaphas, the man bearing the brunt of the ritual calendar, at the council's meeting. It also does not contradict John's claim that Annas was the main priestly official involved. After all, the term "high priest" could just as easily describe Annas as Caiaphas (Chapter 2). Moreover, the rituals of Passover presumably attracted all the priestly groups that maintained the Temple's rituals and sacrifices on weekly rotations during the year. Their number being in the many thousands, they had to manage the innards of many slaughtered lambs over a couple of hours. On the day of preparation for Passover, and Passover itself, we would expect the priests to be overwhelmingly present in Jerusalem and sharing the work, even if the incumbent high priest was overly taxed. Also, if we take Josephus at face value, we could easily arrive at an implausible number of lambs being slaughtered (250,000) and pilgrims accommodated (roughly 3 million). We should accept a council still could meet in Jerusalem and address critical

138   KILLING THE MESSIAH

matters. Many potential participants were already in Jerusalem for Passover. Presumably the chief priests and their allies could arrange a division of labor. Despite Mark and Matthew, we can dismiss the suggestion that all the priests and allied scribes attended Jesus' hearing or took him to Pilate the following morning. A hearing needed only a quorum. After that, only some petitioners and witnesses had to attend the trial before Pilate.[9]

Second, Jesus' prophecies of Jerusalem's destruction are consistent with predictions that other charismatic preachers were making in his lifetime (Chapters 3 and 6). They also cohere with aspects of Jesus' final days on which all Gospels agree: Jesus was posing as a Messianic figure, and Pilate subsequently mocked him as "King of the Jews." A rapid assembling of some chief priests and scribal elites to address the matter is credible. The rabbinic prohibitions on what "the Sanhedrin" could do represent what some Jews believed long after Jesus was dead. When Jesus lived, a council could assemble in haste at Jerusalem on the night of Passover without violating the scruples of many judges. Their views on piety and purity varied.[10]

Third, Jesus' supporters could have learned the gist of what happened at the council shortly after it occurred. The chief priests presumably reported to Pilate a version of what had happened and defended it against subsequent criticisms. The basics would have circulated. Mark reports that various people had also gathered in the courtyard of the high priest's house while a *synhedrion* had apparently assembled in one of the nearby rooms. Most were the chief priests' supporters. But people who were more neutral or at least willing to perform acts of decency for Jesus or his followers were there. The Synoptics' treatment of Joseph of Arimathea hints at people like this. The Gospels even claim that one close follower of Jesus was in the courtyard to acquire information for most of the night, until a rooster crowed the following morning. This was Simon Peter. Mark plausibly reports basic knowledge that circulated among Jesus' followers, even if reworking it. We can doubt the dialogue happened as reported, but its gist of what the council accomplished is credible.[11]

Fourth, parallels between Mark's account and Josephus' reports of actions taken by the chief priests or councils in the 50s–60s probably reflect practices that occurred at Jerusalem during Jesus' lifetime. Jerusalem's royal or priestly elite customarily summoned an advisory *synhedrion* to assess serious criminal affairs, their participants being somewhat flexible. According to Josephus, whose source is unclear, Herod's early career risked being cut short when his opponents objected to his executing brigands as governor of Galilee without a council's hearing. Hyrcanus II, both chief priest and king, assembled a council to assess Herod's conduct. Herod reportedly summoned a *synhedrion* for

Jesus and "the Sanhedrin"

capital cases many times, even if each was populated by people prone to comply with his goals. After 6 CE, high priests could assemble councils at their discretion.[12]

Finally, the Synoptics arguably do not recount a trial of Jesus or a formal conviction before a *synhedrion* at all. What the Synoptics portray is a hearing and interrogation to determine whether Jesus should be deemed liable for a capital charge before Pilate. When its members "judged" Jesus liable for death (Mark 14:64: *enochon einai thanatou*), they were deeming him worthy of a capital charge before the Roman magistrate. The next morning, some of its members gathered to take Jesus to Pilate and serve as petitioners or witnesses, and this event was misleadingly treated by Mark as a second assembling. We know a council sometimes assembled to determine the liability of defendants before bringing them to trial before the prefect (if not whipping or illicitly executing them). As mentioned, Josephus points to such a procedure for a man who publicly proclaimed Jerusalem's destruction right before the First Jewish Revolt.[13]

But where did Jesus' hearing before a *synhedrion* at Jerusalem take place? The Gospels vary in their reports. Matthew (26:57) places Jesus at the house of Caiaphas, the high priest. Mark (14:53) and Luke (22:54) refer to the high priest without naming him. Many surmise the other Synoptics refer to Caiaphas. It would have been at Caiaphas' courtyard house that Simon Peter, who had followed the arresting party, allegedly denied knowing Jesus three times. But John (18:13–14, 24) places Jesus first at the house of Annas, the father-in-law of Caiaphas. The accusers then bring him to Caiaphas, who is presumably nearby, later that night or the following morning. At Annas' house, he is interrogated by a "high priest" (*archiereus*). It is there that John places Simon Peter's denials of Jesus. At first glance, John is hard to reconcile with the Synoptic Gospels. They seem to differ regarding where a council met for Jesus' hearing.

In truth, the unnamed high priest of Mark and Luke is probably Annas. Matthew assumed it would have been Caiaphas and rewrote the sequence accordingly. During Passover week, Caiaphas, the incumbent high priest, faced a massive burden on his time and energy. Foremost responsible for executing and managing Temple ritual, he could not easily conduct a hearing late at night. His father-in-law, Annas, an influential figure, had more flexibility. Just as important, he had the social authority in the eyes of Jerusalem's priestly and scribal elite. The high priest from 6 to 15 CE, he had retained the title long after his deposition by the Romans (Chapter 2). Like other priests and chief priests, he had certain official duties during Passover week. But Caiaphas bore the brunt. As such, Caiaphas was probably not even present. John makes no mention of his being at the hearing. Instead, it describes Jesus as being transported from Annas to Caiaphas afterward. This is consistent with the Synoptic Gospels, which report a meeting of some priests the morning after Jesus' hearing.[14]

As John attests, Jesus was brought in bonds to the house of Annas on the same night that he helped execute Jesus' arrest. It was there that a *synhedrion* was assembling. But where were the houses of Annas and Caiaphas, which were surely close (if not in the same complex)? Specific locations elude us. But by this period, the western hill, especially the Upper City, had overwhelmingly become the residential area for Jerusalem's elite. Being in proximity to the Temple Mount, it housed Hasmonaean and Herodian palaces and was near where Pilate kept his headquarters. On the night of his arrest, we can place Jesus in detainment there (Map 6.1 and Figure 1.4 and Figure 10.2).[15]

Ultimately, we can doubt whether the council's hearing happened as the Gospels report. But we can surmise that one assembled and conducted an inquiry into Jesus' alleged Messianic posturing at the Temple precinct. The chief priests and allied scribes were to determine whether his behavior warranted a capital charge. By doing so, they were fulfilling a serious obligation to pilgrims who sacrificed at the Temple precinct during Passover week.

Jesus' Hearing

Despite discrepancies, the Synoptic Gospels are fairly uniform in communicating what occurred at Jesus' hearing before a *synhedrion*. But they probably contrived much of what its parties reportedly said and did for theological purposes. Some of the most important priests, elders, and scribes were present. But Mark overstates when placing *all* of them there. Mark claims that the petitioners lacked witnesses who could corroborate most accusations. Some reportedly alleged that he had promised to destroy the Temple built by human hands and rebuild it in three days. But since this distorted what Jesus reportedly stated at the Temple precinct, the witnesses disagreed on what exactly he had said. When asked to respond, Jesus was silent. This entire episode is vulnerable to suspicion of being a Markan invention. It aligns too conveniently with the text's overall theology and makes Jesus appear to predict the Temple's destruction in 70. Even so, it also may reflect how Jesus' opponents were misconstruing his prediction of how God's imminent reign would destroy or replace the Temple (Chapter 6).[16]

Jesus and "the Sanhedrin"

Whatever Jesus had said about the Temple, Mark states that he had another serious problem. According to the Synoptics, the chief priest asked Jesus whether he was the Messiah, the son of "the Blessed One." Jesus' contemporaries did not call God "the Blessed One" in their own language. This reflects Mark's emphasis on Jesus' divinely appointed agency and, perhaps, its Greek rendering of an effort to avoid uttering the Hebrew tetragrammaton. It also calls to mind the Messiah and Son of God celebrated by 2 Samuel (7:12–16). According to Mark (14:61–62), Jesus responded, "I am." Since this represents when Mark first portrays Jesus as unambiguously claiming to be the Messiah, some prefer the phrasing of Matthew and Luke: "You say that I am." Then, referencing Daniel 7:13 and Psalms 110:1, Jesus reportedly predicted, "'you will see the Son of Man' seated at the right hand of Power and 'coming with the clouds of Heaven.'" This communicated that he was a divinely appointed Messiah. The concepts of Son of Man, Son of God, and Messiah had considerable overlap among Jesus' contemporaries. They could all refer to a divinely appointed agent who proclaimed an imminent reign of God. But the phrase "Son of Man" could also denote a figure who would return from heaven when the reign of God came. Mark basically indicates that Jesus quoted Daniel to claim that he was such a Messianic figure. In response, the high priest claimed that Jesus had committed blasphemy and tore his garments. When he solicited a decision from the council, all its members judged Jesus "to be liable for death." They deemed him worthy of a capital charge and reportedly began to strike and batter him (Mark 14:62–65; Matt 26:67–68).[17]

As stated, we should be skeptical of Mark's account in all its particulars. But if we accept that any such exchanges happened, what did the council define as blasphemy? Uttering the Divine Name warranted it. But arguments that Jesus blasphemously intoned it while responding to the judges fall short (Mark 14:62; Matt 26:64). Messianic claims were not blasphemous either, even if Sadducees were hostile to them. Since the Greek term for "blasphemy" generally means "insult," maybe the judges found Jesus' statement insulting (not blasphemous). The council also conceivably deemed it blasphemous for someone to claim powers held only by God. A rabbi recorded by the Jerusalem Talmud declared that a person who claimed to be the "Son of Man" was trafficking in blasphemy. This perhaps refers to Jesus himself, or his portrayals by the Gospels. At least, it hints that the council would have seen Jesus' claim of being a heavenly Son of Man as encroaching on God's divinity.[18]

Some texts state that Jesus, acting as a false prophet, was accused by his adversaries of "deceiving" or "seducing" people into false beliefs. These include various Gospels and early Christian writings. Even Lucian, a second-century

Syrian polytheist, implies that Jesus was executed because of his powers of deceit. His statement is consistent with what contemporary Christian authors say. Various texts accuse Jesus of being a sorcerer too. Starting in the second century, Christian sources sometimes blame contemporary Jews for emphasizing such claims of deception and sorcery. These receive elaboration in later rabbinic works and a tale of Jesus' life (the *Toledot Yeshu*) that parodies Gospel material. The *Toledot Yeshu* even accuses Jesus of stealing the name of God from the Jewish Temple and various other misdeeds before being tried by sages and Pilate, stoned, and hanged from a tree. For the later rabbis, deception on sacred matters (being a *mesit* or *maddiah*) and sorcery were capital offences. Jesus' opponents reportedly responded to his preaching and reputation for miracles in such terms, and some Jews may have done so polemically in the generations after his death. Scholars sometimes surmise that deception, or even sorcery, was part of the formal charges at the *synhedrion*'s hearing. Yet nothing from the Gospels indicates this. The claims of the chief priests that Jesus was a "deceiver" of crowds were, if anything, pertinent to their charges of sedition before Pilate (Chapters 9–10).[19]

As noted, John (18:19–24) differs markedly from the Synoptics in describing Jesus' hearing. It suggests that no formal hearing happened at all. Instead, the "high priest" Annas questioned Jesus about his teachings, and Jesus was noncompliant. Even so, John has apparently taken material from the account of the *synhedrion*'s hearing by Mark or a common source and moved it to earlier parts of Jesus' ministry, while adding its own creative layers. For example, John depicts Jesus as being accused by "Jews" of claiming to be the Messiah while making one of his pilgrimages to the Jewish Temple (10:22–39). When he responds by claiming to be the Son of God, they try to arrest and stone him for blasphemy. John's portrayal of such an accusation is consistent with Mark's version of Jesus' hearing.[20]

We have already communicated that the Gospel accounts of what was said and done when the council convened are suspect. They have the goal of casting the chief priests and allied scribes in the worst possible light. But whatever happened, we should emphasize again that the council was assessing Jesus' liability for a capital charge before Pilate. It was not overseeing a formal trial and conviction for blasphemous or sacrilegious acts. Jesus reportedly did not deny any of the accusations made at the hearing. If true, this affirmed for the council's members that his confrontational posturing as a Messiah at the Temple precinct was incendiary. It could incite serious crowd violence and endanger innocent pilgrims. They deemed him liable for a capital charge and prepared to take him to Pilate and petition his court. Whatever their personal motives were, the chief priests were fulfilling a serious

Jesus and "the Sanhedrin"

obligation to Jewish worshipers, Jesus' compatriots. They were confirming the liability of someone who was known to have seriously compromised the safety of people worshiping at the Temple.

In Mark and Matthew, the hearing happens on the same night that Jesus is arrested, after the Passover feast and right when the Feast of Unleavened Bread is starting. Some of its participants reassemble the next morning to bring Jesus to Pilate. Luke (22:66) offers a somewhat different version. It places the hearing of a council on the morning after Jesus' arrest, and from there it brings Jesus directly to Pilate. Luke apparently combines into one meeting what Mark and Matthew record as two. If Annas was the unnamed high priest who oversaw Jesus' condemnation in Mark, that would mean the council had assembled at Annas' house to hold a hearing about Jesus' liability. The following morning, some members of the council gathered to take Jesus to Pilate for trial, but Mark misleadingly treats this as a second formal assembling of the council. Some men who served as Jesus' judges were now acting as petitioners of Pilate's court. After all, they had witnessed the council's proceedings.[21]

The Gospels claim that a serious conflict of interest was in play at Jesus' council hearing. The people judging Jesus had motive to eliminate him. What the Gospels do not state is that the chief priests were fulfilling an obligation to their compatriots and to Roman authority by making an arrest and assessing liability. They do not acknowledge that the chief priests were protecting innocent pilgrims. Even so, we can note some parallels with John the Baptizer's execution by Antipas. Antipas too stood to benefit from John's death. But there is one critical distinction: Herod Antipas' ability to execute John after essentially acting as both prosecution and judge was accepted by Roman authority. A council at Jerusalem did not have the same discretion. It could deem Jesus liable for a capital charge before a prefect. It could not formally try and execute him for one. We have seen how Roman authorities took measures to prevent capital charges from being enacted in their provincial territories in such situations. In other words, even though client kings like Antipas could act on their own conflicts of interest in capital matters, the local courts of ethnic communities in provincial space could not. The Roman governor was to arbitrate. Ultimately, the one advantage that Jesus had over John the Baptizer was that a council did not have license to kill. Its members had to petition their prefect and try Jesus at his court. But to Jesus' misfortune, he ended up crossing paths with a judge who thought his conduct was a capital crime worthy of crucifixion. This was Pontius Pilate.

9

Pilate and Sedition

Marveling at [the Jews'] strength in guarding their laws,
Pilate immediately returned the likenesses [of the emperor
Tiberius] from Jerusalem to Caesarea.

—JOSEPHUS, *Ant.* 18.59

The soldiers landed blows much greater than what Pilate
ordered, and they did not handle gently those who had
clamored with fair measure and were not behaving
violently. The result was that many who were caught
unarmed by men attacking them by design ended up dying
that way, and the rest ran away wounded. So the sedition
ceased.

—JOSEPHUS, *Ant.* 18.62

ACCORDING TO THE Gospels, Pilate did not seek out Jesus. The chief priests and allied scribes organized his arrest and brought him to their prefect, who was in Jerusalem for Passover. But they could not stone him. Roman prefects had authority over capital cases, and the chief priests were petitioners, not judges. As we have seen, a passage from Josephus (*Ant.* 18.63–64) corroborates this testimony, despite its controversial stature. Pilate condemned Jesus on an "indictment [*endeixis*] from the foremost men among us" at Jerusalem (Chapter 7; Appendix 2). Having arrested Jesus, the chief priests had petitioned Pilate's court on a capital charge. Pilate handled such cases. They did not.

Roman judges had tremendous power. Their verdicts had serious consequences. But their petitioners could also be persuasive. They could exploit prior edicts and courtroom decisions to forge legal pathways attractive to judges. They could create situations that made it awkward for governors to rule against them, even if their decisions defied easy prediction. In Judaea,

Roman magistrates thought of the chief priests and scribes as experts in their compatriots' behaviors. They played a key role in communicating to Pilate what words or deeds could incite outbreaks of violence, sedition, or crowd disturbance. They had a huge advantage over Jesus.

Yet Pilate had an agency of his own. He had to decide whether Jesus was guilty and deserved to die. We know he had Jesus crucified. But why? What was Pilate's legal path to condemning Jesus? Did he have one? Various Gospel accounts claim Pilate knowingly killed a guiltless man. Some surmise that he condemned Jesus just to accommodate the chief priests or attending crowd. The chief priests were important, and judges were sometimes swayed by crowds at public trials (though emperors and jurists disapproved). In other words, Pilate had personal motives for having Jesus executed, but a very weak legal basis.[1]

Pilate undoubtedly had personal motives for crucifying Jesus. But we can suspect he had criteria for believing Jesus to be seditionist, even if these were molded by his relationship with the chief priests. Before proceeding to Jesus' trial and Pilate's judgment (Chapter 10), we must examine the agency of governors like Pilate and petitioners like the chief priests. After all, their entanglement with one another killed Jesus. But how did Pilate and Roman prefects in Judaea identify criminal behavior like sedition? How did their relationship with the chief priests affect their understanding? Did prefects define it consistently or with variation? Above all, what does Pilate's pattern of violence as prefect tell us about how he understood it?

Petitioners and Roman Authority: The Example of Babatha

When the chief priests petitioned Pilate, they had advantages over Jesus. A *synhedrion* at Jerusalem had found him worthy of a capital charge, which carried some weight. Pilate also thought of them as experts in the politics of Jerusalem's Temple. The petitioners were arguing that Jesus had committed a criminal deed that warranted death. They were even perhaps nudging him to expand his parameters for what criminal activity was. But how would they do this?

Here the legal activity of Babatha is again instructive. In 124, nearly a century after Jesus' trial, Babatha had a problem. She needed guardians to manage the property of her son after her first husband had died. They were to ensure his proper maintenance from the revenue that the property generated. After all, anyone else she married could abuse her son's assets. The origins of this legal practice are hard to trace. Different societies had their own mechanisms for guardianship. Jewish, Nabataean, Greek, and even Roman roots

146

KILLING THE MESSIAH

are plausible. Even so, the precise origins may not matter. Different legal systems were not isolated. They cross-pollinated, and litigants may not have distinguished among them. In truth, petitioners pressed judges to consider different legal traditions in their decisions about justice. They even prompted judges to reconsider what was authorized by Roman law itself, sometimes despite what statutes and jurists had already declared.[2]

In turn, Roman authorities, not being professional jurists, did not just impose legal concepts on provincials. Aided by their advisers and local legal experts, they worked with what petitioners provided in defense of their own interests. Loosely bound by standing statutes, they could give wide scope to their own worldviews, which petitioners could work to reshape. Given their limited knowledge, we must account for how judges, with their biases as wealthy humans, could be persuaded by petitioners about what was legal or criminal. This made courts and the outcomes of cases into arenas of uncertainty and opportunity, a situation that Babatha tried to leverage. In Roman Egypt, where surviving papyri texts abound, the accretive petitioning of litigants undoubtedly shaped how judges made legal decisions over time.[3]

In truth, the petitioning of Roman provincials like Babatha had a serious impact on legal frameworks in which governors operated. They imparted to judges their own views. Aided by their advisers, judges would then decide whether their views were valid, and perhaps legitimize their future use. But whatever judges decided, they were responding to viewpoints more or less in terms that the litigants had set. Petitioners often communicated (with biases) to Roman judges what their local traditions and precedents were. They also cited previous rulings that Roman judges had made. They shaped what judges knew about legal precedent, often in the absence of regulatory statutes. When combined with the biases and perceptions of judges, such factors created the potential for a vast spectrum of outcomes and determined individual verdicts.[4]

Ultimately Pilate's petitioners helped forge a legal path for him to convict Jesus of a serious crime (Chapter 10). We can surmise that they earnestly believed he had committed one, even if the Gospels treat it as mere pretext. Pilate found the chief priests compelling. But how did he define criminal activity, and what were his powers as prefect in suppressing it?

Governors as Judges

As an equestrian prefect, Pilate was something of a middle magistrate. He governed the district of Judaea, located in the province of Syria. Since he was subordinate to the consular governor of Syria, some even object to calling him a governor. Even so, he had *imperium* (governing authority) in his district. Most surviving testimonies from Roman jurists can be traced to the third century, centuries after Pilate had Jesus executed. But when combined with surviving papyri and inscriptions, we can define his coercive powers as governor and judge.

Proconsular governors were the senior judges in their provinces. Embodying authority there superseded only by the emperor, they could inflict capital punishment even on Roman citizens (*ius gladii*) and issue edicts with legal force. During policing action they could kill people who were visibly engaging in insurrection, brigandage, or rioting without a legal conviction, if doing so would secure peace. When Jesus lived, the governor of Syria had such power in the Roman Levant. As prefect of Judaea, Pilate answered to him.[5]

Whether subordinate magistrates had similar powers in their regions is more ambiguous. Client kings like Antipas surely did. We know that equestrian prefects like Pilate sometimes acquired such powers from the emperor. At least some equestrian officials could execute convicts. The equestrian prefect of Egypt implemented this power in 185. Other equestrian officials put Christians to death (Chapter 11). Prefects of Judaea had this authority. Given Pilate's authority to implement repressive violence in Judaea, we can reasonably describe him as governor of his district.[6]

In Pilate's lifetime, governors had some guidelines for their legal decisions. Laws and statutes had been issued by the emperor or Roman Senate or, further in the past, by republican voting assemblies. Yet many phenomena were not regulated by laws and statutes, and governors needed other legal means. Some provinces had been assigned a "law of the province" (*lex provinciae*). This in theory defined what types of cases a provincial governor would normally judge. In Bithynia it regulated who was eligible for citizenship in cities. The testimony of one of its governors in c. 110, Pliny the Younger, tells us so.

Emperors usually conferred *mandata* upon governors as they embarked for their provinces or districts. These addressed protocols and issues not regulated by standing laws. Governors seeking further direction could write letters to emperors and await responses. Slow technologies of movement could make this undesirable. The senator Pliny, just mentioned, famously published letters he exchanged with the emperor Trajan when he governed Bithynia. In them, Pliny mentions his *mandata* many times. At Hama in Syria, an inscription records guidelines imparted by the emperor Domitian to a procurator. He commands that no one (including soldiers) seize the labor of animals or people without the emperor's approval. His directives were either part of the procurator's *mandata* or from a letter that Domitian sent to him subsequently.

148   KILLING THE MESSIAH

But within such guidelines, governors like Pilate had massive discretionary authority. One weapon in their legal arsenal was the power to issue edicts. Josephus claims that the first prefect of Judaea had "every power." Pilate surely could issue edicts too. Governors sometimes inherited from their predecessors an edict outlining a broad legal framework for judging cases. These were generally consistent in a province. But they could differ among provinces, and governors could always revise their province's edict. A famous example comes from Babatha's documents. Three of them, copies of one another, apparently recorded an edict of the governor of Arabia. It regulated when judges should convict guardians of violating their obligations and what the penalties should be. It famously resembles a formula recorded by the jurist Gaius. A papyrus from Egypt contains an edict issued by a prefect. It specifies that he was to judge cases related to murder, brigandage, armed violence, and other crimes and civil infractions. The rest were to be judged by local courts, unless appealed to him. In a third-century text, a public intellectual in Smyrna (modern Izmer, Turkey) advises citizens to take criminal or capital affairs to the governor. His advice was precisely what governors mandated. A papyrus from the same period assumes that capital cases were handled by governors. Accounts of the trials of Christians do too, even if municipal authorities made the arrest (Chapter 11).[7]

Governors also issued edicts to address specific problems as they arose. Such edicts pertained only so long as the governors who issued them held office. Despite consistencies, a governor's edicts could differ from those of predecessors, successors, or other contemporary governors in critical ways. When a region changed governors, its population could encounter shifts in legal practices. Unfortunately, Pilate's edicts and those of most governors do not survive. But we can surmise that he circulated them and that the chief priests were familiar with them. They presumably stated that any capital cases had to be tried at his court. We have seen how prefects of Judaea normally expected this.

A famous example of a governor's edict involves circumcision. Romans mostly deemed the practice abhorrent. Jurists classified it as genital mutilation, if a mild form. Its punishments were to be consistent with those for castration. By the mid-second century, Roman emperors had issued a rescript permitting Jews to do it for their sons. This indicates that a general ban had been issued by then. Before that, Jews practiced it with little state intervention. Even so, around 130 a Roman governor named Tineius Rufus apparently imposed restrictions or at least convicted and punished some so accused. His main concern may have been the circumcision of the enslaved. But his restrictions were remembered as a universal ban on circumcision or genital mutilation by later rabbinic sources and Latin historiography, even though it was neither. The relationship between any circumcision ban and the Bar Kochba Revolt of 132–135 is still debated.[8]

Because of their overwhelming authority, governors operated with a vast scope for uncertainty and initiative in their decision-making. They often found themselves judging matters not clearly addressed by Roman statutes or *mandata*. Governors could defer to the legal practices of local communities, something that Roman jurists noted. From Egyptian papyri, we know that Roman judges sometimes sought advice from Greek or Egyptian experts or tendered verdicts according to their understanding of provincial legal traditions. The Jerusalem Talmud reports how a woman petitioned the provincial governor after rabbis judged in her disfavor. Babatha kept documents written in Aramaic and inspired by local legal customs; she apparently believed them actionable in Roman courts.[9]

For such reasons, we know that governors could base their decisions on provincial customs and even the desires of influential petitioners. Could Pilate have been motivated by them in capital cases? Some posit that Pilate executed Jesus because a council that the chief priests convened at Jerusalem found him blasphemous. Jesus had not broken any Roman laws or done anything that Romans normally deemed criminal. But Pilate had upheld Jewish custom and accommodated the chief priests and Jewish legal experts. One variation even casts Pilate as an incompetent governor who had needlessly alienated the chief priests. To win them over again, he allowed them to corner him into having Jesus executed. In other formulations, Pilate convicted Jesus of treason or sedition because his eccentric regal claims provided a convenient pretext for conviction. Pilate did not want to oppose the chief priests or the crowd supporting them. He also was taking precautions to prevent Jesus' reputation as "King of the Jews" from inciting social turbulence, independently of his intentions or acts during Passover week. The common factor in all such theories is that Pilate did not deem Jesus criminally guilty of anything but convicted and executed him as a criminal anyway, for his own expedience. The chief priests were more important to him politically than Jesus was, and though innocent, Jesus was worth killing to prevent any possible crowd violence or rioting. We know that some governors knowingly but illicitly convicted innocent people in exchange for bribes. We have witnessed how crowds could sway judges. Possibly Pilate had Jesus executed without believing him guilty of a capital crime. After all, this is what the Gospels claim he did anyhow.[10]

Even so, we can disregard claims that Pilate simply sanctioned a council's conviction, deferred to Jewish law, or caved to political pressure from the chief priests and attending crowds. A council at Jerusalem had not convicted Jesus of any crime at all (Chapter 8). Councils were no longer permitted by Roman authorities to judge capital cases. When Jesus was arrested, the council assembled to assess his liability for a capital charge before a Roman judge. It was not formally convicting him of any crime. There was no conviction for Pilate to uphold in the first place.

In a similar vein, governors often dismissed local legal customs that Romans deemed excessively harsh and sought mitigating advice from their own legal advisers on serious matters. They usually had free defendants convicted of minor infractions beaten with rods. This was also the only punishment inflicted without a trial. Governors and jurists found whipping, let alone execution, too harsh for free men not convicted of an egregious crime. As for crucifixion, they resorted to it to punish sedition and other criminal acts defined as heinous by Roman Italian standards. They conceived of crucifixion as among the most horrific methods of execution, consistent with burning someone alive and even worse than beheading or consignment to mines. All the people Josephus reports being crucified by Roman authorities in first-century Judaea had been sentenced as brigands and insurgents. As governor of Syria (7–4 BCE), Varus inflicted the punishment on 2,000 insurrectionists. In the 40s–50s, magistrates crucified the rebellious sons of Judas the Galilean and the followers of a brigand leader named Eleazer. Right before the First Jewish Revolt, the governor Florus treated a social disturbance that happened in Jerusalem when he took ample sums from the Temple as a general rebellion. He massacred and crucified many civilians, some being of equestrian rank and entitled to appeal to the emperor. Florus undoubtedly abused his power, but his pretext was that he was suppressing an insurrection. Josephus otherwise never indicates that governors crucified people because they had violated local customs or had offended the sensibilities of the chief priests while otherwise being innocent. One reason why Roman prefects prohibited councils at Jerusalem from conducting most capital cases was to prevent this. Governors did execute people convicted of acts of sacrilege, but for them, this involved robbing temples. Jesus did not stand accused of this at all. If the chief priests saw Jesus' posturing as a heavenly "Son of Man" as blasphemous (Chapter 8), it was not sacrilegious by Roman legal standards. To crucify a freeborn man just because his compatriots thought him blasphemous would have offended many Roman governors and jurists. For them, it would have been a visibly violent abuse of power, not justice.[11]

Pilate and Sedition 151

Roman governors were likewise expected by their emperor and superiors to engage in violence needed for keeping peace in the province, no more and no less. Because of their vast scope for identifying and suppressing criminal behavior, ancient and modern sources often treat governors as having a whimsical temperament, a limitless capacity for violent behavior, and little accountability for it. There is some truth in that. Governors could kill people visibly engaged in acts of insurrection, brigandage, or rioting without trying them, if it was necessary for preserving peace. They also had ample grounds for convicting people of criminal behavior and executing them accordingly. Some governors abused their discretionary authority. Tacitus criticizes the governor Felix, notably a judge of the apostle Paul, for his "king-like rule" (*regium ius*). He reportedly imprisoned Paul for two years for dubious reasons. During the lifetime of Jesus and Pilate, a governor in Anatolia named Volesus notoriously executed hundreds of provincials in a single day while posturing as a king. Shortly after Pilate had Jesus crucified, a governor in Egypt named Flaccus classified Jews as seditious without any provocation and had them massacred without a trial. In turn, bringing charges against corrupt violent governors or securing their recall could be very difficult. These often had the means and motives to prevent such measures, which could involve travel to the court of a more senior governor or emperor. Flaccus prevented people from leaving his province to report his corrupt violence. Pilate was known for what provincials like Philo defined as excessive, unjust violence.[12]

Even so, violent governors risked serious consequences if they executed or slaughtered provincials in ways that influential senators, equestrians, or provincial elites deemed unjust or unnecessary. The "kinglike" Volesus just mentioned was condemned and exiled by the Senate for his actions. In Judaea, both Cumanus and Felix faced recall and trial for actions involving bribery and excessive violence during the 50s. After abusing his power in a murderous orgy of unaccountability, Flaccus was arrested in Egypt, brought to Rome, tried, and exiled (and later executed). A governor could never truly know whether excessive cruelty would lead to serious consequences after leaving office or being removed. One reason Pliny wrote to Trajan to seek further guidance about his treatment of Christians was so that he would not expose himself to such consequences. He had already executed some, only to discover that they had committed no criminal misdeeds (other than being Christians), and his actions had encouraged further accusations, often made anonymously. He realized that he risked overstepping and sought the emperor's sanction for his prior acts of violence and others that he might commit. Pliny knew that governors were sometimes punished for unjust convictions and executions. He was aware that a reputation for excessive violence affected the outcomes of extortion trials. Pilate had a proclivity for violence, and the Gospels maintain that the chief priests did apply pressure to have Jesus executed. But we can expect that Pilate would have avoided killing a detained man he did not think had committed a crime. Doing so exposed him to serious consequences.[13]

Such considerations lead to the following questions: Would Pilate have executed Jesus because of a council's recommendation? Would he have imposed a manner of death typically allotted to violent, seditious criminals even without deeming him one? The Gospels' claim that Pilate had Jesus scourged and then executed by crucifixion between two known "brigands" (*leistai*) supports that he was not responding to a charge of blasphemy, as Jews defined it. Pilate must have convicted Jesus of something else, something that some Roman governors defined as seriously criminal behavior. If so, it was not foremost because Jesus' reportedly "royal" aspirations provided a convenient pretext. Pilate must have seen something criminal in what was otherwise the bizarre regal posturing of an eccentric preacher with a dozen or so core followers. He was not just doing a favor for the chief priests or taking a precaution that could prevent a civil disturbance. Instead, the chief priests were arguing that Jesus' behavior made him criminally responsible for endangering innocent people. They had to intervene. Pilate believed they were right.[14]

Roman Governors and Seditious Behavior

Pilate did not have Jesus killed just to satisfy the chief priests. But the chief priests still affected his decision-making. They were petitioners of Pilate's court who were charging Jesus with criminal behavior. For Pilate, these were the most legitimate political authorities and legal experts at Jerusalem. He valued their assessment of social conflicts there. No doubt the chief priests and Pilate could and did sometimes find themselves at odds. But they also represented the established order of governance and wealth in Judaea. Their interests were generally aligned, and they were by necessity political allies (if uneasy ones). These factors raise an obvious question: What role did the chief priests play in how Pilate understood criminal behavior?[15]

Being senior magistrates, Roman governors and their courts often attracted petitioners. Their decisions superseded those of local courts too. Roman laws and edicts usually assigned serious criminal charges and punishments to governors and restricted local courts from intervening. But governors were sometimes harder to access. One had to travel to where they had their headquarters or wait for their periodic journeys through the province

Pilate and Sedition

(assuming Pilate made them). Even then, time and resources were limited. Governors were swamped with petitions and cases. They could hear hundreds in just hours. Given the demands on their attention and time, they could reject a case or solicit another court to take it. Provincials could petition their governor, but they could not ensure his attention. He, his counsel, and his troops were typically dealing with more urgent matters. We do not know whether Jewish provincials in Judaea often brought their own affairs to the courts of prefects like Pilate. But either way, we could expect that Pilate's attention was devoted to maintaining peace and addressing criminal concerns during Passover week in Jerusalem.[16]

Petitioners were not alone in facing complications. Despite their overwhelming power, governors faced them too. Some cases could involve their political connections. This created a real potential for conflicts of interest, despite pretenses of neutrality. Sometimes local courts asserted competencies only governors were supposed to have. This could create awkward situations. Governors also had to judge social phenomena not addressed by standing statutes or widely known precedents. They often operated without clear guidelines, so that much was left to their discretion. As papyri from Egypt show, they tendered verdicts based on their (incomplete) understanding of Roman and local legal precedents, their own moral biases, and their political desires. This is precisely why petitioners who were expert in local politics, familiar with their governor, or adept at creating persuasive legal pathways had a unique advantage. When Pilate became governor of Judaea, this was the legal world he had to navigate.[17]

Such factors meant that Roman governors and judges could have different views on criminal behavior. Sedition and insurrection are cases in point. These were indisputably criminal and punishable by laws against treason and public violence. Their punishments were fairly standard and horrifically severe. Yet even if some acts obviously were sedition, the Romans did not have a comprehensive definition of what it was. It could depend on the perceptions of governors. Moreover, their judgments and acts of violence were expected be what was needed to maintain order and to punish criminal behavior. But what was needed, and what governors defined as criminal, could vary in different places. As they navigated unfamiliar cultures, how governors understood seditious behavior could be shaped by local elites or their courtroom petitioners. In Jesus' case, the petitioners *were* the chief priests.

By the time of Jesus and Pilate, Roman authorities understood sedition as any volatile course of action forbidden by laws against treason or violence, especially when committed by people who did not have Roman citizenship. It was primarily how Roman prefects in Judaea classified social disturbance and justified many of their violent measures. One of a Roman governor's most important tasks was to classify which activities were seditious and to suppress them. Since they embodied the biases of propertied people, they tended to see as seditious any action or person that could upset governing authority and its ordering of (landed) wealth. In practice, the activity of insurrectionists, brigands, and preachers promoting social disturbance could be motivated by the misconduct of the powerful or the rich. But even if the accused genuinely sought justice or relief from poverty for their communities, Roman governors dismissed them as "evil men" engaged in grotesque criminal conduct. Surviving source material from the Roman Empire, include Josephus' writings, overwhelmingly replicates this vantage point.[18]

In response to seditious behavior, governors could inflict mass violence or execute offenders. Sometimes they even did this without courtroom proceedings. When during policing actions they encountered people visibly engaging in violence or seditious activity, they could kill them right then (or immediately after). Otherwise, alleged offenders were supposed to be put on trial. Yet a key problem was that seditious behavior could be hard to define, and governors often had to identify which actions were criminal or seditious without written statutes. Some actions were certainly seditious in the eyes of all Roman governors. Organizing an armed uprising against Roman authorities or their local allies was an obvious example. But some actions did not obviously fit a universal category of seditious behavior. What if a man and his unarmed followers made incendiary statements in a volatile public space? What if their statements or actions could incite violence? Was this sedition? Not all Roman authorities agreed it was.[19]

By the Roman period, many actions could be deemed seditious enough to warrant criminal charges. Few were explicitly forbidden by written statues. Any activity that could undermine the present order of governance and wealth could be classified as seditious by Roman governors, and at their discretion. For them sedition included acts of violence in cities' public spaces. By Jesus' time a law against "assassins" prohibited people from appearing in public armed. This posed a challenge to both Roman authority and municipal governance, even if no violence broke out. Otherwise, acts of sedition, however defined, were clearly prohibited by this law. In Mark (15:7), Barabbas is among the men Pilate convicted of violently engaging in sedition. He had essentially violated the statutes just described.[20]

Of course, sedition was rural too. We have seen how Jesus' Galilee experienced disparities of wealth that could inspire it. Brigandage outside cities was

Pilate and Sedition

prohibited by laws against violence and treason. Roman jurists understood that suppressing bandits or brigands (*latrones* in Latin, *leistai* in Greek), along with other "evil men," was among their primary tasks. Such figures operated (primarily) outside cities and the force of law. Even if they were responding to unjust conditions, Roman and municipal authorities deemed them the scourge of the countryside and cooperated to eliminate them. The two men Pilate crucified with Jesus are identified as brigands by some Synoptics (Mark 15:27; Matt 27:38). When Jesus is arrested in the Gospels, he protests that he is being treated like a brigand accosted by armed men at night.

In other words, organized armed violence in cities and rural areas was indisputably seditious as far as Roman magistrates were concerned. Its culprits were to be tried and normally executed. Roman jurists also believed that people who promoted acts of mass violence were liable. They could be justifiably punished by crucifixion or being thrown to beasts. But there were ambiguities. Did intent matter? What if someone said or did something incendiary before a crowd without intending to foment violence? What if violence broke out anyway? What if it did not? Also, did the potential for crowd violence matter? What if someone said or did something that arguably *could* have led to crowd disturbance? What if no violent outbreak had (yet) occurred? No surviving statute or jurist statement addresses this concretely.

This means that criminal sedition could occupy a vast scope. Roman legal perspectives did not restrict culpability to those who had engineered a civil disturbance. Magistrates could deem culpable anyone whose words or deeds could foreseeably incite violence. It was the charge of governors to rid their province of "evil men." These were any people whose conduct could inspire social disorder. Murderers, bandits, and insurrectionists obviously fit the description. But much depended on the perceptions or motives of individual governors and of the local elites or jurists who advised them. Whether charismatic preachers qualified as such "evil men" was often ambiguous. Armed with discretionary powers, prefects of Judaea responded with some consistency but also considerable variety.

For most Roman prefects of Judaea, prophetic or apocalyptic preachers who organized mass gatherings or marches were seditious. Even if these events were not insurgent by design, they could become so. Governors consistently responded to them with violence. Several episodes from Judaea followed Jesus' death. Around 45, a dissenting preacher named Theudas posed as a prophet and amassed a large following that marched to the Jordan River. He claimed he would part it for crossing. Theudas' unarmed followers had done nothing violent. Yet the prefect Fadus apparently deemed them insurgents and slaughtered them. The Acts of the Apostles suggests how easily Roman authorities could conflate prophetic movements like Theudas' with insurgency or violent insurrection. A scribe named Gamaliel places the activity of Judas the Galilean (Chapter 3), Judas' sons, and Theudas on a continuum of seditious behavior. Gamaliel's speech makes some obvious historical errors and anachronisms (Appendix 1). Even so, he implies that Roman governors typically treated mass gatherings or marches by prophetic preachers as insurgent activity. He even proposes that after Jesus' death his growing numbers of followers might suffer this fate.[21]

Not long after the slaughter of Theudas' followers, a Jew from Egypt gathered a crowd at the Mount of Olives and marched toward Jerusalem. He claimed the walls of Jerusalem would collapse at his command. The governor Felix classified this as seditious and slaughtered his followers. When the Roman historian Tacitus described Felix's activity as "king-like," he perhaps had episodes like this in mind. But Felix's legal justification was that he was suppressing a seditious event as it was taking shape. Actions like this exposed him to criticism and potential charges of excessive violence. But he noticeably never faced dismissal or trial for it. Apparently both Roman authorities and the chief priests deemed his actions warranted and within his policing authority. Instead, Felix was recalled and tried only because he massacred Jews involved in civil strife with local polytheists at Caesarea. His enemies found this choice deserving of prosecution. They apparently had not thought of any prior massacres in this way.

Much more ambiguous were the charismatic preachers who had a small following and were not organizing mass demonstrations or marches. While not posing a massed military threat, their incendiary preaching still could inspire crowd violence at the Temple precinct. While in Jerusalem, Jesus fit this general profile, and he apparently died for it. Even if he had some hundreds of sympathizers there (1 Cor 15:5–6), only a dozen or two core followers were with him at the Temple precinct or his arrest. Yet, intriguingly, various governors are known to have judged other preachers who behaved like Jesus without executing them, and in some instances the chief priests were the ones who made the arrest and brought them to the prefect's court. Shortly before the First Jewish Revolt, a figure named Jesus bar Ananias was preaching at the Temple and adjacent streets. His message prophesied Jerusalem's destruction and, presumably, an imminent reign of God. Josephus reports that "leading community members" responded by arresting him and having him lashed. This suggests that the chief priests had assembled a *synhedrion* to assess his liability for a capital charge. Yet they could not try capital cases or execute their sentences. When they petitioned his court, the governor Albinus questioned Jesus bar Ananias, convicted him of sedition, and had him lashed until disfigured. But Albinus let him go because he was disturbed. The defendant's message and conduct resembled those of Jesus of Nazareth, but Albinus did not execute him. Jesus bar Ananias died during the Roman siege of Jerusalem a few years later. A projectile struck him as he proclaimed his message.[22]

We encounter the same pattern in how the governor Felix reportedly dealt with one of Jesus' most famous advocates, the preacher Paul, sometime in the 50s (for greater detail, Chapter 11). The sole source is Acts of the Apostles (24), whose report aligns with how the Lukan author consistently portrays Jesus' followers as innocuous in the eyes of Roman authorities (even corrupt ones). Its narrative also obviously mirrors what Luke claims about Jesus' trial. It is hard to verify its accuracy, but it casts plausible light on how Roman governors could understand criminal accusations. Felix was the same governor of Judaea who massacred the unarmed followers of an Egyptian Jew who had marched to the walls of Jerusalem. We have seen how Tacitus described him as "king-like" in his unaccountability. Yet, when Roman troops from the Antonia had arrested Paul during a social disturbance at the Temple, Felix was reportedly not so violent. At his court, the chief priests charged Paul with "stirring seditions" (*kinounta staseis*) among Jews and trying to violate the Temple by bringing non-Jews into it. In response, Paul reportedly denied that he had been disputing with anyone publicly or inciting crowd disturbance. He claimed that the petitioners were trying to eliminate him because he was aligned with Jesus' followers. Acts alleges that Felix kept Paul detained for bribes and to placate the chief priests. But he did not convict and execute him. Felix apparently responded violently to mass demonstrations organized by charismatic preachers. But when one made incendiary statements at the Temple precinct alone or with a modest following, he did not.[23]

Of course, there are some widely recognized differences in the activity of Jesus of Nazareth, Jesus bar Ananias, and Paul. Jesus of Nazareth was reportedly making Messianic claims about himself like some other first-century insurrectionists. Jesus bar Ananias and Paul were not. Jesus of Nazareth preached at the Temple in the company of one or two dozen followers. Jesus bar Ananias and Paul apparently did not. Jesus and his followers reportedly engaged in intimidation and leveraged the volatility of the crowds at the Temple precinct for their desired ends. Jesus bar Ananias and Paul did not. Jesus of Nazareth and Jesus bar Ananias were not Roman citizens. In Acts of the Apostles (but not necessarily his letters), Paul is. Even so, the execution of

Jesus of Nazareth, the scourging of Jesus bar Ananias, and the sparing of Paul were to some extent motivated by the perceptions of those who judged them. The governors Pilate, Albinus, and Felix apparently had somewhat different understandings of when incendiary preaching at the Temple precinct was criminally seditious enough to warrant crucifixion. Even when such preaching could inspire crowd violence, Albinus and Felix did not think it demanded execution, or perhaps a conviction at all. Weapons, a mass demonstration, or an obvious attempt to stage insurrection had to be involved. In the absence of these, the governors did not execute preachers who were alone or accompanied by small numbers. They may well have dismissed such a preacher who claimed to be a Messiah or some sort of "King of the Jews" as eccentric or disturbed. They may have disfigured him with the strokes of a rod or the lashes of a scourge. But Pilate did apparently deem such activity seditionist and worthy of crucifixion. What was his relationship with disfiguring, lethal violence?

Pilate's Violence and Chief Priests

How did Pilate define sedition? When were actions seditious? When did they warrant immediate violence, a criminal conviction, or capital punishment? Most of our knowledge of Pilate comes from the Jewish authors Josephus and Philo. Josephus was born in Judaea shortly after Pilate's term as prefect ended. Philo was a contemporary living at Alexandria in Egypt. As important as it is, their testimony does not enable us to make easy sense of Pilate's disposition. They portray a man who is confrontational, imperious, insulting, and at times violent toward the Jews of Judaea writ large. This is a far cry from the pliable Pilate of the Gospels, who has Jesus crucified because the chief priests or attending crowds want it. Such seemingly inconsistent treatments have yielded modern portrayals of Pilate as hostile to Jews, accommodating of the chief priests, an insensitive imperialist, violently aggressive, easily intimidated, woefully incompetent, or marginally effective. But like Gospel accounts of Pilate, Josephus and Philo have their own literary goals. Josephus' focus on Pilate's transgressive behavior fits his narrative arc for escalations in Roman misgovernance preceding the Jewish Revolt. Philo's claim that Pilate was a cruel magistrate who executed people without a trial is what he often says about governors who disrespect Jewish traditions. Even so, the accounts of Philo and Josephus help us understand Pilate's logic in killing people. They enable us to identify a range of behaviors and people that Pilate defined as

Pilate and Sedition 159

seditionist. They also provide glimpses of the impact of his relationship with the chief priests, including Caiaphas and Annas. When we analyze his pattern of violence, it becomes less surprising that he convicted and executed Jesus.[24]

At times, Pilate's relationship with the chief priests was tense. He sometimes engaged in gratuitous conduct that Jews found sacrilegious. But Pilate had some productive points of shared interest with the chief priests too. It is best to think of Pilate and the chief priests as maintaining a tense rapport while they governed. In fact, Pilate apparently refrained from violence when the chief priests mounted resistance to his actions. But he sometimes unleashed it on dissidents who acted without their approval or sympathy. This tendency is important for identifying Pilate's calculations in inflicting repressive violence. He was prone to it as prefect, and Philo condemned him as an unaccountably vicious magistrate. But his violence followed a discernable pattern shaped by his relationship with the chief priests. This does not mean that he had Jesus executed just to satisfy them. It means that Pilate thought people who stirred social disturbances in challenge of their authority were criminals. Killing them served Roman justice and interests in Judaea.[25]

Early in his tenure, Pilate had his soldiers bring standards with images of the emperor to Jerusalem, to be placed in the *praetorium*, formerly Herod's palace. Many Jews considered the images idolatrous. What Pilate was doing was a serious breach, and he apparently knew this. Josephus indicates Pilate aimed to sneak the standards into Jerusalem at night unnoticed, but without success. A crowd of people from Jerusalem and even the countryside gathered at the *praetorium* in Caesarea to petition for their removal. Pilate surrounded the crowd with troops and threatened their execution. According to Josephus, the people proclaimed their willingness to die to prevent the defilement of Jerusalem's sanctity. Some even threw themselves to the ground and exposed their necks. At the crowd's persistence, Pilate decided against mass murder and ordered the standards removed. Josephus states that Jews organized the crowd demonstration. Some infer from this that Annas, Caiaphas, and other chief priests were not providing effective leadership. This could very well be right. But Josephus is known for depicting spontaneous mass demonstrations that prevail through divine intervention, not the machinations of leading figures. He may be minimizing how the chief priests responded. Whatever their role, they at least did not treat the demonstration's organizers as hostile rivals who warranted violence. This factored into Pilate's decision not to react violently.[26]

Later in his tenure, Pilate decorated the *praetorium* of Jerusalem with gold-plated shields. Void of human likenesses, they bore inscriptions suggesting Tiberius' divinity. Philo gives credit to "the many" in selecting four living members of the Herodian dynasty to intervene with Pilate. But they apparently did so as part of a crowd petition that the chief priests supported or did not oppose. Philo even indicates that "those in power" (*hoi en telei*) wrote a letter to Tiberius, who in response pressured Pilate to concede. Pilate had the shields taken to Caesarea and deposited in the Temple to Augustus and Rome there. In this instance, the Herodian dynasts perhaps overshadowed the chief priests. But the fact that all of them deemed the demonstration warranted probably mattered to Pilate. He did not initiate a general massacre.

Sometimes Pilate did massacre or execute people whose behavior he deemed incendiary enough to incite mass rioting, a crowd disturbance, or an insurrection. Notably, however, this occurred when such crowd activity did not involve the leadership or support of the chief priests. It instead happened when dissenting figures were the ringleaders. At some point as prefect, perhaps before the shields incident, Pilate decided to have an aqueduct to Jerusalem built. He funded it from the treasury of the Jewish Temple. His use of such funds attracted criticism, and a hostile crowd gathered near his headquarters in Jerusalem to protest. Even so, Pilate probably had access to this money because the chief priests had coordinated with him or had at least declined to oppose him. Perhaps they were under duress or sought to avoid conflict. But they did not sanction serious opposition to Pilate's decision. In this case, we can assume Annas, Caiaphas, and other senior priests did not lead or support a crowd disturbance but that it was organized by charismatic dissenters who sought to invalidate the chief priests' cooperation with Pilate.[27]

This time, Pilate did get violent. According to Josephus, certain members of the crowd were threatening and insulting. But we can doubt that the crowd's behavior in general was meaningfully different from that in prior incidents. Pilate directed his soldiers to infiltrate in civilian clothes and authorized them to use only clubs. On his order, they started to attack. But a massacre ensued beyond what Pilate intended. In this case, people outside the established Jewish leadership at Jerusalem (including Galileans presumably) had engaged in a mass demonstration. Their demonstration was even antagonistic to the authority of the chief priests, who may not have advocated for them. Pilate responded with repressive violence. Many people died in the slaughter into which it cascaded.

Luke (13:1–2) mentions an act of violence by Pilate at Jerusalem. It may refer to the aqueduct episode, but it could refer to another incident in which Pilate sanctioned mass violence. This incident occurred at the Temple precinct when Pilate massacred Galileans engaged in a mass disturbance beyond the sanction of the chief priests. Whether they were armed is unclear. Episodes

Pilate and Sedition

like this ultimately earned Pilate a reputation for frequent slaughters without a trial according to critics like Philo. Even so, Pilate's justification apparently was that he was confronting crowds of people engaged in seditious or even insurgent activity. Armed with his policing powers as prefect, he had suppressed them immediately. This does not mean he routinely executed people without putting them on trial first. It means he was willing to kill people who were engaged in potentially incendiary demonstrations not sanctioned by the chief priests. Such activity may have attracted the contempt of critics. But it also may have created a decent rapport with the chief priests and won approval from his emperor. Notably, Pilate acted with such violence a full decade before being recalled. He deemed it proportionate and necessary to the demands raised by his turbulent district. Others apparently agreed, until a final act of mass violence ended his career.[28]

Pilate's last documented act of official violence happened in Samaria. Among Samaritans, Mount Gerizim and the site of their destroyed temple was a major pilgrimage site, just as the Temple of Jerusalem was for Jews throughout greater Judaea and in the Diaspora. The temple on Mount Gerizim had been left in ruins by the Hasmonaeans. Both the Herodians and Roman prefects had prevented its subsequent restoration, presumably in part to placate the chief priests of Jerusalem. Even the reign of Herod, who had often recruited Samaritans into his army and coveted their support, did not witness the temple at Gerizim being rebuilt. The dangers posed by social disturbance and incendiary preachers during major festivals there were great. A few years after Pilate executed Jesus, a charismatic preacher claimed he found vessels that had belonged to Moses on Mount Gerizim. He organized a mass march of armed Samaritans to the site. When the armed Samaritans were marching through a village called Tirathana, Pilate massacred them. After this, the priestly elite of the Samaritans brought charges against Pilate before Vitellius, now governor of Syria. They claimed the Samaritan demonstrators had been responding to the extreme violence of Pilate's governance, not rebelling against Roman rule. Unfortunately, Josephus does not share what exactly Pilate had done to the Samaritans previously. But the claim resembles Philo's perception that Pilate was an unwarrantedly brutal and violent governor. The Samaritan petitioners did not deny that Pilate should have slaughtered armed insurgents or demonstrators. But they were asserting that Pilate's unnecessarily violent methods of rule had incited their action in the first place.

Vitellius took the Samaritans' claims seriously. He dismissed Pilate and sent him to Rome for trial. But Pilate was otherwise largely unaccountable for his pattern of mass violence. During his decade of governance, his actions apparently met with approval from the prior governors of Syria and the emperor Tiberius. Otherwise, he had established enough of a rapport with the priestly elite of Jerusalem and had refrained from violence against it. When Pilate massacred Jewish demonstrators at Jerusalem, they apparently had been following charismatics competing with the chief priests for authority. When Pilate was recalled, it was because Samaritan leaders, not the chief priests at Jerusalem, had pressed charges. Pilate apparently believed he had inflicted his acts of violence on seditious criminals. He thought of his violence as proportionate to the stability his district required. No doubt Pilate's social biases affected whom he deemed criminally guilty and what he classified as seditious. But he did not kill people he thought were innocent or harmless or publicly declared to be such. He could face stiff consequences for that.

The chief priests at Jerusalem ultimately had some impact on how Pilate defined criminally seditious behavior. If the chief priests sanctioned relatively peaceful demonstrations as they occurred, Pilate treated these as petitioning him for certain desired ends and refrained from violence. But if charismatic figures not sanctioned by the chief priests organized similar demonstrations or marches, Pilate classified their behavior as seditious and responded violently. If the chief priests themselves identified such behavior as incendiary or subversive, Pilate was inclined to accept their viewpoint and validate repressive violence.

For such reasons Jesus' conduct at the Temple precinct of Jerusalem brought him into Pilate's crosshairs. Jesus was not organizing a mass demonstration. He was not engaging in armed uprising. But he was making incendiary prophecies and provocative, if unenforceable, claims of Messianic kingship while engaging in acts of intimidation with a dozen or so followers. After arresting Jesus, the chief priests asserted his activity could incite serious crowd disturbance. Not all governors would have defined this as seditious. Or if they did, they may have thought a brutal, disfiguring scourge was punishment enough. Some governors might not have deemed Jesus worthy of crucifixion. Pilate did.

The Accusations of the Chief Priests

But what was the charge the petitioners brought against Jesus? If they were accusing Jesus of sedition, on what grounds? The Gospels do not specify what exactly the chief priests had communicated to Pilate. Even so, they bear various traces of claims made by Jesus' opponents. These include accusations he

Pilate and Sedition 163

had acquired influence over large crowds of people through acts of deception or sorcery. In this vein, various polytheist, Jewish, and early Christian sources state that Jesus was accused by his adversaries of "deceiving" people into sacrilegious behavior or even of being a sorcerer (Chapter 8). For the later rabbis, these were capital offenses. Some surmise these were among the main charges Jesus was facing before Pilate. Could they have factored into his death?[29]

To Roman governors, being deceptive or persuasive was not a crime. But if it promoted seditious acts or crowd violence, deception could be integral to criminal charges. In Matthew (27:62–63), the chief priests and Pharisees call Jesus a "deceiver" after his death, but in reference to what he allegedly said at the Temple precinct. In Luke (23:1–2, 5), they claim he misled the people during his actual trial by Pilate. In John (7:12, 45–49), Jesus is accused of "deceiving" the crowds during an arrest attempt at the Temple precinct. When Mark emphasizes how Pilate asked Jesus whether he was "King of the Jews," it implies a concern that Jesus' preaching was seditiously deceptive.

In the eyes of Roman governors, sorcery could be a criminal affair. This was especially so for sorcery that could harm others, particularly emperors. In the second century, a famous North African writer named Apuleius even faced accusations he committed harmful acts (*maleficia*) of magic as part of a broader effort to seduce a widow and take her inheritance. He wrote his *Apology* to defend against such claims. In the Gospels, Jesus' opponents associate his miraculous ability to heal or cast out demons with sorcery. Yet in these accounts, Jesus' "magical" acts normally do not harm anyone, especially Roman authorities. The Synoptics do not link accusations of sorcery made by Jesus' adversaries to his final Passover. Nothing suggests they motivated Pilate.[30]

Did the chief priests and scribes think of Jesus as a deceiver or a sorcerer? Presumably they did. Those who believed his prophecies were false but dangerous thought of him as a deceiver. Those who believed he performed miracles through un-sanctioned means or powers defined him as a sorcerer. Even so, arguments that Pilate executed Jesus strictly for being a deceiver or a sorcerer must rely on later Christian or Jewish traditions. They evade what the Gospels narrate about his death. In Mark, Pilate is foremost interested in whether Jesus is King of the Jews. This suggests that chief priests were accusing him of posturing as a Messiah and proclaiming prophecies at the Temple precinct. Luke (23:2–3) makes explicit what Mark implies, and whether informed by a common source or Luke itself, John places a similar accusation in one of Jesus' earlier pilgrimages to Jerusalem (7:26–27, 41–42).

Jesus' opponents at his trial classified him as someone who deceives people (Chapter 10). But their accusations mostly carried weight with Pilate because

Jesus' actions and prophecies at the Temple precinct had a serious potential to incite crowd violence there. This explains why the Gospels portray the chief priests as pivoting from accusations of blasphemy or deception to sedition. Jesus' deceptive Messianic posturing and predictions about a "reign of God" could, in isolation, be dismissed as the deluded posturing of an eccentric or unstable person. But as far as the chief priests were concerned, Jesus was accountable for endangering innocent people and liable for a capital charge. Being Pilate's main advisers about the practices of Jews at Jerusalem, they were now petitioning Pilate to judge Jesus for sedition.[31] Their accusations had lethal potency.

10

Pilate's Path, Jesus' Trial

Pilate responded to them by saying, "Do you want me to release to you the King of the Jews?" For he knew that the chief priests had handed him over because of their envy.

—MARK 15:9

It was the third hour, and [the soldiers] crucified him. The inscription of the charge against him stated: "King of the Jews."

—MARK 15:25

LONG AGO, ON a spring morning, Pontius Pilate judged Jesus of Nazareth. He had him scourged until the bones were visible through the torn, bloody flesh of his back. He had his lacerated body affixed to a cross shortly after. Jesus died in agony and humiliation as the sun climbed across the Jerusalem sky. He was reportedly killed between two other seditionists. The titulus on his cross read "King of the *Ioudaioi*." While *Ioudaioi* could denote Judaean ethnicity, it also referred to the civic community of worshipers to which Jesus belonged, and we will translate it as "Jews" for present purposes (Chapter 1). These features of Jesus' trial and death inspire nearly universal agreement. Everything else is uncertain. What was Pilate's path to crucifying Jesus?

In the Gospel narratives, Pilate is committed to Jesus' innocence but executes him to indulge the trial's petitioners and audience. The Gospels generally say that Jesus was acquitted by Pilate but tortured and sent to his death anyway. Scholars sometimes accept this premise. But Roman trials did not work like that. Magistrates had many considerations in convicting offenders and passing sentence. Sometimes they wrongfully convicted and executed people, even those they knew to be innocent. But they did not sentence people to death after acquitting them or publicly announcing their innocence. They also were not as easily intimidated as the Gospels suggest. Roman governors normally had a council (*consilium*) of advisers and soldiers at their disposal. They were the intimidators. Even so, all four Gospels say that Pilate did not believe Jesus deserved to die and had him killed unwillingly.[1]

These aspects of the Gospels point to a serious issue. When narrating Jesus' trial and death, they portray Pilate as proclaiming Jesus' innocence and acquitting him immediately before having him crucified (generally Mark 15:1–37; Matt 27:1–54; Luke 22:66–23:47; John 18:28–19:30). Their portrayals defy plausibility. Pilate surely had legal justification for having Jesus executed as a criminal. But what was it? What was Jesus' path to crucifixion?

Jesus before Pilate

Jesus' message was antagonistic to Judaea's governing authorities. He envisioned a reign of God that would elevate the downtrodden. His reported claim of being "King of the Jews" (or "Judaeans") exposed him to criminal conviction. But most pivotal was that he had preached this incendiary message at the Temple precinct during Passover week. Of these three factors, the time and place were arguably pivotal in convincing Pilate to convict and execute. He probably would have crucified Jesus for preaching any incendiary message at the same time and place. If Jesus had been making Messianic prophecies to a small circle of unarmed followers in the Judaean desert, he may never have crossed paths with Pilate at all. The Qumran Jews envisioned a similar divine intervention and invited little repressive violence from Pilate. If Pilate's interrogation of Jesus focused on whether Jesus was "King of the Jews," it was because Jesus' alleged Messianic posturing at the Temple precinct could have triggered crowd violence and mass bloodletting. During Passover week several decades earlier, dissidents who had gathered at the Temple to protest the Herodians' appointment of a chief priest and their execution of dissident sages ultimately incited a crowd to pelt troops with stones. Thousands of people died in the ensuring massacre. Jesus' conduct had a similar potential, and he had even ostensibly leveraged this danger to avoid arrest. If confirmed by Pilate, these factors would make Jesus guilty of criminal behavior.[2]

The morning after their council's hearing, the chief priests brought Jesus to Pilate. Pilate normally spent Passover week at Jerusalem. The influx of pilgrims and the possibilities for social disturbance were serious. Pilate did not travel alone. Along with his advisers, he brought troops from Caesarea, maybe even several thousand. In Jerusalem, Pilate and his troops inhabited the *praetorium* that Herod I had built on the western end. We can place Jesus there the morning he died. Some even localize Jesus' trial to an enclosed

Pilate's Path, Jesus' Trial

courtyard at a gate into Jerusalem located at the *praetorium*'s western end. Pilate could have used it as his tribunal. Perhaps more plausible is that Pilate's tribunal was east of his *praetorium*, at a more central location facing the interior city (Figures 10.1 and 10.2). Either way, the pilgrimage traditions that place his trial at the Church of Ecce Homo, a short distance west of the Temple precinct, are widely recognized as misleading.[3]

When they arrived at Pilate's headquarters, the chief priests petitioned Pilate. As mentioned, Pilate apparently played little role in Jesus' arrest. But he probably anticipated the case based on prior communications from the chief priests and his own sources of information. The chief priests submitted an indictment for trial when they petitioned his court. In Mark and Matthew, Pilate is ready for Jesus' transfer to him: "Binding Jesus, they brought and handed him over to Pilate, and Pilate asked him, 'Are you the King of the Jews.'" The other Gospels variously reworked this basic tradition to portray a Pilate who did not expect the petitioners at all. In John, Pilate even asks them for their charges and initially rejects their petition. He tells them to try Jesus in their own court and learns they are bringing a capital charge (Chapter 8). These elements are consistent with how Luke and John shift responsibility from Pilate to the chief priests and attending crowd. Much more likely is that Pilate anticipated and prioritized the petition. The caseloads for governors could be massive. But the Gospels report that Pilate tried Jesus on very short notice. The petitioners were arguing that Jesus' preaching posed an imminent social threat during Passover week. The prosecution of a reputed seditionist, just apprehended, could not wait.[4]

Once Pilate accepted the case, the trial began. According to John (18:28), Pilate received the petitioners outside his *praetorium*. If they had entered, they would have made themselves impure for their Passover meal. The Mishnah, composed c. 200, notes that images of gods or emperors that polytheists used for worship, contact with corpses, or even just being in the house of a non-Jew could raise purity concerns. Jerusalem was largely absent of human likenesses and polytheist objects. But in Pilate's headquarters people easily encountered polytheist paraphernalia and even corpses. John claims that Pilate did not interrogate Jesus before his accusers. He shifted locations, questioning Jesus in his headquarters and then communicating with the petitioners and crowds waiting outside (John 18:28–19:12). Some accept this scenario. But this would be highly irregular for the *cognitio*, where judges normally interrogated litigants in one another's presence.[5]

What explains this? We have seen how John shifts Jesus' trial and death from Passover to the day of preparation for Passover. It likens Jesus to the

FIGURE 10.1 The *praetorium* of Pilate in Jerusalem, model of Jerusalem in the Second Temple period. Photo by N. Andrade. © Holyland Tourism 1992, Ltd. Courtesy of The Israel Museum, Jerusalem, at the Israel National Museum. Place names inserted by N. Andrade.

FIGURE 10.2 Plan of the Old City of contemporary Jerusalem labeled with ancient place names. © Google Earth. Place names inserted by N. Andrade.

Paschal lamb. The Synoptic Gospels differ by placing the trial after the Passover meal. By making this shift, John stages a paradox: The chief priests and allied scribes prosecute Jesus despite prohibitions against conducting business on the day of preparation for Passover, but they keep rules of purity so that they can sacrifice at the Temple. Even so, Pilate may have wanted to see whether Jesus would confess before conducting a *cognitio* in earnest. He could in theory do this without the petitioners present and in the *praetorium* itself, as John stresses. Since the Gospels agree Jesus did not deny any of the accusations, Pilate may have briefly questioned him in isolation and found him guilty. Yet John oddly claims to record statements made by Jesus and Pilate in the *praetorium*, with no one witnessing. The Synoptics portray Pilate as questioning Jesus in front of the petitioners and, by implication, the public. This would have been typical. Governors' tribunals were often in public areas. We have seen how Judaea's governors did public business just outside the *praetorium*. We can accept that Pilate conducted a *cognitio* on his tribunal there, in full view of petitioners, bystanders, and crowds celebrating the Feast of Unleavened Bread. If the *cognitio* was so brief, it was because Jesus did not deny the accusations and was otherwise uncooperative. Beyond confirming the charges, Pilate had no need to interrogate the petitioners in detail.[6]

The Trial of Jesus

In all the Gospel accounts, Jesus' trial by Pilate focuses on whether he was "King of the Jews." Pilate had surely heard reports of Jesus' Messianic claims. But in Mark's account (15:2–4; Matt 27:11–14) the chief priests accuse Jesus of other unspecified crimes. These plausibly involved the conduct of Jesus' followers at the Temple, but by specifying them Mark conceivably would have undermined the case for Jesus' blamelessness. When Luke, expanding on Mark, mentions that Jesus was accused of deceiving the people (Luke 23:1–2, 5), it points to the incendiary potential of Jesus' preaching. The chief priests and other petitioners were accusing Jesus of sedition.

By all accounts, Jesus did not seek an acquittal. In Mark (15:2–3, with Matt 27:11), Pilate immediately asks Jesus whether he was King of the Jews. Jesus answers, "You are saying it." Otherwise, he does not respond to Pilate's queries or the testimony of the petitioners. According to Luke (23:1–5), the charges were that Jesus was inciting the Jews to large-scale insurrection, hindering the payment of taxes to Caesar, and claiming he was "Christ the King." Even so, Luke is expanding upon the murkier material from Mark to provide clarity or verisimilitude. In Acts of the Apostles, the Lukan author has Paul confront similar charges before Roman magistrates. Informed by known Roman court-room procedures, the author apparently fashioned both trials in a formulaic way. While less detailed, Mark is valid in implying the charges were focused on Jesus' recent activity at the Temple and his Messianic prediction that an imminent reign of God was at hand. Pilate considered the chief priests to be experts in their compatriots' affairs. They asserted that Jesus' activity there could have inspired violence. If true, this was enough to convict and execute for sedition. If Jesus did in fact deny nothing and proved uncooperative, that provided even more justification.[7]

Even so, the Gospels are adamant that Pilate did not consider Jesus a threat. According to them, Pilate denied any justification for convicting Jesus through-out the trial (Mark 15:14; Matt 27:23; Luke 23:4, 13–24; John 18:33–19:12). Not one makes explicit that Pilate convicted Jesus for criminal behavior. They also generally portray Pilate as scheming to have Jesus pardoned by the crowd. We have seen how this has inspired various theories that Pilate did not deem Jesus guilty of any crime. He instead condemned Jesus as "King of the Jews" because he was accommodating the chief priests, placating the attending crowd, or taking precautions against crowd disturbance. But in truth, we should deem the opposite scenario more likely. The chief priests were framing acts they considered blasphemous or deceptive as being seditious by Roman legal standards. They surmised that Jesus' Messianic prophecies and incendi-ary activity at the Temple had endangered pilgrims and worshipers during Passover week. Fulfilling an obligation to curb this danger (and not as a con-venient tactic, as the Gospels claim), they were now pivoting from Jesus' alleged blasphemy to the seditious nature of how he had made his "regal" claims. Their concerns proved even more persuasive to Pilate when Jesus did not deny them.[8]

Such factors explain why Pilate asked Jesus whether he was "King of the Jews" and then mocked him as being one during his torture and execution (Mark 15:26; Matt 27:37; Luke 23:38; John 19:19–22). Pilate was under pres-sure from the chief priests to convict and execute Jesus. Roman judicial biases overwhelmingly favored the landowning elite, and Pilate relied on the chief priests for governance and public order. Such pressure reasonably affected his decision-making. But this does not mean Pilate executed Jesus simply because the chief priests wanted it or exploited Jesus' "royal" claims as a pretext to execute him. Instead, such factors validated for Pilate the legal pathway the petitioners were forging. They motivated Pilate to *convict* Jesus of sedition without any complication, whatever his personal motives were. If the Gospel accounts portray Pilate as insisting on Jesus' innocence and trying to have him pardoned before executing him anyway, it is because their authors were framing Jesus' movement, *their* movement, as accommodating of earthly Roman authority. Representing themselves as unworthy of suspicion or repressive violence from contemporary Roman governors, they depict Jesus as recognizably innocent to Pilate.

Once again we can doubt much of what Mark and the other Gospels say about Jesus' trial by Pilate. But we can accept that Pilate convicted Jesus of sedition in what amounted to a formal, visible declaration of his guilt, and with little hesitation. The execution by crucifixion and mockery as King of the Jews make no sense otherwise. Pilate's reported effort to have Jesus pardoned does not make much sense either. Ultimately, all the Gospels agree that Pilate ordered his soldiers to scourge Jesus and dress him mockingly as a king. They state he had Jesus identified as King of the Jews in public. This means Pilate convicted Jesus of the petitioners' charges and treated him with derision, without any reservation. Pilate did not merely execute Jesus. He had him humiliated and tortured with great animus. Pilate was convinced that Jesus was guilty of a serious, grotesque crime.

For these reasons, we can surmise Pilate had classified Jesus' reported claims of being the Messiah, or "King of the Jews," as seditionist behavior. But this was mostly because Jesus had made these claims at the Temple precinct during Passover week while his followers were engaging in confrontational, inflammatory behavior. There they could have inspired a crowd disturbance that got innocent pilgrims hurt or killed (and may have done so). Finding Jesus guilty of criminal activity, Pilate convicted him and had him summarily executed. If Pilate did in fact entertain pardoning Jesus, it was because he had convicted Jesus of a crime. If he had acquitted Jesus, he would have just released him. There would have been nothing to pardon.

Jesus, Pilate, and Antipas ("Herod")

Most Gospels depict Pilate as the only bearer of Roman authority to judge Jesus on a capital charge. Luke differs in one key respect. It claims that upon learning Jesus was Galilean, Pilate paused his trial and sent him to Herod Antipas (23:7–12), who was in Jerusalem for Passover. By implication, his motive either was to show respect or see whether Antipas would be motivated to execute Jesus himself. The petitioners reportedly repeated their charges and testimonies to Antipas. Jesus again remained silent. Intrigued by Jesus' reputation as a holy man, Antipas hoped to witness some miracles.

Pilate's Path, Jesus' Trial

But he reportedly found Jesus innocent of any criminal behavior. He just had Jesus humiliated, dressed in mockingly splendid cloths, and sent back to Pilate.[9]

If Pilate did send Jesus to Herod Antipas (a contentious issue), we should accept Pilate had convicted Jesus of sedition but wanted to establish a consensus with the dynast of Galilee. In turn, Antipas agreed the conviction was just, despite what Luke reports. He also had a personal stake in the matter. We have seen how Antipas had killed John the Baptizer and pursued Jesus because of their prophetic preaching against his realm's ordering of authority and wealth. If he had Jesus dressed in (mockingly) elegant attire and sent back to Pilate, it was for execution. In Acts (4:27), the Lukan author argues that Antipas and Pilate were both agents of Jesus' death, not reluctant judges. These statements go against the narrative grain of both Luke and Acts and probably reflect their historical relationship with Jesus.

Even so, we should assume this episode never happened. The Lukan author consistently portrays Jesus and his followers as nonthreatening to Roman authorities, and parallels between the trials of Jesus and Paul in Luke and Acts suggest literary intervention. Pilate probably did not bother to send Jesus to Antipas. The two men were reportedly not on amicable terms, and despite Luke's assertions, Pilate did not deem Jesus innocent. He also may have wanted to eliminate Jesus without delay. Luke (13:1–2) even claims that Pilate had at some point slaughtered many Galileans in the Temple precinct, apparently without involving Antipas at all. When he had the titulus on Jesus' cross mock him as "King of the Jews," that may have been intended as an insult to Antipas too. After all, Rome never let Antipas govern Judaea or gave him the title of king. His father, Herod, had been king of the Jews/Judaeans; Antipas was not.[10]

Luke conceivably contrives the episode of Antipas' judgment to reinforce one of its main points: agents of Roman authority saw Jesus as an innocent man. This does not mean Antipas was unaware of what was transpiring. He may have been in Jerusalem for Passover when Jesus was executed. For most Passover weeks, he apparently traveled from his realm to Jerusalem and occupied a palace built by the Hasmonaeans at the northeast end of the Upper City. If he was in Jerusalem during Jesus' arrest, Pilate perhaps maintained some form of communication with Antipas as the situation developed. But ultimately, Pilate took credit for eliminating Jesus as a seditionist threat, just as Antipas had done with John the Baptizer a few years earlier. The two men never anticipated they would earn enduring infamy for what they did.[11]

Sentencing by Pilate

Once Pilate convicted Jesus of sedition, he either had to pass a sentence or grant a pardon. Later Roman jurists understood crucifixion to be a standard punishment for sedition and inciting violent crowd disturbance as well as military desertion or treason. They also believed it the most serious form of capital punishment. It surpassed decapitation, forced labor in mines, and exile to an island. Its only rival was being burned alive. In practice, Roman judges could select punishments based on context and what they deemed appropriate, especially in the absence of clear statutes. They also believed in the moral superiority of landed elites, even when they had committed horrible misdeeds, and there were prohibitions against crucifying them. But the mainstream Roman legal perspectives are clear. Sedition and violent social disturbance were very serious crimes. The brutal punishments of crucifixion and being burned alive were appropriate for these. Long inflicted on enslaved and lowborn insurrectionists, crucifixion was how Roman authorities executed the followers of the charismatic leader Spartacus who had destabilized Italy during the 70s BCE. Just prior to Jesus' lifetime, the Roman governor of Syria had crucified 2,000 people in Judaea he had identified as insurrectionists. The Gospels portray the petitioners at Jesus' trial as seeking execution. But Pilate could have imposed a more moderate sentence. Josephus describes how a governor had a man violently scourged for sedition at the Temple and then released. The Lukan author misleadingly communicates that Pilate wanted to give Jesus a disciplinary flogging with rods before letting him go. But Pilate apparently believed that Jesus was a criminal who deserved crucifixion.[12]

Even so, the Gospels assert Pilate schemed to pardon Jesus because he believed him innocent. In the Synoptics, his mechanism is a customary display of goodwill that involved his releasing a convicted prisoner whom Jewish pilgrims at Jerusalem had selected during Passover week. Papyri from Egypt and other witnesses provide parallels for pardons or commuted sentences. One contains the records of a hearing in which a magistrate pardons a man who deserved to be whipped. In first-century Judaea the governor Albinus sometimes pardoned people of minor crimes while refusing to do so for those who had committed violence. As governor of Bithynia, Pliny encountered people who were convicted of capital charges but had become publicly enslaved instead. Even so, full pardons for capital offenses are hard to corroborate. John (18:39) less plausibly attributes Pilate's decision to long-standing Jewish custom. The Gospels generally agree Pilate offered Jesus as the convict he would release because he believed him innocent. He just needed to get the trial's audience to express consent. If successful, Pilate could justify releasing Jesus without alienating the chief priests. He could do it even though he had convicted him of a crime that normally warranted execution.[13]

In the Roman Empire, crowds communicated through acclamations. People would shout or chant in unison. Political players would treat their chants as expressing public consensus. Of course, acclamations could be misleading. A crowd's desires did not necessarily represent popular will. It could even be loaded with partisans. Even so, the pressures posed by acclaiming crowds were potent. According to most Gospels, Pilate expected the crowd to acclaim in favor of Jesus. After all, the crowds at the Temple had overwhelmingly supported him. But Pilate had miscalculated. The crowd turned hostile to Jesus. How could this happen? How could a crowd of people who reportedly celebrated Jesus at the Temple turn on him?

All four Gospels claim the crowd called for the release of Barabbas, a man arrested among seditionists who had recently engaged in lethal violence (Mark 15:6–15; Matt 27:15–23; Luke 23:18–25; John 18:39–40). They say it also advocated for Jesus' crucifixion. This unexplained shift in crowd favor to some extent reflects the machinations of the Gospels. But we should doubt their claim that the crowds at the Temple precinct had overwhelmingly favored Jesus anyhow. Meanwhile Jesus' main followers had been scattered during his arrest. Now in hiding, they were (almost) entirely absent. Any crowd that did gather at Jesus' trial consisted mostly of curious residents and pilgrims celebrating the Feast of Unleavened Bread. Some were presumably sympathetic to the priests who managed the sacrifices on their behalf. Others were clients of the chief priests and allied scribes. Meanwhile Jesus' core followers were in hiding, and his sympathizers may have been distancing themselves from him too. An important factor is that his conduct at the Temple plausibly infuriated people it had endangered, intimidated, displeased, or disrupted from sacrificing. His own base of support was missing. The people witnessing his trial were largely sympathetic to the chief priests, hostile toward Jesus, or curious bystanders. Few were willing to provide vocal support. The crowd otherwise had its own collective energy. While vulnerable to the prompting of others, it created and followed its own social script. If we accept that a crowd witnessed Jesus' trial and petitioned Pilate at it, we must keep such factors in mind.[14]

Even so, many doubt this episode happened at all. Once again, it fits too neatly into the Gospels' goal of shifting responsibility for Jesus' death from

Roman authorities to figures in Jewish society. The ancient sources do not yield clear precedent for the Passover "amnesty." It seems implausible that Pilate would have released a violent seditionist. The name Barabbas, or Jesus Barabbas in Matthew, is suspiciously like that borne by the figure Jesus bar Ananias. We have seen how he was arrested by the chief priests for seditious preaching but tried, lashed, and released by the governor Albinus in 62. Others notice a resemblance to how a crowd reportedly petitioned Archelaus in 4 BCE for the release of prisoners detained by Herod and to concessions made to Jews at Jerusalem by Vitellius in 37 (Chapter 11). These episodes or their literary presentations could have affected the Gospel accounts.[15]

If we do accept that Barabbas' pardon happened, it probably bore little relationship to Pilate's decision to execute Jesus. Instead, Pilate released a man recently arrested for seditionist behavior, conceivably after having him viciously lashed (though this is not specified by the Gospels). The chief priests and attending crowd may have advocated for it. But there was no "trade-off" between Barabbas and Jesus, and Pilate never intended to release Jesus. The Gospels in turn reworked the episode to portray Pilate as earmarking Jesus for pardon but conceding to the crowd. These narratives often have an impact on modern scholarship. In some interpretations, Pilate pursued an amnesty because he had convicted Jesus of a criminal act only to please the chief priests. Believing Jesus to be innocent, he schemed to have the public pardon him. But we should doubt Pilate ever advocated for Jesus' release. We should instead surmise that Pilate had just extended to the crowd an opportunity to have a convicted seditionist pardoned. He reportedly had some in detainment. Along with Jesus and a person named Barabbas, there were the two men with whom Jesus was crucified. Mark (15:7) also refers to some seditionists with whom Barabbas was affiliated.

Here we can emphasize that Matthew, Luke, and John all portray a Pilate who believes in Jesus' innocence, advocates publicly for it, and has Jesus killed anyway. In these narratives, he concedes to the chief priests and the crowd. Yet the testimony of Mark, which deserves priority, presents a different situation. It bears traces of a Pilate who seeks Jesus' death and perhaps manipulates the crowd into agreeing with him. Mark (15:9) records Pilate as asking, "Do you want me to release the King of the Jews?" Apparently reflecting the same tradition (or Mark itself), John (18:39) retains this phrasing despite portraying a Pilate who believed in Jesus' innocence. Pilate's statement hardly seems to be a sincere endorsement of Jesus' release. Instead, it communicates that Pilate was mocking a man he had just convicted of seditiously claiming to be King of the Jews at the Temple precinct before an audience he expected to share his

Pilate's Path, Jesus' Trial

perspective. He did not expect Jesus to be selected by the crowd. At this juncture, Mark states Pilate could tell that the chief priests had handed Jesus over because they envied him. This in theory explains why he petitioned the crowd to decide Jesus' fate. But it does not explain why Pilate called Jesus "King of the Jews" while allegedly trying to secure his release. Perhaps this reflects a clumsy effort to portray a Pilate who tries to spare Jesus' life. Or Mark may even be depicting Pilate as manipulating the crowd into condemning Jesus even though he believed in his innocence. Mark's goals can be debated. But its testimony points to an earlier gospel tradition in which Pilate displayed Jesus to the crowd in mocking terms as the "King of the Jews." After all, if Pilate called Jesus by his actual name, it surely would have garnered greater sympathy.[16]

Intriguingly, the other Gospels represent Pilate as petitioning for Jesus' release, and some rewrite the Markan testimony to do it. Matthew (27:17) replaces the phrasing "King of the Jews" with Jesus' actual name: Jesus, who is called Messiah/Christ. Luke (23:13–16) goes even further. In keeping with its author's tendency to make Jesus and his followers appear innocuous to Roman authorities, it states Pilate proclaimed Jesus' innocence and expressed his desire to release Jesus (after flogging him). In turn, the crowd vehemently insisted on Barabbas' release. But Mark and John support the premise that Pilate simply asked the crowd if they wanted him to release the "King of the Jews." The crowd responded negatively, just as Pilate had anticipated.[17]

Mark's portrayal of Pilate as wanting Jesus' release and its traces of an earlier tradition that intimates otherwise explains the bizarre progression of what follows. When asking the crowd what should be done with Jesus, Pilate once against refers to him as the "King of the Jews," not by his actual name (Mark 15:12). When the crowd demands his crucifixion, Mark claims Pilate asks what evil Jesus had done to deserve the punishment (15:14). The crowd responds by demanding crucifixion again. This second question, however, makes no sense. By this stage of the trial, Pilate must have already convicted Jesus of sedition, despite Mark's omission of this. If he had not, a pardon would not have been necessary for Jesus' release. Once again, Mark is refashioning a hostile Pilate to make him seem convinced of Jesus' innocence or, alternatively, manipulating the crowd into condemning him. Doing so shifts responsibility from Pilate to the chief priests and attending crowd. The other Synoptics go further. Matthew (27:20–26) largely replicates Mark here, but it again portrays Pilate as referring to "Jesus, who is called Messiah/Christ." It then makes the claim, uncorroborated by the other Gospels, that Pilate washed his hands of any blame for Jesus' death. Taking a different tack,

178   KILLING THE MESSIAH

Luke states (again) that Pilate intended to release Jesus after a flogging but conceded to the crowd's demands (23:18–24).

John's account (18:38–19:16) is similarly inconsistent. First, Pilate proclaims Jesus' innocence and announces his intention to release the "King of the Jews." When the crowd asks for Barabbas, he then has his soldiers dress Jesus in a purple robe, flog him, crown him with thorns, and mock him as a king in the *praetorium*. Once again, we witness traces of Pilate's derision for a man he called "King of the Jews." These are embedded in John's broader attempt to rework Pilate as a figure sympathetic to Jesus. As the episode progresses, John has Pilate twice display Jesus to the crowd outside the *praetorium* and attempt to have him spared. His twofold presentation of Jesus noticeably mirrors, and fulfills, how Jesus was proclaimed the lamb of God twice by John the Baptizer. Pilate first emphasizes Jesus' humanity and says, "Behold the man" (19:5). When he tries to persuade the crowd to have Jesus released, the people reproach him and say if he releases Jesus, then he is not a friend of Caesar. This may reflect John's creative engagement with Luke (23:2), which treats Jesus' regal posturing and opposition to taxes to Caesar as charges brought against him. Pilate then displays him at a place near the *praetorium* called the Stone Pavement (Greek) or Gabbatha (Hebrew/Aramaic). Ironically emphasizing Jesus' regal status, he says, "Behold your king... should I crucify your king?" (19.14-15). Here John's narrative once again points to a source tradition, one shared by Mark, in which Pilate was derisively calling Jesus a king before the crowd. Apparently doing what Pilate wants, the crowd petitions for his crucifixion, and the chief priests maintain they have no king but Caesar.[18]

How reliable are the Gospel accounts of Jesus' condemnation by the crowd? It is hard to tell, and they justifiably attract doubts. They align with the overall goal of the Gospels to shift responsibility from Pilate to the chief priests and the people in Jerusalem witnessing his trial. This shift has had a massive impact on the global history of anti-Semitism. But any crowd that witnessed Jesus' trial was surely populated by some people who were hostile or even endangered by Jesus' Messianic posturing at the Temple precinct. They had encountered disruption, intimidation, the perils posed by crowd disturbance, or even violence when Jesus' followers engaged in their confrontational behavior and incendiary preaching. Serious injuries and deaths, omitted by the Gospel accounts, may have occurred. Some people in the crowd may have been seeking justice, and the chief priests and their supporters were there, while most of Jesus' were not. A hostile cluster plausibly had an influence over neutral or impressionable people, shaped the collective attitude, and motivated acclamations. A crowd conceivably clamored for crucifixion at Pilate's prodding, as the Gospels report. We ultimately do not know. But whatever the Gospels claim, we should accept that Pilate had intended to crucify Jesus in public as "King of the Jews" anyway.

The Gospels agree the crowd selected a man named Barabbas for release. But who was he? The phrasing of Mark's narrative, which the later Gospels avoid, is "There was a man called Barabbas imprisoned with the seditionists who had committed murder during *the sedition*" (15:7). Mark does not indicate that Barabbas himself had committed murder. It just places him within a group that recently committed some fatal violence during seditious activity or a civil disturbance, even if Luke reworks the episode to make Barabbas himself a murderer. Mark here anticipates that readers would know which seditious episode was being described, as though it was mentioned earlier in the narrative. Presumably, the nature of the sedition had been clarified in the source tradition from which Mark was deriving material. It was probably unrelated to Jesus' activity. It could refer to one of the turbulent moments that Josephus and Philo report for Pilate's term as prefect (Chapter 9). But it plausibly happened at the Temple precinct in response to Jesus' activity or coincided with it. We will never know the specifics. But as we have seen (Chapter 6), the activity of Jesus and his followers at the Temple precinct did plausibly inspire an arrest attempt and perhaps even a crowd disturbance. Barabbas' acts of violence could have happened in this context, even if they were unrelated to Jesus' activity.[19]

Mark (15:11) also claims Barabbas was the man the chief priests had preferred for release. If the chief priests were advocating for Barabbas to Pilate, and had gotten the crowd to express this sentiment, Pilate conceivably would have released him. Barabbas had been identified by Pilate as one of many seditionists who had contributed to an outbreak of lethal violence. But Mark never specifies he himself killed anyone. The Gospels are also silent on any violence Barabbas suffered from Pilate and implicitly treat his intact body as the foil to Jesus' lacerated, mutilated one. Yet nothing precludes the possibility that Pilate had Barabbas viciously lashed for his role in a seditious outbreak. Pilate could conceivably release such a person after torturing him, especially if he had not led the civil disturbance or killed anyone with his own hands. We have already noted how papyri from Egypt demonstrate governors sometimes pardoned criminals in the face of crowd petitions. It is even possible that Barabbas had been involved in crowd violence in support of the chief priests in some way, and if so, Pilate would have been even more partial. Pilate conceivably released a seditionist, perhaps in response to advocacy by the chief priests or their allies. He may have had him violently scourged before sparing him, as Albinus would later do to Jesus bar Ananias. But he had no problem with crucifying Jesus. After all, he had convicted Jesus of criminally seditious behavior, and Jesus had not denied it.

Torture, Mockery, and Crucifixion

One of the surest signs of Pilate's animus toward Jesus shines through what he had his soldiers do before Jesus' crucifixion. They scourged him with whips. They then dressed him in a purple mantle and crowned him with thorns. Mimicking their prefect, they mocked Jesus as "King of the Jews." All the Gospels agree this sequence occurred, though they differ on the order. John places it before Pilate's order of crucifixion. The Synoptics place it after. When and how was Jesus tortured?

The Gospels give contradictory accounts of the torture that Pilate inflicted on Jesus. Mark (15:15, 19) and Matthew (27:26, 30) claim Pilate ordered Jesus to be lashed with a whip in preparation for crucifixion (*phrangellosas*) and refer to soldiers' striking his head with a reed staff. John (19:1, 3) specifies that Jesus was whipped (*emastigen*) along with given enduring blows (*rapismata*) from fists or a rod. The leather thongs of such whips were normally fitted with sharp metal or bone at their ends. In Luke (23:16, 22), Pilate offers to have Jesus beaten (*paideusas*) before being released to the crowd. The text does not specify whether the beating was delivered after the crowd refused Jesus. But Luke is probably distancing Pilate from deliberate violence against Jesus in its usual way. Mark is more accurate. After convicting Jesus of sedition, Pilate had him lashed so severely that his torn flesh left the bones in his back exposed, as Albinus did to Jesus bar Ananias several decades later. As Jesus' bleeding, tattered body began to go into shock, Pilate's soldiers dressed him in the purple robe of a king, forced a crown of thorns upon him, and beat him about the head with a reed staff. They reveled in the irony that they had reduced the "King of the Jews" to enslaved abjection. Pilate authorized all of it. For him Jesus was getting what he deserved.[20]

By all accounts, Pilate's execution of Jesus put on display that Jesus had been convicted of seditionist behavior. The Gospels all agree the inscription affixed to Jesus' cross read "King of the Jews," a reference to his Messianic claims. According to John, the chief priests wanted the inscription to read, "This man said he was King of the Jews," but Pilate refused to change the title. John also reports the title was written in Hebrew, Greek, and Latin. Nothing about Pilate's written and verbal association of Jesus with the title "King of the Jews" points to belief in his innocence. It was a public, imperialist, and perhaps racialized humiliation of a man who had proclaimed the imminent reversal of the governing order and its distribution of wealth in Roman Judaea. Jesus had envisioned a reign of God that would rectify the injustices suffered by poor Jews. But for Pilate he had committed a despicable crime. Jesus' followers had intimidated and endangered pilgrims while proclaiming this message. Pilate was reasserting a justice that favored Rome's governing order and the landed wealth of Judaea. Jesus' torn, broken body was a visible sign of that justice for the Passover crowds to witness.[21]

Jesus was paraded from the *praetorium*. Apparently too weak to carry his crossbeam, the soldiers conscripted a certain Simon of Cyrene. At a place outside the city walls called Golgotha, otherwise called the Place of the Skull, Jesus was crucified between two other men. Mark (15:27) describes them as two *leistai*, a term that can refer to bandits or seditionists. Intriguingly, this echoes the language Jesus uses at his arrest: "you came out with swords and clubs to seize me, as though against a *leistes*" (Mark 14:48). In isolation, nothing in Mark's account indicates whether the two *leistai* are affiliated with Jesus. Luke describes them as "evil-doers," and in some manuscripts, they are described as "two other evil-doers" (*kakourgoi*: 23:32). This suggests they had been somehow involved in the context of a sedition which Jesus, also defined as an "evil-doer" by Pilate, had been convicted of inspiring. They may very well have been his opponents, as their mockery would suggest. Otherwise, they had just been arrested and crucified for seditious activity according to the same timeline as Jesus.[22]

As this point, the Gospels continue to corroborate or contradict one another in their usual way. We need not trace them any further. But they agree Jesus died by crucifixion, a punishment of choice that Romans dealt to seditionists, while Roman soldiers kept watch. They had already scourged and mutilated him. They had taken his clothes, leaving his wounds exposed. Now they nailed his wrists to his crossbeam, which they then raised and fixed to a post. They had his feet perforated with nails. His suspension cut off his breathing, blood circulation, and organ functioning. His living body was left hanging for several hours, his corpse for just as long. As he hung suspended just above ground, spectators could gaze on his face in mockery or sorrow. Some taunted him, some tried to ease his suffering. Covered in dust, sweat, and blood, Jesus died in slow agony in the Jerusalem heat. But throughout Jesus' crucifixion, the attitude of Pilate, his judge, was clear from the titulus fixed to his cross. It read: "King of the Jews."[23]

When Jesus died, most of his closest followers were absent. After denying his connection to Jesus, Simon Peter had gone into hiding. So had Jesus' other core followers. Pilate was apparently not interested in detaining them unless they reappeared in public. The chief priests had arrested and brought only Jesus to him. Even so, Jesus' followers did not necessarily know Pilate's intentions at the time. In their uncertainty they remained in hiding. Some devoted women (Mark 15:40; Matt 27:56; Luke 23:49), including Mary Magdalene, attended his execution. Not directly complicit in his seditious activity at the Temple, perhaps they did not fear punishment. Or maybe they kept their distance. Only John (19:26) mentions a follower who saw Jesus die: the unnamed "disciple whom Jesus loved." It is also the only account that places Jesus' mother at the scene. We can doubt they were there at all. Jesus' core followers emerged from hiding and preached publicly only after Pilate's deposition (Chapter 11). Fearing implication, they were absent when Jesus died on his cross. They knew Pilate had Jesus crucified for sedition.

PART V

Aftermaths and Apostles

II

Jesus' Followers on Trial (until 250)

You have heard of my behavior in Ioudaismos some time ago, how I excessively pursued the church of God and ravaged it.

—GALATIANS 1:13

Five times I took 39 strokes from Jews/Judaeans. I received three beatings by rods [from Romans]. Once I was stoned.

—2 CORINTHIANS 11:24–25

THE GOSPELS AGREE that Jesus' closest men deserted him in his hours of death. Beyond John's dubious testimony, nothing places them at Jesus' execution. They feared arrest and hid. Only women connected to them watched him die. Mary Magdalene figures prominently. In the Synoptics, Joseph of Arimathea is the only man who petitions Pilate for Jesus' body or entombs him outside the city walls before the Sabbath. Mark identifies Joseph as a civic councilor (*bouleutes*) of Arimathea, not a member of the *synhedrion* that assessed Jesus' liability at Jerusalem (as commonly surmised). He was not Galilean or a core follower. He may have only been doing a pious deed for a compatriot. John claims a recurring figure named Nicodemos helped bury Jesus too. Simon Peter reportedly visited the tomb after hearing it was empty. All the Gospels associate them with Jesus' burial or visits to his tomb.

When Jesus died, his core followers went into hiding, either in Jerusalem or in Galilee. Pilate apparently did not pursue them. The chief priests did not either. With Jesus dead and Passover week over, they had little interest in his followers. Not knowing this for certain, Jesus' followers feared arrest. But they did not stay in hiding forever. Eventually they began to preach in public, including at the Temple precinct of Jerusalem.[1]

The Acts of the Apostles is our main narrative source for Jesus' followers after his death. They are mostly absent from Josephus, who presumably knew

186   KILLING THE MESSIAH

more about their activity in Jerusalem than his *Antiquities* shares. The historical value of Acts is open to criticism, and its particulars are often questionable. But we can accept it accurately captures the following pattern, in general outline. Prominent figures among Jesus' followers at Jerusalem sometimes suffered violence from the chief priests or Roman authorities, including Agrippa I, for preaching in public. Even so, they also preached without arrests, prosecution, or violence for stretches of time. Arrests and violence were occasional and selective. Executions were even rarer. How did Jesus' followers go from fearing violence to preaching in the open? Why did their public preaching attract only occasional arrests or executions? How did Roman governors and their views on sedition affect this pattern?

The Acts of the Apostles

The Acts of the Apostles is our main narrative source for Jesus' followers. But how reliable is it? One issue is that it is hard to date. The Lukan author wrote both Luke and Acts. But when? Many theories place it in the 80s–90s. Arguments also exist for shortly after 62, when its storyline terminates. It never mentions the execution of Jesus Christ believers at Rome in 65, which in some traditions killed Simon Peter and Paul. Quite a few scholars place the text in the early second century for various reasons. Among them are signs its author consulted the letters of Paul and Pliny the Younger. Intriguingly, both Luke and Acts record the activity of a Temple commander and his attendants. This is a post unknown before c. 50 but mentioned several times by Josephus. The Lukan author's references may reflect access to Josephus' works, like its treatment of the prophet Theudas and Judas the Galilean (Appendix 1). The author conceivably wrote Luke and Acts in the 90s at the earliest.[2]

Another issue is that the historical accuracy of Acts is often questionable. Its sources are often unclear, and whether it distorts them is hard to gauge. Acts occasionally refers to historical events or chronological markers. This would suggest sound sources or reliability. But the Lukan author often crafts episodes of arrest and trial to frame Jesus' followers as harmless to Roman authority. We have already seen how Luke reworks Mark to portray a Pilate, and even an Antipas, who are committed to Jesus' innocence. The trial of Paul before Roman governors in Acts also mirrors what Luke depicts Jesus facing. Even if the Lukan author did not write Luke and Acts simultaneously, Acts portrays Roman or Herodian authorities as mostly sparing Jesus' followers. It may not accurately represent the charges against them or their treatment. We must weigh the historical value of Acts' courtroom scenes against its literary goals. Statements ascribed to judges and litigants, and even entire scenes, may be fabricated. Some scholars surmise much of Acts is unreliable, especially when uncorroborated by other sources.[3]

A related issue is how the Lukan author routinely shifts the blame for violence against Jesus' followers from Romans to Jews. We have already noted how Luke exceeds Mark, its main source, in portraying Pilate and even Antipas as convinced of Jesus' innocence and outmaneuvered by chief priests who want Jesus dead. Acts displays this same tendency. It consistently depicts a form of criminal classification in which Jews seek and inflict capital punishment, or even extralegal murders, on Jesus' followers while Roman authorities (even corrupt ones!) play a mitigating role. Paul's letters sometimes contravene what Acts claims. Paul writes about receiving lashes from leaders of Jewish communities on five occasions (2 Cor 11:24–25), but not executions. He also mentions being flogged with rods several times, presumably by Roman judges, and stoned by unspecified people, perhaps extralegally. The tendency in Acts to depict Jews in murderous pursuit of Jesus' followers renders many uncorroborated legal encounters suspect. It also may be ascribing to first-century Jews forms of large-scale pursuit and violence that second-century Roman and municipal authorities undertook against Christians. As we will see, its notorious portrayal of Stephen's stoning is uniquely questionable.[4]

Another issue is that the first half of Acts has very few chronological markers. Its various references to historical persons or events ostensibly support its reliability. Midway through its narrative (16:10), the author famously introduces himself as a figure in it by referring to Paul and himself as "we." From there, the chronological signposting increases somewhat. Yet prior to that most markers consist of references to Herodian kings or Roman magistrates. The passage of time preceding the reign of Herod Agrippa (41–44) is often hard to discern. The text mentions various governors of the 40s–50s. But its opening sequences do not mention Pilate, even though he had just executed Jesus when its narrative begins. It seldom specifies who the high priest is.[5]

A final challenge, already mentioned, is the general lack of external corroboration. Acts is often a solitary witness for the actions of Jesus' followers. Other accounts rarely support it, and its sources are not always clear. At times Acts bears signs of combining historical and contrived material. It also shifts the timeline for historical sequences. It seems to rework certain material from the writings of Paul or Josephus and sometimes creates contradictions while doing so. We have seen how Acts misdates the activity of the insurgent Judas the Galilean and the preacher Theudas (5:36–37). It places the death of Agrippa I at the wrong location. As we will see, what Paul says about his own early career is not always what Acts asserts.

Despite these problems, we can surmise the Lukan author was engaging with prior source traditions for some arrests and legal encounters Jesus' followers faced and not inventing them from whole cloth. Its narrative sometimes makes incidental references to people or events corroborated by other sources. Acts reworks these traditions to portray Jewish leaders as aggressively hostile and Roman authorities as more well-disposed, just like Luke. But its narrative does capture some basic circumstances for when some leading figures among Jesus' followers began to preach at the Temple precinct and suffer repressive violence. It can help us understand how legal authorities were interacting with them if we work to distinguish its plausible components from obviously anachronistic or tendentious ones. We can surmise that Roman authorities or the chief priests sometimes arrested and put on trial leading followers of Jesus when their preaching potentially incited social disturbance. But Jesus' followers often preached without encountering repression at all.[6]

Preaching in Jerusalem: Pilate to Agrippa I

Acts bears no clear chronological markers between Jesus' death (probably in April 33) and the reign of Agrippa I over greater Judaea (41–44). But a skeleton of activity for Jesus' followers and their encounters with repressive violence can be outlined. After Pilate left Judaea in late 36, Jesus' followers were dealing with Roman magistrates who had narrower definitions of criminally seditious behavior. As long as Jesus' followers did not organize mass demonstrations, confrontational encounters, or violent activity, they mostly preached their message in public without being arrested or executed. Meanwhile the chief priests hesitated to prosecute them before Roman prefects. They instead resorted to corrective measures that sometimes involved corporal punishment, but not executions.

When Lucius Vitellius became consular governor of Syria, he had an immediate impact on the fate of Jesus' followers. Vitellius arrived in Syria in 35. By late 36 an embassy of Samaritan elites petitioned him and accused Pilate of being an unusually violent governor. His conduct had allegedly incited the mass armed march to Mount Gerizim and the slaughter that followed. Vitellius took the allegations seriously. He sent Pilate to Rome for trial (Chapter 9). Despite the later Christian traditions that Pilate became a Jesus Christ believer or killed himself, we really know nothing about him from this point on. After Jesus died in the spring of 33 or so, his followers had to fear Pilate for a few years, but not much longer. The Roman authorities who managed Judaea were changing. How they defined sedition could have changed too.

Jesus' Followers on Trial (until 250) 189

Even so, establishing the precise timeline for the activity of Jesus' followers after his death is hard. They apparently were in hiding for some time. They were presumably recruiting followers through their personal and social contacts. They established communities of Jesus Christ believers throughout greater Judaea and adjacent parts of Syria, including Damascus. But they hesitated to preach publicly. Acts contains few signs of dating for what it records, and these raise doubts. In its account, Jesus appeared to his core followers in hiding for 40 days before ascending to heaven. They then celebrated in public at the Pentecost (Acts 1–2), where the Holy Spirit enabled them to preach in all the languages of Jerusalem's pilgrims. Whether Jesus' followers began preaching in public, especially at the Temple, so early after Jesus' death is doubtful. Act's opening sequences never once mention Pilate as an active magistrate. Jesus' followers probably did not preach publicly in Jerusalem until Pilate left Judaea in late 36 or so.[7]

If at all accurate, Acts arguably corroborates this theory. In a rare reference to priestly authority in Jerusalem during the 30s, it places Annas "the high priest," Caiaphas, John, Alexander, and other members of the priestly family at Peter's arrest and questioning (4:6). Here Acts does not call Caiaphas "high priest" and apparently places the episode shortly after 36, when the terms of Pilate and Caiaphas had ended and high priests were being rapidly appointed and demoted. Yet how the Romans were governing Jerusalem and Judaea at this time is unclear. Apparently combining different source traditions, Josephus misleadingly claims Vitellius visited Jerusalem twice as governor of Syria, during Passover of 36 and 37. We should instead surmise that Vitellius had Pilate and Caiaphas dismissed in 36 without visiting Jerusalem at all. In place of Caiaphas, he appointed his brother-in-law Jonathan, a son of Ananus the "high priest." The following Passover, in 37, he visited the city in response to the conflict between Antipas and Aretas (Chapter 2). He appointed a certain "Marcellus" or "Marullus" prefect of Judaea and restored the priestly vestments to the chief priests, which the Roman garrison at the Antonia had previously kept. He also replaced the high priest Jonathan with his brother Theophilus.[8]

Vitellius' priestly appointments perhaps help us understand the conditions in which leading figures among Jesus' followers preached publicly and maybe suffered occasional retributive violence. But this is only if we accept the historical validity of the violence that Acts links to the proto-martyr Stephen. Vitellius may have ended Jonathan's brief term as high priest because a *synhedrion* extralegally executed some of Jesus' followers in Jerusalem in 36–37. This would suggest that Jesus' followers seized the opportunity to preach at the Temple after Pilate and Caiaphas were dismissed in 36. But in turn Jonathan and the chief priests had begun to try capital cases against them that involved accusations of sedition (among other charges). We will see how the *synhedrion* assumed this extralegal authority in 62 to execute James, apparently Jesus' brother, during a transition between Roman prefects. In 36–37, it conceivably did the same.[9]

A key problem is that it is hard to find corroboration for what Acts says about the preaching of Jesus' followers between Jesus' death and the reign of Agrippa I over greater Judaea (41–44). In basic summary, Acts claims Peter and Jesus' inner circle first preached to 120 people in an undisclosed place (the Temple?) and then conspicuously at the Pentecost, with the Temple implied. Thereafter, Peter and John preached at the Temple, where they were arrested by the chief priests, the *strategos* of the Temple, and some Sadducees. The chief priests convened a *synhedrion*, which released Peter and John with a warning, inflicted no punishment, and notified no Roman authorities. When Peter and some companions again preached at the Temple precinct, the chief priests put them in jail. They tried them before another *synhedrion* at Jerusalem for teaching in Jesus' name after being forbidden to do so. Convicting them, the council had them lashed but decided not to execute them. When some of Jesus' followers kept preaching in public, the council reportedly made an example of Stephen, a follower of Jesus who was also active at the Temple. After hostile worshipers seized him there, a council sentenced him and stoned him to death. Stephen's activity incited the broad pursuit of Jesus' followers by allies of the chief priests at Jerusalem, who began to invade their homes to arrest them. The pursuit was so intense that they fled and preached elsewhere in Judaea and Samaria. Meanwhile a Pharisee named Saul who was intimately involved in Stephen's death (but soon to be a Jesus Christ believer called Paul) participated in a broad effort to arrest and execute Jesus' followers. Amid their preaching, Jesus' followers managed to blame Jews in general for Jesus' death despite otherwise acknowledging Pilate and Antipas were most responsible (7:51–53; 4.27).[10]

Such is the report of Acts. But its portrayal of Stephen's death is dubiously aligned with how it depicts Jews (and not Romans) as murderously pursuing Jesus' followers. We will learn how the preacher Paul (2 Cor 11:30–32; Gal 1:13–23) became a Jesus Christ believer in Damascus by 37–38, where Acts (9) places Jesus' followers by that time. Acts (7:58; 8.1–3) alone claims that Paul, being an agent of the chief priests named Saul, attended Stephen's stoning, pursued Jesus' followers, and invaded their homes. Such claims are uncorroborated by Paul's own letters.[11]

Jesus' Followers on Trial (until 250)

If Acts poses so many problems, what can we surmise about the repressive violence Jesus' followers faced at Jerusalem during the mid- to late 30s? If anything, it is that the preaching of Jesus' leading followers at the Temple precinct, especially during important festivals, raised many of the same concerns that Jesus' preaching did during his final Passover. The chief priests in fact had a serious obligation to keep their compatriots safe from violence during the Temple's ritual calendar. If possible, they avoided the intervention of Roman troops. But when the chief priests convened a *synhedrion* to evaluate an incendiary preacher, they could not have it authorize capital punishment. Instead, they brought charges before a Roman magistrate. The sort of arrest, questioning, and, in some instances, lashing reported by Acts has basic support from Paul's own testimony about lashes he received from Jewish community leaders (2 Cor 11:24–25). It is corroborated by Josephus, who reports that the chief priests had Jesus bar Ananias arrested, lashed, and then tried before the governor Albinus in 62 or so. In turn Albinus had him mutilated with scourges but declined to execute him. After Pilate's dismissal, Roman prefects apparently hesitated to execute Jesus' followers or likeminded preachers at Jerusalem for criminal behavior, unless their activity had serious insurrectionist or rioting potential.[12]

If Pilate's successors hesitated to execute followers of Jesus for preaching in public, under Agrippa I we witness a return to Pilate's pattern of conduct. An observant Jew like his predecessor Antipas, Agrippa I was the Roman governor and client king of greater Judaea from 41 to 44. As such, he had a vast remit for executing incendiary preachers who threatened the stability of his governance or Judaea's ordering of wealth. Nothing supports that he pursued Jesus' community of followers in general. But he apparently executed a few select leaders for sedition, much like Pilate and Antipas before him.[13]

Before becoming king, Agrippa I spent a few years as "ethnarch" of the former territories of Philip the Tetrarch and then Antipas. But in 41, the emperor Claudius conferred upon him almost all the remaining territory once ruled by his grandfather Herod I along with the title of king. Agrippa then traveled to Judaea to govern. He encountered only limited intervention from Vibius Marsus, the governor of Syria. He even appointed and deposed Jerusalem's chief priests, as Roman prefects had formerly done. But despite his autonomy, nothing suggests that he indiscriminately punished Jesus Christ believers. If Acts is accurate, Agrippa executed Jesus' follower James and targeted Simon Peter for death (12:1–19). His justification, most probably, was that their public preaching could incite outbreaks of crowd violence. But like Pilate, he did not pursue Jesus' followers beyond that.[14]

Agrippa reigned over greater Judaea for three years. When he died in 44, Roman governors from Italy were once again appointed by emperors to govern Judaea. These continued to prohibit a *synhedrion* from managing capital cases, and unlike Pilate, Antipas, and Agrippa, they apparently did not execute even leading followers of Jesus charged with sedition. This may explain why no council at Jerusalem or Roman governor in Judaea put to death the preacher Paul. Paul was never judged by Agrippa I, and when he was most prominent, Roman governors of Judaea generally refrained from executing Jesus' followers just for incendiary preaching at the Temple if no violence broke out. But when Jesus was alive, he crossed paths with a governor who dealt with the issue more aggressively. This was Pilate.

Paul, Persecutor and Apostle

So far, we have said little about the most intriguing preacher to emerge after Jesus' crucifixion. This is of course Paul, a Pharisee who became one of Jesus' most vocal followers (Phil 3:5; Acts 23:6, 26:5). Yet he engaged in public preaching for decades without being executed by a Roman governor like Jesus. Why is this?

To understand Paul's early career, we best use his own surviving letters. These survive in the New Testament, though many scholars doubt some letters attributed to him are his. Otherwise, we must rely on Acts, which is sometimes inconsistent with Paul's actual writing. In his letters, Paul describes himself as pursuing followers of Jesus in vague terms. He merely claims he was "a pursuer of the church" and someone who "excessively pursued the church of God" (Phil 3:6; Gal 1:13). But he never mentions making arrests or attending extralegal executions. Otherwise, Paul's letters refer to lashes he received on five occasions for his public preaching (2 Cor 11:24) from leaders of local Jewish communities, but not to executions. Acts (7:58–8:3; 22:3–4) alone portrays Paul as attending the murder of Stephen, invading people's homes, and living in Jerusalem after relocating there from Tarsus. Acts is also solitary in placing Paul's such activity in Jerusalem. We have seen how Acts consistently portrays Jews, not Romans, as pursuing Jesus' followers. This and the lack of corroboration raise doubts.[15]

Because of such issues, Paul's early life and even the circumstances under which he became a Jesus Christ believer are hard to discern. But his own letters suggest that he was in Damascus, not Jerusalem, when he was "excessively pursuing the church" and that a divine revelation happened to him there. There he probably was endeavoring to arrest and prosecute leading followers of Jesus who engaged in inflammatory public preaching. In one letter (Gal 1:17), he states that after his conversion, "I did not go to Jerusalem to the apostles before me, but I went out to Arabia and returned back again to Damascus." He also went to Jerusalem three years after becoming a Jesus Christ believer, when he was "still unknown by face to the churches of Judaea in Christ" that had "heard that the one who once pursued us now preaches the faith he once was attacking" (Gal 1:22–23). Paul's testimony in Galatians constantly orients him toward Damascus. It communicates that he was unknown to Jesus' followers in Jerusalem after his becoming a follower of Jesus. If anything, it places Paul in Damascus when he first pursued Jesus' followers in the mid-30s and joined them.

Likewise, Paul's testimony and Acts are inconsistent in how they treat Paul's famous escape from Damascus. When Paul describes the event (2 Cor 11:32–33), he states, "in Damascus, the ethnarch of king Aretas guarded the city of Damascus to lay hold of me, and through a window, I was let down from the wall in a basket and escaped his hands." The reference to Aretas IV dates the episode between 36 and 40. Philip the Tetrarch died in 34. Shortly after, Aretas defeated Antipas in Philip's former territory in an event that can be securely placed in 36. Until 40, when Aretas died, his army controlled territory as far north as Damascus. Paul's statement from 2 Corinthians refers to an event best dated to 37. He is probably describing how he departed Damascus and traveled into Arabia (Gal 1:16–17) or Jerusalem (Gal 1:18–19). His letter mentions no plot to kill him. It only declares that Aretas' army was preventing him from departing through the gates. Acts alone claims that Paul's clever exit from Damascus enabled him to evade a murderous plot of his Jewish opponents (Acts 9:23–26). Some members of the Jewish leadership at Damascus were plausibly petitioning the Nabataean ethnarch to arrest and judge Paul on charges of seditious behavior that stemmed from his public preaching. Paul took measures to avoid detection. But no one was planning to kill him in cold blood.[16]

Altogether Paul's own letters indicate that his pursuit of prominent preachers among the followers of Jesus happened in Damascus in the mid-30s. His activity in Jerusalem, even whether he was living there, is much harder to verify, despite what Acts claims. After briefly pursuing followers of Jesus who publicly preached their message in Damascus, he became one of them. In 37 he evaded Nabataean soldiers to exit the city, and he preached in Arabia and, it seems, visited Jerusalem to consult with James, the brother of Jesus (Gal 1:18–22).

Paul's career as both pursuer and pursued suggests that any violence Jesus' followers encountered after his execution involved sporadic attempts by the chief priests, leaders of local Jewish communities, or Roman authorities to curb the public preaching of individual leaders as it happened. While weighing various considerations, they acted if they believed that someone's preaching could foreseeably incite violence at Jerusalem's Temple precinct or public spaces in cities like Damascus. Such violence would, of course, invite the unwelcome scrutiny of Roman or Greek municipal authorities. Little supports that they defined simply believing in Jesus' Messianic, divinely mandated stature or assembling in a house to celebrate it as criminally seditionist in themselves. The chief priests and other Jewish leaders selectively arrested public preachers or leading figures and had them lashed or brought them to trial before a Roman governor. But they did not execute many (if any) of them. Best dated sometime after 90, Acts is the only text written by the earliest generations of Jesus Christ believers that portrays their adversaries, including Paul, as trying to eradicate their community. Its treatment is suspect.

When Paul publicly preached in Jesus' name in ways that could incite social disturbance, he risked being arrested, tried, and executed for criminally seditionist behavior, just as Jesus had been. But much depended on the individual perspectives of Roman authorities. According to Acts, the chief priests and their allies aggressively petitioned Roman governors to have him tried for capital crimes. But he was apparently never tried before Agrippa I, who, like Pilate, tended to punish such activity more harshly than many governors. Otherwise, no governor of Judaea in whose court Paul appeared ever convicted or executed him. According to Acts, this was because he appealed his case to the emperor, a privilege enjoyed by Roman citizens, and was transported to Rome. Yet Acts also insists that Roman authorities did not believe Paul's activity to be criminal and refrained from executing him even before his appeal. Paul himself likewise indicates Roman or municipal authorities punished him with flogging but never executed him (2 Cor 11:24–25). Otherwise early Christian traditions place his execution among those initiated by the emperor Nero in Rome in 65, which arguably marks a pivotal shift in how Roman authorities confronted communities of Jesus Christ believers and subsequent Christians. Despite similarities in their public preaching, Jesus and Paul were tried by different judges. Paul never crossed paths with Pontius Pilate or Agrippa I. If he did, he might not have survived it.

After Agrippa I

In 44 Agrippa I unexpectedly died. Governance of Judaea once again fell to magistrates of equestrian rank dispatched from Italy. Unlike Agrippa, these hesitated to put Jesus' followers to death for sedition when they preached their message in public. Meanwhile no council at Jerusalem could execute figures for blasphemy or seditious preaching. If one did, the high priest was held accountable by Roman authorities.[17]

A moment in which a *synhedrion* at Jerusalem tried and executed a man actually supports this. In c. 62, the governor Festus died while in office, and the emperor dispatched his replacement, Albinus, to Judaea. While Albinus was on his way, the high priest Ananus, a son of the same Ananus involved in Jesus' trial, convened a council and had James, identified as the brother of Jesus by Josephus' surviving text, charged with some crime. The council convicted him and had him stoned to death. James presumably had been preaching at the Temple, like other leading followers of Jesus charged with seditious behavior. James' death represents how Jesus' followers maintained a public presence at Jerusalem. They competed with the chief priests for authority, and as municipal leaders recognized by Rome, the chief priests sometimes arrested them for inciting social disturbance. But such activity does not reflect a sustained pursuit of Jesus' followers. In fact, some Jews of Jerusalem communicated to Agrippa II what had occurred and traveled toward Alexandria to inform Albinus that a *synhedrion* had executed a person without his approval. Albinus then wrote a threatening letter to Ananus, and Agrippa II deprived him of the high priesthood. Festus apparently had not allowed a council at Jerusalem to put people to death, and Albinus did not either. This same Albinus did not execute Jesus bar Ananias when the chief priests arrested him and charged him with seditious behavior, though he had him brutally scourged. Clearly, he prohibited municipal authorities at Jerusalem from inflicting capital punishment.[18]

The activity and trials of Paul during the 50s, as reported by Acts, also have a bearing on this issue. If accurate, Acts' testimony supports that Roman governors continued to demand capital cases. While at Jerusalem, Paul was reportedly seized by compatriots from Asia Minor and accused of bringing a non-Jew to the Temple's interior courts. When a visible fracas occurred, the Roman garrison at the Antonia intervened, detained him, and brought him to its barracks. The cohort's tribune did not deem Paul's activity seditious offhand, but seeking clarification from his accusers, he had Paul led before a council (Acts 21–23 generally). When Paul's statements triggered a violent dispute, the Roman garrison again intervened and transferred him to the governor Felix at Caesarea (23).

This episode of Acts invites scrutiny. As usual, it portrays Jesus' followers as nonthreatening to Roman authorities while making Jews most responsible for violence against them. We should perhaps accept that the Lukan author contrived much of it. But it accurately reports that Paul's opponents had to prosecute him for seditious activity at the Temple precinct before the Roman governor. Whatever may have happened when a council convened, it had no competency to execute him. Instead, the chief priests reportedly deemed Paul worthy of capital charges and then petitioned Felix. Among the accusations was that Paul was "inciting sedition [*staseis*] for all the Jews/Judaeans in the world" (Acts 24.1–9).

Acts' account of Paul's trials before Roman governors like Felix inspires hesitation. It draws obvious parallels with Jesus' trial before Pilate in Luke, and once again the Lukan author portrays Jesus' followers as innocuous to Roman authority. But Acts represents Roman authorities as reluctant to convict or execute Paul on charges of sedition. It reports Felix heard the case but refused to tender a verdict until the tribune who had arrested him could testify. Despite being corrupt, he did not execute Paul as a favor to the chief priests. After two years of delay, Festus became governor of Judaea and judged the case (Acts 24). However questionable the particulars may be, Acts portrays a *synhedrion* as not empowered to execute on capital charges. It had to bring capital charges before the governor. It also points to concerns that the chief priests had about Paul's ostensibly incendiary preaching at the Temple precinct. In response, Paul reportedly insisted before the governor that he had committed no wrong against the "law of the Jews," the Temple, or Caesar (25:8). He was arguing that he was not inciting sedition at all. Ultimately Paul evaded judgment from Festus by appealing to the emperor as a Roman citizen.[19]

Despite Paul's appeal to the emperor, Acts portrays Agrippa II as hearing the charges against Paul at Festus' behest while visiting Caesarea (25:10–26:32, with 22:25–29). After Paul makes his case, Agrippa proclaims his innocence. But even if he had found him guilty, neither Festus nor Agrippa arguably had any authority to punish him (at least, in the narrative of Acts). We can once again suspect the episode was contrived by the Lukan author. We have already noted the parallel with Pilate's decision to send Jesus to Antipas in Luke (23:6–12). While emphasizing that Roman governors deemed Jesus and his followers innocent of any seditious crimes, the Lukan author perhaps takes the extra step of portraying Herodian dynasts who share the belief. Even so, its claim that Roman governors prevented councils from executing offenders is correct. If tried by Roman governors in Judaea, Paul obviously was not executed by them either. His own testimony instead suggests he was flogged with rods by Roman magistrates and then released (2 Cor 11:24–25).

Despite the problems posed by Acts, its reports of capital cases are instructive. They point to how Roman authorities were managing repressive violence in Judaea after the reign of Agrippa I. They continued to prohibit a *synhedrion* at Jerusalem or municipal leaders elsewhere to have discretion over capital cases, including those that involved seditiously public preaching. They also typically refrained from killing incendiary preachers for sedition, unless they had initiated acts of mass violence, accumulated arms, organized mass demonstrations, or inspired an actual social disturbance (Chapter 9). Preachers who publicly proclaimed an incendiary message without being accompanied by a mass following were often spared, though perhaps flogged or lashed. Unlike Pilate, governors like Felix (active 52–60), Festus (60–62), and Albinus (62–64) hesitated to execute them. Otherwise, Acts exaggerates the coercive violence undertaken by chief priests at Jerusalem or community leaders in Damascus, which is often hard to corroborate. These sometimes acted against leading preachers who appeared to incite social disturbance or outbreaks of violence. But even then, they still had to bring charges before Roman governors who were reluctant to execute, and Acts' report of consistent, widespread persecutory conduct toward Jesus Christ believers is unfounded. This is perhaps why Paul did not die in Jerusalem, as Jesus did.

Trials and Executions of Early Christians: A Comparative Context

After the confrontations narrated by Acts, there is an unsettling quiet. For the next 200 years, only periodically are Roman governors on record as judging Jesus Christ believers. It was only by the mid-to-late second century or so (as scholars now increasingly surmise) that Jesus Christ believers had so differentiated themselves from Jews that they were meaningfully Christians. (Scholars still debate how this happened.) But however classified, violence by the Roman state against them remained sporadic. Most governors had no interest in pursuing Christians or even hearing cases brought against them. Their activity is beyond the chronological scope of this study. Still, the inconsistency of Roman governors in judging and executing Christians highlights a key aspect of how Roman prefects behaved toward Jesus, his followers, and dissident preachers like them. Much was contingent on the moral biases and legal perspectives of Roman governors, who differed in what they viewed as seditious behavior. Yet there was a key difference. Governors of Judaea like Pilate had to decide whether incendiary preaching in a politically turbulent space was seditionist. Those who subsequently executed Christians in the provinces were formulating different opinions about whether being Christian, assembling with Christians, and refusing to worship traditional gods were seditionist behaviors.

The executions of early Christians by Roman governors point once again to the governors' vast discretion. Before 250 Roman magistrates judged and executed Christians only sporadically. The insurgencies of the First Jewish Revolt (66–74), the diasporic rebellions (115–117), and the Bar Kochba Revolt (132–135) may have even made them more well-disposed toward Jesus Christ believers than they were toward many other Jews. These in turn increasingly distanced themselves from their compatriots until they, as Christians, belonged to entirely different communities. But altogether, the inconsistency with which Christians had fatal confrontations with Roman authority helps illuminate the legal pathways that did prove lethal.[20]

In 250, the emperor Decius mandated that all Romans worship polytheist gods. In c. 300, Diocletian and his co-ruling emperors issued edicts against Christianity specifically and initiated a general spate of arrests and executions. But before that, devotees of Christ mostly conducted their affairs as small exclusive communities resembling voluntary associations in urban centers. Local connections that they forged through organic social means won them converts. But they also attracted resentment or suspicion from their neighbors, who created noxious stereotypes and sometimes sought to prosecute them. By the second century, polytheists even construed Christians and their hostility to traditional gods as signs that they were a faction that incessantly sowed sedition against broader communities.[21]

After the timeline recorded by Acts, such factors sometimes proved fatal for Christians. But much depended on the orientations of individual governors. Some defined the habitual, quotidian activities of Christians in themselves as criminally seditious. Others did not. The first recorded large-scale prosecution and execution of Jesus Christ believers or Christians happened after the infamous fire of Rome in 64. Christians would remember this episode as a serious persecution, and in their memories it carried off both Peter and Paul. As the second-century historian Tacitus reports, the emperor Nero spuriously blamed "Christians" of Rome for the fire. While this provided justification for their trials and executions, Tacitus hints that Roman authorities thought of their simply being "Christian" as habitually criminal behavior. He claims they were convicted not so much of arson as of their "hatred of the human race" (*odio humani generis*), or in other words their reputation for habitual, seditious plotting. Some suggest that Tacitus' information is anachronistic. Certain people (spuriously) convicted and executed for the fire may have happened to be Jesus Christ believers. But they were not being targeted as "Christians," as they were during Tacitus' lifetime. Others surmise that Nero was hostile to Jesus Christ believers; Tacitus inaccurately connects his violence to the fire. However we understand Tacitus, a basic point remains: Pilate had executed Jesus for sedition because his activity had the potential to inspire social instability. But at some point in the first or second century, Jesus Christ believers or Christians were at times being executed for this same potential even if they had not engaged in incendiary public preaching. Some Romans simply viewed their very identities and habitual rejection of traditional gods as criminal behavior.[22]

For the next two centuries, reports about the executions of Christians focused on certain cities in the provinces at certain times. Roman governors did not uniformly target Christians. Christians were not consistently being tried and executed throughout the Roman Empire. Christian communities that suffered a spate of executions were not necessarily being targeted for a protracted time. Very often Christian communities that suffered violence were behaving just like Christians living elsewhere who did not. Such inconsistencies reflect the moral biases and legal perspectives of different governors who determined whether a Christian community suffered violence at a given time or place. A governor might harm local Christians, but his successors or his neighboring governors might not.

If Roman prefects of Judaea had different definitions of seditious preaching before 65, provincial governors after that disagreed as to whether simply being Christian was seditious. We witness the dilemma in the next serious prosecution of Christians on record after the executions in Rome under Nero. Unfortunately, the precise circumstances under which a bishop of Antioch named Ignatius was tried and executed, reportedly during the reign of Trajan, are very difficult to reconstruct. Many letters attributed to him may not be authentic. But we can focus our attention on another documented moment of prosecution and execution with which the reign of Trajan will forever be associated. This involved Pliny the Younger during his time as the Roman proconsul in Bithynia (111–113) and is documented by his letter exchange with the emperor Trajan.[23]

Certain aspects of Pliny's activity warrant emphasis. First, polytheists had petitioned his court to judge people suspected of practicing Christianity. Beyond that, he did not arrest Christians on his own initiative. As had been the case with Jesus, local elites had done the work of collecting intelligence, organizing arrests, and bringing the accused to the governor for trial. Second, Pliny was deeply in doubt about what the crimes of the Christians were. He even stated that he did not know whether they stood accused of bearing the name or of actual criminal acts. Even so, he believed being Christian did involve some sort of habitually criminal or seditious behavior. The petitioners of his court were charging the defendants with being Christians but with no specific act. At trial, he initially condemned and sentenced (apparently to execution) those who repeatedly admitted being Christian. As the successes of the petitioners apparently led to more charges, Pliny followed a procedure similar to those used by subsequent Roman judges. He spared those who denied being Christian and showed it by worshiping polytheist gods. He ordered persisting offenders to be imprisoned until he could get further directions from the emperor Trajan. Despite his uncertainties, Pliny recognized being Christian as a criminal offense, especially when prompted by petitioners. This was so even when he discovered that their activities otherwise involved no conspiracy to organize social disturbance or armed insurgency.[24]

The subsequent prosecutions and executions of Christians betray similar patterns. Local polytheists petitioned, and a governor then judged whether being Christian was a seditious act. Otherwise governors or their officers actively sought out Christians, especially as military policing became more robust and invasive for civilians. During the reign of Antoninus Pius (137–161), Justin Martyr criticized the execution of Christians at Rome and met a similar fate himself shortly thereafter. In his *Apologies*, he countered Roman authorities who classified Christian allegiance as criminal or seditious behavior. His response was that Christians were good, law-abiding people who should not be executed simply because of the name "Christian." He and other Christian apologists criticized Roman judges for indulging their biases and disregarding expectations that they dispense justice, not cruelty.[25]

Clearly, some Roman governors agreed with Justin's sentiment. According to Tertullian, some governors of Africa Proconsularis had Christians tried and executed. But others deemed charges against them to have no merit. For them, being Christian was not in itself a seditious act. A Christian who had not committed a recognizably criminal deed was to be spared. One governor provided guidance to a defendant about how to get acquitted. Another simply acquitted. One released a Christian who promised to apostatize and pursued the matter no further. Another had the indictment destroyed when the petitioner did not appear.[26]

After Justin Martyr and Tertullian, martyr acts provide many of the surviving accounts of Christian trials. Their dating and historical accuracy are much debated. Only a few texts describing the executions of Christians before 250 can be securely placed before the fourth century. Whether they are based on actual trial transcripts is a contentious issue. Even so, they reflect common long-standing assumptions about Roman governance and legal decision-making whose features Christian authors were reworking or exaggerating for their desired ends. In many key texts, we witness municipal leaders bringing accusations and Roman judges determining criminal liability and deciding whether to execute.[27]

Letters attributed by the fourth-century historian Eusebius to Christians from Lyons and Vienne who underwent serious trials in 177 are good examples. They clarify that Roman magistrates intervened in the activities of Christians in response to petitions by local elites and on the grounds that being Christian was a seditious act. According to the letter, a military tribune, instigated by local leading men, arrested local Christians and had them imprisoned. At trial, the governor was interested only in whether the people confessed to being Christian. He was not swayed when advocates argued that Christians were moral, law-abiding people who committed no criminal acts. As the convicts were being sentenced to beheading or to death by beasts, the governor sent a petition to the emperor for further direction. The response of the emperor maintained those who denied being Christian would be spared.[28]

Our next text, *The Acts of the Scillitan Martyrs*, is framed as the transcript of a case that occurred at Carthage in North Africa in 180 under the Roman governor Saturninus. When asked to renounce their Christian allegiance, the defendants maintained they had engaged in no criminal activity. Their refusal to swear an oath by the emperor's genius and their insistence on proclaiming themselves Christian led to their execution. The governor defined their activity as against "the Roman way of life" (*Romanorum morem*). It is hard to date the text before the fourth century in any of its surviving variations. Yet it is consistent with second-century witnesses like Pliny, Justin Martyr, and Tertullian in pointing to a simple fact: some governors killed Christians for being intrinsically seditious; others did not.[29]

The Passion of Perpetua contains the compelling narration of a woman imprisoned and then executed at Carthage in 203. According to her, the procurator Hilarianus exhorted her to have mercy on her father and her son by making a sacrifice for the health of the emperor. When she refused, the procurator asked her if she was a Christian, and she responded that she was. The procurator condemned her to death. Finally, *The Martyrdom of Polycarp*, perhaps dated to the third century, communicates how the municipal police at Smyrna arrested the bishop Polycarp and transferred him to the governor for execution. The initial arrest was reportedly motivated by the hostility of local polytheists. But once charges were brought to the governor, he recognized Polycarp's Christian affiliation as seditionist.[30]

Some governors were clearly willing to recognize being Christian as an actionable offense. Yet their conduct disguises the hosts of governors who did not and whose inaction the historical texts do not explicitly record. After all, before 250 no edict prohibited people from being Christian or forced them to worship polytheist gods. Whether being Christian was criminally seditious varied according to the perceptions of Roman judges, who responded in different ways. Some governors accepted petitions from provincials who accused others of being Christian. Others declined. Some actively pursued Christians. Others acquitted them outright. Even the emperors were inconsistent. Centuries after Pilate crucified Jesus, men like him continued to forge their legal pathways unabated.

The Trials of Jesus and of Early Christians

The executions of Jesus Christ believers and Christians between 65 and 250 happened largely because some governors understood simply being Christian and refusing traditional gods to be habitually seditious. The petitioners of their courts certainly thought of them that way. But in their own lifetimes, Jesus and his immediate followers did not face execution for this reason. Instead, authorities were debating whether their public acts and statements were criminally seditionist. What they said, how they said it, where they said it, and whether these factors combined could incite social disturbance or crowd violence were at issue. But there is also some continuity. In the two centuries or so after Jesus' followers began their public preaching, Roman governors continued to differ in their opinions about the legal validity of prosecuting, sentencing, and executing Christians. Some were aggressive in accepting petitioners and inflicting coercive violence. Others did not think Christians were seditionist criminals.

But a key shift had occurred. During the lifetime of Jesus and its immediate aftermath, uncertainties abounded about how governors should respond to public and incendiary preaching. Was it seditious or not? They were not very concerned with what Jesus or his followers believed or practiced on a quotidian basis. But they were concerned with what they said in public, how they said it, and its potential for fomenting social disturbance. As communities of Jesus Christ believers and then Christians came to populate most urban areas of the Roman Empire, the focus shifted to whether simply being and practicing as a Christian (and refusing traditional gods) was seditious and warranted the intervention of judges. Roman governors continued to differ in how they approached this issue, but the violent debate had changed. Jesus' death was determined by who was governor when he preached at the Temple precinct. Different governors did not execute other men, including Jesus' followers, who did the same. But after that, the fates of so many Christians pivoted on whether a governor defined being Christian as habitually seditious activity. Their fate was determined by who governed their province and the legal pathway he forged.

Epilogue

CROSSING PATHS WITH PILATE

Ordering Jesus scourged, [Pilate] handed him over to be crucified.

—MARK 15:15

LONG AGO, ON a spring morning in Jerusalem, a Roman governor passed judgment on a mysterious preacher. The preacher was brutally affixed to a cross shortly after. The effects of this verdict have reverberated throughout the world. They have shaped two millennia of history. Today billions of people embrace the executed convict as their savior. His judge is remembered as his impious murderer. The Nicene Creed names only one man for crucifying Jesus of Nazareth: Pontius Pilate.

Was Jesus a seditionist? He was, in Pilate's eyes. Through his words and deeds he had ostensibly incited violence at the Temple precinct during Passover week. His preaching and activity suggested Messianic or regal aspirations. Yes, the chief priests saw Jesus as an imposter and a competitor for authority. But they also had an obligation to his compatriots to protect them at the Temple. They tried to arrest him while he preached, and they desisted when they sensed this could create turmoil and violence. They instead captured him at night at his camp outside Jerusalem and brought him to the house of Annas, the (former) high priest. At a council hearing, they found him liable for a capital charge. But they did not have the legal authority to try and convict him of a capital crime. They had to bring him to Pilate. To his point Pilate had played almost no role in collecting information on Jesus or arresting him. But Pilate had a vested interest in judging people accused of sedition by the chief priests. He already had jailed Barabbas and the two men who would die with Jesus, all seditionists. Pilate surmised that Jesus was a man of such character. He accepted the case and interrogated the defendant, who denied nothing. Jesus died horrifically hours later.

Epilogue

If Jesus had been tried by a different governor, he may have survived his final Passover week. He was not being accused of armed insurrection or revolutionary insurgency. His core following was relatively small. He reportedly claimed to be "King of the Jews" (or "Judaeans"), but he had no obvious earthly means to be king. Some governors would have dismissed the claim, in isolation, as coming from an unbalanced eccentric. But Jesus had posed as a prophet and even the Messiah while predicting a reign of God that would disturb the governing order. He had done so at the Temple while accompanied by his core followers. His words and deeds could have inspired crowd violence and gotten innocent people hurt or killed, whatever his intentions. They may not have raised concerns elsewhere. But at the Temple precinct, they had a real lethal potential. Jesus was even apparently leveraging the specter of civil violence to avoid arrest by the chief priests. The chief priests had to act. They arrested Jesus outside of town, brought him to their prefect, and accused him of posing as a Messiah at the Temple. In response, Pilate mocked him as "King of the Jews" and had him crucified. But Jesus' message was not Pilate's only concern. It may not even have been his main one.

Pilate did not have Jesus executed simply because the chief priests, allied scribes, or crowd at his trial wanted it. He did not order Jesus' death while believing him innocent of criminal behavior. Yes, Pilate's understanding of seditious behavior in Judaea was shaped by what the chief priests said and did. It was molded by who and what they sanctioned or opposed. Crowd violence at the Temple was a serious concern. But governors and judges had to justify their violence on legal grounds, as flexible and shifting as these could be. Their violence had to be what social stability demanded. This elastic principle governed how they defined seditious behavior. It informed how they sometimes brutally suppressed insurgent threats. It shaped whether they convicted defendants of capital crimes. In Judaea, it made prophetic and Messianic preaching at the Temple precinct very suspect, especially during holidays. But governors faced serious consequences if they overstepped. They could be dispossessed and banished for excessive violence. They sometimes responded to active insurgents or insurrectionists with slaughter. But overwhelmingly they killed the arrested after convicting them of a crime at trial. Pilate faced consequences for his repressive violence only after governing for a decade and after slaughtering armed seditionists. He was no stranger to violence. But he did not just kill visibly innocent men. At Jesus' trial, the chief priests claimed Jesus had endangered pilgrims at the Temple precinct. Pilate concluded they were right. When he had Jesus crucified, he did it because he believed that Jesus committed a grotesque crime that warranted a grotesque death.

The chief priests and allied scribes at Jerusalem played a role in Jesus' death. But in doing so, they were fulfilling their obligations as the governing elite at Jerusalem. Yes, the Gospels portray them as eliminating a rival. Yes, the chief priests represented the ordering of authority and wealth in Roman Judaea that Jesus opposed. But they were not just acting on their own political motives. They had to ensure their compatriots could participate in Passover week at the Temple without being harmed, and Jesus' conduct there could have incited outbreaks of uncontrolled violence. It comes as no surprise that the Gospels ascribe uniquely selfish motives to the chief priests. But in truth, they were acting like other municipal leaders in the Roman Empire who were responsible for protecting innocent people.

Pilate was the one who judged Jesus guilty and deserving of crucifixion. He did not need much convincing. He too embodied the order of governance and wealth in Roman Judaea. He did not hesitate to eliminate anyone who inspired crowd violence in opposition to it. Jesus had done just that. Pilate responded by mocking him repeatedly as "King of the Jews." He selected a public form of execution doled out to the most malignant criminals. He had Jesus executed alongside what he deemed to be other such men. Pilate never believed in Jesus' innocence, despite what the Gospels say. Jesus was just one of many seditious men he executed during a Passover week, and with a valid legal basis. Pilate did not foresee that billions of people would embrace Jesus as a divine king sent from heaven even 2,000 years later. He had no idea he was judging the most famous trial the world had ever witnessed. But if anything, history has been much kinder to him than to Jesus' compatriots. The Gospel narratives have long been a basis for anti-Jewish hate. Each spring the timing of Easter haunts the holiday of Passover.

Jesus was crucified because he crossed paths with Pilate. Many different governors might have acquitted, spared, flogged, or scourged him. But they would have left it to Herodian dynasts like Antipas or Agrippa I to kill him. Without Pilate, Jesus may have lived out his normal lifespan, his iconic execution never happening. But Jesus' judge was not Felix, Festus, or Albinus. These reportedly refused to execute Paul or Jesus bar Ananias for their incendiary preaching. Conceivably they would have acquitted Jesus. Or they would have flayed his flesh with the scourge, leaving him alive and tattooed by scars. But Jesus' judge was Pontius Pilate. Jesus committed an act of sedition. Pilate forged his path to crucifying him.

APPENDIX I

Policing, Arresting Parties, and the New Testament Gospels

The dates of the New Testament Gospels, their sources, and their relationships to one another are heavily debated (Chapter 4). So is their value for understanding Jesus' preaching and death in historical terms. One key problem is related to a goal the Gospels share: they all shift the responsibility for Jesus' death from Roman authorities to the chief priests (or in John, "the Jews"). But what does this mean for Jesus' arrest, trial, and death? Pilate had Jesus crucified. But did the chief priests organize his arrest and bring him before a council (*synhedrion*)? Or was this contrived by the Synoptics or their sources?

The chart below repeats schematically how I understand the dates, relationships, and sources for the Gospels and Acts (Chapter 4). As noted, current and future work on Marcion's Gospel may warrant serious revision:

	Date	Sources
Mark	shortly before or after 70 CE	Paul's letters?
Matthew	late first/early second century	Mark, Modest-sized Q
Luke/	early to mid-second century (or	Mark, Matthew, Modest-sized Q,
Acts	slightly earlier)	Josephus (probably)
John	mid-second century	Mark, the Synoptics, or common sources

My views on Luke and Acts warrant additional comment. Their dates occupy a vast chronological spectrum in scholarly debate. Even without the complications raised by the relationship between Marcion's Gospel and Luke, different theories offer dates ranging from the 60s to the early second century (Chapters 4 and 11). Scholars also differ on whether the Lukan author had read Paul, Pliny, or Josephus, which has bearing on the dating. Even so, I agree with the premise that the Lukan author relied on Josephus for some historical information (even if distorting it or making errors). Most notably, it

208 *Appendix 1*

portrays a Pharisee named Gamaliel as making strange errors when describing the mass movement of the prophet Theudas and the children of Judas the Galilean. In the setting of Acts, Gamaliel's monologue chronologically precedes the activity of Theudas but describes it as a past event. It also dates the activity of Theudas (c. 45) before that of Judas the Galilean and by extension well before when Fadus was governor (Acts 5:35–37). This most plausibly reflects a garbled engagement with Josephus' *Antiquities*, which describes Fadus' suppression of Theudas' movement and then mentions Judas the Galilean. Josephus clearly knew the proper chronological order, but the Lukan author was apparently confused by how Josephus' text sequenced them or accidently conflated Judas with his sons, who died shortly after Theudas. Luke's reference to the census of Quirinius and temporal markers for John the Baptizer align with material from *Antiquities* 18 too. In Appendix 2, we discuss how the Lukan author possibly consulted and serves as a key witness for Josephus' *Testimonium Flavianum*.[1]

The Gospel portrayals of policing and arrest similarly support a late dating for Luke and Acts and dependence on Josephus. They also indicate that the chief priests were exercising standard policing obligations of municipal elites in the Roman Empire by organizing Jesus' arrest. Mark and by extension Matthew recount an armed band rapidly assembled by the chief priests. This aligns with local policing procedure in the provinces during Jesus' lifetime. Municipal councilors or magistrates were usually responsible for such measures, among their other duties. But while reworking Mark's narrative, Luke depicts magistrates (*strategoi*) who specialize in policing and command subordinates. This became more typical in the Roman Empire after the mid-first century. John places a Roman cohort and tribune at Jesus' arrest, which is more standard in the second century (Chapter 7). The Gospels' treatment of policing supports their notional dating. They also support the validity of Mark's portrayal of Jesus' arrest by the chief priests, who provided municipal governance at Jerusalem.[2]

The Lukan author's unique references to a *strategos* (or *strategoi*) of the Temple are arguably anachronistic. Luke places multiple *strategoi* at Jesus' arrest. In Acts, one *strategos* detains his followers Peter and John and is accompanied by "retainers" (*hyperetai*), which some misleadingly call "temple police" or "temple guards." Yet *strategoi* are absent from other passages of Luke and Acts that depict tense confrontations or arrests. The Lukan author apparently inserted them into some existing traditions, but not consistently.[3]

Aside from the Lukan author, the main surviving source for the *strategos* of the Temple is various passages from Josephus, whose narrative never mentions one being active before 50. The position apparently took shape a decade or two after Jesus' crucifixion and seems to be the *sagan* mentioned in Mishnaic passages. The War Scroll, which is difficult to date, refers to some sort of deputy of the chief priest when portraying an eschatological battle. But this is not an unambiguous reference to any contemporary position at the Temple itself. More probably, the *strategos* of the Temple was established in the mid-first century, as Josephus best supports. This would be consistent with when municipal governments in Roman provinces generally started to appoint officials to specialize in policing and suppressing brigands.

Appendix 1

The testimony of Josephus regarding the Temple *strategos* also has implications for how we understand the work of the Lukan author. As mentioned, the Lukan author was apparently familiar with municipal policing practices of the late first century. But the fact that Luke inserts such *strategoi* into the Markan tradition of Jesus' arrest is consistent with the premise that the Lukan author was influenced by Josephus. This same influence could explain why Luke "corrects" Mark's errors in its treatment of the death of John the Baptizer (Chapters 3 and 5) and offers further support that Luke and Acts were written after Josephus' *Jewish War* (c. 75) and even his *Antiquities* (written in 93–94) were circulating.[4]

Such trends in local policing in the Roman Empire have a bearing on how we understand John's portrayal of Jesus' arrest by Roman soldiers. This probably reflects John's refashioning of a basic tradition reflected by the Synoptic narratives according to contemporary paradigms of the mid-second century. It suggests John's account does not reflect an independent tradition for Jesus' arrest that has more historical validity than what the Synoptics report. It also renders more plausible the Synoptic portrayals of the chief priests as organizing Jesus' arrest. Such actions were among the duties fulfilled by municipal elites of the Roman provinces in the early first century. As the municipal elites of Jerusalem, the chief priests acted on a recognizable obligation to the Romans and their compatriots by arresting Jesus.

APPENDIX 2

Josephus on Jesus

There was at this time Jesus, a wise man, if we should actually call him a man. For he was the doer of extraordinary deeds, a teacher of those who enjoy receiving the truth. He attracted many Jews and many from the Greek community. He was the Christ. When Pilate condemned him to the cross at the indictment of our foremost men (*protoi*), those who were foremost in treasuring him did not stop. For living once again he appeared to them on the third day, according to how the divine prophets predicted these and a host of other marvels about him. The tribe of those called Christians after him have not vanished even now.

This brief description of Jesus that survives in Josephus' *Antiquities* (18.63–64) potentially offers crucial testimony that Jesus was prosecuted before Pilate by the priestly elite of Jerusalem (Chapter 7). But it poses many complications, and its authenticity is heavily disputed. Here we briefly outline reasons why we can accept the passage as mostly authentic.[1]

An expanded version of the disputed passage that survives in Slavonic manuscripts was clearly made by medieval Christian hands. The disputed passage itself appears in all the Greek manuscripts but could have been inserted by a Christian before Eusebius quoted it several times c. 300. Scholars often note the following premises against its authenticity:

- It seems inconsistent with the material that proceeds and follows in *Antiquities*.
- It suggests that Jesus was more than human and states that "he was the Christ." It also claims that Jesus appeared alive to his followers on the third day after his death.
- Christian authors do not cite the existing passage before Eusebius (early fourth century). In the third century, Origen stated that Josephus did not believe Jesus was the Messiah while asserting he was a source for John the Baptizer and Jesus' brother James.

Appendix 2

In support of the passage's authenticity, with some modifications, scholars often note the following premises:

- Even when it compliments Jesus as Christ, it deviates from how Christian interpolators would have described him. It calls him a "wise man" who did "amazing deeds." It also uses the term *hedone* (which had negative connotations among Christians) for the enjoyment with which his followers embraced his message and describes him as founding "a tribe" (*phylon*).
- It states Jesus built a following among Jews and Greeks. This seems inconsistent with the Gospels' reports but reflects how a Jew of the late first century may have understood Jesus' contemporary believers.
- Its phrasings are mostly consistent with Josephus' style of Greek.
- Sometimes episodes in *Antiquities* do not mesh thematically with material surrounding it. The disputed passage is not unique in that respect.

From such premises, many surmise Josephus' original passage had a neutral tone. Some posit a negative one.[2]

A recent, in-depth analysis of parallels between the passage and how Luke portrays the resurrected Jesus' appearance to followers at Emmaus (24.18–27) has yielded the following suggestions:[3]

- Josephus composed the entire passage himself, without interpolations.
- Josephus acquired his material from a Christian source.
- Seemingly Christian material could have been written by someone who did not believe Jesus was a Messiah. The apparent reference to Jesus as "Christ" simply used Jesus' known second name to distinguish him from other people named Jesus. The reference to the resurrection reflects the vantage point of Jesus' followers, not Josephus.

In my view, it is best to accept that the passage was mostly composed by Josephus and had encountered Christian reworking by c. 300, though we cannot know what material (if any) was removed. Josephus' original described Jesus as a wise man reputed to be the Christ, and a Christian interpolator tweaked the statement to say Jesus was the Christ.[4] The following factors favor this viewpoint:

- It explains the passage's overall consistency with Josephus' style.
- It accommodates the variances between the style and content of this passage (as it survives) from those surrounding it or focusing on Pilate in *Antiquities* 18. While having his own language style and thematic goals, Josephus did not always impose these on his sources or work them into a seamless thread. In *Antiquities* Josephus sometimes replicates or adapts the style, viewpoint, or themes of his sources, and he primarily assembles them in chronological order, not thematically.[5]

Appendix 2

- It would explain why Origen states that Josephus did not believe Jesus was Christ and why Jerome and Michael the Syrian, when attesting the passage as mediated by Eusebius, claim it described Jesus as someone who was believed to be the Christ. Michael the Syrian also in fact supports that Josephus described Pilate as crucifying Jesus due to the accusation of leading men. A scribal error in the transmission of the Syriac translation of Eusebius' *Church History* makes Michael's passage appear to say otherwise. Agapius contains only a paraphrase, not a better reading.[6]
- It would explain the overtly Christian elements of the passage as it now survives, particularly its identification of Jesus as Christ.
- It aligns with *Antiquities* 20.200, where Josephus refers to Jesus as "Jesus, the one called Christ." The statement is generally (and justifiably) regarded as authentic.[7]

Likewise, the correspondences between Luke 24:18–27 and Josephus' passage can be explained by the Lukan author's dependence on Josephus (Appendix 1). In the Lukan passage, Jesus' disciples describe him as a prophet without specifying that he is the Messiah (24:19). The resurrected Jesus rebukes them and states that Jesus is the Christ (24:26). The Lukan author plausibly embedded key aspects of Josephus' passage into a narrative of what the resurrected Jesus said and did for his followers. If so, this author was responding to how it treated Jesus as merely a sage reputed to be the Christ by having Jesus identify himself as Christ. Josephus' statement that Jesus appeared to his followers three days after his death is conceivably authentic and reflects the vantage point of Jesus' followers (not his own). Luke 24:18–27 in this case would be a witness for Josephus' passage before Christian doctoring made it specify that Jesus was Christ.

APPENDIX 3

Greek and Hebrew/Aramaic Names

In general, I have rendered the names of people from the Greek texts of the New Testament or Josephus according to their commonly Anglicized forms. Corresponding Hebrew/Aramaic forms for the following names that frequently recur in the book are from Ilan (2002).

New Testament/Josephan Form	Hebrew/Aramaic Name
(Anglicized)	
Ananias	Hananiah
Annas/Ananus	Hanan
Barabbas	Abba
Caiaphas	Qaifa
Jesus	Yeshu
John	Yohanan
Judas	Yehudah
Mary	Mariam/Miriam
Simon	Shimon

APPENDIX 4

Note on Texts, Translations, and Abbreviations

For the New Testament, I used Nestle-Aland, *Novum Testamentum Graece*, 28th revised edition (Stuttgart: Deutsche Bibelgesellschaft, 2012). For the Hebrew Tanakh and Greek Septuagint, respectively, I consulted A. Alt et al., *Biblia Hebraica Stuttgartensia*, 5th ed. (Stuttgart: Deutsche Bibelgesellschaft, 1997) and A. Rahlfs and R. Hanhart, *Septuaginta: Id est Vetus Testamentum Graece iuxta LXX interpretes*, 2nd ed. (Stuttgart: Deutsche Bibelgesellschaft, 2006). In general, translations of passages from the Hebrew Tanakh and New Testament are modified forms of the *New Revised Standard Version Bible (NRSV)* (1989) as they have been reproduced in *The New Oxford Annotated Bible: New Revised Standard Version*, 5th ed. (2018); *The Jewish Annotated New Testament*, 2nd ed. (2017); or in the Greek-English version of Nestle-Aland (2012). For Josephus, I used the edition of Benedikt Niese, *Flavii Josephi Opera*, 7 vols. (Berlin: Weidmann, 1887–1895) and consulted the translations of Thackeray (Loeb), Whiston, and when available, Brill's *Josephus: Translation and Commentary* series. For other Greek and Latin texts, I used OCT, Teubner, GCS, SC, and other standard editions and consulted Loeb or other standard translations. For the Mishnah and Tosefta, I consulted Philip Blackman, *Mishnayoth*, 3rd ed. (New York: Judaica Press, 1963–64) and Saul Lieberman, *Tosefta*, 3 vols. (Jerusalem: Wahrmann, 1955–73). Translations of Hebrew/Aramaic texts generally are variations on those from Blackman (1963–64), Chapman-Schnabel (2019), Martínez and Tigchelaar (1998), or Charlesworth (1993–), which also reproduce the original text.

For in-text citations and footnotes, "classical" authors and texts in Greek or Latin are abbreviated according to the standards of *The Oxford Classical Dictionary*, 4th ed. (Oxford: Oxford University Press, 2012). The one exception is the use of *War* for Josephus' *Bellum Judaicum*. Abbreviations for biblical, Qumran, and early Christian authors are from the *SBL Handbook of Style*, 2nd ed. (Atlanta, GA: SBL, 2014). References to papyrus documents are from *Checklist of Editions of Greek, Latin, Demotic, and Coptic Papyri, Ostraca, and Tables*, 5th ed. (Oakville, CT: American Society of Papyrologists, 2001). In instances of duplication and conflict, I have followed this order of preference: *Dictionary*, then *Handbook*, then *Checklist*. For material not found in these or alternative abbreviations I use, the reader should note the following:

<u>Ancient Authors</u>
Jos., *Ant.* = *Antiquitates* (*Antiquities*)
    Life = *Vita* (*Life*)
    War = *Bellum Judaicum* (*Jewish War*)
<u>Modern Publications</u>
CIIP = *Corpus Inscriptionum Iudaea/Palaestinae*
FIRA = S. Riccobono et al., *Fontes iuris romani antejustiniani*, 3 vols. (Florence: Barbèra, 1940–43).
Greek Constitutions = James Oliver, *Greek Constitutions of the Early Roman Emperors from Inscriptions and Papyri* (Philadelphia: American Philosophical Society, 1989).
JAJ = *Journal of Ancient Judaism*
JSHJ = *Journal for the Study of the Historical Jesus*
Lex Irnitana = Julián González and Michael Crawford, "The Lex Irnitana: A New Copy of the Flavian Municipal Law," *JRS* 86 (1986): 147–243.
NOAB = Michael Coogan et al., *The New Oxford Annotated Bible: New Revised Standard Version*, 5th ed. (Oxford: Oxford University Press, 2018).
JANT = Amy-Jill Levene and Marc Zvi Brettler, *The Jewish Annotated New Testament*, 2nd ed. (Oxford: Oxford University Press, 2017).

All dates are CE unless indicated otherwise. For clarity, I always mark single-digit years as BCE or CE (6 CE, for example). In general, names are transcribed according to their form in the text being discussed. But see Appendix 3 for more information.

Notes

INTRODUCTION

1. For the Gospels' shifting blame from Romans to Jews: Winter (1974); Bermejo-Rubio (2014a), esp. 11–27, (2018b) 119–338; Greenberg (2014), esp. 16–17; Crossan (1995); Ehrman (2016) 156; Brandon (1968a) 21–82, (1968b) 81–139; Fredriksen (2000) 115–22; Elliott (2019) 32–35; Aslan (2013) 114–15; Stegemann (2002), (2010) 353–82. Winter (1974) 208; Betz (2007) 9–10 for impact on the Holocaust. For Christian memories of Pilate and related legal paradoxes: Dusenbury (2021).

2. For detailed inquiry into Jesus' final Passover and sources: Brown (1994); Chapman-Schnabel (2019); Schnabel (2018). My book is indebted to their learnedness for much of its information. For a variety of scholars' perspectives: 3–6, n. 4–11, this chapter.

3. Dusenbury (2021): works attributed to Pilate; many appear in Ehrman-Pleše (2011), (2014). On the apocryphal Gospels: 72–73, n. 1, Chapter 4. Parts II–III delve into scholarship on Mark, but also see nn. 7, 9, this chapter.

4. Blinzler (1969), esp. 245–356 is influential; with variations: Sherwin-White (1963) 1–48; Bammel (1984b) 434–50 (esp. 434–35); Krimphove (1997) 233; Schnabel (2018) 256–83; Reiss (2021). Also, 5, n. 8, this chapter. Without trial/conviction: Crossan (1995) 117; Agamben (2015), refuted by Dusenbury (2017); Aslan (2013) 112, 117–18.

5. *b. Sanh.* 43a. Powell (1994) 205–6 endorses this flawed theory. For older theories, Bickerman (2007) 731–32. For Talmudic material: Schäfer (2017) 129–52, 191–260 (esp. 132–34). On the Gospels and crucifixion: nn. 9–12, this chapter; n. 14, Chapter 4.

6. Peasant prophet: Horsley (1987), (2014), esp. 160–67, with (2011), esp. 187–204, (2012); Reinbold (1994) 311–16. As Cynic or sage: Borg (1994) 47–61, 112–17; Crossan (1991) 355–60, 367–76, (1995) 58–65, 105–17; Borg-Crossan (2006). Challenge to Roman authority: Aslan (2013) 115–17; Reinbold (1994), esp. 311–16, (2006) 100–101, 134–47;

Webb (2009b) 740–57; Dunn (2003) 794–80; Schuol (2007) 193–201; Cook (2011) 199–203; Theobald (2022), esp. 723–26.

7. Winter (1974), esp. 27–89; Zeitlin (1964) 161–179; Cohn (1971) 171–77; McLaren (1991) 96–101; Thiessen-Merz (1998) 458–59; Egger (1997) 195–200, 208–214; Demandt (1999) 170–72; Ehrman (1999) 221–23, (2016) 148–152; Betz (2007), esp. 82–86 (shared expectations of chief priests and Pilate), with Boer (2007) 163–64; Allison (2010) 234–40; Watson (1995) 122–23, 174; Destro-Pesce (2014) 125–29; Bond (1998) 198–200, (2012) 161–62; Greenberg (2014) 249–53; Stegemann (2010) 380–82; Joseph (2016) 25–27. Distorted memories: Ehrman (2016) 148–77. Pilate's hesitation: Lémonon (2007) 259; Joseph (2016) 25–27.

8. Strobel (1980) 116–31; Sanders (1985) 294–318; Hengel-Schwemer (2019) 639–40; Smith (2018) 165–70; Wright (1998); Wenham (2021) 217–20, Keener (2009) 316–20; Sloyan (2006) 100–103; Bovon (2006) 49–50; Bryan (2005) 56–62; Liebs (2012) 110–11; Smith (2018) 68–79, 165–70, on Pilate's desire to placate chief priests; Keener (2016), on Pilate's hesitation. For Jesus as disturbed: Meggitt (2007), critiqued by Fredriksen (2007). Confession (*confessus*), uncooperative conduct (*contumacia*): Schuol (2007) 193; Niemand (2007) 420, 495–96.

9. Bermejo-Rubio (2014a), (2018b) 1–338, with (2013b), (2014b), (2015), (2016), (2018a), (2019), Bermejo-Rubio-Zeichmann (2019), preceded by Brandon (1968a), esp. 1–24, 322–58 (1968b), esp. 140–50. For theories since the 1770s, Bammel (1984a). Martin (2014) suggests Jesus anticipated a heavenly battle; response by Fredriksen (2015).

10. Fredriksen (1999) 232–34, 240–41, 250–59, (2008), esp. 269–71, (2018) 43–73 (esp. 67–73), with (2000), (2015).

11. Elliott (2019), esp. 38–39; Cohick (2008) 122, 129–31; Burchard (1993) 66–67; Vermes (1993) x; Bond (2004) 67–69, (2012) 143–45; Crossley-Myles (2023) 207–10, 228–32. My viewpoint is especially indebted to these arguments.

12. Observed, by Fredriksen (2007) 271, (2018) 40–41, 56–58. Also nn. 9–10, this chapter; n. 11, Chapter 9.

13. For example, Allison (1998) 75–78, (2010) 5–16; Bock-Webb (2009) 7; Carrier (2014), reviewed by Gullotta (2017), on "historicist" versus "mythicist," along with Lataster (2019); Keener (2009) 1–32, (2019). Supporting Jesus' historical existence: Ehrman (2012); Casey (2014); Bermejo-Rubio (2018b) 65–72. The scope of the present book prevents my joining the mythicist-historicist debate. I believe that Jesus existed historically based on Paul's letters, the Gospels, and other ancient witnesses like Tacitus (15.44) and Josephus (*Ant.* 20.197–203), and the more controversial Jos., *Ant.* 18.63–64 (Chapters 3–6; Appendix 2).

14. While learned, Blinzler (1969) and various articles of Bammel-Moule (1984) pit Jesus against Jewish society. Sloyan (2006) 1–10, 103–13; Bermejo-Rubio (2013b), esp. 189–95, (2014a) 102–3; Bond (2004) 9–14 comment on such tendencies, including in some late 20th- and 21st-century publications. On the "Jewishness" of Jesus in scholarship: Crossley (2014); Arnal (2014); Meyer (2020). Judas and the

Notes

chief priests trying to spare Jesus: Cohn (1971) 71–93; Greenberg (2014), esp. 130–54, 266–69. Also 2, n. 1, this chapter.

15. On Pilate's alleged testimony: 3, n. 3, this chapter. For Caiaphas' moral obligations and motives: Bond (2004) 9–72, esp. 9–14, 67–69, (2012) 143–44; Fredriksen (1999) 252–55, (2018) 70–72.

CHAPTER I

1. For Pompey's triumph: Jos., *Ant.* 14.54–79; Plut., *Pomp.* 45; for priestly families, Jos., *Ant.* 20.248–50. The term "client kingdom" is controversial: Kaizer and Facella (2010); Baltrusch-Wilker (2015). For client kings under Augustus: Marshak (2015) 3–24; Ish-Shalom (2021). On Hasmonaean and Herodian Judaea, with relevant references: Grabbe (2020). Czajkowski-Eckhardt (2021) 42–46, 88–93 address Josephus on Herod. Josephus' arguments about Jews and Roman governance: Rajak (2002) 65–103.

2. The dates for many historical events between 40 BCE and 39 CE are debated. Mahieu (2012) is detailed, but not beyond critique; Grabbe (2020) 27–33. Unless stated otherwise, we use conventional dates.

3. Andrade (2013), (2014).

4. MacDonald (2009); Fisher (2015). On Arabic script: Nehmé (2010). On Roman Palestines: Butcher (2003) 86; Isaac (2017) 123–24.

5. Cimadomo (2019) 88–180 (esp. 92–97); Dan-Nodet (2017); Roller (2018) 905; Isaac (2017) 131–32. For "Greek cities": Jos., *War* 2.97, 7.364, *Life* 32–42, 67, 134; *BNJ* 90.136. For demoniac at Gerasa (Mark 5:1–20; Luke 8:26–39) or Gadara (Matt 8:28–34).

6. Cohen (2006); Andrade (2013) provide treatment.

7. For definitions of Judaea: Rosenfeld (2000); Bernett (2007) 23–26; Andrade (2010); Isaac (2017) 137–43. Census, Galilee, Judaea: Luke 2:39, also 5:17; Matt 2:22–23, 3:1, 3:5; 4:25, 19:1–2; Mark 3:7–8.

8. Hasmonaeans and definitions: Leibner (2021); Van Maaren (2022) 114–25. For Hasmoneans: Berlin-Kosmin (2021). For "the Jewish/Judaean land": Strabo, 16.2.21; Jos., *Ant.* 13.395–97; 14.74–76, 87–91, 15.328–30; *War* 1.155–57, 166–70; *Life*, 346–9. Governing the following paragraph, esp. on temples and statues: Bernett (2007), esp. 23–26, 338–39; Andrade (2010). Jesus as *Ioudaios*: John 4:8–10. On Philistia/Palestine: Isaac (2017) 123–24.

9. Mason (2007); Esler (2009); Schwartz (2009); Freyne (1999); Satlow (2014); Grabbe (2020) 7–13; Miller (2014); Rotman (2021), who frames as a civil or juridical community of worship.

10. Pummer (2009), (2016); Hengel-Schwemer (2019) 149–55; Meier (1991) 3.532–49; Staples (2021), esp. 54–86 on Samaritans, Israelites, and Jews. For references from Josephus: *Ant.* 8.306–12, 321–28; 10.288–91. For impurity and Good Samaritan: Crossley-Myles (2023) 172–74.

Notes

11. For coins: Hendin (2021) 193–275; Ariel-Fontanille (2012). Meshorer (2001), with 73–78; Ariel-Fontainelle (2012) 40 on whether taxes and dues in Tyrian shekels were obligatory (*m. Šeqal.* 2.4; *m. Bek.* 8.7). On likenesses and imperial cult: Bernett (2007).

12. For this section, Netzer (2006), esp. 3–240, (2018), Magness (2012) 133–91, with Patrich (2019) on Caesarea; Porat (2015–) on the Herodeion; Galor-Bloedhorn (2013) 63–112, Magness (2024) 154–291 on Jerusalem, govern my summary of Herod's building projects. Rocca (2007); Marshak (2015) govern my reflections on Herod as king.

13. On Samaria: Jos., *Ant.* 16.292–98; *War* 1.403; Caesarea: *Ant.* 15.331–41; *War* 1.408–16. Patrich (2019) 8 (Acts 23:35) on the *praetorium*, with Bond (1998) 5–7; Zeichmann (2018) on auxilia. Jos., *Ant.* 20.173; *War* 2.266: conflict at Caesarea. Pilate's inscription: *CIIP* 2.1277.

14. Netzer (2006) 119–78; Magness (2012) 133–91, (2024) 154–291, with references at n. 12, this chapter. On Herod as devout: Marshak (2015) 273–334. References: Jos., *Ant.* 15.318–20; *War* 1.402–3, 5.161–83, with *War* 2.301 and nn. 3 and 6, Chapter 10 on palace; Jos., *Ant.* 15.380–425; *War* 5.184–247 on Temple; Philo, *Gai.* 212; Jos., *Ant.* 15.417, *War* 5.194; *CIIP* 1.2 on prohibition; Acts 28–29 on Paul; Jos., *Ant.* 15.403–9; *War* 5.238–47 on Antonia.

15. On Temple/pilgrimage: Goodman (2009), with (2007) 55–60; Schwartz (2014) 63–65. Keddie (2019) 161–96, (2021) 179–86, with Ex 30:12–13; Deut 14:22–29; Lev 27:30; Num 18:23–29; Girardin (2022) 85–122 (esp. 86–92), 222–360, on taxes, tithes, fines, and commercial ventures. Lapin (2017a), (2017b): the Temple's land and agricultural means. Evans (1992a), Snodgrass (2009) 455–60; Klawans (2006) 222–41; Charlesworth (2014) 160–64; Joseph (2016) 95–104 on criticisms of priests. On chief priests, scribes, and landed interests aligned with the Herodians-Romans: Horsley (1987), esp. 285–317, (2011), esp. 155–204, (2012), esp. 111–49, (2014), esp. 26–53; Crossley-Myles (2023) 76–126; Bond (2004), (2011) at length.

16. The scholarship on empires, ancient and modern, is vast. Foremost informing my perceptions in this and following paragraphs: Ando (2000); Mattingly (2011); Lavan-Payne-Weisweiler (2016); Bang-Bayly (2011); Bang-Bayly-Scheidel (2021). For the Roman Middle East: Millar (1993); Butcher (2003); Andrade (2013); Sommer (2018). On client kings as peers/competitors of Italian governors, Ish-Shalom (2021).

17. For ancient empires, n. 16, this chapter. Roman Judaea: Goodman (1987), (2007); McLaren (1991); Schwartz (2001) 49–99, (2014) 59–74; Grabbe (2020), with 14, 20–25, 31–35, nn. 1, 12, 14, 18–23, this chapter; Chapters 2, 8–9 generally.

18. Governing Herod's reign and its aftermath, for the preceding and following paragraphs: Rocca (2007); Marshak (2015); Wilker (2007). For Roman imperialism: Goodman (2007) 379–423; Schwartz (2001) 30–108; Hengel-Schwemer (2019) 41–128. For Roman violence in relation to Jesus' ministry: Horsley (1987) 20–58, (2011) 17–42, (2012) 79–92, (2014), esp. 54–79. On genital episode: Crossley-Myles

Notes

223

(2023) 196. References to Josephus: *Ant.* 14.57–79, 92–104, 271–491, 17.250–70, 18.120–22; *War* 1.141–54, 162–222, 2.39–51.

19. Goodman (1987) is the key work, but see Bond (2004) 36, 168–70. On Herod's relationship with Hasmonaeans and priests: Marshak (2015) 110–38, 306–309; Rocca (2007) 281–87. On Herodian legitimacy among Jews: Wilker (2007) 290–316. Also at 20–25, nn. 12–14, this chapter; Chapters 2–3, 5.

20. Sacrilege by Romans: Jos., *War* 2.223–32, 293–308; *Ant.* 20.105–17. Goodman (2007) 55–60, (2009); Schwartz (2014) 63–65; Marshak (2015) 303–9. This aspect of the Temple looms large in many accounts of Jesus' death. For example, Fredriksen (1999), (2018) and references at nn. 6–9, 11, Introduction. On violence at the Temple and conflicts between Galileans and Samaritans: Jos., *Ant.* 17.206–19, 250–270, 20.118–36; *War* 2.4–12, 2.39–51.

21. On this and following paragraph: Andrade (2010). For calendars: Kushnir-Stein (2005). For violence: Philo, *Gai.* 200–3; Jos. *Ant.* 19.300–2, 20.1–5.

22. On statuary and violence: Jos., *War* 2.266, 7.23, 37–39; *Ant.* 18.457–80, 20.173. Jensen (2010) 9–34, 126–85, (2012); Keddie (2019) 71–110 govern this and following paragraphs, along with Myles (2019) on class in Jesus' Judaea, Crossley-Myles (2023) 39–49 on Galilee's situation, and various articles on Judaea/Galilee from Blanton-Choi-Lieu (2022). For class in antiquity: Ste. Croix (1983); Rose (2012), esp. 1–55 (which justifies usage of the concept). For Jesus as galvanizing village communities: n. 23, this chapter.

23. Experiences: Crossley (2015) 23–24; Crossley-Myles (2023) 45; Keddie (2018). Keddie (2019); Myles (2019); Crossley-Myles (2023), esp. 39–49 on economic relations govern this and following paragraphs. Horsley (1987), esp. 187–284, (2011), esp. 67–149, (2012), esp. 43–155, (2014) 25–49, 105–27 on Jesus, grievances of villagers in Galilee, and the priestly and scribal elite. Also Borg (1994) 105–17; Crossan (1991), esp. 359–60; Borg-Crossan (2006) 39–52.

CHAPTER 2

1. Diversity of Jews: Goodman (2007), (2009), (2010); Meier (1991–) 3.269–514; Eckhardt (2012), esp. Goodblatt (2012); Stern (2011); Schwartz (2014) 66–70. For "dissenters" and "sectarians": Newman (2006), esp. 121–25 (though my "dissenters" are Newman's sectarians); Schnabel (2018) provides comprehensive background on all the people and places from Jesus' Passion narrative (the following chapters owe it many debts). For the Romans, Herodians, and chief priests and allied scribes as cooperating rulers and landed interests, references at n. 15, Chapter 1; n. 20, this chapter. The views and practices of Jews regarding purity, too diverse and intricate to explore in this book, are treated by Furstenburg (2023), with Magness (2011) passim (esp. 6–8).

2. Some key works on the First Jewish Revolt are Goodman (2007); Mason (2016); Rogers (2021). It and other first-century insurgencies figure prominently in most

224   *Notes*

narratives of Jesus: nn. 6–11, Introduction. For references, Jos., *War* 2.408–10, 441–42; 4.147–57, 177–85, 305–25.

3. Goodman (1987) 164–67 critiques Josephus' claim. Also Mason (2016) 110–12; Vanderkam (2004) 479–82. On Josephus' self-portraits, Mason (2003) 55–146, esp. 121–31; Rajak (2002) 144–73. Key references: Jos., *War* 2.566–646, 3.132–408, 5.362–419, 6.106–111; *Life* (generally).

4. Mason (2003), (2009), (2016); Schwartz (2007), (2013), (2016) govern my understanding of Josephus' value and limitations. On Josephus and priests, McLaren (2016).

5. Jos., *Ant.* 18.257–309, esp. 273; *War* 2.184–203; Philo, *Gai.* 225–43, esp. 223–24. For detailed analysis of the episode, Bernett (2007) 264–87. On elite involvement, Bond (2004) 88; Girardin (2022) 324–38 (at 326). See 62–63, nn. 16–17, Chapter 3; n. 21, Chapter 9 for works on Jesus or his Judaea that address the Caligula episode, and n. 26, Chapter 9 on spontaneous demonstrations.

6. Bermejo-Rubio (2019); Bermejo-Rubio-Zeichmann (2019) for example.

7. Primary treatments governing this section: Jensen (2010), esp. 135–77, (2012); Keddie (2019) 51–58; Taylor (1997) 235–59; Marcus (2018) 58–59, 98–112. Also at 33–35, nn. 22–23, Chapter 1. Tiberias' burial sites: Jos., *Ant.* 18.38.

8. Philip's death, Judas the Galilean: Jos. *Ant.* 17.271–72, 18.4, 18.106; *War* 2.56. Insurgents and Judas the Galilean, 62–63, nn. 16–17, Chapter 3.

9. At 57, n. 8, Chapter 3; 92, nn. 11–13, Chapter 5. On Antipas' deposition and death, Jos., *Ant.*, 18.240–56.

10. For wealth and coordination, 28–29, 31–32, nn. 15, 19–20, Chapter 1; 37, n. 1, this chapter; 152, 158–59, nn. 15, 24, Chapter 9.

11. Vanderkam (2004) 394–490; Bond (2004) 23–49; Metzner (2010) 11–34, 53–61; Goodman (1987) 29–134, Marcus (2000–2009) 1100–1102; McLaren (1991) 201–8, govern this section. Jos., *Ant.* 7.365–66: weekly rotation. Rotation and festivals: Mason (2001) 5; Hengel-Schwemer (2019) 165–69, Metzner (2010) 11–34, 56–57. Houses: Magness (2012) 143–46, (2024) 240–46, with n. 16, this chapter. Also at 28–29, 31–32, nn. 15, 19–20, Chapter 1; 45–47, nn. 13–16, this chapter.

12. On criticisms, Evans (1992a); at length, Horsley (1987) 275–317, (2011), (2012), (2014), esp. 32–36; Snodgrass (2009) 455–60, 462–76; Charlesworth (2014) 160–64; Crossley-Myles (2023) 79–126, 201–7; Borg-Crossan (2006). Keddie (2019) 1–196, Girardin (2022) 85–122 (esp. 86–92), 222–360 for how the elite generated wealth. Key texts: *m. Keritot.* 1.7; *t. Menah* 13.21–22; 1QpHab 8.8–12, 9.4–5, 10.1, 12.10; 4QpNah Fr. 3–4, 1.11; CD 6.16, 21. Also at 28–29, 33–35, nn. 15, 22–23, Chapter 1; n. 18, Chapter 4; nn. 11–13, Chapter 6.

13. Sanders (1992) 78–80, 92–102, 119–45; Bond (2004) 44–47, 67–69, (2012) 144; Fredriksen (1999) 252–55, (2018) 70–72 on obligations. Key references are: Jos., *Ant.* 3.224–57, 7.365–66; *War* 5.219, 231–38. For numbers of animals/people: Jos., *War* 2.280, 6.423–26, but qualified by Lapin (2017a), esp. 424–26 (2017b), who places 62,000 pilgrims at Jerusalem per year, others in the hundreds of thousands. Also Crossley-Myles (2023) 194. Magness (2024) 252–53 treats

pilgrim numbers and remains of slaughtered animals. For Passover feast, 118–19, n. 2, Chapter 7.

14. Bond (2004) 42–43; Vanderkam (2004) 420–24 govern this and the following paragraph. Annas' appointment: Jos., *Ant.* 18.26. Annas as "high priest": John 18:12–24; Luke 3:2; Acts 4:6. For the chief priests as a civic council, Violante (2021) 171–81.

15. Bond (2004) 40–44; Metzner (2010) 67–79; Vanderkam (2004) 426–35, 476–82, with Jos., *Ant.* 18.35, govern this and the following paragraphs. A less common theory is that Caiaphas was appointed by Pilate, who would have started governing in 19. See 49–50, n. 20, this chapter.

16. Josephus on Ananus' descendants and tomb: *War* 2.256, 5.506; *Ant.* 20.198–203. *CIIP* 461, 463, 534, 3295; Vanderkam (2004) 423–24, 435–36; Bauckham (2011), with Bond (2004) 1–8, Magness (2024) 270–72 on ossuaries. Schnabel (2018) 125–29; Smith (2018) 101–4, discuss theories about houses. On James: 135–36, 195.

17. Keith (2011) 71–124, 177–88, (2020), esp. 15–38 governs this section. Also Meier (1991–) 3.289–487, 549–59; Newman (2006), esp. 121–25. On Jesus' literacy based on comparanda from Egypt, Huebner (2019a) 76–80.

18. Jos., *Ant.* 18.16–17; *War* 2.164–65. Klawans (2006) 169–70; Magness (2011) 6–7; Schnabel (2018) 80–81; Meier (1991–) 3.389–488; Newman (2006) 73–82. On Sadducees and the Messiah, Knohl (2022), with 100–108 on beliefs.

19. Jos., *Ant.* 18.12–15; *War* 2.162–63. On Pharisees, Neusner-Chilton (2007); Mason (2009) 185–238; Meier (1991–) 3.289–388; Newman (2006) 52–72; Schnabel (2018) 83–84. On Pharisees and rabbis, Lapin (2012) 45–50 (with a critical perspective). Developments after 70: Fredriksen (1999) 10–11; Meier (1991–) 3.298–301, 335–40; Marcus (2000–2009) 519–24; Keith (2020) 130–39. Jensen (2013); Dunn (2006); Keener (2009), 223–32: Pharisees, purity, archaeology in Galilee. Keith (2020), esp. 130–51 develops how Jesus and scribes were locked in debate from the initial phases of his public preaching (138–39 explore what Jesus shared with Pharisees); also Le Donne (2011). On *qorban, JANT* 84; Marcus (2000–2009) 452.

20. Bond (1998), with 1, n. 1 on chronology and Lémonon (2007); Carter (2003), with 3–5, along with Chapman-Schnabel (2019) 167–98 on different representations; Demandt (1999) are foremost treatments that govern this section. Also Gers-Uphaus (2020); Krieger (1995). Most scholars, including those referenced here, are now critical of the ruthlessly violent Pilate based on his portraits from Philo and Josephus or the often hypothesized link with the emperor Tiberius' henchman Sejanus: Bond (1998) 21–23, but see Aslan (2013) 112, 116–17; Greenberg (2014) 107–30. My treatment synthesizes scholarly observations I deem correct. See also 158–62, nn. 24–28, Chapter 9. On later memories of Pilate, Dusenbury (2021).

21. For inscription, *CIIP* 2.1277; Amorai-Stark (2018), Eck-Ecker (2023) on the ring; Szanton et al. (2019), Magness (2024) 253–54, 261–62 on the street and aqueduct (with 160, n. 27, Chapter 9); Bond (1998) 21–23, Webb (2009b) 707–14; Hendin (2021) 279–81, Jensen (2010) 194–99 on the coins. On Pilate's and material traces, Chapman-Schnabel (2019) 158–66.

Notes

22. Prefect and "governor": Eck (2007) 29–39. Also Chapman-Schnabel (2019) 159–60; Czajkowski (2020) 90–93. On Pilate's intelligence, Bermjeo-Rubio (2019); Bermejo-Rubio-Zeichmann (2019).

CHAPTER 3

1. Keddie (2018), esp. 268–76 emphasizes how eschatological prophecies discouraged military insurgency. For dissenters: n. 1, Chapter 2. For commonalities among "religious organizers": Crossley-Myles (2023) 47–126; references from the following sections.

2. Crossley (2015) 71–76; Crossley-Myles (2023) 99–126 (with "revolutionary millenarianism"); Keddie (2018) on reversal; Kosmin (2018) 137–86, with Portier-Young (2011), on Seleucid time and apocalyptic resistance. Jesus' quotation: Mark 14:62, with Matt 26:64, Luke 22:69. On "Son of Man": 67–68, n. 28, this chapter; "millenarianism": Allison (1998), (2010).

3. Keddie (2018), esp. 268–76 on prophecies discouraging insurgency. For varieties of Messiahs: Collins (2010b); Fredriksen (1999) 123–29, 212–13, (2018) 109–14. On Bar Kochba: Mor (2016) 137–45.

4. Magness (2002) 32–47 with (2011) passim, (2012) 108–32; Crawford (2019) 115–265 ("a scribal library with a sectarian component" quotes one of her chapter subtitles). Most documents appear in the Discovery in the Judaean Desert series. For critical editions and translations: Charlesworth (1993–). Easily consultable for nonliterary texts are Martínez and Tigchelaar (1998); Vermes (2004) (for English). Charlesworth (1992); Hempel (2010); Collins (2010a); Crawford (2019) govern my discussion.

5. Collins (2010a) 1–87; Crawford (2019) 269–320, with references from prior note, govern this and following paragraphs. Also Hempel 2010 (in which Fabry 2010); Girardin (2022) 361–70. References: 1QS, esp. 6, CD 13–14 (celibates in towns and camps, work, and wealth distribution); CD 6.12–21, 7.6–7, 15.5, 16.10–12, 12.1, 18–19 (married in towns and cities, procreation, charitable redistribution); 1Q28 2.12–22, 4Q174 (Messiahs); 1QS 5.15–26, 9.1–11; CD 12.22, 14.18–19 (judgment).

6. Taylor (2012), esp. 195–201; Crawford (2019) 269–320 govern this and the following discussion. References: Jos., *Life* 11–12, *War* 2.119–62; Philo, *Prob.*, 75–91, *Hypothetica* 11.1–8. Also, n. 8, this chapter.

7. Particularly Collins (2010a) 122–65; Taylor (2012); Magness (2002), esp. 39–43; Crawford (2019) 269–320 for this paragraph.

8. This and the following paragraphs engage with Collins (2010a) 149–50; Taylor (2012), esp. 195–201; Klawans (2006) 111–74; Regev (2019) 9–11; Rietz (2006); Von Weissenberg (2010); Crawford (2019) 206–8, 286–90; Magness (2016); Czajkowski-Eckhardt (2021) 42–26. Josephus on Essenes, Herodian dynasts, and the Temple: *Ant.* 15.371–79, 17.345–48, 18.18–22; purity, Hasmonaeans, and lack of

Notes 227

insurgency: Philo, *Prob.*, 91. Qumran and Temple offerings: CD 6.12–18, 11.19, 16.13. As Herodians: Taylor (2012) 109–30.

9. Klawans (2006) 145–74; Collins (2010a) 154–56; Regev (2019) 9–11 discuss. Prophesied king: 4Q252, 5, with Taylor (2012) 126–28.

10. On Temple: Klawans (2006) 158–60; Regev (2019) 11. References: unique righteousness: 1QS 8.5–6; Temple's priestly order: CD 6.12–18; tax: 4Q159; wealth collection: 1QpHab 8.8–12, 9.4–5, 10.1, 12.10; 4QpNah Fr. 3–4, 1.11; CD 6.14–21; imposters: 1QpHab 8–9; Temple maintenance and Temple Scroll: 11 QT, with Schiffman-Gross (2021) 2–5, Magness (2024) 161; judgment: 11 QT(19) 29.8–10; sanctity: CD 11.19, 12.1, 16.13. On offerings to God: 1QS 8.4–10, 9.3–5; Philo, *Prob.*, 75; Collins (2010a) 149–50; Klawans (2006) 145–74, esp. 164–66; Regev (2019) 9–11. On tithes and taxes: Girardin (2022) 361–70. On Temple as central: Goodman (2009), (2010).

11. Taylor (1997); Marcus (2018), with *JSHJ* 19.1 (2021), esp. Aldinolfi-Taylor (2021); Fredriksen (1999) 184–97; Destro-Pesce (2021); Meier (1991) 1.19–233; Bermejo-Rubio (2013a); Crossley-Myles (2023) 50–73 govern the following paragraphs. Location: Matt 3:1–7; Mark 1:4–5; Luke 3:1–3; John 3:22–24, 4:1–3. For hypotheses on background: Crossley-Myles (2023) 57–58.

12. For authenticity of Jos. *Ant.* 18.116: Marcus (2018) 125–27. Against it: Nir (2012). References: Matt 3:1–7; Mark 1:4–10; Luke 3:3, with John 3:22–4:3. On Elijah and John's diet and camel attire: Fredriksen (1999) 186; Marcus (2018) 46–61, esp. 56–57; Taylor (1997) 34–42.

13. Gospel references: Mark 1:9–11; Matt 3:13–17; Luke 3:21; John 3:22–4:3. Taylor (1997) 15–48; Marcus (2018) 27–45, 62–97; Destro-Pesce (2021), esp. 97–102, 149–96; Webb (2009a). On baptism of Jesus: Ehrman (1999) 93, (2016) 211–14; Crossley-Myles (2023) 66–69. Bermejo-Rubio (2013a); Allison (2010) 204–20 on continuity between John the Baptizer and Jesus. On Jesus' claiming Messianic recognition from John: Ferda (2020); Destro-Pesce (2021) 117–20, 164–76.

14. Taylor (1997), esp. 15–48, 109–11, 132–44; Marcus (2018), esp. 8–35, 62–80, 134; Destro-Pesce (2021) 76–78; Bond (2004) 55–56; Webb (2009a), esp. 120; Joseph (2016) 103–104 govern my discussion. For world's end, encompassing fire: Mark 1:7–8; Matt 3:11; Luke 3:7–9, 16–17; John 1:33; 1QS 3.4–12, 4.4–25, 5.13–14; 1QH 11.29–36, 14.17–19, 16.10–19.

15. For this and next paragraph: Kokkinos (1989); Taylor (1997) 255–59; Mahieu (2012) 414–15, 470–71; Marcus (2018) 99–112, 120–24; Bowersock (1983) 65. Visi (2020) places John's death in 35–36, after Jesus' crucifixion, on the grounds that Josephus' implied chronology suggests that Antipas' marriage happened shortly before his defeat in 36. But we cannot fix the wedding so precisely or late. References: Mark 6:17–29; Matt 14:3–12; Jos., *Ant.* 18.109–26, 136–37; Chapter 5.

16. Naturally, these insurgencies often elicit comparisons and contrasts with Jesus' activity (however understood). Just for example: Brandon (1968a) (1968b); Horsley (1987) 28–120, (2011) 73–87, (2012) 88–95, (2014), esp. 24–53; Bermejo-Rubio (2014a),

Notes

16. (2018b) 323–35; Fredriksen (1999) 166–71, 248–49 (2018) 173–76; Aslan (2013) in general; Crossley-Myles (2023), esp. 4–8. Also references at nn. 6–9, Introduction.

17. Jos., *Ant.* 17.271–84, 18.4–10, 23–25, 20.102; *War* 2.55–64, 118, 7.253–62; also Acts 5:37. Judas the Galilean often attracts commentary in treatments of Jesus or first-century Judaea. Vermes (2005) 85–86, 165–67; Horsley (1987) 50–54, 77–89, (2011) 75–76, (2012) 90, (2014) 64–65 (who deems him non-insurgent); Mason (2016) 245–254; Goodman (1987) 93–96, (2007) 395–96; Bermejo-Rubio (2014a) 29–32, with n. 113, (2018b) 330–33; Aslan (2013) 44–50; Girardin (2022) 298–305, with 305–25 on taxes in Judaea.

18. Jos., *War* 2.433–449, 7.253–62; Magness (2019) on Masada.

19. Brighton (2009), esp. 141–50; Mason (2016) 254–57. For references: Jos., *War* 2.255–56, 425, 4.398–409, 7.252–454; *Ant.* 20.162–64.

20. Jos., *War* 4.128–61, esp. 160–61; Mason (2016) 444–50.

21. For references, nn. 6–9, Introduction; nn. 2–3, Chapter 2; n. 17, this chapter.

22. Jos., *War* 2.258–63; *Ant.* 20.97–99, 167–72, with Acts 5.34–39. For scholarship on Josephus' testimony on these figures, n. 21, Chapter 9.

23. Jesus as a Jew of the Second Temple period has been a particular focus of recent decades. Influential are Vermes (1973), (1993), Sanders (1985) (1992); Meier (1991–), with a focus in Crossley-Myles (2023) 156–77. Hengel-Schwemer (2019) still insist Christianity starts when Jesus began his eschatological preaching. Crossley (2014), (2021); Arnal (2014) critique scholarly views on Jesus as a Jew while stressing that it should be non-controversial. Meyer (2020) examines the theological implications of Jesus as Jew.

24. On birth/chronology: Vardaman-Yamauchi (1989); Meier (1991) 1.371–433; Humphreys (1992); Kidger (1999); Brown (1993); Mahieu (2012) 235–488; Schnabel (2018) 141–42; Nicholl (2015); Huebner (2019a) 31–50. For Quirinius' career and governorship of Syria, Dabrowa (1998) 21–30, (2011).

25. Schnabel (2018) 141–42 reconciles Luke 3:23 and John 2:20 and places Jesus' first preaching in 27 by dating from Tiberius' assuming tribune and proconsular powers in 13. But see Mahieu (2012) 454–60, 465–68 for different possible interpretations of these passages. On the difficulty of using John's reference for Jesus' chronology: Culpeper (2019). Bond (2013) explores why a precise date between 29 and 34 is elusive. For John on Jesus in Jerusalem: 2:13, 5:1, 6:4, 11:55–19:14.

26. On Jesus' preaching: Fredriksen (1999) 191–97; Destro-Pesce (2021) 181–87, 191–96; Crossley-Myles (2023) 35–59, 130–35; Horsley (1987), (2011), (2012), (2014) generally. Followers: Meier (1991) 3.19–124; Fredriksen (1999) 204–10; Crossley-Myles (2023) 75–98. For John the Baptizer, see at 59–62, nn. 11–14, this chapter. For what Jesus shared with the Qumran Jews, John the Baptizer, Pharisees, and Galilean Jews, see at 48–49, n. 19, Chapter 2; 81–82, n. 18, Chapter 4. On the archaeology of first-century Nazareth: Dark (2023) 135–63.

27. Jesus and John on Temple, sacrifices, purity: Fredriksen (1999) 191–97, 207–14, (2018) 47–48; Chapters 4, 6. On Kingdom of God, Meier (1991–) 2.237–506 (esp.

Notes 229

237–70); Allison (2010) 164–203. For reign of God: Bond (2012) 89–90; for empire/dictatorship: Crossley-Myles (2023), esp. 105.

28. Son of Man: Aslan (2013) 105–7, 172–73; Keener (2009) 200–202; Dunn (2003) 724–64; Burkett (1999); Collins-Collins (2008) 75–100 (on Ezekiel, 75); Meier (1991–) 3.621–26; Allison (2010) 267–74; Marcus (2000–2009) 528–32; Bond (2012) 100–1; and now, in great detail Bauckham (2023–), with emphasis on return from heaven. Messiah: Collins-Collins (2008) 48–174, Hengel-Schwemer (2001), with n. 3, this chapter. On whether Jesus called himself the Messiah (despite not being a Davidic warrior): Fredriksen (1999) 249–52, (2018) 68; Ehrman (1999) 216; Brown (1994) 476–80; Crossley-Myles (2023) 121–25. For Jesus as Messianic preacher: 75, n. 7, Chapter 4.

29. Horsley (1987), esp. 149–284, (2011), esp. 111–49, (2012), 67–149, (2014), esp. 108–27; Bermejo-Rubio (2018a), (2018b) 169–80 on political, earthly Kingdom of God. Fredriksen (1999) 119–54, (2018) 67–73; Hengel-Schwemer (2001) 63–69, 207–30; Dunn (2003) 759–62 on Messianic reception and biblical templates. For varied interpretations of Jesus' activity: 3–6, n. 4–11, Introduction; 110, n. 17, Chapter 6.

CHAPTER 4

1. Ehrman (2003) introduces apocryphal gospels and apostolic acts; many appear, in original language or translation, in Schneemelcher-Wilson (1991–1992), Ehrman-Pleše (2011), (2014). The Gospel of Thomas, a sayings Gospel, provides no narrative of Jesus' death (Gagné 2019). The Gospel of Peter, which some construe as important (Crossan (1991) 462–66, (1995), 223–28), offers no material preceding the New Testament Gospels and exceeds even John in shifting blame to "the Jews." Brown (1994) 1317–49; Ehrman (2003) 16–24; Ehrman-Pleše (2011) 371–87 (esp. 373–75).

2. For debates and theories on the Synoptic problem: Porter-Dyer (2016). Robinson et al. (2000); Fledderman (2005) on theoretical reconstructions of "Q." Eve (2021) accessibly introduces Luke's dependence on Mark and Matthew. Bird (2014) 123–62 develops a compelling theory for Luke's engagement with Mark and Matthew, with Matthew and Luke also sharing a basic Q-source. For John and Synoptics: 101–102, n. 4, Chapter 6.

3. For differing views on Marcion's Gospel in relation to the New Testament (and Luke in particular): BeDuhn (2013), esp. 93–97; Roth (2015); Vinzent (2014), with (2019), (2023), (2024); Klinghardt (2015); Lieu (2015) 183–241; *NTS* 63.2: 318–34. Also see Appendix 1.

4. For recent re-evaluation of Christianity as truly a second-century phenomenon and the impact of second-century Christians on the textual sources: Arnal (2011), (2014); Vinzent (2019), (2023), (2024); Vearncombe-Scott-Taussig (2021). I thank Philip Harland and Heidi Wendt for helpful conversation.

Notes

5. Fredriksen (1999) 10–11, 34–41, (2008), (2018) 14–73; Bermejo-Rubio (2014a), (2018b) 34–41; Ehrman (2016) 131–78; Keener (2009) 71–162; Allison (2010) 1–31; Crossley-Myles (2023) 10–20 inform the material in this paragraph. On the tax: Heemstra (2010). On rejection of Jesus as Messiah: Ehrman (2016) 152. On Gospels minimizing conflicts with Romans, exaggerating those with Jews: Winter (1974) consistently; also Brandon (1968a) 221–81, (1968b) 81–139; Fredriksen (1999) 115–20; Bermejo-Rubio (2014a), (2018b) 119–338; Elliott (2019) 32–35 Greenberg (2014), esp. 16–17, 19–53 (43–47 on Septuagint/Greek); Crossan (1995), at length. For Aramaic in Jesus' Judaea: Gzella (2015) 225–37, (2021) 105–50. Also see 1–2, n. 1, Introduction.

6. For peasant sage/prophet: Borg (1994); Crossan (1991), (1995), critiqued by Allison (1998), esp. 10–32, 113–28, (2010) 31–163. For criticisms of criteria of authenticity: Keith-Le Donne (2012), with Keith (2020) 73–84; Bermejo-Rubio (2018b) 93–118; Crossley (2015) 35–55; Crossley-Myles (2023) 10–20.

7. Allison (1998) 39–171, (2010) 31–164; Fredriksen (1999) 78–154; Bird (2014) 27–54; Hengel-Schwemer (2001) 1–80, 165–230, (2019) 427–52, 487–580; Keener (2009) 71–162 for a gospel tradition; for overlapping traditions: Destro-Pesce (2017) 135–202. For Gospels and first-century Roman biography: Keener (2019), Bond (2020). For eschatological or millenarian Jesus: Ehrman (1999), (2016); Allison (1998), (2010); Fredriksen (1999) 155–259, (2018); Hengel-Schwemer (2001), (2019) 487–582; Keener (2009) 33–45, 238–82; Crossley-Myles (2023). For impact of second-century Christians: 73–74, n. 4, this chapter. On Paul and letters: Schellenberg and Wendt (2021). On "the Gospel": n. 8, this chapter.

8. 1 Thess 4:15–17, Mark 13:24–27; 1 Thess 5:1–3, Matt 24:43/Luke 12:39; 1 Thess 2:14–16, Matt 5:11–12/Lk 6:22–23; 1 Thess 4:15–17, Matt 24:30; 1 Cor 11:23–26, Mark 14:22–25. Allison (1998) 125–26, (2010) 49–50; Bird (2014), esp. 29–30; DPL 474–92; Theobald (2014), with a critical vantage point; Thompson (2022) govern this paragraph. For eyewitnesses: Bauckham (2017), esp. 155–82 (Peter); but also Ehrman (2016) 87–130. On Peter, Mark, and (un)reliability of memory: Bond (2015). For Papias: Carlson (2021), esp. Fr. 4, 6. On "the Gospel" of Paul and Mark: Mason (2009) 282–302. Regarding Pauline influence on Mark: Marcus (2000); Crossley (2012); Wischmeyer-Sim-Elmer (2014); Becker-Engberg-Pedersen (2014); Wendt (2021) stake various positions. For impact of second-century Christians: 73–74, n. 4, this chapter.

9. Allison (2010) 392–423, with 399, nn. 55–56; Reinbold (2006) 129, Boring (2015) 91–107 on 1 Thess 2:14–16 as authentic; also Webb (2009b) 671–74; Thompson (2022), esp. 389–91. Pauline references: Rom 3:25; 1 Cor 10:16; 11:25, 27; Gal 6:17. For Passion narrative: Thiessen (1991) 166–99; Borg-Crossan (2006) ix, Dunn (2003) 765–69; Bauckham (2017) 183–84; M. L. Soards in Brown (1994) 1492–554; Collins (2007) 621–27; Keener (2009) 305–7; Allison (2010) 387–415; Marcus (2000–2009) 924–29; Theobald (2022) 46–188. For the narrative's probable tendentious focus on the chief priests' culpability: Reinbold (1994), esp. 306–25,

with Bultmann (1968) 262–84, Mack (1988) 247–312; Crossan (1988); Bond (2020) 106–15. On not dying in Passover week: Bond (2013); n. 2, Chapter 7. On crucifixion: n. 14, this chapter.

10. Sloyan (2006) 7–14, 103–7 captures the problem posed by the Gospels. For the Gospels as historical sources: Keener (2009) 71–162, (2019). Theobald (2022) 56–60, with Fredriksen (1999) 256, *JANT* 99, 727–30 on how Gospel sequences fulfill many of the Psalms and prophecies from Isaiah. For views on continuity between the theologies of Jesus and the Gospels: Goodacre (2006); Marcus (2000–2009) 776–80, 927–29; Allison (2010) 78–82, 244–47, 252–53, 286–87, 388–89; Kinman (2009) 396–405; Theobald (2022). Also 103–4, n. 6, Chapter 6.

11. On dating Mark: Kloppenborg (2005); Kimondo (2018); Collins (2007) 11–15; Marcus (2000–2009) 37–40.

12. Schneider (1984); Heusler (2000) generally; Bickerman (2007) 754–64 on Mark, Luke, and Roman legal procedure in this and the following paragraph. On Gospels' altering Mark: Greenberg (2014), esp. 38–40; Aslan (2013) 114–15 for example.

13. My approach in this and following paragraphs owes much to Bermejo-Rubio (2014a), esp. 11–34, (2018b) 119–338; Allison (1998), (2010); Greenberg (2014) 15–16, 43–47 even if differing in conclusions. On particular matters, I have often been aided by Meier (1991–), Brown (1994), Bond (1998); Marcus (2000–2009); Collins (2007); Bock-Webb (2009), Schnabel (2018), Chapman-Schnabel (2019) and works referenced in nn. 6–11, Introduction; nn. 5, 7 this chapter. On Mark 14:61–62: 141, n. 17, Chapter 8.

14. Governing this and the following paragraph, for example, are Bermejo-Rubio (2014a), esp. 20, (2018b) 147–51; Fredriksen (1999) 8–9, (2018) 40–41, 57; Bird (2014) 26–90 on early traditions of the Gospel.

15. Paul's references to crucifixion: Rom 6:6; 1 Cor 1:23, 2:2, 2:8; 2 Cor 13:4; Gal 2:19, 3:1, 6:14. See n. 9, this chapter on authenticity of 1 Thess 2:14–16.

16. On Pilate's phrasing: Bond (1998) 110–11, (2020) 257–58, 263–66, who suggests Pilate is manipulating the crowd, with Horsley (2014) 162; Carter (2003) 69–74; Blinzler (1969) 306–7.

17. References: Matt 1:1–17; Luke 3:23–38; Mark 10:46–52, 11:9–10, with Mark 12:35–38 (descended from David or not); Mark 10:23–31, 41–45; 12:1–12; 13:1–2 (judgment). On biblical exemplars: Dunn (2003) 759–63; Allison (2010) 388–89.

18. Allison (2010) 352–68, on Leviticus 19; Keener (2009) 207–12 on property, tax collectors, and "sinners"; Klawans (2006) 237–38; Girardin (2022) 371–75; Crossley-Myles (2023) 76–126 (with 85–86 on tax collectors and sinners) treat Jesus on wealth distribution and Jewish piety, and many of the Gospel quotations cited. For chief priests as facilitating Roman-Herodian rule: Horsley (1987), esp. 285–317, (2011), esp. 87–108, 155–178, (2012), esp. 95–149 (2014), esp. 26–53; Evans (1992a) 243; 25–29, n. 15, Chapter 1, n. 12, Chapter 2. Josephus on *protoi: Ant.* 18.7, 273, with 18.64(?); Goldberg (2022) 19. Matt 17:24–27 obviously refers to Roman taxation after 70 under the guise of the Temple tax: Keddie (2019) 194. For

232 *Notes*

commentary on Markan passage: Marcus (2000–2009) 720–40, 805, 810–13, 851–60. On Jesus, scribes, and Qumran sectarians: Rietz (2006); 48–49, nn. 17–19, Chapter 2; 54–59, nn. 4–10, Chapter 3.

19. Coded statements: Bermejo-Rubio (2014a) 62, (2018b) 198–206. Taxes: Mark 12:17; Matt 22:21; Luke 20:25. King of the Jews: Mark 15:3; Matt 27:11; Luke 23:3; 68, n. 29, Chapter 3, 110–11, nn. 16–17, Chapter 6.

20. References: Mark 5:1–20, Matt 8:28–34, Luke 8:26–39. Since all three Gospels indicate Jesus had crossed the Sea of Galilee to reach the location, both Gadara and Gerasa are possible as destinations. But all the narratives assume immediate proximity to the sea, and Matthew's makes more geographical sense. Matthew accordingly reworked Mark's reference to Gerasa. *NOAB* 1794, 1837–38, 1883–84; *JANT* 27, 79, 130; Marcus (2000–2009) 341–42.

21. As noted by Bermejo-Rubio (2014a) 13; Horsley (2014) 102–3; *NOAB* 1837–38, 1884; *JANT* 27, 79, 130; Marcus (2000–2009) 341–53. On military in Judaea, Zeichmann (2018).

22. Bermejo-Rubio (2014a) 13; Horsley (2014) 102–3 on anti-imperial messaging.

CHAPTER 5

1. Czajkowski (2016) on Herod's courts; Taylor (1997) 235–50 on no cohesive movement. On coordination: 89, n. 6, this chapter.

2. Mason (2003) 161–62; Marcus (2000–2009) 396–404, (2018) 58–59, 98–112; Jensen (2010) 94–98, 112–14; Aslan (2013) 73–74; Taylor (1997) 235–50 govern this and following paragraphs. For different understanding: Mahieu (2012) 416–17.

3. Jos., *Ant.* 18.116–19, 136–37, with *War* 7.163–77; For excavations: Vörös (2019), (2022). Luke and Josephus: Mason (2003) 251–96, (2022), esp. 212–31; Appendix 1.

4. On this pattern: Greenberg (2014) 161–64.

5. On movement and ambiguous statements: Bermejo-Rubio (2014a) 13, 61–62, (2018b) 170–72, 206–10, with Hengel-Schwemer (2019) 368–70; Jensen (2010) 110–14, governs this paragraph and what follows. Mark 3:6–7, 4:33–35; 6:45; 8:26–30; 9:30–31.

6. All Israel: Fredriksen (1999) 180–84, 238–40; Allison (1998) 141–45, (2010) 50–51; Dunn (2003) 506–15; Horsley (1987), esp. 167–208, (2011), (2012), (2014). On Jesus at Caesarea Philippi: 91, n. 10, this chapter. For a different outlook on Pilate, Antipas, and intelligence coordination: Bermejo-Rubio (2019); Bermejo-Rubio-Zeichmann (2019).

7. Governing this paragraph and what follows, see references at n. 2, this chapter; Bond (2020) 178–89.

8. Mason (2003) 251–96, (2022), esp. 212–31; Appendix 1.

9. Mark 8:15–16, with Matt 16:11–12; Luke 12:1. Marcus (2000–2009) 507 on leaven. Greenberg (2014) 16 on episode and Synoptic alterations.

Notes   233

10. Movement and secrecy: Bermejo-Rubio (2014a) 61, (2018b) 170–72, 208; Mark 8:27–38, Matt 16:13–28, Luke 9:18–27; Jensen (2010) 110–12. On the "Messianic secret": Marcus (2000–2009) 525–27. On Luke 23:6–12: 93, n. 14, this chapter; 172–73, n. 9, Chapter 10.

11. Schnabel (2018) 95–96; Meier (1991) 3.560–65; Wilker (2007) 305–9; Greenberg (2020) 161–63 on this episode and Synoptic alterations.

12. Meier (1991–) 3.560–65; Marcus (2000–2009) 249–50, with comments on possible Markan contrivance.

13. Jensen (2013); Dunn (2006), on material culture.

14. In greater detail, 172–73, n. 9, Chapter 10.

15. On birth: Ehrman (2020) 130–36; Brown (1993) 1–232 (in detail).

CHAPTER 6

1. At 75–77, nn. 7–9, Chapter 4; 118–19, n. 2, Chapter 7.

2. On the various "circles" of Jesus' followers, Meier (1991) 3.19–124; Fredriksen (1999) 204–10; Crossley-Myles (2023) 75–98 (with critical commentary on crowds at 90–91).

3. Final Passover: Mark 11–15; Matt 21–27; Luke 19–24. Earlier pilgrimage: Luke 2:41–51. Acclaim: Mark 11.8–10; Matt 21:8–11. John's testimony: 2:13, 6:4, 11:55 (Passovers), 7:2–10:42 (Tabernacles), 5:1 (festival).

4. On secret messages: Bermejo-Rubio (2014a) 11, 55, (2018b) 170–72; Bauckham (2017) 187–89; Marcus (2000–2009) 778, 948. References: Mark 11:1–11: Matt 21:1–10; Luke 19:29–37. Mark not specifying one pilgrimage: Crossley-Myles (2023) 74. John reworking Mark (or a common source): Greenberg (2020); Anderson et al. (2016), with North (2016); Charlesworth-Pruszinski (2019) and esp. Daise (2019) on Jesus' confrontation with moneychangers at the Temple; Becker-Bond-Williams (2021) and esp. Bond (2021), with Thatcher (2016), Destro-Pesce (2017) 176–202, on the Passion narratives. All Israel: 89, n. 6, Chapter 5. John the Baptizer: Mark 1:4–11; Matt 3; Luke 3:21–22; John 1:19–34.

5. Fredriksen (1999) 218–25, (2008), (2018) 14–22, 43–73; Hengel-Schwemer (2019) 362 on John on Jesus' earlier pilgrimages. Key references from John: 2:13, 5:1, 6:4, 7:2–10:42, 11:55 (pilgrimages to Jerusalem); 7:1, 10–13, 25, 32, 45–52 (interest in arresting Jesus). John's claims (8:59, 10:31, 11:8) that the chief priests pondered having Jesus stoned are tendentious, and Roman authorities prohibited it (Chapter 8).

6. Gospel passages: Mark 11:9–10; Matt 21:9; Luke 19:38; John 12:13. Ehrman (1999) 210–11, (2016) 159–63; Fredriksen (1999) 250–52, (2018) 66, 69, 72; Cohick (2008) 120–22; Bond (2012) 137–38; Crossley-Myles (2023) 198–201 discuss issues of size, regality, and possible link to death. On doubts the event occurred: Collins (2007) 513–14; Hengel-Schwemer (2019) 585–86; Kinman (2009) 383–87. Catchpole (1984) doubts Messianic implications are historical. For possibility of a modest following: Ehrman (2016) 162; Kinman (2009) 396–418 (who defends that Jesus

234   *Notes*

imitated Zechariah). Chapter 4, at 77, n. 10 for history, theology, and links to Zech 9:9. Mirroring Pilate: Kinman (2009) 415–18.

7. Bermejo-Rubio (2014a) 11, 55, (2018b) 170–72; Bauckham (2017) 187–89; Marcus (2000–2009) 778, 948. Clandestine movements: Mark 11:1–11: Matt 21:1–10; Luke 19:29–37; with John 7:10–11. Passover meal arrangements: Mark 14:12–16, with Matt 26.17–19; Luke 22:7–13.

8. For emulation of Jeremiah 7:3–20: Horsley (1987) 297–300, (2011) 172–73, (2014) 121; Snodgrass (2009) 466; Charlesworth (2014) 160–64; Smith (2018) 106–8; Crossan (1995) 50–65; Marcus (2000–2009) 784–85; Collins (2007) 527–31. Suppression of moneychangers and vendors: Mark 11:15; Matt 21:12; Luke 19:45; John 2:15 (Jesus with cord whip). Hideout of brigands: Mark 11:17, Matt 21:13; Luke 19:46 citing Jr 7:11; on translation, see citations of Horsley above. For "small change collectors" and people carrying "vessels of priestly tithes": Keddie (2021) 182–86.

9. Brandon (1968a), esp. 322–58, (1968b) 140–50; Bermejo-Rubio (2014a) 10, 77, 83, with (2018b) 170–72, discuss armed possibility; on collective action, Elliott (2019); Crossley-Myles (2023) 207–210. Fredriksen (1999) 207–14, 225–32, (2008) 264–65, (2015) 348, (2019) 43–51 emphasizes the many factors that raise doubts about the event. Cohick (2008), esp. 121–24; Horsley (2014) 72–74; Greenberg (2014) 174–75; Snodgrass (2009) 434–39, 448–54; Theobald (2022) 724 govern the following on size and absence of response. On Levites as guards: Sanders (1992) 82 on Philo, *Spec. Leg.* 1.156; Schnabel (2018) 92; Metzner (2010) 53–57.

10. Fredriksen (1999) 207–14, 225–32, (2008) 264–65, (2015) 348, (2018) 43–51, who, like Charlesworth (2014), emphasizes that Jesus was an observant Jew, though Joseph (2016) 136–67 argues that Jesus opposed animal sacrifice (unlikely in my view). Collins (2007) 527–29; Snodgrass (2009) 434–39 also discuss the objections against historicity.

11. Ehrman (1999) 207–8, 213–14, (2016) 165; Crossley-Myles (2023) 201–7; with n. 12, this chapter, governing this paragraph. For criticisms of wealth and the chief priests by Jews: 44–45, n. 12, Chapter 2; 55–59, nn. 5, 10, Chapter 3; 81–82, n. 18, Chapter 4; Evans (1993), (1997a), (1997b); Joseph (2016) 136–67. Elliott (2019) 25, 38–39; Cohick (2008) 122, 129–31 on priests, scale, and crowd violence.

12. Sanders (1985) formulates that Jesus was symbolically enacting an eschatological moment, not condemning the Temple or its priests. Likewise, Schnabel (2018) 156–62; Bond (2012) 139–42 summarizes arguments that Jesus was not hostile to the Temple's activity; Joseph (2016) 136–67 sees the episode as symbolic, but against the Temple's management and animal sacrifices. Klawans (2006), esp. 222–41; Magness (2012) 156, (2024) 224–25; Snodgrass (2009) 462–73, esp. 469–70; Charlesworth (2014) 160–64; Keddie (2021), with n. 11, this chapter, govern my following narrative. For tithes and taxes: Keddie (2019) 176–96, (2021) 179–86; Girardin (2022) 85–122 (esp. 86–92), 222–360. For critiques of the existing theories: Regev (2019) 21–34, who sees Jesus as protesting the corrupting power of money circulated by the unrighteous.

Notes

235

13. *m. Šeqal.* 1:3, 5:3–4, 6:5; Lapin (2017a), esp. 444–45, (2017b) 249–50; Keddie (2019) 161–75, (2021) 179–85, with 185 on tithes; n. 12, this chapter.

14. For sword (*hereb*): Bermejo-Rubio (2014a) 10, 24–25, 38–42, 56, 83, (2018b) 210–15, 284–86; Martin (2014). For sacrificial knife (*makelet*): Fredriksen (2015) 323, (2018) 63–64.

15. For whether the prediction refers to the Temple: Regev (2019) 115–16; Collins (2007) 601–2; Kloppenborg (2005) 429–35. Witnessing Jesus' activity: Matt 21:12–16, Luke 20:45–47. What power?: Mark 11:27–33; Matt 21:23–27; Luke 20:1–8. Vine farmers parable: Mark 12:1–12, Matt 21:33–46, Luke 20:9–19. Caesar's coin: Mark 12:13–17, with Matt 22:15–22; Luke 20:20–26. Messiah not descended from David: Mark 12:35–37; Matt 22:41–46; Luke 20:41–44. Destruction of Jerusalem/Temple: Mark 13:1–2, Matt 24:1–2, Luke 21:5–6. Mount of Olives: Mark 13:3; Matt 24:3; Luke 21:37. For Mark 12:35–37 being based on the Septuagint: Marcus (2000–2009) 846–47; Collins (2007) 579–82; Greenberg (2014) 43–45. Mark's placement of Jesus' statements: Crossley-Myles (2023) 210–14.

16. Ehrman (1999) 157–59 (against Temple prediction); Borg (1994) 112–16, Crossan (1991) 355–59, (1995) 58–65 (against Messianic claims); Fredriksen (1999) 207–14, 225–32, (2018) 43–73. On Paul's omission: Fredriksen (2015) 319, (2018) 23–29, 50–51.

17. Jesus as king among contemporary claims of kingship: Horsley (1987) 52–58, (2011) 81–86, (2012) 87–95, (2014) 38–40; Bermejo-Rubio (2014a) 10–14, 25–26, 28–34, (2018b) 188–97, 323–32; Fredriksen (1999) 166–71, 248–49, (2018) 173–76. Jos., *War* 2.55–62, *Ant.* 17.271–84. On Messiah: Collins (2010b); Hengel-Schwemer (2001) 1–80, 165–230; Fredriksen (1999) 123–29, 212–13, (2018) 109–14; Crossley-Myles (2023) 213–14. Pilate's mockery of Jesus as "King of the Jews" is widely considered a reference to the concept of Messiah. See nn. 4–11, Introduction.

18. Josephus and prophets: Horsley (1987) 20–58, (2011) 81–86, (2012) 87–95, (2014) 38–40; Marcus (2000–2009) 871–73; *Ant.* 20.97, 160–61, 167–72; *War* 6.285–309. Also see at 81–83, nn. 17–18, Chapter 4; 155–57, nn. 21–22, Chapter 9. Temple: 11 QT(19) 29:8–10; 4QFlor; 1 En 90, 28–29, 91:12–13; 2 Sam 7:12–16; Zech 6:12. Sanders (1985) 77–90; Ehrman (1999) 157–59, 213–14; Evans (1992b); Ådna (2000); Allison (2010) 43; Hengel-Schwemer (2001) 188–92; Marcus (2000–2009) 1013–15; Rietz (2006); Keener (2009) 250–53; Crossley-Myles (2023) 215–17 make observations about Temple prediction. But see Regev (2019) 38–39.

19. On Passover: Borg-Crossan (2006) 110; Keener (2009) 372–75; Brown (1994) 1372–73; n. 2, Chapter 7. Passover lamb: John 1:35, 19:14–15, 19:36–37; n. 4, this chapter.

20. Fredriksen (1999) 222–33, 255–56, (2018) 52–64; Elliott (2019), esp. 26–36 on Gospel portrayals, crowd shifts, and crowd dynamics. On crowd autonomy: Myles (2020); Crossley-Myles (2023) 207–10, 230–31. Chief priests' obligations: Bond (2004) 44–47, 67–69, (2012) 144; Fredriksen (1999) 252–55, (2018) 70–72. See also n. 13, Chapter 2.

21. Massacres and Pilate in Josephus: *Ant.* 17.206–19, 250–70, 18.60–62, *War* 2.4–12, 39–51, 175–77. Hengel-Schwemer (2019) 612 on Roman troops escalating; Bond

Notes

(2004) 46 on Herodian troops at Temple. Problems posed by Jesus' numbers: Bond (2004) 67–69, (2012) 143–45, with n. 11, this chapter. For Pilate's violence: 158–62, nn. 24–28, Chapter 9. On Josephus and Luke, Appendix 1.

22. Elliott (2019) 25, 28–31, 38; Cohick (2008) 122, 129–31; Crossley-Myles (2023) 206 govern this paragraph. On Mark and "not during the festival": Marcus (2000–2009) 933–34; Collins (2007) 624.

23. Greenberg (2020) 358–68, 381–83. Also n. 4, this chapter.

24. Bermejo-Rubio (2014a) 9, 14, 33–34, 54, (2013b), esp. 134, (2018b), 147–68; Aus (1998) 136–37; Elliott (2019) 36–37; Cohick (2008) 122, 129–31; Marcus (2000–2009) 1029; Crossley-Myles (2023) 207–10, 230–31 govern this and the following paragraph.

25. Hillner (2015) 48–63; Robinson (2007) 113–14; 124, n. 8, Chapter 7. On Felix: Acts 24:27; Tacitus, *Hist.* 5.9. On crucifixion as standard for sedition: 7, n. 12, Introduction; 150–52, n. 11, 14, Chapter 9; 174, n. 12, Chapter 10.

26. Men crucified with Jesus: Mark 15:27, Matt 27:38, Luke 23:32 (*kakourgoi*); John 19:18. As noted by Bermejo-Rubio (2013b) 130, (2018b) 147–68; Crossley-Myles (2023) 207–10. Other manuscripts have a different ordering: "others, two evil-doers": Fitzmyer (1981–1985) 2.1499.

27. On traces from the Gospels and lack of coherent picture: Bermejo-Rubio (2014a), (2018b) 119–332.

CHAPTER 7

1. On the scholarship on Judas: Crossan (1995) 71–75; Meier (1991) 3.141–45, 209–211; Allison (2010) 68–69. Reassessing Judas' role: Greenberg (2014), esp. 131–54, with 7–8, n. 14, Introduction.

2. For this and next paragraph, Synoptics: Mark 14; Matt 26; Luke 22; John: 13, 18, 19:14, with Ehrman (1999) 215; Fredriksen (2015) 321; Brown (1994) 1350–76; Greenberg (2020) 577–89; Keener (2009) 372–75; Marcus (2000–2009) 931–32, 944. The Synoptics specify a Paschal feast (*Pascha*) that would have included a Passover lamb. For arguments favoring John: Brown, Greenberg, and Marcus above. Bond (2012) 148–50 summarizes why many scholars favor John and discusses Mark 15:42–46. Schnabel (2018) 145–47 suggests that discrepancies in the Gospels reflect different dates for Passover maintained by the chief priests (predominantly Sadducees) and the Pharisees. Blinzler (1969) 101–25 discusses theories that the arrest preceded Passover; Bond (2004) 70–71, 180, (2012) 148–49, (2013), with bibliography, prefers this dating; also Fredriksen (2018) 72. In support of Passover meal: 1 Cor 5:7, 11:23–25; Allison (2010) 411–15; Bird (2014) 29; Crossley-Myles (2023) 217–19 and esp. Jeremias (1966) 16–25, 41–61 (with 74–78 stressing how people could buy a shroud for Jesus and bury him on Passover); Collins (2007) 623–24, who notes the leniency of Lev 23:7–8; Hengel-Schwemer (2019) 615–20. On "not during the festival": n. 22, Chapter 6. For commitments of the chief priests during Passover: 136, n. 6, Chapter 8.

Notes 237

3. Fuhrmann (2012) 44–87 governs my discussion about "civilian policing." As relating to Hellenistic-Roman Judaea: Bickerman (2007) 728–29.

4. Fuhrmann (2012) 53, n. 33 (Jesus' arresting party), 55–60, 66–67 (municipal elites and policing). For chief priests as *boule* (municipal council): Violante (2021) 181–91.

5. On municipal police officers: Fuhrmann (2012) 55–87; Schnabel (2018) 91; Brown (1994) 1430–31. *Strategos*: Luke 22.4, 22.52; Acts 4:1–3, 5:21–24; Jos. *Ant.*, 20.131, 20.208, *War* 2.409, 6.294. *Hyperetai*: Acts 5:22, 26; John 7:32, 45–46, 18:3, 12. *Lex Ursonensis* c.5.2–4 (CIII) in Crawford (1996) 409, 428; *Lex Irnitana* 19.5–13. Josephus on priests' organizing armed bands: *Ant.* 20.179–81, 200–3; *War* 6.300–9.

6. Winter (1974) 61–69; Bermejo-Rubio (2016), esp. 315–16, (2018b) 286–90; Fredriksen (2000) 115–20, (2018) 60, 65; Martin (2014) 5–6; Greenberg (2014) 195–197. For chief priests and armed bands: Bourgel (2012) 504–6 on Jos., *Ant.* 20.179–81. On Herodian troops: Blinzler (1969) 95–98; Schnabel (2018) 93–94, 218, with critique by Keener (2009), 375–77; Brown (1994) 248. Josephus uses this terminology (*War* 2.11) for troops mustered by the Herodians before the Romans made lesser Judaea into provincial territory. But see Mason (1974) 85, 99–100.

7. Fuhrmann (2012) 52, n. 33 on policing procedure and Gospel dates. Similarly, Keener (2009) 375–76; Crossan (1995) 80–81; Joseph (2016) 19–23, for example. For theological motives: Brown (1994) 250; Reinbold (2006) 125–26.

8. Hengel-Schwemer (2019) 624–25 on house of chief priest. On imprisonment: Hillner (2015), esp. 48–63; Brélaz (2021) 487, 493–94 govern this paragraph. On theories that Roman troops transferred Jesus to the chief priests: Cohn (1971) 71–93; Brown (1994) 250–51; Greenberg (2014) 266–69. Tacitus on Felix: *Hist.* 5.9.

9. Reinbold (2006) 129; Allison (2010) 392–423, with 399, nn. 55–56; Boring (2015) 91–107.

10. Appendix 2 on relevant references and expanded arguments. Josephus on *protoi*: *Ant.* 18.7, 273; Fredriksen (1999) 247–49, (2018) 70; Chapman-Schnabel (2019) 187–88 (who discuss *endeixis*).

11. Grünewald (2004), esp. 91–109 on *leistai* in Judaea. Also, Fredriksen (2018) 46. On seditionists/brigands: 115–16, nn. 26–27, Chapter 6; 154–55, n. 20, Chapter 9; 181, n. 22, Chapter 10.

12. Fredriksen (1999) 232–34, 240–41, 250–59, (2015), (2018) 65, 72; Cook (2011) 199–203; Sanders (1985) 302–4; Reinbold (2006) 95–101 on Jesus arrested alone. For theories that some of Jesus' companions were crucified with him: Bermejo-Rubio (2013b), (2018b) 141–68.

CHAPTER 8

1. Governing this and following paragraphs on Babatha: Czajkowksi (2017), with 133–64 on non-Roman arbitration; Esler (2017), (2019) on ethnographic approaches to the Nabataean documents P. Yadin 1–4, with (2017) 28–64 on Nabataeans; Czajkowski-Eckhardt (2018) 7–17. For courts in Roman Judaea: Czajkowski

238   *Notes*

(2020). Civic council of Petra, P. Yadin 12; marriage document, P. Yadin 10; Titus Haterius Nepos, P. Yadin 23, 25–26. Assyrian language: *Dig.* 45.1.1, 6. Courts at Qumran: CD 9–12. Also, n. 9, Chapter 9.

2. Grabbe (2008); Czajkowski (2020) 93–95, with Sanders (1992) 472–88; Smith (2018) 123–39; Rocca (2007) 267–72; McLaren (1991) 211–21; Bond (2004) 167, n. 2 on *synhedria* as ad hoc advisory councils. As distinct from the *boule*: Violante (2021) 181–91. For Cyrene: *Greek Constitutions*, nos. 8–12; for Irnitana: *Lex Irnitana*, 89–90.

3. For example, Heusler (2000) 194–95; Webb (2009b) 729–30; Chapman-Schnabel (2019) 201–8. See *Greek Constitutions*, nos. 8–12, esp. lines 62–71.

4. Governing this and the following paragraph: Blinzler (1969) 229–44; Brown (1994) 361–72 (747 on John's audience); Chapman-Schnabel (2019) 15–30, 42–44, 86–90; Piattelli (1999); Santalucia (1999) 100–102; Fuhrmann (2012) 54 on Qumran Jews as a "closed society." For *apokteinai* and arguments that the chief priests/Sanhedrin could execute people for breaches of sanctity: Giovannini-Grzybek (2008), esp. 11–32, Riess (2021), esp. 86. Qumran witnesses: CD 9–12. *Scroll of the Fasts* (Megillat Ta'anit) 6 [13–15]: Beyer (1984) 356; Chapman-Schnabel (2019) 25–26. Executions for entering Temple's inner court: *CIIP* 1.2, Philo, *Gai.*, 212; Josephus, *War* 5.193–94, 6.124–26 (Jewish authorities), *Ant.* 15.417. Stephen: Acts 6:8–8:1. Paul's trial: Acts 21–24 generally. James' trial: Jos., *Ant.* 20.200–3; for dispute over identity, n. 18, Chapter 11. Greek intellectual: Philostr., *Soph.* 1.532. Executed Roman soldiers: Bammel (1984b) 438 on Jos., *War* 2.246, with 231; *Ant.* 20.136. Scourging and release by Albinus: Jos., *War* 6.300–309.

5. Stephen: Acts 6:8–8:1; Mahieu (2012) 516–17. Sanhedrin's powers: *y. Sanh.* 1.1 (18a, 42–43), 7.2 (21b, 52–53); *b. Avod. Zar.* 8b. On John 8:53: Brown (1994) 368. On Stephen and Paul: 190, nn. 10–11, Chapter 11.

6. Mark 14:53–65, 15:1–2; Matt 26:57–27:4. For harmonizing and preferring Mark: Hengel-Schwemer (2019) 625–34; Schnabel (2018) 222–52; Metzner (2010) 119–37; Blinzler (1969) 134–244; Catchpole (1971); Schubert (1984); Betz (2007) 55–86; Bock (2009); Joseph (2016) 19–25. Favoring John: Millar (1990); Bond (2004) 71, (2012) 155–57; Greenberg (2014) 200–225. Dismissal: Winter (1974), esp. 33–34; Cohn (1971) 94–141; Fredriksen (1999) 222–23, 254–55, 258, (2018) 60–61 (who emphasizes the ritual commitments of the chief priests); Mack (1988) 293–95; Crossan (1991) 375–76, (1995) 100–117; Stegemann (2002), (2010) 353–82, esp. 368–69; Borg-Crossan (2006) 128; Horsley (2011) 186, (2014) 159; Collins (2007) 699–700; Niemand (2007) 409–11; Bermejo-Rubio (2018b) 305–10; Destro-Pesce (2014) 125–29; Sloyan (2006) 36–47; Reinbold (1994) 308–9; Crossley-Myles (2023) 226–27. For various positions: Thiessen-Merz (1998) 460–65; Brown (1994) 1.328–29; Marcus (2000–2009) 525–28 ("Messianic secret"), 1126–30; Broer (2007). All these many references govern the paragraphs in his section.

7. *m. Sanh.* 4.1. Chapman-Schnabel (2019) 54–56; Schnabel (2018) 231–33; Brown (1994) 358–59, 420–23; Keener (2003) 1092–93, 1100, (2009) 313–16. On

Notes

239

sources: Borg-Crossan (2006) 128; Sloyan (2006) 36–37; Bermejo-Rubio (2018b) 305–10; Blinzler (1969) 174–83 (discussing prior scholarship). On anachronism: Bourgel (2012) 507–13; Weeden (2003). Jesus bar Ananias: Jos., *War* 6.300–309.

8. For Christological purposes of Mark's *synhedrion*: Marcus (2000–2009) 1000–1013 (esp. 1010–13), with 525–27 on the "Messianic secret." Also references at nn. 6–7, this chapter. On whether Mark's narrative reflects anti-Judaism: Hengel-Schwemer (2001) 131–64; Marcus (2000–2009) 929–30; Matthews (2013) 59–72, regarding Acts of the Apostles, is relevant.

9. Priests: *Aristeas* 95; Jos., *Ap.* 2.108, with Sanders (1992) 78–79. On Annas' role: Bond (2004) 72. On Josephus, lambs, numbers of pilgrims, and remains of slaughtered animals: 45, n. 13, Chapter 2.

10. Blinzler (1969) 216–29; Brown (1994) 358–59, 420–23; Chapman-Schnabel (2019) 55; Schnabel (2018) 232–33: Marcus (2000–2009) 1126–30.

11. Hengel-Schwemer (2019) 633–34; Keener (2009) 316; Bauckham (2017) 170–79; Bock (2009) 607–9. Joseph of Arimathea: Mark 15:43; Matt 27:57; Luke 23:50–51. Bond (2012) 154–55 supports historical outline, doubts dialogue.

12. Grabbe (2008) 9–11; Marshak (2015) 78–82; McLaren (1991) 67–79 discuss the episode's general historicity. Jos., *Ant.* 14.163–78 (Herod executes the council's members at 175); *War* 1.204–11 (where a *synhedrion* is implied). On the source: Ilan (2018); Czajkowski-Eckhardt (2021) 31, n. 12. Sanders (1992) 482–83; Smith (2018) 127–28 record *synhedria* being summoned to assess criminal affairs. Jos, *Ant.* 15.173, 17.46, 89–131; *War* 1.620, 640.

13. Bock (2009) 604–6; Bickerman (2007) 733–36; Piattelli (1999) 78–84; Santalucia (1999) 100–104; Smith (2018) 140–47; Chapman-Schnabel (2019) 15–31 (esp. 30–11); Metzner (2010) 105–19; Joseph (2016) 19–25; Cohick (2008) 126, who stresses the chief priests saw Jesus' activity as seditionist.

14. Bond (2004) 72, on Annas. Also 137–38, n. 9, this chapter.

15. Magness (2012) 143–46, (2024) 240–46 (on the wealthy Western Hill/Upper City); Schnabel (2018) 125–29; Smith (2018) 101–2 discuss theories about where the houses of Annas and Caiaphas were located (and whether they occupied the same courtyard house complex).

16. Temple, three days: Mark 14:56–58, with Matt 26:59–62; statement at the Temple: Mark 13:2, Matt 24:2, Luke 21:5–6, though see John 2:19. Brown (1994) 455–50; Collins (2007) 699–703. For Jesus' reported prediction of the Temple's destruction: 109–11, nn. 15–18, Chapter 6.

17. Brown (1994) 467–70 ("Blessed One"); Sloyan (2006) 37–44; Bock (2009) 630–38; Collins (2007) 704–7; Greenberg (2014) 47. On intertext with 2 Sam 7:12–16: Allison (2010) 287. The high priest's question and Jesus' response: Mark 14:61–62, with Matt 26:64; Luke 22:67–70. For alternate phrasing: Bovon (2006) 41; Marcus (2000–2009) 1004–6. On the Hebrew tetragrammaton, Andrade (2015). On Son of Man, Son of God, and Messiah: Collins-Collins (2008) 48–174; Brown

240   *Notes*

(1994) 506–15; Hengel-Schwemer (2001) 63–80, 208–30; Bock (2009) 638–56; Bauckham (2023–), who stresses heavenly return.

18. Bock (2009) 609–60; Collins (2006); Schnabel (2018) 243–47; Chapman-Schnabel (2019) 98–129 (with sources); Brown (1994) 530–47; Joseph (2016) 24–25, with references from n. 28, Chapter 3, govern the following. Uttering the Divine Name and blasphemy: Philo, *Moses*, 2.203–8; Jos., *Ant.* 4.198–202; *m. Sanh.* 6:4, 7:5. Powers held by God: Philo, *Dream*, 2.219–32, *Dec.* 61–63; *y. Taan.* 2.1 (65b, 61–71), on which Schäfer (2017) 218–19. Also, Ehrman (1999) 220, (2020) 115; Knohl (2022) on Sadducees; Brown (1994) 488–89; Chapman-Schnabel (2019) 105; Schnabel (2018) 246–47; Bock (2009) 610–13 on "I am" and divine name. For insult: Bickerman (2007) 733–34.

19. Chapman-Schnabel (2019) 130–39 for sources, with 63–77 on *m. Sanh.* 7. Deceiving/seducing: Matt 27:62–63, Luke 23:1–2, 5; John 12:45–49. Jewish sources: Jos., *Ant.*, 18.63–64, if authentic; *b. Sanh.* 43a, 107b. Lucian: *Peregr.* 12. Sorcery: Mark 3:22, Matt 12:22–24, Luke 11:14–15. Justin Martyr: *Dial.* 69.7; Origen, *Celsus*, 1.6, 38, 68; *b. Sanh.* 43a, 107b. On *Toledot Yeshu*: Schäfer (2017) 105–28; Meerson-Schäfer (2014), esp. 64–70, 82–100. On deception: Strobel (1980) 61–94; Betz (2007) 55–99; Hengel-Schwemer (2019) 632–33; Krimphove (1997) 183–84; Schnabel (2018) 237–39; Bond (2012) 156–157; Welch (2006) (sorcery). Also, 162–64, nn. 29–31, Chapter 9.

20. Greenberg (2020) 458–63 on John 10:22–39. For John's engagement with Mark and Synoptics: n. 4, Chapter 6.

21. Schnabel (2018) 251–52; Blinzler (1969) 210–15, who posits one extended session; references at 136, n. 6, this chapter.

CHAPTER 9

1. Crowds: *CJ* 9.47.12, with *Dig.* 48.8.16, 49.1.12; Justin Martyr, *Apol. Mai.* 68.8. Aubert (2002) 124–25; Bovon (2006) 50; Hengel-Schwemer (2019) 640; Bickerman (2007) 762–63. On such an understanding of Jesus' execution: 3–5, nn. 4, 7–8, Introduction.

2. Czajkowski (2017), esp. 26–133, 167–98, with Czajkowski (2020) 90–93; Czajkowski-Eckhardt (2018) esp. 7–17; Bryen (2012), (2013), esp. 43–48 govern the present and following discussion.

3. Czajkowski (2017), esp. 107–32, 167–98; Czajkowski-Eckhardt (2018), esp. 7–17; Bryen (2012), esp. 795–803, (2013), esp. 43–48 for observations here and in following paragraph.

4. The vast discretionary powers of Roman governors are often discussed. Sherwin-White (1963) 1–48; Ste. Croix (2006) 114–17; Heusler (2000) 197–217; Liebs (2012) 103; Aubert (2002) 99; Nogrady (2006) 24–25; Bryen (2014) 246–53. See 145–50, 154, nn. 2–3, 5, 9, 11, 19, this chapter.

Notes 241

5. Bérenger (2014), 63–102, 171–265 governs what follows in this section, with Eck (2007) 1–52; Czajkowski (2020) 90–93. Senior judges: P. Euphrates 3.12; authority in provinces: *Dig.* 1.16.8 and 1.18.4; *ius gladii: Dig.* 1.18.6.8.

6. Venturini (1999); Santalucia (1999); Bickerman (2007) 743–47; Eck (2007) 1–52; Czajkowski (2020) 90–93. *Ius gladii* for equestrian prefects: *IGLS* 6.2796, *CIL* 9.5439, 2.484; Christian sources: *Perp.* 6.3; Eusebius, *Hist. Eccl.,* 5.1; in Egypt: P. Petaus 9; in Judaea: Jos., *War*, 2.117, *Ant.* 18.2.

7. *Lex provinciae* and *mandata*: Pliny, *Ep.* 10.22, 30, 56, 96, 110–11, 114; *Greek Constitutions*, no. 40 (Domitian); "every power": Jos., *Ant.* 18.2; *Gaius* 1.6: *ius ediciendi*; P. Yadin 28–30 with *Gaius* 4.47 on governor of Arabia; Egyptian papyrus: P. Yale 3.162=SB 12.10929, with P. Oxy 17.2104; Philostr., *Sophists* 1.532: intellectual. Chapman-Schnabel (2019) 208–10; Bickerman (2007) 743–47 on the sources. The governors in Egypt accepted cases from diverse people, not just Roman citizens. Bryen (2012) 781–82, 786–88; (2013), esp. 43–48.

8. Abusch (2003) on circumcision laws; Mor (2016), 13–145 on causes for the Bar Kochba Revolt. Permission for sons: *Dig.* 48.8.11.1; ban on mutilation (*mutilare genitalia*): *HA Had.* 14.

9. On judges, Sherwin-White (1963) 1–48; Heusler (2000) 197–217; Liebs (2012) 103; Aubert (2002) 99. For Egypt: Bryen (2012), esp. 796–97, (2013), esp. 179–86, with (2014) 246–53; Dolganov (2019); Czajkowski (2017) 179–80; Czajkowski-Eckhardt (2018), esp. 9, 16; Chapman-Schnabel (2019) 147–49. Jurists on governors' decisions and local traditions: *Dig.* 1.3.32–40, 22.1.1, 25.4.1.15; experts (*nomikoi*) from Egyptian papyri: P. Oxy 2.237, 36.2757, 42.3015. On Jerusalem Talmud and Aramaic documents: *y. Meg.* 3:2(74a); Czajkowski (2017) 109–15, 130–2, 163–64.

10. Pliny, *Ep.* 2.11 for bribes; see 3–6, nn. 4–11, Introduction. Smith (2018) 68–79, 165–70 on desire to win over chief priests. On crowds: 145, n. 1, this chapter.

11. Bryen (2012) 796–97, with (2013) 46–47; Dolganov (2019) governing this paragraph. Dismissing local customs: P. Oxy. 2.237; whipping: P. Oxy. 9.1186, *Dig.* 47.10.45; advisers: P. Oxy. 17.211, with Bermejo-Rubio (2019a), (2018b) 311–17; sacrilege: *Dig.* 1.18.13, 48.13.4.2; crucifixion as most serious: *Dig.* 48.19.28, *FIRA* 2.405 with Aubert (2002) 120–27; Cook (2014). For blows without a trial: Sherwin-White (1963) 27; Bryen (2012) 783. On crucifixion as standard for sedition, brigandage, and similar crimes: *Dig.* 48.19.28, 38; *FIRA* 2.405–10, 414; Chapman-Schnabel (2019), 602–24, 640–53; Jos., *War* 2.75, 241, 253, 293–308, *Ant.* 17.295, 20.102, 129, 160–62; 7, n. 12, Introduction; 152, n. 14, this chapter; 174, n. 12, Chapter 10.

12. Corke-Webster (2017) generally governing the paragraph, with 376 on Volesus and Sen., *Ira* 2.5.5. Also, Ste. Croix (2006) 114–15. For Felix: Tac., *Hist.* 5.9, with n. 21, this chapter. For Philo on Pilate: *Gai.* 302. On bringing charges against corrupt magistrates and challenges: Carter (2003) 53–54; Bryen (2012) 783–84. On Flaccus: Philo, *Flaccus*; Van der Horst (2003). On ostensible unpredictability of judges: 146, nn. 3–4, this chapter.

13. Corke-Webster (2017), esp. 389–90 on Pliny. Volesus: Tac., *Ann.* 3.68; Cumanus and Felix: Jos., *Ant.* 20.118–36, 173–78, with Tacitus, *Ann.*, 12.54, who conflates the two events. Pliny on Christians: *Ep.* 10.96; unjust convictions: *Ep.* 2.11; reputation for violence: *Ep.* 3.9.1–2.

14. Relevance of brigands: Bermejo-Rubio (2014a), (2018b) 119–332, with (2013b). See also at 7, n. 12, Introduction; 150, n. 11, this chapter; 174, n. 12, Chapter 10.

15. The unequal cooperation between prefects like Pilate and the chief priests, and the chief priests' role as local experts, have been widely explored. For example, Bond (1998) 17–19; Fredriksen (1999) 254–55; Carter (2003) 47–49; Skinner (2010) 14–22; Horsley (1987) 285–317, (2011) 187–204, (2012), esp. 145–49, (2014), esp. 33–36; Smith (2018) 80–117. Also at 25–34, nn. 15–19, 22, Chapter 1; 43–46, 50–51, nn. 11–15, 22, Chapter 2; 153, n. 17, this chapter.

16. Bryen (2012) 773, (2013) 19: in 209, the governor of Egypt heard over 1,800 in a three-day span. For limited demand for Roman magistrates among Jews, Czajkowski (2020) 91–93.

17. For this and next paragraph, Bryen (2012), (2013) (Egypt), (2014) 246–53 on provinces generally; Eck (2007) 1–52, Skinner (2010) 14–22, Czajkowski (2020) 90–93 (Judaea under Pilate); Bond (1998), Lémonon (2007) on Pilate. Czajkowksi (2017) on Judaea in the time of Babatha. See also 145–50, 154, nn. 2–3, 5, 9, 11, 19, this chapter. Different definitions of criminal behavior in different places: *Dig.* 47.2.9–10; 48.19.16.9.

18. On sedition (*seditio* or *stasis*), treason (*maiestas*), and violence (*vis*): Chapman-Schnabel (2019) 210–42 (sources); Robinson (1995) 78–80; Aubert (2002), esp. 120–27 (with a focus on Jesus); Cook (2011) 199–203; Dormeyer (2000) (*stasis*); Schnabel (2018) 262–65. The Markan author and Josephus often use *stasis*, a common Greek term for "sedition" or "insurrection," to describe the destabilizing activity to which Pilate and other prefects responded violently. Also n. 20, this chapter.

19. Nogrady (2006) 24–25, who stresses trials for the arrested; Ste. Croix (2006) 115; Liebs (2012) 109; Heusler (2000) 197–214; Bérenger (2014) 237–64; Aubert (2002), esp. 98–99.

20. For this and following paragraphs: Cook (2011) 199–203; Aubert (2002), esp. 120–27; Chapman-Schnabel (2019) 201–42 on *maiestas*; Sherwin-White (1963) 1–24. Assassins: *Dig.* 48.8.1; *seditio* under Augustus: *Dig.* 48.6 generally, with *Dig.* 48.4.1; acts of *seditio*: *Dig.* 48.6.3; 49.1.16. Bandits, brigands, and "evil men" (*homines mali*): *Dig.* 1.18.13; 48.13.4; 48.8.1, 48.6.3. On Barabbas: 114–15, n. 24, Chapter 6; 175–79, nn 15–19, Chapter 10. On *actores seditionis*: *Dig.* 48.6.3; 48.8.3; 48.19.38; *FIRA* 2.407.

21. The following paragraphs feature widely explored examples. See references at nn. 16–22, Chapter 3. Some treatments are Horsley (1987) 20–52, (2011) 73–87, (2014) 26–79; Mason (2003), (2016); Goodman (1987) 80, 92–93, (2007) 386; Chapman-Schnabel (2019) 122–26, 153–97; Broer (2007) 157–65; Bermejo Rubio (2014a), esp. 31, 37, 63–64, (2018b) 323–32; Fredriksen (1999) 149–51, (2018) 173–78;

Notes 243

Greenberg (2014) 71–88; Crossley-Myles (2023) 4–8. For Theudas: Jos., *Ant.* 20.97–102; Acts 5.34–39, whose flawed testimony perhaps misunderstands Josephus; Mason (2003) 276–82, (2022) 221–31; Gregory (2016) 106–7. For the Egyptian: Jos., *Ant.* 20.167–72; *War* 2.261–63. For Felix: Jos., *Ant.* 20.173–78; Tac., *Hist.* 5.9, with *Ann.*, 12.54, which conflates events recorded by Jos., *Ant.* 20.118–36, 173–78.

22. Jesus bar Ananias: Jos., *War* 6.300–9. This figure's trial is often compared and contrasted with Jesus' in the literature. Governing the next few paragraphs are Chapman-Schnabel (2019) 123–27, 149–51; Brown (1994) 367–68; Horsley (2011) 171–72, (2012) 145–46, (2014) 159; Webb (2009b) 738–39; Bond (2004) 66–67, (2012) 143–45; Fredriksen (1999) 228. Also key are Sanders (1985) 304–6; Broer (2007) 165–67; Stegemann (2010) 376–79; Reinbold (1994) 314–16, (2006) 95–101 who stress that different numbers of followers attracted different punishments, if not different arresting authorities. For the various "circles" of Jesus' followers: n. 2, Chapter 6.

23. Acts of the Apostles 21–24 generally, esp. 24. For historical and literary issues: 195–96, n. 19, Chapter 11. For Felix, 155–56, n. 21, this chapter. On characterizations of Roman governors: Yoder (2014).

24. On Josephus: Mason (2009) 18–24; Schwartz (2007). On Philo: Bond (2004) 31–33. For Pilate's poor relations with chief priests: Smith (2018) 68–79. For Pilate as unrelentingly cruel: Aslan (2013) 112–18; Greenberg (2014) 107–30. Bond (1998), esp. 24–95, (2004) 50–55, Skinner (2010) 14–22; Carter (2003); Lémonon (2007); Horsley (2011) 183–86 (2014) 158–62 and others have a more balanced perspective. See Pilate's characterizations at 49–50, n. 20, Chapter 2.

25. Blinzler (1969) 282; Lémonon (2007) 259; Joseph (2016) 25–27; Keener (2016) on Pilate's hesitation or resistance to pleasing chief priests. Bond (1998) 49–93, (2004) 50–55 foremost governs this paragraph. Pilate's sacrilegious actions and the responses of Jews have attracted ample coverage. For example, Bond (1998) 24–95; Lémonon (2007) 125–60; Webb (2009b) 714–25; Smith (2018) 68–78; Schnabel (2018) 98–101; Chapman-Schnabel (2019) 167–92 (with 188–92 on Samaritans); Horsley (1987) 90–110, (2011) 156–61, (2014) 63–64, 78; Vanderkam (2004) 431; Girardin (2022) 328–32; Schwartz (2013) 115–21, who suggests that Philo (on shields) and Josephus (on standards) report the same incident. Also references from nn. 4–11, Introduction. For Philo on Pilate: *Gai.* 302.

26. Foremost governing this and following paragraphs are Bond (1998) 24–95; Lémonon (2007) 125–60; Webb (2009b) 714–25; Smith (2018) 68–78; Schnabel (2018) 98–101; Chapman-Schnabel (2019) 167–92 (with 188–92 on Samaritans); Horsley (1987) 90–110, (2011) 156–61, (2014) 63–64, 78; Vanderkam (2004) 431; Girardin (2022) 328–32; Schwartz (2013) 115–21, who suggests that Philo (on shields) and Josephus (on standards) report on the same incident. Also references from nn. 4–11, Introduction. Goodman (1987) 29–50; Horsley (1987) 90–110; (2011) 156–61, (2014) 63–64, 78 on lack of leadership. Bond (2004) 51; Metzner

244 Notes

(2010) 80–81; McLaren (1991) 84 on spontaneous demonstrations as Josephus' choice of rhetoric. For Josephus' passages: *Ant.* 18.55–59; *War* 2.169–74; for Philo's: *Gai.* 299–308.

27. Jos., *Ant.* 18.60–62; *War* 2.175–77. Bond (1998) 92–93, (2004) 50–55 on impact of leadership of chief priests. Temple money: Bond (1998) 92–93, (2004) 52–53; Lémonon (2007) 157–58; Metzner (2010) 82; McLaren (1991) 85–87. On aqueduct: Magness (2024) 253–54, 61–62.

28. Bond (1998) 194–96. Mason (2003) 283 surmises that Luke possibly refers to Pilate's massacre of Samaritans. Governing the following paragraphs on Pilate's slaughter of Samaritan insurgents: Jos., *Ant.* 18.85–89; Chapman-Schnabel (2019) 188–92; n. 26, this chapter. For Herod and Samaritans, 21–24, 31–32, n. 12–13, 18–20, Chapter 1.

29. On deception/seduction, 142–44 n. 29, Chapter 8; Chapman-Schnabel (2019) 130–39; Sherwin-White (1963) 24–25; Schneider (1984); Bond (2012) 157, 161; Joseph (2016) 25–27. For relationships with sedition, n. 31, this chapter.

30. Rives (2011); Pellecchi (2012); *FIRA* 2.407, 409. For demons: Mark 3:22; Matt 12:22–24; Luke 11:14–15.

31. This pivot from blasphemy/deception to sedition has attracted widespread comment. Strobel (1980) 116; Sherwin-White (1963) 46–47; Hengel-Schwemer (2019) 632–33; Betz (2007) 55–99; Bond (2012) 157, 161; Joseph (2016) 25–27; Schnabel (2018) 265. Also 3–6, nn. 4–11, Introduction; n. 29, this chapter; n. 8, Chapter 10.

CHAPTER 10

1. Bermejo-Rubio (2018b) 311–17, (2019) on *consilium*.

2. My perspective owes many debts to Elliott (2019), esp. 24–25, 38; Cohick (2008), esp. 122, 129–31; Vermes (1993) x (which I paraphrase here); Crossley-Myles (2023) 228–32; Fredriksen (1999) 235–60, esp. 232–34, 240–41, 250–59, (2018) 43–73 (esp. 67–73); Ehrman (1999) 207–26, (2016) 131–78. It also has benefited from the detailed studies of Chapman-Schnabel (2019) 198–298; Schnabel (2018) 251–86; along with references from nn. 4–11, Introduction. Disturbance at the Temple: Jos. *Ant.* 17.206–219, *War* 2.4–12, with Bond (2004) 46.

3. Gibson (2009) 96–98; Smith (2018) 154–55; Schnabel (2018) 133–36 for gate; whether this is the Gate of the Essenes is debated; Magness (2024) 161–62. For east of the *praetorium*: Hengel-Schwemer (2019) 638. For discussion of the *praetorium*'s location and Jesus' trial: Blinzler (1969) 256–59; Brown (1994) 706–10; Schnabel (2018) 131–33; Magness (2024) 236–37. Pilate's need to be in Jerusalem during festivals is noted by Bond (1998) 7–8 and much of the literature at nn. 4–11, Introduction. Also n. 14, Chapter 1.

4. Mark 15:1–2; Luke 23:1–2; John 18:28–32 (on which 135, n. 4, Chapter 8). For Pilate's intelligence gathering: Bermejo-Rubio (2013b), (2018b) 290–93, 299–304,

Notes   245

(2019); Bermejo-Rubio-Zeichmann (2018); Bond (2012) 161–62. Bickerman (2007) 748–53 on indictment. On rates of petitions: 152–53, n. 16, Chapter 9.

5. On prohibition: Brown (1994) 744–47; Schnabel (2018) 254–55; Blinzler (1969) 276. Images of gods: *m. Avod. Zar.* 3.1–4, with Jos., *Ant.* 18.55–59; *War* 2.169–74; corpses: Num 19:16, 31:19; *m. Ohal.* 17.5, 18.7. Accepting John: Blinzler (1969) 276–83; Smith (2018) 155–60; Schnabel (2018) 267–68. Ehrman (2016) 154; Cohn (1971) 151–55 note how strange John's portrayal is.

6. Paradox: Brown (1994) 745. Lack of denial and cooperation: Schuol (2007) 193; Niemand (2007) 420, 495–96. Implausibility: Ehrman (2016) 158. Location of tribunal: Jos., *War*, 2.301; *Ant.* 17.222; Philo, *Gai.*, 299–306; Bond (2004) 8; Schnabel (2018) 131–33; with detail, Blinzler (1969) 346–56.

7. Heusler (2000) 46–182; Brown (1994) 767, 779 on Acts and Luke. On the charges in Luke: Sherwin-White (1963) 24–25; Schneider (1984); Joseph (2016) 25–27. See Acts 24:1–9, 25:7–9.

8. Strobel (1980) 116; Sherwin-White (1963) 46–47; Hengel-Schwemer (2019) 632–33; Betz (2007) 55–99; Bond (2012) 157, 161; Schnabel (2018) 265; Joseph (2016) 25–27, who emphasizes the compatibility of the chief priests' and Pilate's views. For theories on Pilate's decision-making: 3–6, nn. 4–11, Introduction; nn. 15, 24–25, Chapter 9.

9. Brown (1994) 778–86; Bickerman (2007) 758–61; Jensen (2010) 114–22; Skinner (2010) 79–80; Wilker (2007) 108–30; Schuol (2007) 190, 200; Chapman-Schnabel (2019) 269; Schnabel (2018) 269–71 discuss possible historicity and govern this section. Greenberg (2014) 242–44, 268–71 theorizes that Antipas pressured Pilate to kill Jesus.

10. Matthews (2010), esp. 6–20, 30–43, (2013) 45–56; Brown (1994) 779; Heusler (2000) 46–182 on similarities with trials in Acts. Cohick (2008) 117 on titulus.

11. Bond (1998) 8; Schnabel (2018) 134; Magness (2024) 175 on Antipas' palace. See Jos., *Ant.* 20.189–90.

12. Ancient witnesses: *Dig.* 48.19.1–2, 11, 13, 28, 38; *FIRA* 2.405–10, 414; Jos, *Ant.* 17.295; *War* 6.300–9; Luke 23:15–16, 22. For material on crucifixion: Chapman-Schnabel (2019) 299–754; Cook (2014). For favoritism toward landed elite in punishments: Aubert (2002), esp. 101; Robinson (2007) 61, 105–8; Harries (2007) 5–7, 33–38. See 7, n. 12, Introduction; 150, n. 11, Chapter 9.

13. Mark 15:6; Matt 27:15; Luke 23:18–24. Hengel-Schwemer (2019) 640; Brown (1994) 816–17; Schnabel (2018) 271–72; Chapman-Schnabel (2019) 264–66; Collins (2007) 713–16. Papyrus: P. Flor. 61; Albinus: Jos., *Ant.* 20.208–9, 215; Pliny, *Ep.* 10.31–32.

14. Crowd populated by allies of priests: Hengel-Schwemer (2019) 641–42. For example, Mark 15:11. Shifting allegiances: Fredriksen (1999) 222–23, 255–56, (2018) 52–63; Elliott (2019), esp. 26–36. On crowd autonomy and agency: Myles (2020); Crossley-Myles (2023) 207–10, 230–31.

15. Winter (1974) 131–43. Also Fredriksen (1999) 222–23, (2019) 67–73; Bourgel (2012) 513–16; Sloyan (2006) 49–51; Horsley (2011) 183–84; Greenberg (2014)

256–57; Cohn (1971) 164–69; Aus (1998) 135–70 on Jos., *Ant.* 17.204, *War* 2.4. For Vitellius' visit: 189, n. 8, Chapter 11.

16. Bond (1998) 110–11, (2021) 257–58, 263–66; Greenberg (2020) 529–30; Horsley (2014) 161. Also Collins (2007) 720; Marcus (2000–2009) 1036–38 on the logic of petitioning the crowd. See 79–80, n. 16, Chapter 4.

17. Bond (1998) 94–193; Sloyan (2006) 55–96; Carter (2003) on variations on how the Gospels portray Pilate.

18. Keener (2003) 1123–32 on John 19:4–16. On Lamb of God: John 1:29, 36.

19. Hengel-Schwemer (2019) 641; Schnabel (2018) 103–4 on Barabbas. On "the sedition," the references from n. 24, Chapter 6 govern my views.

20. Blinzler (1969) 321–22, with *CT* 8.5.2, 9.35.2 on outfitted whips; Schnabel (2018) 276, 284–85; Bovon (2006) 51.

21. Mark 15:26; Matt 27:37; Luke 23:38; John 19:19–21. Park (2019) 120–30 on titulus and racial discourse. For influence on viewers: n. 10, Introduction.

22. Mark 15:20–30; Matt 27:31–40; Luke 23:26–41. Crossbeam and fatigue: Schnabel (2018) 283, 289–90. On the *leistai/kakourgoi*: Bermejo-Rubio (2013b), esp. 130, with (2018b), 141–68. The other dominant phrasing is "others, two evil-doers."

23. Mark 15:26; Matt 27:37; Luke 23:38; John 19:19–20, which notes that the titulus featured Hebrew, Latin, and Greek. On crucifixion: Cook (2014), esp. 430–35; Schnabel (2018) 293–96, with medical bibliography; Chapman-Schnabel (2019) 653–57. The use of nails is supported by the discovery of a crucified corpse outside Jerusalem in 1968.

CHAPTER 11

1. Joseph of Arimathea and burial: Mark 15:43; Matt 27:57; Luke 23:50–51; John 19:38, with McCane (2003) 89–108; Gibson (2009) 127–48; Magness (2011) 164–71, (2024) 283–85; Crossley-Myles (2023) 238–43. Simon Peter: Luke 24:12; John 20:2–6. Nicodemos: John 19:39, with John 3:4, 7:50. Hiding in Jerusalem: Luke 24; John 20; in Galilee: Matt 28:16; Mark 16:7; John 21. Public preaching: Acts 1–4; Luke 24:53. Asiedu (2019), esp. 21–128 on Josephus and Jesus' followers. Also, n. 2, Chapter 7.

2. Keener (2012–2015) 1.383–389, (2020) 46–48; Strong (2021) discuss factors supporting an early date. For possible dependence on letters of Paul or Pliny: Smith-Tyson (2013) 5–14; Matthews (2013), 22–23; Bilby (2017); Phillips (2017); Mount (2021). For dependence on Josephus: Mason (2003) 251–96, (2022), esp. 212–31; Gregory (2016) 106–7 summarizes recent arguments. For the Temple commander: Appendix 1.

3. Matthews (2010), esp. 6–20, 30–43, (2013) 45–56; Heusler (2000) 46–182; Brown (1994) 767, 779. Parsons (2008) 16–17 suggests that Luke and Acts could have been written decades apart. For general unreliability: Smith-Tyson (2013). But Keener (2012–2015), with 550–81 on unity of Luke-Acts, and (2020) in favor of reliability.

Notes

4. Matthews (2010), esp. 6–20, 30–43, (2013) 45–56. On Roman authorities: Yoder (2014). On lashing/flogging and punishment: Fredriksen (2017) 81–82; Ehrman (2018) 180–81; Schellenberg (2021) 130–33. Deut 25:3 limits the number of strokes/blows to 40; the Septuagint translation assumes whipping. For differing views on anti-Judaism in Acts: Matthews (2013) 59–72; Keener (2012–2015) 1.459–77. On violence and anachronism: Shaw (2018) 233–35, Brélaz (2019) 501–2; Mount (2021) 35–36. On criminal classification, Williams (2024).

5. For chronological markers: Hemer (1987) 159–253; Mahieu (2012) 489–526; Keener (2012–15) 1.196–220, (2020) 20–22. On "we" passages: Wedderburn (2002). Chief priests: Acts 4:6; 23:3.

6. Hemer (1987) 159–253; Keener (2012–15) 1.196–220, (2020) 20–22 emphasize factors favoring historical validity.

7. Schwemer (2011) 170–77; Smith-Tyson (2013) 3 for Christian communities. On Pilate's fate and later traditions: Dusenbury (2021).

8. Nodet (2011); Mahieu (2012) 515–16. Relevant passages of Josephus: *Ant.* 18.89–95, 123, 237. For Marcellus and Marullus as the same: Bond (1998) 8.

9. Mahieu (2012) 516–17.

10. Bond (2004) 73–82; Fredriksen (2017) 61–62, (2018) 24–25, 128–30, 144–53. For citations: Acts 1:12–15 (Mount of Olives, house), 2 (Pentecost), 3 (Temple, with arrest), 4 (before the *synhedrion*); 5:12–42 (lashed/flogged by *synhedrion*); 6:8–8:1 (Stephen); 8:1–40 (persecution).

11. Matthews (2010), esp. 6–20, 30–43; Smith-Tyson (2013) 2–3, 84–92; Fredriksen (2018) 129–31 notes additional problems with Acts' account.

12. Fredriksen (2017) 82–93 (lashing on 82), (2018) 128–32, 144–52 on punishment.

13. Schwartz (1990); Wilker (2007) 144–91 govern this section.

14. Schwartz (1990) 119–24, 208–212; Wilker (2007) 164–78. Agrippa I, chief priests: Jos., *Ant.* 18.237–56, 19.256–77, 297–98, 312–16, 326–27, 338–342.

15. Fredriksen (2017) 82–93 (lashing on 82), (2018) 128–32, 144–52; Hengel-Schwemer (1997) 35–50 (who consider broad pursuit of Jesus' followers in Jerusalem possible); Ehrman (2018) 180–81; Schellenberg (2021) 130–33 on lashing/flogging; Smith-Tyson (2013), esp. 2–3, 106–21 on Paul's letters versus Paul in Acts. But see 73–76, nn. 4 and 8, Chapter 4 on the intervention of second-century Christians in Paul's letters. For recent approaches to Paul's biography: Schellenberg-Wendt (2021), with Mount (2021) 35–36, Schellenberg (2021) 126–27 on weaknesses of Acts. For key observations on the verb dioko (pursue, prosecute legally), Williams (2024) 6–9.

16. Campbell (2002), with (2021) 270–73; Bunine (2006). Also Hengel-Schwemer (1997) 106–13; Schwemer (2011) 170–77; references from nn., 11, 15, this chapter. For different reconstructions of Paul's early chronology: Dunn (2009) 497–511, 601–22; Riesner (1998) 1–89, with n. 15, this chapter. On Paul's death in Rome or elsewhere: Wright (2018) 391–97; Eus., *Hist. Eccl.* 2.25.

17. Eck (2007) 26–51; Czajkowski (2020) 90–93 on magistrates in Judaea.

Notes

18. Jos., *Ant.* 20.197–203, with *War* 6.300–9; McLaren (2001), with Brown (1994) 367–68; Joseph (2016) 25. Most accept the reference to Jesus as authentic: Paget (2010) 192–99. But see List (2024). On James and his disputed ossuary: Vermes (2005) 125–30; Magness (2011) 145, 174–80, (2024) 285–87.

19. Heusler (2000) 46–182; Wilker (2007) 265–83 (272 notes how appeal to the emperor supersedes judgment); Smith-Tyson (2013) 265–304; Brélaz (2021) 492–93, 498–500; Schellenberg (2021) 126–27: historicity and literary purpose. Matthews (2010), esp. 6–20, 30–43, (2013) 45–56 on Roman authority as innocuous. On Agrippa II generally: Jacobson (2019). On Paul, Felix/Festus, and the *synhedrion*: Brown (1994) 367 and 155–57, nn. 21, 23, Chapter 9.

20. Ste. Croix (2006); Barnes (1968); Moss (2012); Ehrman (2018) 180–206; Rebillard (2015), (2017), (2021); Bryen (2014); Kinzig (2021) govern this section. For Jesus Christ believers and Jews: 74–75, nn. 4–5, Chapter 4.

21. Rives (1999); Ando (2000) 207–9, (2012) 134–41; Potter (2014) 237–40. For small, exclusive communities: Kloppenborg (2019), (2020). For "atheism": Minucius Felix, *Octavius* 8–12; Lucian, *Alex.* 25; *Peregr.* 11–14. On *stasis*: Origen, *Cels.* 3.5–6, 8; 8.2, 13, 15, 49–50. Ste. Croix (2006) 133–39.

22. Tac., *Ann.* 15.44; Eus., *Hist. Eccl.* 2.25. For debate about legal logic and historicity of the executions at Rome: Ste. Croix (2006) 108–9; Shaw (2015), (2018); Jones (2017); Meier (2021); Nogrady (2006) 48–56; Ehrman (2018) 198–200; Liebs (2012) 114–24.

23. Eus., *Hist. Eccl.* 3.36; Moss (2012) 52–58 on Ignatius. On Ignatius' letters: Vinzent (2019) 266–464, (2023) 248–87. For Pliny: *Ep.* 10.96–97.

24. Corke-Webster (2017) governs this paragraph. Also Sherwin-White (1967) 171–79; Ehrman (2018) 183–86; Liebs (2012) 125–38 (esp. 136–37).

25. Rebillard (2015) for the agency of governors in North Africa. On military policing: Fuhrmann (2012) 201–39. On Justin's *Apologies*: Minns-Parvis (2009); Moss (2012) 79–88. On Christian criticisms of legal proceedings and unfairness: Bryen (2014). Relevant passages: Justin Martyr, *Apol. Mai.* 4.2–7, 7.1–5; *Apol. Min.* 1–2.

26. Tert., *Scap.* 4; Ste. Croix (2006) 117–18; Moss (2012) 10; Bryen (2014) 262–63.

27. Rebillard (2021); Huebner (2019b).

28. Eus., *Hist. Eccl.* 5.2. Moss (2012) 100–121; Ehrman (2018) 200–201.

29. Text in Musurillo (1972) 68–69; Moss (2012) 125–30; Rebillard (2021) 52–56, 85, 93–123.

30. Heffernan (2012); Gold (2018) on Perpetua. Musurillo (1972), 2–21, Moss (2012) 129–44, with 58–76 on Polycarp.

APPENDIX I

1. Mason (2003) 251–96 (esp. 276–82), (2022), esp. 212–31; Smith-Tyson (2013) 70–71; Gregory (2016) 106–7. For early date and independence from Josephus: Keener (2012–15), (2020); Strong (2021). Josephus on Theudas: *Ant.* 20.97–102.

Notes

2. Fuhrmann (2012) 47–87, esp. 53, n. 33.

3. Brown (1994) 1430–31 provides the ancient references here and the next paragraph; Schnabel (2018) 91 on *hyperetai*. References with *strategos*: Luke 22.4, 22.52; Acts 4:1–3, 5:22–26. Retainers in John: 7:32, 45–46; 18:3, 12. Arrests without *strategos*: Luke 20:18–19; Acts 7:8–8:1, 20–22.

4. On the dating of Josephus' works: Rajak (2002) 195–96, 237–38. On *strategos*: Jos., *Ant.* 20.131, 208; *War* 2.409, 6.294; 1QM 2:1–2.

APPENDIX 2

1. For authenticity, with some reworking: Meier (1991) 1.56–88; Paget (2010) 185–265; Bermejo-Rubio (2014b), with (2018b) 49–54; Whealey (2003), (2007), (2008), (2016) Theobald (2022) 202–7; Chapman-Schnabel (2019) 187–88. For inauthenticity: Feldman (2011); Hopper (2014). Van Voorst (2000) 81–103, esp. 88–94 frames key issues. Also Brown (1994) 373–76; Mason (2003) 225–36; Bond (2004) 60–62; Fredriksen (1999) 247–49. The bibliography is massive; works cited here have relevant references, and my translation is a variation on theirs.

2. Van Voorst (2000) 88–94; Paget (2010) 199–246 provide the main points for authenticity/inauthenticity summarized here. Mason (2003) 225–36, esp. 227 for inconsistency with surrounding material. Bermejo-Rubio (2014b), with (2018b) 49–54, argues that Josephus saw Jesus as a seditionist and notes that the portrayal of Jewish involvement in Jesus' death could involve Christian reworking. For Eusebius: *Hist. Eccl.* 1.11.7; *Dem. Ev.* 3.5.106; *Theoph.* 5.44; for Origen: *Cels.* 1.47; *Comm. Matt.* 10.17.

3. Goldberg (2022).

4. Bermejo-Rubio (2014b) 334–36; Whealey (2008), (2016) 345–47. This understanding is supported by references to Josephus' passage made by Jerome, Michael the Syrian, and Agapius, ostensibly via Eusebius.

5. While Schwartz (2016) denies the authenticity of 18.63–64 (45), he insightfully notes many instances in which Josephus' arrangement of sources into chronological or thematic units was not seamless (36–44). Also, Paget (2010) 222–26. For Josephus' use of the phrasing of sources: Czajkowski-Eckhardt (2021) 18–19.

6. For Jerome: *Vir. Ill.* 13.5. Whealey (2008), esp. 581 on Origin-Jerome-Michael, with 586, 589 on the scribal error that affected Michael's Syriac text, which is at Chabot (1899–1910) 4.91: lw (not) for l-h (him as direct object). This seemingly small error changes the statement that Pilate crucified Jesus ("him") because of the testimony of leading men to his doing it *not* because of their testimony.

7. Paget (2010) 191–99. Some however challenge authenticity. Most recently, List (2024).

Bibliography

Abusch, Ra'anan. 2003. "Negotiating Difference: Genital Mutilation in Roman Slave Law and the History of the Bar Kokhba Revolt," in Peter Schäfer (ed.), 71–91. *The Bar Kokhba Reconsidered: New Perspectives on the Second Jewish Revolt against Rome*. Tübingen: Mohr Siebeck.

Ådna, Jostein. 2000. *Jesu Stellung zum Tempel: Die Tempelaktion und das Tempelwort als Ausdruck seiner messianischen Sendung*. Tübingen: Mohr Siebeck.

Agamben, G. 2015. *Pilate and Jesus*, trans. Adam Kotsko. Stanford: Stanford University Press.

Aldinolfi, Federico and Joan Taylor. 2021. "Catching John in Four Nets? Competition, Qumran, Sacramentalism, and Messianism," *JSHJ* 19: 74–98.

Allison, Dale. 1998. *Jesus of Nazareth: Millenarian Prophet*. Minneapolis, MN: Fortress.

Allison, Dale. 2010. *Constructing Jesus: Memory, Imagination, and History*. Grand Rapids, MI: Baker Academic.

Amarelli, Francesco and Francesco Lucrezi. 1999. *Il Processo contro Gesù*. Naples: Jovene Editore.

Amorai-Stark, Shua. 2018. "An Inscribed Copper-Alloy Finger Ring from Herodium Depicting a Krater," *IEJ* 68.2: 208–20.

Anderson, Paul et al. 2016. *John, Jesus, and History*. Vol. 3: *Glimpses of Jesus through the Johannine Lens*. Atlanta, GA: SBLPress.

Ando, Clifford. 2000. *Imperial Ideology and Provincial Loyalty to the Roman Empire*. Berkeley: University of California Press.

Ando, Clifford. 2012. *Imperial Rome, AD 193 to 284: The Critical Century*. Edinburgh: University of Edinburgh Press.

Andrade, Nathanael. 2010. "Ambiguity, Violence, and Community in the Cities of Judaea and Syria," *Historia* 59.3: 342–70.

Andrade, Nathanael. 2013. *Syrian Identity in the Greco-Roman World*. Cambridge: Cambridge University Press.

Andrade, Nathanael. 2014. "Assyrians, Syrians, and the Greek Language in the Late Hellenistic and Roman Imperial Periods," *JNES* 73.2: 299–317.

Andrade, Nathanael. 2015. "The Jewish Tetragrammaton: Secrecy, Community, and Prestige among Greek-Writing Jews of the Early Roman Empire." *JSJ* 45: 198–223.

Ariel, Donald and J.-Ph. Fontanille. 2012. *The Coins of Herod: A Modern Analysis and Die Classification*. Leiden: Brill.

Arnal, William. 2011. "The Collection and Synthesis of 'Tradition' and the Second-Century Invention of Christianity," *Method and Theory in the Study of Religion* 23.3: 193–215.

Arnal, William. 2014. *The Symbolic Jesus: Historical Scholarship, Judaism, and the Construction of Contemporary Identity*. London: Routledge.

Asiedu, F. B. A. 2019. *Josephus, Paul, and the Fate of Early Christianity*. Lanham, MD: Lexington Books.

Aslan, Reza. 2013. *Zealot: The Life and Times of Jesus of Nazareth*. New York: Random House.

Aubert, Jean-Jacques. 2002. "A Double Standard in Roman Criminal Law? The Death Penalty and Social Structure in Late Republican and Early Imperial Rome," in Jean-Jacques Aubert and Boudewijn Sirks (eds.), 94–133. *Speculum iuris: Roman Law as a Reflection of Social and Economic Life in Antiquity*. Ann Arbor: University of Michigan Press.

Aus, David. 1998. *Caught in the Act, Walking on the Sea, and the Release of Barabbas Revisited*. Atlanta, GA: SBL.

Baltrusch, Ernst and Julia Wilker. 2015. *Amici—socii—clientes? Abhängige Herrschaft im Imperium Romanum*. Berlin: Topoi.

Bammel, Ernst. 1984a. "The Revolution Theory from Reimarus to Brandon" in Bammel and Moule (eds.), 11–68.

Bammel, Ernst. 1984b. "The Trial before Pilate," in Bammel and Moule (eds.), 415–52.

Bammel, Ernst and C. F. D. Moule. 1984. *Jesus and the Politics of His Day*. Cambridge: Cambridge University Press.

Bang, Peter Fibiger and C. A. Bayly. 2011. *Tributary Empires in Global History*. Basingtoke, Hampshire: Palgrave Macmillan.

Bang, Peter Fibiger, C. A. Bayly, and Walter Scheidel. 2021. *The Oxford World History of Empire*, 2 vols. New York: Oxford University Press.

Barnes, T. D. 1968. "Legislation against the Christians," *JRS* 58: 32–50.

Bauckham, Richard. 2011. "The Caiaphas Family," *JSHJ* 10: 3–31.

Bauckham, Richard. 2017. *Jesus and the Eyewitnesses: The Gospels as Eyewitness Testimony*. 2nd ed. Grand Rapids, MI: Eerdmans.

Bauckham, Richard. 2023. *"Son of Man."* Grand Rapids, MI: Eerdmans.

Becker, Eve-Marie, Helen Bond, and Catrin Williams. 2021. *John's Transformation of Mark*. London: T&T Clark.

Becker, Eve-Marie, Troels Engberg-Pedersen, and Mogens Müller. 2014. *Mark and Paul*. Berlin: de Gruyter.

BeDuhn, Jason. 2013. *The First New Testament: Marcion's Scriptural Canon*. Salem, OR: Poleridge.

Bérenger, Agnès. 2014. *Le métier de gouverneur dans l'empire romain: De César à Dioclétien*. Paris: Boccard.

Berlin, Andrea M. and Paul J. Kosmin. 2021. *The Middle Maccabees: Archaeology, History, and the Rise of Hasmonaean Kingdom*. Atlanta, GA: SBL Press.

Bermejo-Rubio, Fernando. 2013a. "Why is John the Baptist Used as a Foil for Jesus? Leaps of Faith and Oblique Anti-Judaism in Contemporary Scholarship," *JSHJ* 11: 170–96.

Bermejo-Rubio, Fernando. 2013b. "(Why) Was Jesus the Galilean Crucified Alone? Solving a False Conundrum," *JSNT* 26.2: 127–54.

Bermejo-Rubio, Fernando. 2014a. "Jesus and the Anti-Roman Resistance: A Reassessment of the Arguments," *JSHJ* 12: 1–105.

Bermejo-Rubio, Fernando. 2014b. "Was the Hypothetical 'Vorlage' of the 'Testimonium Flavianum' a 'Neutral Text'? Challenging the Common Wisdom in 'Antiquitates Judaicae' 18.63–64," *JSJ* 45.3: 326–65.

Bermejo-Rubio, Fernando. 2015. "La pretensión regia de Jesús el Galileo: Sobre la historicidad de un motivo en los relatos evangélicos," *Studia Historica, Studia Antiqua* 33: 135–67.

Bermejo-Rubio, Fernando. 2016. "Between Gethsemane and Golgotha, or Who Arrested the Galilean(s)? Challenging a Deep-Rooted Assumption in New Testament Research," *Annali di storia dell'esegesi* 33: 311–39.

Bermejo-Rubio, Fernando. 2018a. "Is the Kingdom of God/Heaven a Promised Land? Traces of a Material View in Jesus of Nazareth's Eschatology," *Forma Breve* 15: 81–98.

Bermejo-Rubio, Fernando. 2018b. *La invención de Jesús de Nazaret: Historia, ficción, historiografía*. Madrid: Siglo XXI España.

Bermejo-Rubio, Fernando. 2019. "Was Pontius Pilate a Single-Handed Prefect: Roman Intelligence Sources as a Missing Link in the Gospels' Story," *Klio* 101.2: 505–42.

Bermejo-Rubio, Fernando and Christopher Zeichmann. 2019. "Where Were the Romans and What Did They Know? Military and Intelligence Networks as a Probable Factor in Jesus of Nazareth's Fate," *SCI* 38: 83–115.

Bernett, Monika. 2007. *Der Kaiserkult in Judäa unter den Herodiern und Römern: Untersuchungen zur politischen und religiösen Geschichte Judäas von 30 v. bis 66 n. Chr.* Tübingen: Mohr Siebeck.

Betz, Otto. 2007. *Der Prozess Jesu im Licht jüdischer Quellen*. Basil: Brunnen Verlag Giessen.

Beyer, Klaus. 1984. *Die aramäischen Texte vom Toten Meer*. Göttingen: Vandenhoeck & Ruprecht.

Bickerman, Elias. 2007. *Studies in Jewish and Christian History*. Ed. Avram Tropper. Leiden: Brill.

Bilby, Mark. 2017. "Pliny's Correspondence and the Acts of the Apostles: An Intertextual Relationship," in Verheyden and Kloppenborg (eds.), 147–70.

Bird, Michael. 2014. *The Gospel of the Lord: How the Early Church Wrote the Story of Jesus*. Grand Rapids, MI: Eerdmans.

Blanton, Thomas IV, Agnes Choi, and Jinyu Liu. 2022. *Taxation, Economy, and Revolt in Ancient Rome, Galilee, and Egypt*. London: Routledge.

Blinzler, Josef. 1969. *Der Prozess Jesu*. 4th ed. Regensburg: F. Pustet. An English translation of the shorter 2nd edition is *The Trial of Jesus*. Westminster, MD: Newman, 1959.

Bock, Darrell. 2009. "Blasphemy and the Jewish Examination of Jesus," in Bock and Webb (eds.), 589–667.

Bock, Darrell L. and Robert L. Webb. 2009. *Key Events in the Life of the Historical Jesus: A Collaborative Exploration of Text and Coherence*. Tübingen: Mohr Siebeck.

Bond, Helen. 1998. *Pontius Pilate in History and Interpretation*. Cambridge: Cambridge University Press.

Bond, Helen. 2004. *Caiaphas: Friend of Rome and Judge of Jesus?* Louisville, KY: Westminster John Knox.

Bond, Helen. 2011. "The Herods, Caiaphas, and Pontius Pilate," in Keith and Hurtado (eds.), 219–48.

Bond, Helen. 2012. *The Historical Jesus: A Guide for the Perplexed*. London: Bloomsbury.

Bond, Helen. 2013. "Dating the Death of Jesus: Memory and the Religious Imagination," *NTS* 59: 461–75.

Bond, Helen. 2015. "Was Peter Behind Mark's Gospel?," in Helen Bond and Larry Furtado (eds.), 45–60. *Peter in Early Christianity*. Grand Rapids, MI: Eerdmans.

Bond, Helen. 2020. *The First Biography of Jesus: Genre and Meaning in Mark's Gospel*. Grand Rapids, MI: Eerdmans.

Bond, Helen. 2021. "The Triumph of the King: John's Transformation of Mark's Account of the Passion," in Becker, Bond, and Williams (eds.), 251–68.

Borg, Marcus. 1994. *Jesus in Contemporary Scholarship*. Valley Forge, PA: Trinity Press International.

Borg, Marcus J. and John Dominic Crossan. 2006. *The Last Week: The Day-by-Day Account of Jesus' Final Week in Jerusalem*. San Francisco: Harper.

Boring, M. Eugene. 2015. *I & II Thessalonians*. Louisville, KY: Westminster John Knox.

Bourgel, Jonathan. 2012. "Les récits synoptiques de la Passion préservent-ils une couche narrative composée à la veille de la Grande Révolte Juive?," *NTS* 58: 503–21.

Bovon, Francois. 2006. *The Last Days of Jesus*. Trans. Kristin Hennessy. Louisville, KY: Westminster John Knox.

Bowersock, Glen. 1983. *Roman Arabia*. Cambridge, MA: Harvard University Press.

Brandon, S. G. F. 1968a. *Jesus and the Zealots*. New York: Scribner.

Brandon, S. G. F. 1968b. *The Trial of Jesus of Nazareth*. New York: Stein & Day.

Brélaz, Cédric. 2021. "The Provincial Contexts of Paul's Imprisonments: Law and Criminal Enforcement in the Roman East," *JSNT* 43.2: 485–507.

Brighton, Mark. 2009. *Sicarii in Josephus' Jewish War: Rhetorical Analysis and Historical Observations*. Atlanta, GA: SBL.

Broer, Ingo. 2007. "The Death of Jesus from a Historical Perspective." In Tom Holmén (ed.), 145–68. *Jesus from Judaism to Christianity: Continuum Approaches to the Historical Jesus*. London: T&T Clark.

Brown, Raymond. 1993. *The Birth of the Messiah: A Commentary on the Infancy Narratives in the Gospel of Matthew and Luke*. New York: Doubleday.

Brown, Raymond. 1994. *The Death of the Messiah*. 2 vols. New York: Doubleday.

Bryan, Christopher. 2005. *Render unto Caesar: Jesus, the Early Church, and the Roman Superpower*. Oxford: Oxford University Press.

Bryen, Ari. 2012. "Judging Empire: Courts and Culture in Rome's Eastern Provinces," *Law and History Review* 30.3: 771–811.

Bryen, Ari. 2013. *Violence in Roman Egypt: A Study in Legal Interpretation*. Philadelphia: University of Pennsylvania Press.

Bryen, Ari. 2014. "Martyrdom, Rhetoric, and the Politics of Procedure," *CA* 33:2: 243–80.

Bultmann, Rudolf. 1968. *The History of the Synoptic Tradition*. Trans. John Marsh. 2nd ed. New York: Harper & Row.

Bunine, Alexis. 2006. "La date de la première visite de Paul à Jérusalem," *RB* 113.3: 436–56.

Burkett, Delbert. 1999. *Son of Man Debate: History and Evaluation*. Cambridge: Cambridge University Press.

Burchard, Christoph. 1993. "Jesus of Nazareth," in Jürgen Becker (ed.), 15–71. *Christian Beginnings: Word and Community from Jesus to Post-Apostolic Times*. Trans. Annemarie S. Kidder and Reinhard Krauss. Louisville, KY: Westminster John Knox.

Butcher, Kevin. 2003. *Roman Syria and the Near East*. London: British Museum Press.

Campbell, Douglas. 2002. "An Anchor for Pauline Chronology: Paul's Flight from 'The Ethnarch of King Aretas' (2 Corinthians 11:32–33)," *JBL* 121.1–2: 279–302.

Campbell, Douglas. 2021. "Chronology," in Schellenberg and Wendt (eds.), 265–86.

Carlson, Stephen. 2021. *Papias of Hierapolis, Exposition of Dominical Oracles: The Fragments, Testimonia, and Reception of a Second-Century Commentator*. Oxford: Oxford University Press.

Carrier, Richard. 2014. *The Historicity of Jesus: Why We Might Have Reason for Doubt*. Sheffield: Phoenix Press.

Carter, Warren. 2003. *Pontius Pilate: Portraits of a Roman Governor*. Collegeville, MN: Liturgical.

Casey, Mark. 2014. *Jesus: Evidence and Argument or Mythicist Myths*. London: Bloomsbury.

Catchpole, D. R. 1971. "The Problem of the Historicity of the Sanhedrin Trial," in Ernst Bammel (ed.), 47–65. *The Trial of Jesus: Cambridge Studies in Honour of C. F. D. Moule*. Cambridge: Cambridge University Press.

Catchpole, D. R. 1984. "The 'Triumphal' Entry," in Bammel and Moule (eds.), 319–34.

Chapman, David and Eckhard J. Schnabel. 2019. *The Trial and Execution of Jesus: Texts and Commentary*. Revised ed. Peabody, MA: Hendrickson. Originally 2015, Tübingen: Mohr Siebeck.

Chapman, Honora H. and Zuleika Rodgers. 2016. *A Companion to Josephus*. London: Wiley-Blackwell.

Charlesworth, James H. 1992. *Jesus and the Dead Sea Scrolls*. New York: Doubleday.

Charlesworth, James H. 1993–. *The Dead Sea Scrolls: Hebrew, Aramaic, and Greek Texts with English Translations*. Tübingen: Mohr Siebeck.

Charlesworth, James H. 2006. *Jesus and Archaeology*. Grand Rapids, MI: Eerdmans.

Charlesworth, James H. 2014. *Jesus and Temple*. Minneapolis, MN: Fortress.

Charlesworth, James and Jolyon Pruszinksi. 2019. *Jesus Research: The Gospel of John in Historical Inquiry*. London: T&T Clark.

Cimadomo, Paolo. 2019. *The Southern Levant during the First Centuries of Roman Rule (64 BCE–135 CE): Interweaving Local Cultures*. Oxford: Oxbow.

Cohen, Getzel. 2006. *The Hellenistic Settlements in Syria, the Red Sea Basin, and North Africa*. Berkeley: University of California Press.

Cohn, Haim. 1971. *The Trial and Death of Jesus*. New York: Harper and Row.

Cohick, Lynn. 2008. "Jesus as King of the Jews," in S. McKnight and J. B. Modica (eds.), 111–32. *Who Do My Opponents Say I Am? An Investigation of the Accusations against the Historical Jesus*. London: Bloomsbury.

Collins, Adela Yarbo. 2006. "The Charge of Blasphemy in Mark 14:64," in Van Oyen and Shepherd (eds.), 149–70.

Collins, Adela Yarbo. 2007. *Mark: A Commentary*. Minneapolis, MN: Fortress.

Collins, Adele Yarbro and John Collins. 2008. *King and Messiah as Son of God: Divine, Human, and Angelic Messianic Figures in Biblical and Related Literature*. Grand Rapids, MI: Eerdmans.

Collins, John J. 2010a. *Beyond the Qumran Community: The Sectarian Movement of the Dead Sea Scrolls*. Grand Rapids, MI: Eerdmans.

Collins, John J. 2010b. *The Scepter and the Star: Messianism in Light of the Dead Sea Scrolls*. 2nd ed. Grand Rapids, MI: Eerdmans.

Cook, John Granger. 2011. "Crucifixion and Burial," *NTS* 57: 193–213.

Cook, John Granger. 2014. *Crucifixion in the Mediterranean World*. Tübingen: Mohr Siebeck.

Corke-Webster, James. 2017. "Trouble in Pontus: The Pliny-Trajan Correspondence on the Christians Reconsidered," *TAPA* 147: 371–411.

Crawford, M. H. 1996. *Roman Statutes*. 2 vols. London: ICS.

Crawford, Sidnie White. 2019. *Scribes and Scrolls at Qumran*. Grand Rapids, MI: Eerdmans.

Crossan, John Dominic. 1988. *The Cross That Spoke: The Origins of the Passion Narrative*. San Francisco: Harper & Row.

Crossan, John Dominic. 1991. *The Historical Jesus: The Life of a Mediterranean Jewish Peasant*. San Francisco: Harper.

Crossan, John Dominic. 1995. *Who Killed Jesus? Exposing the Roots of Anti-Semitism in the Gospel Story of the Death of Jesus*. San Francisco: Harper.

Bibliography

Crossley, James. 2012. "Mark, Paul, and the Question of Influences," in Michael Bird and Joel Willitts (eds.), 10–30. *Paul and the Gospels: Christologies, Conflicts, and Convergences*. London: T&T Clark.

Crossley, James. 2014. "A Very Jewish Jesus: Perpetuating the Myth of Superiority," *JSHJ* 11: 109–29.

Crossley, James. 2015. *Jesus and the Chaos of History: Redirecting the Life of the Historical Jesus*. Oxford: Oxford University Press.

Crossley, James. 2021. "Editorial: Next Quest for the Historical Jesus," *JSHS* 19: 261–64.

Crossley, James and Robert Myles. 2023. *Jesus: A Life in Class Conflict*. Winchester, UK: Zerobooks.

Culpeper, R. Alan. 2019. "John 2:20, 'Forty-Six Years': Revisiting J. A. T. Robinson's Chronology of Jesus' Ministry," in Charlesworth and Pruszinksi (eds.), 142–54.

Czajkowski, Kimberley. 2016. "Justice in Client Kingdoms: The Many Trials of Herod's Sons," *Historia* 65.4: 473–96.

Czajkowski, Kimberley. 2017. *Localized Law: The Babatha and Salome Komaise Archives*. Oxford: Oxford University Press.

Czajkowski, Kimberley. 2020. "Law and Romanization in Judaea," in Czajkowski, Eckhardt, and Strothmann (eds.), 84–100.

Czajkowski, Kimberley and Benedikt Eckhardt. 2018. "Law, Status, and Agency in the Roman Provinces," *Past & Present* 241.1: 3–31.

Czajkowski, Kimberley, Benedikt Eckhardt, and Meret Strothmann. 2020. *Law in the Roman Provinces*. Oxford: Oxford University Press.

Czajkowski, Kimberly and Benedikt Eckhardt. 2021. *Herod in History: Nicolaus of Damascus and the Augustan Context*. Oxford: Oxford University Press.

Dabrowa, Edward. 1998. *The Governors of Roman Syria from Augustus to Septimius Severus*. Bonn: Habelt.

Dabrowa, Edward. 2011. "The Date of the Census of Quirinius and the Chronology of the Governors of Syria," *ZPE* 178: 137–42.

Daise, Michael. 2019. "Jesus and the Historical Implications of John's Temple Cleansing," in Charlesworth and Pruszinksi (eds.), 203–22.

Dan, Anca and Etienne Nodet. 2017. *Coelé-Syrie*. Leuven: Peeters.

Dark, K. R. 2023. *Archaeology of Jesus' Nazareth*. Oxford: Oxford University Press.

Demandt, Alexander. 1999. *Hände in Unschuld: Pontius Pilates in der Geschichte*. Köln: Böhlau Verlag.

Destro, Adriano and Mauro Pesce. 2014. *La morte di Gesù: Indagine su un mistero*. Milan: Saggi Rizzoli.

Destro, Adriano and Mauro Pesce. 2017. *From Jesus to His First Followers: Continuity and Discontinuity, Anthropological and Historical Perspectives*. Leiden: Brill.

Destro, Adriano and Mauro Pesce. 2021. *Il Battista e Gesù: Due movimenti giudaici nel tempo della crisi*. Rome: Carocci.

Bibliography

Dolganov, Anna. 2019. "Reichsrecht and Volksrecht in Theory and Practice: Roman Justice in the Province of Egypt (P.Oxy. II 237, P.Oxy. IV 706, SB XII 10929)," *Tyche* 34: 27–60.

Dormeyer, Detlev. 2000. "*Stasis*-Vorwürfe gegen Juden und Christen und Rechtsbrüche in Prozessverfahren gegen sie nach Josephus' *Bellum Judaicum* und Mark 15, 1–20 parr.," in Jürgen U. Kalms (ed.), 63–77. *Internationales Josephus-Kolloquium Aarhus 1999*. Münster: Lit Verlag.

Dunn, James. 2003. *Jesus Remembered*. Grand Rapids, MI: Eerdmans.

Dunn, James. 2006. "Did Jesus Attend the Synagogue?," in Charlesworth (ed.), 206–22.

Dunn, James. 2009. *Beginning from Jerusalem*. Cambridge, UK: Eerdmans.

Dusenbury, D. L. 2017. "The Judgement of Pontius Pilate: A Critique of Giorgio Agamben," *Journal of Law and Religion* 32.2: 340–65.

Dusenbury, D. L. 2021. *The Innocence of Pontius Pilate: How the Roman Trial Shaped History*. New York: Oxford University Press.

Eck, Werner. 2007. *Rom und Judaea: Fünf Vorträge zur römischen Herrschaft in Palaestina*. Tübingen: Mohr Siebeck.

Eck, Werner and Avner Ecker. 2023. "Not a 'Signet Ring' of Pontius Pilate," *'Atiquot* 100: 89–96.

Eckhardt, Benedikt. 2012. *Jewish Identity and Politics between the Maccabees and Bar Kokhba: Group, Normativity, and Rituals*. Leiden: Brill.

Egger, Peter. 1997. *"Crucifixus sub Pontio Pilato": Das "Crimen" Jesu von Nazareth im Spannungsfeld römischer und jüdischer Verwaltungs- und Rechtsstrukturen*. Münster: Aschendorff.

Ehrman, Bart. 1999. *Jesus, Apocalyptic Prophet of the New Millennium*. Oxford: Oxford University Press.

Ehrman, Bart. 2003. *Lost Christianities: The Battles for Scripture and the Faiths We Never Knew*. New York: Oxford University Press.

Ehrman, Bart. 2012. *Did Jesus Exist? The Historical Argument for Jesus of Nazareth*. New York: HarperOne.

Ehrman, Bart. 2016. *Jesus before the Gospels: How the Earliest Christians Remembered, Changed, and Invented Their Stories of the Savior*. New York: HarperOne.

Ehrman, Bart. 2018. *The Triumph of Christianity*. New York: Simon & Schuster.

Ehrman, Bart. 2020. *The New Testament: A Historical Introduction to the Early Christian Writings*. 7th ed. New York: Oxford University Press.

Ehrman, Bart and Zlatko Pleše. 2011. *The Apocryphal Gospels: Texts and Translations*. New York: Oxford University Press.

Ehrman, Bart and Zlatko Pleše. 2014. *The Other Gospels: Accounts of Jesus from Outside the New Testament*. New York: Oxford University Press.

Elliott, Neil. 2019. "Jesus, the Temple, and the Crowd: A Way Less Traveled," in Robert Myles (ed.), 15–53. *Class Struggle in the New Testament*. Lanham, MD: Lexington Books.

Esler, Philip. 2009. "Judean Ethnic Identity in Josephus' *Against Apion*," in Zuleika Rodgers, Margaret Daly-Denton, and Anna Fitzpatrick-McKinley (eds.), 73–91. *A Wandering Galilean: Essays in Honour of Sean Freyne*. Leiden: Brill.

Esler, Philip. 2017. *Babatha's Orchard: The Yadin Papyri and an Ancient Jewish Family Tale Retold*. Oxford: Oxford University Press.

Esler, Philip. 2019. "Female Agency by the Dead Sea: Evidence from the Babatha and Salome Komaïse Archives," *DSD* 26: 362–96.

Evans, Craig. 1992a. "Opposition to the Temple: Jesus and the Dead Sea Scrolls," in Charlesworth (ed.), 235–53.

Evans, Craig. 1992b. "Predictions of the Destruction of the Herodian Temple in the Pseudepigrapha, Qumran Scrolls, and Related Texts," *JSP* 10: 89–147.

Evans, Craig. 1993. "Jesus and the 'Cave of Robbers': Toward a Jewish Context for the Temple Action," *BBR* 2: 92–110.

Evans, Craig. 1997a. "From 'House of Prayer' to 'Cave of Robbers': Jesus' Prophetic Criticism of the Temple Establishment," in Craig Evans and Shemaryahu Talmon (eds.) 417–42. *The Quest for Content and Meaning: Studies in Biblical Intertextuality in Honor of James A. Sanders*. Leiden: Brill.

Evans, Craig. 1997b. "Jesus' Action in the Temple: Cleansing or Portent of Destruction?," in Bruce Chilton and Craig Evans (eds.), 395–439. *Jesus in Context: Temple, Purity, and Restoration*. Leiden: Brill.

Eve, Eric. 2021. *Solving the Synoptic Puzzle: Introducing the Case for the Farrer Hypothesis*. Eugene, OR: Cascade.

Fabry, Heinz-Josef. 2010. "Priests at Qumran: a Reassessment," in Hempel (ed.), 243–62.

Feldman, Louis. 2011. "On the Authenticity of the *Testimonium Flavianum* Attributed to Josephus," in Elisheva Carlebach and Jacob Schacter (eds), 11–30. *New Perspectives on Christian Relations*. Leiden: Brill.

Ferda, Tucker. 2020. "The Historicity of Confusion: Jesus, John the Baptist, and the Construction of Identity," *JBL* 139.4: 747–67.

Fisher, Greg. 2015. *Arabs and Empires before Islam*. Oxford: Oxford University Press.

Fitzmyer, Joseph. 1981–85. *The Gospel According to Luke: Introduction, Translation, Notes*. 2 vols. Garden City, NY: Doubleday.

Fledderman, Harry. 2005. *Q: A Reconstruction and Commentary*. Leuven: Peeters.

Fredriksen, Paula. 1999. *Jesus of Nazareth, King of the Jews: A Jewish Life and the Emergence of Christianity*. New York: Knopf.

Fredriksen, Paula. 2000. *From Jesus to Christ: The Origins of the New Testament Images of Jesus*. 2nd ed. New Haven, CT: Yale University Press.

Fredriksen, Paula. 2007. "Why Was Jesus Crucified, but His Followers Were Not?," *JSNT* 29.4: 415–19.

Fredriksen, Paula. 2008. "Gospel Chronologies, the Scene in the Temple, and the Crucifixion of Jesus," in Fabian Udoh et al. (eds.) 246–82. *Redefining First-Century Jewish and Christian Identities: Essays in Honor of Ed Parish Sanders*. Notre Dame, IN: Notre Dame University Press.

Fredriksen, Paula. 2015. "Arms and the Man: A Response to Dale Martin's 'Jesus in Jerusalem: Armed and Not Dangerous,'" *JSNT* 37.3: 312–25.

Fredriksen, Paula. 2017. *Paul: The Pagan's Apostle*. New Haven, CT: Yale University Press.

Fredriksen, Paula. 2018. *When Christians Were Jews: First Generation*. New Haven, CT: Yale University Press.

Freyne, Sean. 1999. "Behind the Names: Galileans, Samaritans, *Ioudaioi*," in Eric M. Meyers (ed.), 39–56. *Galilee through the Centuries: Confluence of Cultures* Winona Lake, IN: Eisenbrauns.

Fuhrmann, Christopher. 2012. *Policing the Roman Empire: Soldiers, Administration, and Public Order*. Oxford: Oxford University Press.

Furstenburg, Yair. 2023. *Purity and Identity in Ancient Judaism: From the Temple to the Mishnah*. Trans. Sara Tova Brody. Bloomington: Indiana University Press.

Gagné, André. 2019. *The Gospel According to Thomas*. Turnhout: Brepols.

Galor, Katharina and Hanswulf Bloedhorn. 2013. *The Archaeology of Jerusalem: From the Origins to the Ottomans*. New Haven, CT: Yale University Press.

Gers-Uphaus, Christian. 2020. "The Figure of Pontius Pilate in Josephus Compared with Philo and the Gospel of John," *Religions* 11: 1–24.

Gibson, Shimon. 2009. *The Final Days of Jesus: The Archaeological Evidence*. New York: HarperCollins.

Giovannini, Adalberto and Erhard Grzybek. 2008. *Der Prozess Jesu: Jüdische Justizautonomie und römische Strafgewalt: Eine philologisch-verfassungsgeschichtliche Studie*. Munich: Vögel.

Girardin, Michael. 2022. *L'offrande et le tribut: Histoire politique de la fiscalité en Judée hellénistique et romaine (200 a.C.–135 p.C.)*. Bordeaux: Ausonius.

Gold, Barbara. 2018. *Perpetua: Athlete of God*. New York: Oxford University Press.

Goldberg, G. L. 2022. "Josephus's Paraphrase Style and the *Testimonium Flavianum*," *JSHJ* 20: 1–32.

Goodacre, Mark. 2006. "Scripturalization in Mark's Crucifixion Narrative," in Van Oyen and Shepherd (eds.), 33–48.

Goodblatt, David. 2012. "Varieties of Identity in Late Second Temple Judah (200 BCE–135 CE)," in Eckhardt (ed.), 11–28.

Goodman, Martin. 1987. *The Ruling Class of Judaea: The Origins of the Jewish Revolt against Rome*. Cambridge: Cambridge University Press.

Goodman, Martin. 2007. *Rome and Jerusalem: The Clash of Ancient Civilizations*. London: Allen Lane.

Goodman, Martin. 2009. "Religious Variety and the Temple in the Late Second Temple Period and Its Aftermath," *JJS* 60.2: 202–13. Reprinted in Stern 2011, 21–37.

Goodman, Martin. 2010. "The Qumran Sectarians and the Temple in Jerusalem," in Hempel (ed.), 275–92.

Grabbe, Lester. 2008. "Sanhedrin, Sanhedriyyot, or Mere Invention," *JSJ* 29: 1–19.

Grabbe, Lester. 2020. *A History of the Jews and Judaism in the Second Temple Period*. Vol. 3: *The Maccabaean Revolt, Hasmonaean Rule, and Herod the Great (175–4 BCE)*. London: T&T Clark.

Greenberg, Gary. 2014. *The Judas Brief: A Critical Investigation into the Arrest and Trials of Jesus and the Role of the Jews*. New York: Pereset.

Greenberg, Gary. 2020. *The Case for a Proto-Gospel: Recovering the Common Written Source behind Mark and John*. New York: Peter Lang.

Gregory, Thomas. 2016. "*Acts and Christian Beginnings*: A Review Essay," *JSNT* 39.1: 97–115.

Grünewald, T. 2004. *Bandits in the Roman Empire: Myth and Reality*. Trans. J. Drinkwater. London: Routledge.

Gullotta, Daniel. 2017. "On Richard Carrier's Doubts: A Response to Richard Carrier's *On the Historicity of Jesus: Why We Might Have Reason for Doubt*," *JSHJ* 15: 310–46.

Gzella, Holger. 2015. *A Cultural History of Aramaic: From the Beginnings to the Advent of Islam*. Leiden: Brill.

Gzella, Holger. 2021. *Aramaic: A History of the First World Language*. Trans. Benjamin Suchard. Grand Rapids, MI: Eerdmans.

Harries, Jill. 2007. *Law and Crime in the Roman World*. Cambridge: Cambridge University Press.

Heermstra, Marcus. 2010. *The Fiscus Judaicus and the Parting of the Ways*. Tübingen: Mohr Siebeck.

Heffernan, Thomas. 2012. *The Passion of Perpetua and Felicity*. New York: Oxford University Press.

Hemer, Colin. 1987. *The Book of Acts in the Setting of Hellenistic History*. Tübingen: Mohr Siebeck.

Hempel, Charlotte. 2010. *The Dead Sea Scrolls: Texts and Contexts*. Leiden: Brill.

Hendin, David. 2021. *Guide to Biblical Coins*. 6th ed. New York: Amphora.

Hengel, Martin and Anna Maria Schwemer. 1997. *Paul between Damascus and Antioch: The Unknown Years*. Louisville, KY: Westminster John Knox.

Hengel, Martin and Anna Maria Schwemer. 2001. *Der messianische Anspruch Jesu und die Anfänge der Christologie: Vier Studien*. Tübingen: Mohr Siebeck.

Hengel, Martin and Anna Maria Schwemer. 2019. *Jesus and Judaism*. Trans. Wayne Coppins. Waco, TX: Baylor University Press.

Hillner, Julia. 2015. *Prison, Punishment, and Penance in Late Antiquity*. New York: Cambridge University Press.

Heusler, Erika. 2000. *Kapitalprozesse im Lukanischen Doppelwerk: Die Verfahren gegen Jesus und Paulus in exegetischer und rechtshistorischer Analyse*. Münster: Aschendorff.

Hopper, Paul. 2014. "A Narrative Anomaly in Josephus: *Jewish Antiquities* xviii:63," in Monika Fludernik and Daniel Jacob (eds.), 147–69. *Linguistics and Literary Studies: Interfaces, Encounters, Transfers*. Berlin: de Gruyter.

Horsley, Richard. 1987. *Jesus and the Spiral of Violence: Popular Jewish Resistance in Roman Palestine*. New York: Harper & Row.

Horsley, Richard. 2011. *Jesus and the Powers: Conflict, Covenant, and the Hope of the Poor*. Minneapolis, MN: Fortress.

Horsley, Richard. 2012. *The Prophet Jesus and the Renewal of Israel: Moving beyond a Diversionary Debate*. Grand Rapids, MI: Eerdmans.

Horsley, Richard. 2014. *Jesus and the Politics of Roman Palestine*. Columbia: University of South Carolina Press.

Huebner, Sabine. 2019a. *Papyri and the Social World of the New Testament*. New York: Cambridge University Press.

Huebner, Sabine. 2019b. "Soter, Sotas, and Dioscorus before the Governor: The First Authentic Court Record of a Roman Trial of Christians?," *JLA* 12.1: 2–24.

Humphreys, Colin J. 1992. "The Star of Bethlehem, a Comet in 5 BC, and the Date of Christ's Birth," *TynBul* 43.1: 31–56.

Ilan, Tal. 2002. *Lexicon of Jewish Personal Names*. Pt. 1: *Palestine, 330BCE–200CE*. Tübingen: Mohr Siebeck.

Ilan, Tal. 2018. "Josephus's 'Samias Source,'" in Michael Satlow (ed.), 197–217. *Strength to Strength: Essays in Honor of Shaye Cohen*. Providence, RI: Brown Judaic Studies.

Isaac, Benjamin. 2017. *Empire and Ideology in the Greco-Roman World: Selected Papers*. Cambridge: Cambridge University Press.

Ish-Shalom, Tal. 2021. "Provincial Monarchs as an Eastern *Arcanum Imperii*: 'Client Kingship,' the Augustan Revolution, and the Flavians," *JRS* 111: 153–77.

Jacobson, David. M. 2019. *Agrippa II*. London: Routledge.

Jensen, Morten Hørning. 2010. *Herod Antipas in Galilee: The Literary and Archaeological Sources on the Reign of Herod Antipas and Its Socio-economic Impact on Galilee*. 2nd ed. Tubingen: Mohr Siebeck.

Jensen, Morten Hørning. 2012. "Rural Galilee and Rapid Changes: An Investigation of the Socio-economic Dynamics and Developments in Rural Galilee," *Biblia* 93.1: 43–67.

Jensen, Morten Hørning. 2013. "Purity and Politics in Herod Antipas' Galilee: The Case for Religious Motivation," *JHSJ* 11: 3–34.

Jeremias, Joachim. 1966. *The Eucharistic Words of Jesus*. New York: Scribner.

Jones, C. P. 2017. "The Historicity of the Neronian Prosecution: A Response to Brent Shaw," *NTS* 63: 146–52.

Joseph, Simon. 2016. *Jesus and the Temple: The Crucifixion in Its Jewish Context*. Cambridge: Cambridge University Press.

Kaizer, Ted and Margherita Facella. 2010. *Kingdoms and Principalities in the Roman Near East*. Stuttgart: Steiner.

Keddie, Anthony. 2018. *Revelations of Ideology: Apocalyptic Class Politics in Early Roman Palestine*. Leiden: Brill.

Keddie, Anthony. 2019. *Class and Power in Roman Palestine: The Socioeconomic Setting of Judaism and Christian Origins*. Cambridge: Cambridge University Press.

Keddie, Anthony. 2021. "Beyond the 'Den of Robbers': The Dialectics of Sacred and Profane Finances in Early Roman Jerusalem," in Francesca Mazzilli and Dies van der Linde (eds.), 169–90. *Dialectics of Religion in the Roman World*. Stuttgart: Steiner.

Keener, Craig. 2003. *The Gospel of John: A Commentary*. 2 vols. Peabody, MA: Hendrickson.

Keener, Craig. 2009. *The Historical Jesus of the Gospels*. Grand Rapids, MI: Eerdmans.

Keener, Craig. 2012–15. *Acts: An Exegetical Commentary*. 4 vols. London: Baker.

Keener, Craig. 2016. "What Is Truth: Pilate's Perspective on Jesus in John 18:33–38," in Anderson et al. (eds.), 77–94.

Keener, Craig. 2019. *Christobiography: Memory, History, and the Reliability of the Gospels*. Grand Rapids, MI: Eerdmans.

Keener, Craig. 2020. *Acts*. Cambridge: Cambridge University Press.

Keith, Chris. 2011. *Jesus' Literacy: Scribal Culture and the Teacher from Galilee*. London: T&T Clark.

Keith, Chris. 2020. *Jesus against the Scribal Elite: The Origins of the Conflict*. Revised ed. London: T&T Clark.

Keith, Chris and Larry Hurtado. 2011. *Jesus among Friends and Enemies: A Historical and Literary Introduction to Jesus in the Gospels*. Grand Rapids, MI: Baker.

Keith, Chris and Anthony Le Donne. 2012. *Jesus Criteria and the Demise of Authenticity*. London: T&T Clark.

Kidger, Mark. 1999. *The Star of Bethlehem: An Astronomer's View*. Princeton, NJ: Princeton University Press.

Kimondo, Stephen Simon. 2018. *The Gospel of Mark and the Roman-Jewish War of 66–70 CE: Jesus' Story as a Contrast to the Events of the War*. Eugene, OR: Pickwick.

Kinman, Brent. 2009. "Jesus' Royal Entry into Jerusalem," in Bock and Webb (eds.), 383–429.

Kinzig, Wolfram. 2021. *Christian Persecution in Antiquity*. Trans. Markus Bockmuehl. Waco, TX: Baylor University Press.

Klawans, Jonathan. 2006. *Purity, Sacrifice, and the Temple: Symbolism and Supersessionism in the Study of Ancient Judaism*. Oxford: Oxford University Press.

Klinghardt, Matthias. 2015. *Das älteste Evangelium und die Entstehung der kanonischen Evangelien*, vols. 1–2. Tübingen: Franke.

Kloppenborg, John. 2005. "*Evocatio deorum* and the Date of Mark," *JBL* 124.3: 419–50.

Kloppenborg, John. 2019. *Christ's Associations: Connecting and Belonging in the Ancient City*. New Haven, CT: Yale University Press.

Kloppenborg, John. 2020. "Recruitment to Elective Cults: Network Structure and Ecology," *NTS* 66.323–50.

Knohl, Israel. 2022. *The Messiah Confrontation: Pharisees versus Sadducees and the Death of Jesus*. Trans. David Maisel. Lincoln: University of Nebraska Press.

Kokkinos, Nikos. 1989. "Crucifixion in 36: The Keystone for Dating the Birth of Jesus," in Vardaman and Yamauchi (eds.), 133–64.

Kosmin, Paul. 2018. *Time and Its Adversaries in the Seleucid Empire*. Cambridge, MA: the Belknap Press of Harvard University Press.

Krieger, Stefan Klaus. 1995. "Pontius Pilatus: Ein Judenfeind? Zur Problematik einer Pilatusbiographie," *BN* 78: 63–83.

Bibliography

Krimphove, Dieter. 1997. *"Wir haben ein Gesetz" . . . Rechtliche Anmerkungen zum Strafverfahren gegen Jesus*. Münster: LIT.

Kushnir-Stein, Alla. 2005. "City Eras on Palestinian Coinage," in Christopher Howgego et al. (eds.), 157–61. *Coinage and Identity in the Roman Provinces*. Oxford: Oxford University Press.

Lapin, Hayim. 2012. *Rabbis as Romans: The Rabbinic Movement in Palestine, 100–400 CE*. Oxford: Oxford University Press.

Lapin, Hayim. 2017a. "Feeding the Jerusalem Temple: Cult, Hinterland, and Economy in First-Century Palestine," *JAJ* 8: 410–53.

Lapin, Hayim. 2017b. "Temple, Cult, and Consumption in Second Temple Judaism," in Oren Tal and Zeev Weiss (eds.), 241–54. *Expressions of Cult in the Southern Levant in the Greco-Roman Period: Manifestations in Text and Material Culture*. Turnhout: Brepols.

Lataster, Raphael. 2019. *Questioning the Historicity of Jesus: Why a Philosophical Analysis Elucidates the Historical Discourse*. Leiden: Brill.

Lavan, Myles, Richard Payne, and John Weisweiler. 2016. *Cosmopolitanism and Empire: Universal Rulers, Local Elites, and Cultural Integration in the Ancient Near East and Mediterranean*. New York: Oxford University Press.

Le Donne, Anthony. 2011. "The Jewish Leaders," in Keith and Hurtado, 199–218.

Leibner, Uzi. 2021. "Galilee in the Second Century BCE: Material Culture and Ethnic Identity," in Berlin and Kosmin (eds.), 123–44.

Lémonon, Jean-Pierre. 2007. *Ponce Pilate*. Paris: Les Éditions de l'Atelier.

Liebs, Detlef. 2012. *Summoned to the Roman Courts: Famous Trials from Antiquity*. Trans. Rebecca Garber and Carole Curten. Berkeley: University of California Press.

Lieu, Judith. 2015. *Marcion and the Making of a Heretic: God and Scripture in the Second Century*. New York: Cambridge University Press.

List, Nicholas. 2024. "The Death of James the Just Revisited," *JECS* 32.1: 17–44.

MacDonald, M. C. A. 2009. "Arabs, Arabias, and Arabic before Late Antiquity," *Topoi* 16: 277–332.

Mack, Burton. 1988. *A Myth of Innocence: Mark and Christian Origins*. Philadelphia: Fortress.

Magness, Jodi. 2002. *The Archaeology of Qumran and the Dead Sea Scrolls*. Grand Rapids, MI: Eerdmans.

Magness, Jodi. 2011. *Stone and Dung, Oil and Spit: Jewish Daily Life in the Time of Jesus*. Grand Rapids, MI: Eerdmans.

Magness, Jodi. 2012. *The Archaeology of the Holy Land: From the Destruction of Solomon's Temple to the Muslim Conquest*. Cambridge: Cambridge University Press.

Magness, Jodi. 2016. "Were Sacrifices Offered at Qumran? The Animal Bone Deposits Reconsidered," *JAJ* 7: 5–34.

Magness, Jodi. 2019. *Masada: From Jewish Revolt to Modern Myth*. Princeton, NJ: Princeton University Press.

Bibliography

Magness, Jodi. 2024. *Jerusalem through the Ages: From Its Beginnings to the Crusades.* New York: Oxford University.

Mahieu, Bieke. 2012. *Between Rome and Jerusalem: Herod the Great and His Sons in Their Struggle for Recognition: A Chronological Investigation of the Period 40 BC–39 AD with a Time Setting of New Testament Events.* Leuven: Peeters.

Marcus, Joel. 2000. "Mark—Interpreter of Paul," *NTS* 45: 473–87.

Marcus, Joel. 2000–2009. *Mark.* 2 vols. New York: Doubleday.

Marcus, Joel. 2018. *John the Baptizer in History and Theology.* Columbia: University of South Carolina.

Marshak, Adam. 2015. *The Many Faces of Herod the Great.* Grand Rapids, MI: Eerdmans.

Martin, Dale. 2014. "Jesus in Jerusalem: Armed, Not Dangerous," *JSNT* 37.1: 3–24.

Martínez, F. G. and Eibert, J. C. Tigchelaar. 1998. *The Dead Sea Scrolls: Study Edition.* 2 vols. Leiden: Brill.

Mason, Hugh. 1974. *Greek Terms for Roman Institutions: A Lexicon and Analysis.* Toronto: University of Toronto Press.

Mason, Steve. 2001. *Flavius Josephus: Translation and Commentary.* Vol. 9: *Life of Josephus.* Leiden: Brill.

Mason, Steve. 2003. *Josephus and the New Testament.* 2nd ed. Peabody, MA: Hendrickson.

Mason, Steve. 2007. "Jews, Judaeans, Judaizing, Judaism: Problems of Categorization in Ancient History," *JSJ* 38: 457–512.

Mason, Steve. 2009. *Josephus, Judea, and Christian Origins.* Peabody, MA: Hendrickson.

Mason, Steve. 2016. *A History of the Jewish War,* A.D. *66–74.* New York: Cambridge University Press.

Mason, Steve. 2022. "Was Josephus a Source for Luke-Acts?," in Joseph Verheyden et al., 199–244. *On Using Sources in Graeco-Roman, Jewish, and Early Christian Literature.* Leuven: Peeters.

Matthews, Shelly. 2010. *Perfect Martyr: The Stoning of Stephen and the Construction of Christian Identity.* New York: Oxford University Press.

Matthews, Shelly. 2013. *The Acts of the Apostles: Taming the Tongue of Fire.* Sheffield: Phoenix Press.

Mattingly, D. G. 2011. *Imperialism, Power, and Identity: Experiencing the Roman Empire.* Princeton, NJ: Princeton University Press.

McCane, Bryon. 2003. *Roll Back the Stone: Death and Burial in the World of Jesus.* Harrisburg, PA: Trinity.

McLaren, James. 1991. *Power and Politics in Palestine: The Jews and the Governing of Their Land 100 BC–AD 70.* Sheffield: Academic Press.

McLaren, James. 2001. "Ananus, James, and Early Christianity: Josephus' Account of the Death of James," *JTS* 52.1: 1–25.

McLaren, James. 2016. "Josephus and the Priesthood," in Chapman and Rodgers, 273–81.

Meerson, Michael and Peter Schäfer. 2014. *Toledot Yeshu: The Life Story of Jesus.* Tübingen: Mohr Siebeck.

Meggitt, Justin. 2007. "The Madness of King Jesus: Why Was Jesus Put to Death, but His Followers Were Not?," *JSNT* 29.4: 379–413.

Meier, John. 1991–. *A Marginal Jew: Rethinking the Historical Jesus*. 5 vols. New York: Doubleday.

Meier, Mischa. 2021. *Die neronische Christenverfolgung und ihre Kontexte*. Heidelberg: Universitätsverlag Winter.

Meshorer, Ya'akov. 2001. *A Treasury of Jewish Coins from the Persian Period to Bar Kokhba*. Jerusalem: Yad Ben-Zvi Press.

Metzner, Rainer. 2010. *Kaiphas, der Hohepriester jenes Jahres: Geschichte und Deutung*. Leiden: Brill.

Meyer, Barbara. 2020. *Jesus the Jew in Christian Memory: Theological and Philosophical Explorations*. Cambridge: Cambridge University Press.

Millar, Fergus. 1990. "Reflections on the Trial of Jesus," in P. R. Davis (ed.), 133–63. *Essays in Honour of Geza Vermes*. Sheffield: Sheffield University Press.

Millar, Fergus. 1993. *The Roman Near East, 31 B.C.–A.D. 337*. Cambridge, MA: Harvard University Press.

Miller, David. 2014. "Ethnicity, Religion, and the Meaning of *Ioudaios* in Ancient 'Judaism,'" *CurBR* 12.2: 216–65.

Minns, Denis and Paul Parvis. 2009. *Justin, Philosopher and Martyr: Apologies*. Oxford: Oxford University Press.

Mor, Menahem. 2016. *The Second Jewish Revolt: The Bar Kokhba War, 132–136 CE*. Leiden: Brill.

Moss, Candida. 2012. *Ancient Christian Martyrdom: Diverse Practices, Theologies, and Traditions*. New Haven, CT: Yale University Press.

Mount, Christopher. 2021. "Acts," in Schellenberg and Wendt, 123–41.

Musurillo, Herbert. 1972. *The Acts of the Christian Martyrs*. Oxford: Clarendon.

Myles, Robert. 2019. *Class Struggle in the New Testament*. Lanham, MD: Lexington Books.

Myles, Robert. 2020. "Crowds and Power in the Early Palestinian Tradition," *JSHJ* 18: 124–40.

Nehmé, Laïla. 2010. "A Glimpse of the Development of the Nabataean Script into Arabic Based on Old and New Epigraphic Material," in M. C. A. MacDonald (ed.), 47–88. *The Development of Arabic as a Written Language*. Oxford: Archaeopress.

Netzer, Ehud. 2006. *The Architecture of Herod, the Great Builder*. Tübingen: Mohr Siebeck.

Netzer, Ehud. 2018. *The Palaces of the Hasmonaeans and Herod the Great*. Jerusalem: Israel Exploration Society.

Neusner, Jacob and Bruce Chilton. 2007. *In Quest of the Historical Pharisees*. Waco, TX: Baylor University Press.

Newman, Hillel. 2006. *Proximity to Power and Jewish Sectarian Groups of the Ancient Period: A Review of the Lifestyle, Values, and Halakah in the Pharisees, Sadducees, Essenes, and Qumran*. Leiden: Brill.

Nicholl, Colin. 2015. *The Great Christ Comet: Revealing the True Star of Bethlehem*. Wheaton, IL: Crossway.

Niemand, Christoph. 2007. *Jesus und sein Weg zum Kreuz: Ein historisch-rekonstruktives und theologisches Modellbild*. Stuttgart: Kohlhammer.

Nir, Rivka. 2012. "Josephus' Account of John the Baptist: A Christian Interpolation?," *JSHJ* 10: 32–62.

Nodet, Etienne. 2011. "Josephus and Discrepant Sources," in Menahem Stern, Pnina Stern, and Jack Pastor (eds.), 259–77. *Flavius Josephus: Interpretation and History*. Leiden: Brill.

Nogrady, Alexander. 2006. *Römisches Strafrecht nach Ulpian: Buch 7 bis 9 De officio proconsulis*. Berlin: Duncker & Humblot.

North, Wendy E. S. 2016. "Points and Stars: John and the Synoptics," in Anderson et al. (eds.), 119–32.

Paget, James Carleton. 2010. *Jews, Christians, and Jewish Christians in Antiquity*. Tübingen: Mohr Siebeck.

Park, Wongi. 2019. *The Politics of Race and Ethnicity in Matthew's Passion Narrative*. Cham, Switzerland: Palgrave Macmillan.

Parsons, Mikeal. 2008. *Acts*. Grand Rapids, MI: Baker Academic.

Patrich, Joseph. 2019. *A Walk to Caesarea: A Historical-Archaeological Perspective*. Jerusalem: Israel Exploration Society.

Pellecchi, Luigi. 2012. *Innocentia Eloquentia est: Analisi giuridica dell'Apologia di Apuleio*. Como: New Press Edizioni.

Phillips, Thomas E. 2017. "How Did Paul Become a Roman 'Citizen'? Reading Acts in Light of Pliny the Younger," in Verheyden and Kloppenborg (eds.), 171–89.

Piattelli, Daniela. 1999. "*Lo portarono da Caifa, sommo sacerdote* (Matth. 24,57): La giurisdizione del Sinedrio," in Amarelli and Lucrezi (eds.), 65–84.

Porat, Roi. 2015–. *Herodium: Final Reports of the 1972–2010 Excavations Directed by Ehud Netzer*. Jerusalem: Israel Exploration Society.

Porter, Stanley and Bryan Dyer. 2016. *The Synoptic Problem: Four Views*. Grand Rapids, MI: Baker.

Portier-Young, Anathea. 2011. *Apocalypse against Empire: Theologies of Resistance in Early Judaism*. Grand Rapids, MI: Eerdmans.

Potter, David. 2014. *The Roman Empire at Bay, AD 180–395*. Abingdon: Routledge.

Powell, Enoch. 1994. *The Evolution of the Gospel: A New Translation of the Gospel with Commentary and Introductory Essay*. New Haven, CT: Yale University Press.

Pummer, Reinhard. 2009. *The Samaritans in Flavius Josephus*. Tübingen: Mohr Siebeck.

Pummer, Reinhard. 2016. *The Samaritans: A Profile*. Grand Rapids, MI: Eerdmans.

Rajak, Tessa. 2002. *Josephus: The Historian and His Society*. 2nd ed. London: Duckworth.

Rebillard, Éric. 2015. "Popular Hatred against Christians: The Case of North Africa in the Second and Third Centuries," *Archiv für Religionsgeschichte* 16.1: 283–310.

Rebillard, Éric. 2017. *Greek and Latin Narratives about the Ancient Martyrs*. Oxford: Oxford University Press.

Rebillard, Éric. 2021. *The Early Martyr Narratives: Neither Authentic Accounts nor Forgeries*. Philadelphia: University of Pennsylvania Press.

Regev, Eyal. 2019. *The Temple in Early Christianity: Experiencing the Sacred*. New Haven, CT: Yale University Press.

Reinbold, Wolfgang. 1994. *Der älteste Bericht über den Tod Jesu: Literarische Analyse und historische Kritik der Passionsdarstellungen der Evangelien*. Berlin: de Gruyter.

Reinbold, Wolfgang. 2006. *Der Prozess Jesu*. Vandenhoeck & Ruprecht.

Reiss, Werner. 2021. "The Trial of Jesus Revisited," in Andrea F. Gatzke, Lee L. Brice, and Matthew Trundle (eds.), 83–99. *People and Institutions in the Roman Empire: Essays in Memory of Garrett G. Fagan*. Leiden: Brill.

Riesner, Rainer. 1998. *Paul's Early Period: Chronology, Mission, Theology*. Trans. Doug Stott. Grand Rapids, MI: Eerdmans.

Rietz, Henry. 2006. "Reflections on Jesus' Eschatology in Light of Qumran," in Charlesworth (ed.), 186–205.

Rives, James. 1999. "The Decree of Decius and the Religion of the Roman Empire," *JRS* 89: 135–54.

Rives, James. 2011. "Magic in Roman Law: The Reconstruction of a Crime," in J. A. North and S. R. F. Price (eds.), 71–108. *The Religious History of the Roman Empire: Pagans, Jews, and Christians*. Oxford: Oxford University Press.

Robinson, O. F. 1995. *The Criminal Law of Ancient Rome*. Baltimore: Johns Hopkins University Press.

Robinson, O. F. 2007. *Penal Practice and Penal Policy in Ancient Rome*. London: Routledge.

Robinson, James et al. 2000. *The Critical Edition of Q*. Minneapolis, MN: Fortress.

Rocca, Samuele. 2007. *Herod's Judaea: A Mediterranean State in the Classical World*. Tübingen: Mohr Siebeck.

Rogers, Guy. 2021. *For the Freedom of Zion: The Great Revolt of Jews against Romans, 66–74*. New Haven, CT: Yale University Press.

Roller, Duane. 2018. *A Historical and Topographical Guide to the Geography of Strabo*. Cambridge: Cambridge University Press.

Rose, Peter. 2012. *Class in Archaic Greece*. Cambridge: Cambridge University Press.

Rosenfeld, Ben-Zion. 2000. "Flavius Josephus and Portrayal of the Coast (Paralia) of Contemporary Roan Palestine: Geography and Ideology," *JQR* 91.1–2: 143–83.

Roth, Dieter. 2015. *The Text of Marcion's Gospel*. Leiden: Brill.

Rotman, Yuval. 2021. "Between *Ethnos* and *Populus*: The Boundaries of Being a Jew," in Jonathan Price, Margalit Finkelberg, and Yuval Shahar (eds.), 203–22. *Rome: an Empire of Many Nations: New Perspectives on Ethnic Diversity and Cultural Identity*. Cambridge: Cambridge University Press.

Sanders, E. P. 1985. *Jesus and Judaism*. Philadelphia: Fortress.

Sanders, E. P. 1992. *Judaism: Practice and Belief, 63 BCE–66 CE*. London: SCM.

Santalucia, Bernardo. 1999. "Lo portarono via e lo consegnarono al governatore Ponzio Pilato (Matth. 27,2): La giurisdizione del prefetto di Giudea," in Amarelli and Lucrezi (eds.), 85–104.

Bibliography

Satlow, Michael. 2014. "Jew or Judaean?," in Caroline J. Hodge et al. (eds.), 165–75. *"The One Who Sows Bountifully."* Providence, RI: Brown Judaic Studies.

Schäfer, Peter. 2017. *Jesus im Talmud.* 3rd ed. Tübingen: Mohr Siebeck. An English version of an earlier edition is *Jesus in the Talmud.* Princeton, NJ: Princeton University Press, 2007.

Schellenberg, Ryan. 2021. "Beatings and Imprisonment," in Schellenberg and Wendt (eds.), 123–41.

Schellenberg, Ryan and Heidi Wendt. 2021. *T&T Clark Handbook to the Historical Paul.* London: T&T Clark.

Schiffman, Lawrence and Andrew Gross. 2021. *The Temple Scroll.* Leiden: Brill.

Schnabel, Eckhard. 2018. *Jesus in Jerusalem: The Last Days.* Grand Rapids, MI: Eerdmans.

Schneemelcher, Wilhem and R. McL. Wilson. 1991–92. *New Testament Apocrypha.* Rev. ed. 2 vols. Cambridge, UK: James Clarke.

Schneider, Gerhard. 1984. "The Political Charge against Jesus (Luke 23:2)," in Bammel and Moule (eds.), 403–15.

Schubert, K. 1984. "Biblical Criticism Criticised: With Reference to the Markan Report of Jesus' Examination before the Sanhedrin," in Bammel and Moule (eds.), 385–402.

Schuol, Monika. 2007. *Augustus und die Juden: Rechtsstellung und Interessenpolitik der kleinasiatischen Diaspora.* Frankfurt: Antike Verlage.

Schwartz, Daniel. 1990. *Agrippa I: The Last King of Judaea.* Tübingen: Mohr Siebeck.

Schwartz, Daniel. 2007. "Composition and Sources in *Antiquities* 18: The Case of Pontius Pilate," in Zuleika Rodgers (ed.), 125–46. *Making History: Josephus and Historical Method.* Leiden: Brill.

Schwartz, Daniel. 2009. " 'Judaean' or 'Jew'? How Should We Translate *Ioudaios* in Josephus?," in Jörg Frey, Daniel Schwartz, and Stephanie Gripentrog (eds.), 3–27. *Jewish Identity in the Greco-Roman World.* Leiden: Brill.

Schwartz, Daniel. 2013. *Reading the First Century: On Reading Josephus and Studying Jewish History of the First Century.* Tübingen: Mohr Siebeck.

Schwartz, Daniel. 2016. "Many Sources but a Single Author: Josephus' *Jewish Antiquities*," in Chapman and Rodgers (eds.), 36–58.

Schwartz, Seth. 2001. *Imperialism and Jewish Society, 200 B.C.E. to 640 C.E.* Princeton, NJ: Princeton University Press.

Schwartz, Seth. 2014. *The Ancient Jews from Alexander to Muhammad.* Cambridge: Cambridge University Press.

Schwemer, Anna Maria. 2011. "Die ersten Christen in Syrien." In Dmitrij Bumazhnov and Hans Reinhard Seeliger (eds.), 169–94. *Syrien im 1.-7. Jahrhundert nach Christus.* Tübingen: Mohr Siebeck.

Shaw, Brent. 2015. "The Myth of the Neronian Persecution," *JRS* 105: 73–100.

Shaw, Brent. 2018. "Response to Christopher Jones: The Historicity of the Neronian Persecution," *NTS* 64: 231–42.

Bibliography

Sherwin-White, A. N. 1963. *Roman Society and Roman Law in the New Testament.* Oxford: Clarendon.

Sherwin-White, A. N. 1967. *Fifty Letters of Pliny.* Oxford: Oxford University Press.

Skinner, Matthew. 2010. *The Trial of Narratives: Conflict, Power, and Identity in the New Testament.* Louisville, KY: Westminster John Knox.

Sloyan, Gerard. 2006. *Jesus on Trial: A Study of the Gospels.* 2nd ed. Minneapolis, MN: Fortress.

Smith, Dennis and Stephen Tyson. 2013. *The Acts and Christian Beginnings: The Acts Seminar Report.* Salem, OR: Poleridge.

Smith, Mark. 2018. *The Final Days of Jesus: The Thrill of Defeat, the Agony of Victory.* Cambridge, UK: Lutterworth.

Snodgrass, Klyne. 2009. "The Temple Incident," in Bock and Webb (eds.), 429–80.

Sommer, Michael. 2018. *Roms orientalische Steppengrenze: Palmyra—Edessa—Dura-Europos—Hatra: Eine Kulturgeschichte von Pompeius bis Diocletian.* 2nd ed. Stuttgart: Steiner.

Staples, Jason. 2021. *The Idea of Israel in Second Temple Judaism: A New Theory of People, Exile, and Israelite Identity.* Cambridge: Cambridge University Press.

Ste. Croix, G. E. M. de. 1983. *The Class Struggle in the Ancient Greece World: From the Archaic Age to the Arab Conquests.* Ithaca, NY: Cornell University Press.

Ste. Croix, G. E. M. de. 2006. *Christian Persecution, Martyrdom, and Orthodoxy.* Oxford: Oxford University Press.

Stegemann, E. Wolfgang. 2002. "Wie im Angesicht des Judentums historisch vom Tod Jesu sprechen? Vom Prozess zu den Passionserzählungen der Evangelien," in Gerd Häfner and Hansjörg Schmid (eds.), 23–52. *Wie heute vom Tod Jesu sprechen? Neutestamentliche, systematisch-theologische, und liturgiewissenschaftliche Perspektiven.* Freiburg: Katholische Akademie.

Stegemann, E. Wolfgang. 2010. *Jesus und seine Zeit.* Stuttgart: Kohlhammer.

Stern, Sacha. 2011. *Sects and Sectarianism in Jewish History.* Leiden: Brill.

Strobel, August. 1980. *Die Stunde der Wahrheit: Untersuchungen zum Strafverfahren gegen Jesus.* Tübingen: Mohr Siebeck.

Strong, Karl Leslie. 2021. *Dating Acts in Its Jewish and Greco-Roman Contexts.* London: Bloomsbury.

Szanton, Nahshon et al. 2019. "Pontius Pilate in Jerusalem: The Monumental Street from the Siloam Pool to the Temple Mount," *Tel Aviv* 46.2: 147–66.

Taylor, Joan. 1997. *The Immerser: John the Baptist within Second Temple Judaism.* Grand Rapids, MI: Eerdmans.

Taylor, Joan. 2012. *The Essenes, the Scrolls, and the Dead Sea.* Oxford: Oxford University Press.

Thatcher, Tom. 2016. "The Passion of Jesus and the Gospel of John: Progress and Prospects," in Anderson et al. (eds.), 141–71.

Theobald, Michael. 2014. "Die Passion Jesu bei Paul und Markus," in Wischmeyer, Sim, and Elmer (eds.), 244–82.

Bibliography

Theobald, Michael. 2022. *Der Prozess Jesu: Geschichte und Theologie der Passionserzählungen*. Tübingen: Mohr Siebeck.

Thiessen, Gerd. 1991. *The Gospels in Context: Social and Political History in the Synoptic Tradition*. Trans. Linda M. Maloney. Minneapolis, MN: Fortress.

Thiessen, Gerd and Annette Merz. 1998. *The Historical Jesus: A Comprehensive Guide*. Trans. John Bowden. Minneapolis, MN: Fortress.

Thompson, Michael. 2022. "Paul and Jesus," in Matthew Novenson and R. Barry Matlock (eds.), 389–405. *The Oxford Handbook of Pauline Studies*. Oxford: Oxford University Press.

Van der Horst, P. W. 2003. *Philo's Flaccus: The First Pogrom*. Leiden: Brill.

Vanderkam, James C. 2004. *From Joshua to Caiaphas: High Priests after the Exile*. Minneapolis, MN: Fortress.

Van Maaren, John. 2022. *The Boundaries of Jewishness in the Southern Levant, 200 BCE–132 CE: Power, Strategies, and Ethnic Configurations*. Berlin: de Gruyter.

Van Oyen, Geert and Tom Shepherd. 2006. *The Trial and Death of Jesus: Essays on the Passion Narrative in Mark*. Leuven: Peeters.

Van Voorst, Robert E. 2000. *Jesus Outside the New Testament: An Introduction to the Ancient Evidence*. Grand Rapids, MI: Eerdmans.

Vardaman, Jerry and Edwin M. Yamauchi. 1989. *Chronos, Kairos, Christos: Nativity and Chronological Studies Presented to Jack Finegan*. Winona Lake, IN: Eisenbrauns.

Vearncombe, Erin, Bernard Scott, and Hal Taussig. 2021. *After Jesus before Christianity: A Historical Exploration of the First Two Centuries of Jesus Movements*. New York: HarperOne.

Venturini, Carlo. 1999. "Nota introduttiva: La giurisdizione criminale in Italia e nelle province nel primo secolo," in Amarelli and Lucrezi (eds.), 1–38.

Vermes, Geza. 1973. *Jesus the Jew: A Historian's Reading of the Gospels*. London: Collins.

Vermes, Geza. 1993. *The Religion of Jesus the Jew*. Minneapolis, MN: Fortress.

Vermes, Geza. 2004. *The Complete Dead Sea Scrolls in English*. Rev. ed. New York: Allen Lane.

Vermes, Geza. 2005. *Who's Who in the Age of Jesus*. London: Penguin.

Verheyden, Joseph and John Kloppenborg. 2017. *Luke on Jesus, Paul, and Christianity*. Leuven: Peeters.

Vinzent, Markus. 2014. *Marcion and the Dating of the Synoptic Gospels*. Leuven: Peeters.

Vinzent, Markus. 2019. *Writing the History of Early Christianity*. Cambridge: Cambridge University Press.

Vinzent, Markus. 2023. *Resetting the Origins of Christianity: A New Theory of Sources and Beginnings*. Cambridge: Cambridge University Press.

Vinzent, Markus. 2024. *Christ's Torah: the Making of the New Testament in the Second Century*. Abingdon, Oxon: Routledge.

Violante, Donata. 2021. "Gerusalemme: Storia e caratteri di una *polis*," in Luigi Gallo and Stefania Gallotta (eds.), 161–96. *Administration, Politics, Culture, and Society of the Ancient City*. Rome: Bretschneider.

Visi, T. 2020. "The Chronology of John the Baptist and the Crucifixion of Jesus of Nazareth: A New Approach," *JSHJ* 18: 3–34.

Vörös, Győző. 2019. *Machaerus III: Final Report on the Herodian Citadel 1968–2018*. Milan: Edizioni Terra Santa.

Vörös, Győző. 2022. *Machaerus: The Golgotha of John the Baptist*. Budapest: MMM Kiadó.

Watson, Alan. 1995. *The Trial of Jesus*. Athens: University of Georgia Press.

Webb, Robert. 2009a. "Jesus' Baptism by John: Its Historicity and Significance," in Bock and Webb (eds.), 95–150.

Webb, Robert. 2009b. "The Roman Examination and Crucifixion of Jesus: Their Historicity and Implications," in Bock and Webb (eds.), 669–775.

Wedderburn, A. J. M. 2002. "The 'We'-Passages in Acts: On the Horns of a Dilemma," *Zeitschrift für die neutestamentliche Wissenschaft und die Kunde des Urchristentums* 93: 78–98.

Weeden, Theodore. 2003. "Two Jesuses: Jesus of Jerusalem and Jesus of Nazareth," *Forum* 6.2: 137–77.

Weissenberg, Hanne Von. 2010. "The Centrality of the Temple in 4QMMT," in Hempel (ed.), 293–305.

Welch, John W. 2006. "Miracles, *Maleficium*, and *Maiestas* in the Trial of Jesus," in Charlesworth (ed.), 349–83.

Wendt, Heidi. 2021. "Secrecy as Pauline Influence on the Gospel of Mark," *JBL* 140.3: 579–600.

Wenham, David. 2021. *Jesus in Context: Making Sense of the Historical Figure*. Cambridge: Cambridge University Press.

Whealey, Alice. 2003. *Josephus on Jesus: The Testimonium Flavianum Controversy from Late Antiquity to Modern Times*. New York: Peter Lang.

Whealey, Alice. 2007. "Josephus, Eusebius of Caesarea, and the *Testimonium Flavianum*," in Christfried Böttrich and Jens Herzer (eds.), 73–116. *Josephus und das Neue Testament*. Tübingen: Mohr Siebeck.

Whealey, Alice. 2008. "The Testimonium Flavianum in Syriac and Arabic," *NTS* 54: 573–90.

Whealey, Alice. 2016. "The *Testimonium Flavianum*," in Chapman and Rodgers (eds.), 345–55.

Wilker, Julia. 2007. *Für Rom und Jerusalem: Die herodianische Dynastie im 1. Jahrhundert n. Chr*. Frankfurt: Verlage Antike.

Williams, Jeremy. 2024. *Criminalization in Acts of the Apostles: Race, Rhetoric, and the Prosecution of an Early Christian Movement*. Cambridge: Cambridge University Press.

Winter, Paul. 1974. *On the Trial of Jesus*. 2nd ed. Rev. and ed. T. A. Burkill and Geza Vermes. Berlin: de Gruyter.

Wischmeyer, Oda, David Sim, and Ian Elmer. 2014. *Paul and Mark*. Berlin: de Gruyter.

Bibliography

Wright, Nicholas. 1998. *Jesus and the Victory of God*. Minneapolis, MN: Fortress.

Wright, Nicholas. 2018. *Paul: A Biography*. New York: HarperOne.

Yoder, Joshua. 2014. *Representatives of Roman Rule: Roman Provincial Governors in Luke-Acts*. Berlin: De Gruyter.

Zeichmann, Christopher. 2018. "Military Forces in Judaea 6–130 CE: The *Status Quaestionis* and Relevance for New Testament Studies," *CurBR* 17: 86–120.

Zeitlin, Solomon. 1964. *Who Crucified Jesus?* 5th ed. New York: Bloch.

Index

For the benefit of digital users, indexed terms that span two pages (e.g., 52–53) may, on occasion, appear on only one of those pages.

Acts of the Apostles, 24–25, 32, 46–47, 93, 123, 135–136, 155–158, 170–171
    date and composition, 185–188
    Josephus, 186–187
    Paul, 192–194
    violence, 188–197
Agrippa I, Herod, 42, 93, 185–188, 190–192, 194–195
Agrippa II, Herod, 20, 94, 195–196
Albinus, Lucceius, 135–136, 156–158, 174–176, 179–180, 191
Annas/Ananus (high priest, 6–15), 8, 43–48, 124, 158–160, 189
    Jesus' arrest and hearing, 136–140
Ananus bar Ananus (high priest, 62), 38, 46–47, 63–64, 195
Antipas (Herod), 14–16, 30, 39–42, 44–45, 48–51, 76–79, 143, 172–173
    John the Baptizer, 59–62, 86–94
    Mark, 86–94
    Luke/Acts, 91–93, 172–173, 186–187, 189–193, 196
Archelaus, Herod, 14–16, 24, 30–32, 175–176
Aretas IV, 42, 61–62, 189, 193

Augustus (emperor), 16, 21, 29–31, 46, 134
auxiliary troops, 21–24, 84

Babatha, 132–133, 145–146, 148–149
Bar Kochba Revolt, 53–54, 73–75, 79, 132, 148–149, 198
blasphemy, 16–17, 110, 131, 141–143, 149–152, 163–164, 171, 194–195
brigands, 18, 35, 52, 59, 115, 118–126, 138–139, 147–155, 208

Caiaphas (high priest 18–36), 8, 36, 43–48, 50, 124, 127, 158–160, 189–190
    Jesus' arrest and hearing, 136–140
Caligula (emperor), 33, 39–40, 42
chief priests, *see also* Caiaphas, Annas, 1–9, 24–35, 71, 74, 76–80
    First Jewish Revolt, 37–39
    Herod I/Herodians, 25–30
    festivals/sacrifices, 45
    obligations, 42–48, 102–103, 106–108, 111–113, 117–126
    Pilate/Romans, 37–40, 49–51, 54, 144–182, 185–206

276 Index

chief priests (*continued*)
synhedria and Jesus, 131–143
Temple, 25–29, 42–48, 97–117
Temple tax, 25–29, 42–43, 104–107
tithes, 25–29, 42–43, 104–105,
107–108
Christians, *see also* Jesus Christ believers,
13–14, 65–67, 72–75, 197–203
courts
Herodian dynasts, 88
Jerusalem, 131–143
local/municipal/*synhedria*, 131–143
Nabataean kings, 132–133
Pilate/Roman governors, 144–182

Damascus, 14, 189–190, 192–194
Dead Sea Scrolls (*see* Qumran texts)
deception (crime), 141–142, 163–164

Egypt (Roman), 146–149, 153,
174–175, 179–180
Essenes, *see also* Qumran Jews, 52, 54–59,
66–67
Eusebius of Caesarea, 201, 211, 213

Fadus, Cuspius, 64–65, 155–156, 207–208
Felix, Marcus Antonius, 24, 63–65, 115,
124, 151–152, 156–158, 195–197
Feast of Unleavened Bread, 45, 111–112,
118–119, 136, 143, 167–170, 175
Festus, Porcius, 24, 195–197, 206
First Jewish Revolt, 31–33, 37–39, 46–47,
63–64, 135–136, 150, 156–159, 198
Gospels, 74, 79, 84, 123
Florus, Gessius, 31, 150

Galilee
Antipas, 40–42, 86–94, 133
Herod I, 32–35
Jesus, 86–94
Gadara, 17, 33, 83
Gerasa, 17, 33, 83

Gospel of John
arrest of Jesus, 46, 118–127, 208–209
baptism, 66
date, 73, 77–78, 207
death of Jesus, 46, 111–112, 115,
180–182, 185
Mark, 73, 77–78, 80, 101–103
preaching of Jesus, 66, 101–102, 114
synhedrion, 131, 135–140
Synoptic Gospels, 73, 77–78, 80,
101–103
trial of Jesus, 163, 166–178
Gospel of Luke
Acts of the Apostles, 157, 172–173,
186–188, 195–196, 207–209
arrest of Jesus, 123–127, 207–209
census, 17, 24
chronological markers, 61, 66
date, 73, 77–78, 207–209
death of Jesus, 180–182
Josephus, 61, 66, 88
Mark, 48, 73, 75–84, 87–94, 109–110,
123–127, 141–143, 163, 165–172,
186–187
preaching of Jesus, 81–83, 101,
108–115
synhedrion, 131–143
trial of Jesus, 163, 166–167, 170–172,
175–177, 187
Gospel of Mark
arrest of Jesus, 118–127, 207–209
Antipas, 39–41, 61–62
date, 6, 73, 207
death of Jesus, 180–181
Herodians, 41, 57, 92
Jesus at Temple, 97–115
Jesus in Galilee, 86–94
Passion Narrative, 76–79
preaching of Jesus, 67–68, 71–94,
97–115
synhedrion, 43, 131–143
trial of Jesus, 165–180, 186–187

Gospel of Matthew
 arrest of Jesus, 118, 121–124, 126–127,
  207–208
 date, 73, 207
 death of Jesus, 155, 180–182
 Herod I, 93–94
 Mark, 48, 73–84, 87–92, 104–115,
  118–127, 136–143, 154–155, 163,
  166–182
 preaching of Jesus, 82, 97, 104,
  109–115
 synhedrion, 136–138, 141, 143
 trial of Jesus, 163, 166–178
Gospels, *see also* Gospel of John, Gospel
  of Luke, Gospel of Mark, Gospel of
  Matthew
 apocryphal, 3, 72–73
 dates, 72–73, 207–209
 Synoptics, 48, 73–84, 87–92, 104–115,
  118–127, 136–143, 154–155, 163,
  166–182
Gratus, Valerius, 36, 46

Hasmonaeans, 13–14, 17–25, 31–33,
  44–45, 48, 57–59, 152, 161, 173
Herod I
 building, 20–29
 effects of reign, 14, 30–35, 138–139
 Gospel of Matthew, 93–94
 Herod Agrippa I (*see* Agrippa I)
 Herod Agrippa II (*see* Agrippa II)
 Herod Antipas (*see* Antipas)
 Herod Philip (*see* Philip the Tetrarch)
 high priests (*see* Annas/Ananus,
  Caiaphas, chief priests)
 Hyrcanus II (*see* John Hyrcanus II)

insurgency/insurrection, *see also* First
  Jewish Revolt; Bar Kochba
  Revolt; policing; sedition
 Antipas, 41
 Egyptian, 64, 156–157

Herod I and aftermath, 31–34, 41,
  50–51, 54, 62–65, 84, 110–111, 174
 Jesus of Nazareth, 4–6, 105, 108,
  170–171, 205
 Judas the Galilean, 35, 41, 48–49,
  62–64, 150, 155–156, 186–187, 208
 sicarii, 46–47, 63
 Theudas, 64–65, 155–156, 186–187, 208
 Zealots, 63–64
Ioudaioi, 19–20, 76–77, 79, 165–166, 173,
  185, 195–196, 205

James (apostle), 93, 191
James, brother of Jesus, 46–47, 135–136,
  189–190, 193, 195, 211
Jerusalem, *see also* Temple
 pilgrimage, 25–29, 32–35, 39–40, 45,
  81–84, 101–114, 140–143, 163
 praetorium, 24, 50, 103–104, 124, 159,
  166–170, 178, 181
Jesus of Nazareth
 arrest, 118–127
 burial, 118–119, 185
 crowds, 97–117, 175–180
 crucifixion, 180–182
 dissenter, 65–68, 81–83
 followers, 66–67, 75–76, 81–82, 97,
  118–127, 195–198
 Jew, 65–68, 105–106
 Josephus' *Antiquities*, 211–213
 Messiah, 4–6, 60–68, 73–83, 110–117,
  137–143, 157–162, 172–178, 205
 secrecy, 72–76, 91, 111–112
 synhedrion, 131–143
 Talmud, 3–4, 141
 Temple of Jerusalem, 4–9, 42, 81–82,
  92–93, 97–117, 140–143, 157–182,
  204–206
 trial by Pilate, 1–9, 165–182
 wealth, 81–83, 104–108
Jesus bar Ananias, 136–137, 156–158,
  175–176, 179–180, 191, 195, 206

278   *Index*

Jesus Christ believers, *see also* Christians
Jews (see *Ioudaioi*)
John (*see* Gospel of John)
John the Baptizer
    death, 14, 40–42, 60–61, 86–91, 94,
       143, 173, 209
    preaching, 35–39, 59–62, 81–82,
       84–85, 178, 208
John Hyrcanus II, 13–14, 31–32, 138–139
Joseph of Arimathea, 138–139, 185
Josephus
    Acts of the Apostles, 121–122, 186,
       207–209
    Ananus/Annas, 46–48
    Antipas, 40–41, 87–91
    biases, 38–39
    Caiaphas, 46–48
    Essenes, 56–57
    First Jewish Revolt, 37–39
    Herod I, 21–25
    insurgents/insurrections, 62–64
    Jesus, 125, 144, 211–213
    John the Baptizer, 61–62, 65–66,
       87–91
    Judaea and Roman governance, 137–139,
       148–150, 153–154, 156–157, 174
    Luke, 61, 88, 91, 113, 121–122, 186,
       207–209
    Messiah, 110–111
    Pilate, 50, 113, 125, 144, 158–162
    scribes, 48–49
    works, 38
Judaea
    Greater Judaea, 13–20, 29–39, 62–63,
       82–84, 93, 161, 188–192
    Lesser Judaea, 13–20, 30–35, 41, 55–63,
       133–134
    Roman district, 18–19, 30–31, 50–51,
       60, 146–162
Judaeans (see *Ioudaioi*)
Judas the Galilean (*see* insurgency/
    insurrection)

Judas Iscariot, 7–8, 118
Justin Martyr, 200–201

legions, 21–24, 31, 73, 83–84
Lukan author, *see also* Acts of the
    Apostles; Gospel of Luke
    Josephus, 61, 88, 91, 122, 186,
       207–209
    themes of Luke and Acts, 93, 121–122,
       157, 170–171, 173, 186–187, 196,
       207–209
Luke (*see* Gospel of Luke)

maiestas (*see* treason)
Marcion, 73–74, 207–208
Mark (*see* Gospel of Mark)
Mary Magdalene, 181–182, 185
Masada, 21, 37–38, 63
Matthew (*see* Gospel of Matthew)
Messiah
    definition, 35–37, 47–48, 53–56,
       58–60, 109–110
    Jesus, 4–6, 60–68, 73–83, 110–117,
       137–143, 157–162, 172–178, 205
    Josephus, 110–111
    King of the Jews, 4–5, 157–158, 172,
       176–178, 205
    Son of Man, 67–68, 81, 108,
       141–142
Mishnah, 48–49, 107–108, 133–134,
    136–137, 167
Mount Gerizim, 18–21, 32, 161, 188

Nabataeans, 16–17, 29, 31, 42, 61–62,
    132–133, 145–146, 193

Passover/Pesach
    background, 45, 118–119
    chief priests, 97–116, 136–140, 143,
       189, 191
    Jesus, 2, 4–8, 66, 72–73, 76–77,
       97–116, 163, 166–181

Index

pilgrims, 97–116, 122, 166–181
Pontius Pilate, 1, 5–7, 13, 50, 144, 149,
 152–153, 166–181
Temple, 13, 31, 66, 97–116
Paul
 Acts of the Apostles, 24–25, 32, 123–124,
  135, 173, 186–187, 190–191
 Agrippa II, 24, 196
 Damascus, 190–194
 Felix, 24, 115, 151, 157–158, 170–171,
  195–196
 Festus, 24, 196
 James, brother of Jesus, 193
 Jerusalem/Temple, 25, 32, 108–110, 123,
  135, 190–191, 195–196
 lashes/punishment, 122, 187, 191–192
 letters, 75–77, 79, 101, 110, 119, 122,
  124–125, 187, 192–194
Peraea (Transjordan), 17–18, 29, 32–33,
 40–41, 59–61, 102
Peter (*see* Simon Peter)
Pharisees
 background, 36–37, 41–43, 48–49
 Jesus, 62–63, 66–67, 74, 81–82, 86,
  88–92, 163, 208
 Paul, 190, 192
Philip the Tetrarch, 14–16, 30, 41, 61–62,
 87–91, 191, 193
Philo of Alexandria
 Caligula, 39
 Essenes, 56
 Pilate, 151, 158–160
Pliny the Younger, 147, 151–152, 174–175,
 186, 199–200
policing, 121–124, 147, 154, 156, 160–161,
 200, 205, 208–209
Pompey, Gnaeus, 13–14, 16–18, 24–25,
 29, 31, 33
Pontius Pilate
 career, 24, 49–51, 61, 89, 160–161
 duties, 21–24, 29–30, 101–104,
  108–109, 133, 144–164

relationships, 36–40, 44–51, 65–66,
 87–93, 113, 122–124, 131–136,
 160–162
sedition, 115–117, 144–164, 204–206
trial of Jesus, 1–9, 13–16, 20–24,
 36–42, 52–68, 71–85, 97–113,
 125–126, 133–143, 165–182, 204–206
violence, 19–20, 59–60, 113, 115–117,
 160–162

Quirinius, Publius Sulpicius, 30–31,
 62–63, 207–208
Qumran, 36–37, 44–45, 52–59
Qumran Jews, *see also* Essenes, 37, 52–61,
 66–67, 81–82, 106–111, 133, 135, 166
Qumran texts, 44–45, 54–59

rebellion/revolt (*see* insurgency/
 insurrection)

Sabinus (procurator), 31–32, 84
Sadducees, 36–37, 41–43, 48–49, 91, 141,
 190
Samaria/Samaritans, 13–14, 17–21, 29–32,
 51, 161–162, 188, 190
Sanhedrin, *see also* courts, 3–4, 8, 76–77,
 131, 133–138
scribes, *see also* chief priests, Essenes,
 Pharisees, Sadducees
 background, 48–49
sedition (*seditio/stasis*), *see also*
 insurgency/insurrection
 definitions, 135, 144–145, 149–159,
  165–182, 188–203
 John the Baptizer, 86–91
 Jesus, 2–9, 77–79, 101, 114–117, 126,
  141–142, 162–182
 Pilate, 115–117, 122, 144–182, 204–206
seduction (crime), *see also* deception,
 141–142, 163
Sepphoris, 40, 89
sicarii (*see* insurgency/insurrection)

Index

Simon Peter, 43–47, 75–76, 126–127,
138–139, 181–182, 185–186, 189,
198–200
sorcery, 141–142, 162–163
Stephen (protomartyr), 135–136, 187,
189–190, 192
synhedrion (*see* courts)
Syria (province), 13–31, 39–51, 62–66,
83–84, 89, 133–142, 146–162, 174,
188–191

Talmud, 3–4, 48–49, 141, 157
Temple of Jerusalem, *see also* chief priests
Antiochus IV, 53
Caligula, 39
commerce, 25–29, 34, 42–43,
104–108
destruction, 19, 37–38, 74–79, 109–111,
136–137, 140
Herod's rebuilding, 14, 20, 24–29,
32–34, 66
Jesus, 4–8, 42, 63–68, 74, 92–93,
97–117, 121–122, 141–143, 156–164,
166–180, 204–206

management, 8–9, 14, 18–19, 43–50,
54–56, 106–108, 121–124, 135–140,
145, 186, 191
Qumran Jews, 56–59
Pilate, 160–162, 173
rituals, 40–41, 45, 47–48, 54, 60–61,
67, 119–121, 137–140, 167–170
tax, 24–29, 42–43, 104–108
violence/disturbance, 13–14, 31, 51, 54,
63, 71–72, 84, 112–116, 125–127,
150–158, 166–174, 185–196
Tertullian, 73, 200–201
Theudas (*see* insurgency/insurrection)
Tiberias, 40–41, 89
Tiberius (emperor), 13, 24, 50, 61, 65–66,
159–162
Transjordan (*see* Peraea)
treason (*maiestas*), 5, 149, 153–155, 174

Vitellius, Lucius, 31, 62, 65–66, 161–162,
176, 188–190
Volesus Messalla, 151–152

Zealots (*see* insurgency/insurrection)